Andrew Henry

ANDREW

MINE AND MOUNTAIN MAJOR

Jelm Mountain Publications

HENRY

by

Margaret Hawkes Lindsley

Laramie, Wyoming 1990

Andrew Henry
Mine and Mountain Major

Copyright 1990
By Margaret Hawkes Lindsley

All rights reserved. No part of this book may be reproduced or transmitted in any form or by any means, electronic or mechanical, including photocopying, recording or by any information storage and retrieval system without written permission from the author, except for the inclusion of brief quotations in a review.

Library of Congress Cataloging-in-Publication Data
Lindsley, Margaret Hawkes, 1919
   Andrew Henry : mine and mountain major / by Margaret Hawkes Lindsley.
      p.   cm.
   ISBN 0-936204-78-8 (pbk.)
   ISBN 0-936204-79-6 (hrd.)
   1. Henry , Andrew, b. ca. 1775—Fiction.   I. Title.
PS3562.I5126A85 1990
813'.54—dc20   90-42009

ISBN 0-936204-78-8 softcover
ISBN 0-936204-79-6 hardcover
Jelm Mountain Publications
209 Park Street
Laramie, Wyoming 82070

Dedicated
To All My Family

CONTENTS

Contents	Page
Foreword	ix
Prologue	3
Chapter 1	5
Chapter 2	21
Chapter 3	33
Chapter 4	51
Chapter 5	68
Chapter 6	86
Chapter 7	105
Chapter 8	122
Chapter 9	144
Chapter 10	161
Chapter 11	177
Chapter 12	197
Chapter 13	214
Chapter 14	232
Chapter 15	251
Chapter 16	268
Chapter 17	288
Chapter 18	303
Chapter 19	324
Chapter 20	342
Recollections	359
Interview	361
Epilogue	365
Appendix	367
Letter	368
Photos	369
Maps	371

FOREWORD

There once was a man named Andrew Henry, frontiersman, lead miner, fur trader, explorer. He left no personal diaries, journals or memoirs. Only one letter in his distinctive handwriting has survived.

"It is a privilege to work on the handwriting of an historical figure whose personality and character has been deduced heretofore from writings and descriptions of his accomplishments by others," stated Barbara Finch, Certified Graphoanalyst, concluding her examination of the photostatic copy of Andrew Henry's letter to Francis Valle preserved in the Fur Trade Collection of the Missouri Historical Society. "The subject was an extraordinary man in 1810 and would be so today.

"A. Henry had a good mind, active, flexible and versatile . . . caught on quickly and could move from one topic to another without confusion . . . strong analytical ability combined with a questioning mind . . . was endowed with aptitudes in many fields, strong in business, cultural and scientific areas, but also able to handle mechanical principles and use hand and eye coordination for manual dexterity.

"Emotionally responsive, he delighted in all his senses, had an eye for beauty, an appreciative palate, a taste for good design and texture, musical appreciation and skill. The appreciation made him a delightful guest and thoughtful host.

"He took special care of his personal appearance, was a candid person, a caring person, with a cheerful, optimistic disposition. Confidence in himself and his ability to work through difficulties made him prefer company of like personalities.

"Almost totally without greed, he would balance need with methods of acquisition. An honorable man, he was true to himself and avoided shady practice. What gains he husbanded, whether it was cash, property or knowledge. No wild frontiersman was A. Henry, nor a gambler, but rather a polished gentleman."

This is the story of that A. Henry's life, woven together from the known events, situations and people of his time and place in history. All the characters in this biographical novel were real people, or are based on real people. As far as historical records can substantiate, they are in the right places, doing the right things, on the right dates.

In over thirty years of meticulous research into those historical records, the steady emergence of additional sources and documentation have been a boon. Original documents of the period, whenever possible, have been relied on as source material: diaries, journals, personal letters, memoranda, legal papers, ledgers, military records, deeds, plats, land records, census, church, genealogical and fraternal records, newspapers and magazines of the period, family Bibles, memoirs and oral histories.

There are no absolute truths in history; only certain evidence to be measured against other evidence. New evidence, a different viewpoint, will still provide no absolute truths.

ANDREW HENRY

Prologue

September has come to the mountains. In a small protected valley near a gleaming stream that runs bright and clear, where there is grass in abundance, with easy access to a look-out spot that commands all approaches, a buckskin-clad man squats on his heels chiselling letters into a rock. The rock is part of a shallow outcropping and its base, like those of its fellows clustered nearby, is out of sight, deep underground.

Not far away, another man in buckskins, cross-legged on the ground, is using the blade of his hunting knife to scrape the fat from the beaver pelt he has stretched on a round frame of willows. A third man, in worn woolen pants, faded blue woolen shirt, is patching a pair of moccasins, humming softly to himself, his back against one of the rocks.

One of the horses staked out in the luxuriant grass lifts his head and snorts. The other horses perk up their ears. Every man halts what he is doing.

Major Andrew Henry pauses on his way up the hillside. He is pleased to see the alertness of his men. Three months ago they learned to grab up their guns without pausing, and so they do now. He watches as the men locate the object noted by the horses, one of their little group who comes striding into camp as his companions lay aside their guns, within easy reach.

Wet to the waist, the newcomer drops his catch of pelts to be fletched and the beaver tail to be roasted, then leans over the carver's shoulder to look at the lettering just completed on the rock: Camp Henry Sept 1810.

The Major continues on up the hillside, passing another rock with the fresh chipped names of Henry, Hoback, Jackson, McBride and Cather. He strolls on up to the look-out point, savoring this day. The high slopes no longer have the misty blue look of August, nor does the light in the wooded parks and vales wear summer's veil of lavender. Instead, the air has a sparkle, reminding him of a good wine.

September has polished the atmosphere to crystal clearness. It was like a superb magnifying glass, bringing into arm's reach a horizon two-day's travel away. The aspen are leafed in gold. Here and there, one leaf, then another drops silently into the knee-high grass, ripely nutritious and yellow as a double eagle. Over there, where the Snake River comes out of the mountains, the slopes have been brushed with scarlet.

Here, the chokecherries are a maroon, ripe and plentiful. He pops a handful into his mouth, chews thoughtfully, spits out the pits. More choke than cherry. Those serviceberries over there, velvety-looking blue, they are too bland. Put the two together, though, they'd give them something to go with the meats simmering in the stew pot.

The Major lets his gaze sweep the vista before, then props his rifle against a nearby aspen, removes his headgear. One-handed, he picks a few serviceberries, several handsful of chokecherries, drops the berries into the floppy, worn felt.

At mid-day, the sun on a man's back is too warm, he decides, seeking the shade. In the mornings and evenings, it is never warm enough. Even on a perfect day like this, there's a touch of melancholy to it, knowing that winter lies just ahead.

Those men down there - - they hadn't flinched at the prospect he had offered them. A wealth of beaver for the taking but no way out until spring. Colter had said a man could winter in this place. He should know. He'd been here in the winter himself, thousands of miles from civilization. There was no white man alive who knew more about Stony Mountains than Colter. By this time next year, if he lived that long, the Major thought he might have filled in a gap or two on Colter's map.

The Major let his gaze sweep the horizon again, seeing only the comparative calm so welcome after one of the bloodiest spring in fur trapping history, taking time to admire the beauty of the Tetons, so close at hand.

Standing on 44th parallel, looking east, further and further to the east, remembering, going back in his mind's eye, Major Andrew Henry retraced the steps that had brought him here to Camp Henry in September of 1810.

Chapter 1

Andrew Henry was descended from Celtic folks who had been moving West along the 45th parallel for some four thousand years. His more immediate ancestors were dissident Scots holding fast to their religious reformation covenant.

These Covenanters, or Reformed Presbyterians, practiced a brand of orthodox Calvinism banned by the Established Church of Scotland. When the outlawed preachers continued to hold forbidden meetings in secret glens, their followers were rounded up, banished from Scotland.

By 1750, several thousand of the Reformed Presbyterians had chosen to settle in Pennsylvania, the most democratic of all the American Colonies. In 1751, the Reverend John Cuthbertson began ministering to a widely scattered congregation. Heir to the black robes of Geneva, the righteousness of John Knox, he brought to them the steely words of Moses, the songs of David, the wisdom of Jesus, delivered in the raspy burr of Scotland, and a stentorian voice all his own.

For the next 40 years, Cuthbertson preached to, baptized, catechized, married and buried members of his flock. In a succession of small notebooks he recorded the named of 5,000 people and the 70,000 miles of travel involved in ministering to them.

One of the congregations he visited on a fairly regular basis was the Middle Octoraro Society, Lancaster County, Pennsylvania. For his activities among that congregation, the doughty Cuthbertson's entry for November 23/24, 1763, noted, that, from home, he "rode 17 miles — married George Henry and Margaret Young."

At the time Andrew Henry's parents were being married in eastern Pennsylvania, which is divided by a mountain range, the section west of the mountains was being fought over in the French and Indian War. Following Bouquet's victory at Bushy Run that year, settlers began moving into western Pennsylvania.

George and Margaret Henry took up land in the frontier county of Fayette where Andrew Henry was born sometime between 1773 and 1778. During this period, government was in a state of flux, record keeping haphazard. The shots fired at Lexington and Concord had upset the status quo from Canada to Georgia. Families, friends and neighbors found themselves hatefully at odds.

Under the British, the bulk of the Indians had been pushed back from the settlements. After the fighting began between

Britain and the American Colonies, the British got most of the tribes lined up in war paint on their side. Welcoming the opportunity to eliminate the settlers and regain their lands, the Indians tomahawked and terrorized folks in remote settlements.

During the border wars of the American Revolution, there were times when Henry's folks had to stand and fight; times when they had to run, and times when they had to do both, just to stay alive. Very early in life, Andrew Henry learned that survival on the frontier was a chancy thing.

Every able-bodied man had to have some warrior skills. Boys learned to load and fire a musket, to use the bow and arrow, the hatchet and the knife. Men and women, boys and girls, all learned to look and listen for Indian sign.

The minister usually doubled as the schoolmaster but even the most literate of his pupils had to depend more on observation and experience than books for education. Youngsters learned from their parents or someone else in the settlement through formal and informal on-the-job training in spinning, weaving, blacksmithing, leather-making, farming.

Andrew Henry was raised in such a setting by God-fearing, respectable parents. He and his two older sisters were brought up to be industrious, mannerly and literate. By the time he was eighteen, he had also learned to fend for and defend himself, with rifle, knife, fists and feet.

When he announced his intention to marry, he didn't anticipate any opposition from his parents. George and Margaret Henry had already seen their daughter Nancy married to a Buchanan, taking up the burden of bringing up a family in a log cabin before she was sixteen.

They had no quarrel with Andrew Henry's wish to marry at eighteen. Most couples they knew married before they were out of their teens, welcomed the arrival of children, the pioneer's work force. The quarrel arose because they did not approve the girl and said so harshly. Angered, their son had some hard words of his own for them.

Andrew Henry did not marry the girl. He did leave home. It was said "He did not thereafter hold any communication with his family."

By then he had been provided with a measure of formal education and a seemly background of culture. He had a prepossessing self-assurance that was as welcome at a social gathering in a genteel parlor of civilization as in the defense of a one-room log cabin under siege in a frontier clearing.

Lean, well-built, muscular, a good rider and marksman, he had learned to be resilient and resourceful. On his own, making his way in the world, he learned of the opportunities to be found further west. In 1796 both Kentucky and Tennessee, recently freed of French, English and Indian control, were opened for occupation.

Andrew Henry liked what he heard about Tennessee. Andrew Jackson, a leading citizen of Nashville, was in Philadelphia, the new nation's capitol, as the representative to Congress from Tennessee. He was seeking buyers for his nearly 30,000 acres of land, settlers to establish prosperous communities. Since Colonial days, men had speculated in land. The successful profited financially, advanced socially. Pennsylvanians, well-to-do and not so well-to-do, optimistic about achieving a similar success, headed for the extolled Tennessee countryside.

Andrew Henry was one of those who made his way to Nashville. Still a frontier town, but a growing one, it had been named for two North Carolina brothers, Governor Abner Nash and General Francis Nash. The settlers, now they no longer had to huddle close together for mutual defense from Indian harassment, were spreading out. In the fertile, gentle rolling land watered by the great Cumberland River, where they could find hardwood and game in abundance, they were building frame houses instead of rude log cabins.

For a literate young man, used to hard work, there was employment to be had in Nashville. For an ambitious young man, however, there could be no way of ignoring the magic word 'Missouri.'

"Dan'l Boone's got his own settlement in Missouri," land-hungry men told him. "His boy, Dan'l Morgan, went out in '95, made a deal with the Dons. The hull Boone family's moved there. No taxes, they say, and lots of free land."

When business men spoke in hushed tones in the tavern, loudly at the racetrack and convivially at social gatherings, Andrew was attentive. "Cape Girardeau's the place. The Dons are giving Americans land grants by the square mile — rich farmland near the Mississippi. Free tools and supplies."

"The Dons want a buffer between them, the British an' the Injuns," said the tavern owner. He leaned forward confidentially. "Anyone tell you the Dons would expect you to join their Church?"

When Andrew Henry shook his head, the tavernkeeper advised, "If I was a young feller like you, doin' jest fine here in Nashville, I'd go talk to the Presbyterian minister. I've heard tell he gets letters from folks who've gone to Missouri. A smart feller, he could tell you what's what in Missouri. No sense goin' off on a wild goose chase on jest anybody's say so."

Might be a good idea, Andrew Henry agreed, thanking the man. One of the reasons Presbyterians required an educated clergy was so they could be helpful in worldly as well as spiritual matters.

He already knew the Reverend Craighead was an educated man. The son, grandson and great-grandson of Presbyterian ministers, Craighead was a born teacher, fluent in Latin, Greek and French.

When Andrew Henry called on the Reverend Craighead, "Missouri may be under Spanish rule but the people and culture are French," said the minister, savoring the opportunity to guide and direct an intelligent young man. "Judge Hugh Brackenridge sent his boy to Ste. Genevieve for some of the polish missing in Pittsburgh. The day the youngster arrived, his foster mother insisted he be made a Catholic." He paused. "Joe Fenwick was invited to move there by officials who knew he was both Catholic and wealthy. He has two sons about your age, one an established doctor, the other in training. Both should prosper for doctors are scarce there. However," he shook his head, "I seriously doubt Americans of any Protestant persuasion would be welcome for long — unless they converted."

Andrew had a lot of questions, incisive, direct and relevant. Reverend Craighead, recognizing the momentum of ambition, was not inclined to be discouraging.

"Exposure to other peoples and cultures can benefit a young man of good character," mused Craighead. "If a Connecticut Yankee, married to a Philadelphia Quaker, can do all right among the Catholics of Missouri, maybe that's the place for you. Moses Austin just might be able to use someone of your caliber in his operations." The minister introduced Andrew to a man-of-affairs in Nashville who did business with Austin. He described how the 35-year old Austin had made a reconnaissance of the great lead fields in south-eastern Missouri during the winter of 1796-1797, worked out a partnership with two local officials, and in 1798 obtained a nine-square-mile land grant which included the old workings of Mine á Breton, and moved his family to Missouri.

"Austin's going to have a regular American settlement there. He's using some slave labor, like he did in his lead operations in Virginia, but he's also employing Americans. He's taking on men who have had some frontier experience and won't be scared off by the Osage. He's not going to depend on the Dons to stop the Osage raids. They let that Loramie con them into giving land to his Shawnees and Delawares ten-fifteen years ago, thinking they'd put the run on the Osage. Hasn't worked out that way. Austin figures a twenty-pounder and a few good men with rifles the best way to handle any Osage trouble."

Andrew Henry, who had spent most of his working life with rifle in hand or within reach, said bluntly, "Is he making money — or just surviving?"

"Last I heard he was carting out lead by the wagonload, building a sawmill, laying out a grist mill, and already has a general store and a blacksmith shop. What he needs, though, is someone to ride herd on his Americans. They're an unruly lot." The man-of-affairs gave Andrew Henry a searching glance. "Do you think you could?"

"Just for fun? or for pay?" said Andrew Henry with a grin. "I've done both."

"For pay, of course," said the man-of-affairs shortly, wincing at the thought of doing either one.

The young Pennsylvanian packed up his assets, which weren't all that much. In 1800, a man could go from place-to-place in comparative safety and comfort as long as he had such necessities as ample powder and lead, some axe heads, a couple extra knives, a tinderbox, and a container for water.

Andrew Henry liked to tuck in a whetstone, some horseshoes and nails, a little bar of iron, a file, an awl and some salt, as well as an extra pair of boots or moccasins. He wrapped his books carefully along with his violin, putting Robert Burns' Poems in a separate, handy package so he could browse through his favorites without unpacking the lot.

When he stopped off to thank the Reverend Craighead for his help, the minister said approvingly, "I see you plan to make music wherever you go. You and your violin will find a welcome in Ste. Genevieve. The folks there are much given to dancing.

"That's as may be," said Andrew. "It's Austin I'll be seeking out, not fiddlin' functions."

"You'll find him in residence at Ste. Genevieve. It's the shipping point for his lead. A more comfortable place for his family to live, as well, until he gets a home built for them at Mine a Breton."

They shook hands and the Reverend Craighead, watching the Pennsylvanian ride off, was joined in the driveway by his young son, Alexander, who said, "Is he going off to fight the Indians?"

"Andrew Henry is on his way to make something of himself. Just as you will be doing some day." He put his arm about the boy's shoulder, turned him toward the house. "Come. I'll show you on the map where he will be going. It can be your geography lesson for today."

The geography lesson for Andrew Henry was considerably more strenuous and time-consuming. Trained in wilderness fighting and survival, he met each day with the self-confidence and ability of the experienced rover who took pains to assure he would reach his goal alive and well.

The day did come, on a stretch of the El Camino Real, when he felt he should soon come in sight of Ste. Genevieve. He had been trotting along steadily since early morning, halting only to water and rest his horse. The afternoon sun was approaching the horizon.

He had met only one other traveller, a foppish-looking fellow with an aristocratic profile whose gaze swept over him in a cataloging fashion as he passed him on handsome bay horse going at a fast clip in the other direction.

For a moment he considered hailing him to find out from the stranger the remaining distance, the accommodations to be found. He was looking forward to a hot bath, someone else's cooking and a comfortable bed. From the way the fellow looked askance at him, however, he might just have spurred his horse to put more distance between himself and a rough-looking frontier type.

Andrew Henry had to admit to himself he couldn't fault anyone for being a bit wary of his appearance. When he had shaved that morning, the sliver of a mirror had given him an unflattering glimpse of a gaunted-down, sun-blackened rover who just might be mistaken for one of those rib-stomping, eye-gouging brawlers, unpredictable as the weather, who were to be found on the leading edge of the westward movement, combative toward life in general.

On impulse, he suddenly decided to exchange his worn moccasins for the boots he'd won in a game of chance off a bored New Orleans gentleman whiling away his exile in New Madrid. They were the best footwear he'd ever owned. Much to the loser's chagrin, the boots had fit, soft and supple as a pair of gloves. They still did but his horse gave him a sidelong glance when he remounted. Even he seemed to think it was going to require more than fine boots to improve his appearance.

Perhaps it would be just as well to camp out another night, dig out his best bib-and-tucker and ride into Ste. Genevieve looking less like a hard-bitten backwoodsman. Just up ahead, he could see a little clearing and down among some trees the brook he had forded a couple times already. As he moved toward the promising campsite, he realized he was being followed. Even as he entered the clearing, the stalker was moving into concealment behind a stand of trees, quietly but not quietly enough.

Smoothly, he slid off his horse and began setting up his camp. He held up his water bottle, made a show of shaking it, picked up an iron kettle, looked toward the tree-shaded brook. Putting his horse between him and the unknown menace, he eased himself into the woods.

For a few moments the clearing was occupied only by his horse, then Andrew Henry reappeared prodding a discomfited young man ahead of him with his rifle barrel. "You'll get slim pickin's out of ambushing me."

"I wasn't ambushing you," protested his captive. "I was just looking you over. Before I could come forward and bid you 'good evening,' you sly up on me like a slithering Osage."

"Turn around so I can look *you* over," said Andrew Henry sardonically. "Keep your hands away from that belt knife and sit over there." He motioned toward a handy fallen-tree trunk. "Now tell me why you passed me at a gallop a while ago and the next thing I know you're 'slying up' on me."

"Slying up?" his prisoner repeated in mild inquiry as he seated himself with lithe grace, stretching out narrow, high-arched moccasined feet that were the only incongruous note in the impeccable attire of a stylish French gentleman of the Middle Valley. The face was frank and open as he asked in all seriousness, "That is not precise? Sly, it is a noun?"

"An adjective," said Andrew Henry blandly. "As in 'sly boots.'"

"Boots?" the young man paused in his pursuit of an extemporaneous lesson in colloquial English. He leaned forward to stare at Andrew Henry's feet. "Mon Dieu! Riding boots!" he said indignantly, pointing. "In riding boots, you sly up on me — non, non! Sneak, that is the word — sneak in riding boots —" he paused, his barely noticeable French accent giving a piquant turn to his phrasing. "You frown, M'sieu?" he raised quizzical dark eyebrows over intent brown eyes. "Ah, the noun, it is an insult? Oui. *You* are not a sneak. But in riding boots — incredible! You did 'sneak up' on me without a sound — that is right?"

"It appeared that you might be a *sneak*, up to no good," said Andrew Henry drily. The effervescent fellow looked to be about his own age, and disarmingly self-possessed. "What've I got that you want? My horse?"

"Certainly not. After I passed you, it came to me. Half a mile down the road. You travel with books. And a violin."

"What were you planning to do with my violin after you made off with it? Do you play?"

"Terribly," said the young man candidly. Looking at his captor, fit and spare and radiating energy, he shook his head ruefully. "I'm not as good a woodsman as I thought or I wouldn't be sitting here with you holding that rifle on me. What do you want of me? My horse?"

"I just want to go on about my business," said Andrew Henry firmly. "So let's cut out all this fiddle-faddle and — "

"But it is the fiddle that is needed!" exclaimed the young man with a singularly captivating smile. Because the man travelled with books and a violin, he'd tentatively put him in the category of 'scholar' and therefore, possibly, a 'gentleman'. The low, pleasant voice speaking in words shaped and rounded by schooling were more prepossessing than intimidating. He noted with approval that, as the whimsical response registered, the clean-shaven face remained impassive, but the cool, considering blue-gray eyes showed warm-sparkling centers.

"I'm in charge of the commandant's ball. We've got more violins than violinists," he said blithely. "I've been riding all over the countryside trying to locate somebody to play at the ball tonight. Pierre is off on a keelboat trip. 'Tiste is visiting his cousin in Kaskaskia. You possess a violin. It is to be supposed you know how to play one?"

"I fiddle some," said Andrew Henry, finding the fellow more mettlesome than nettlesome, "but for fiddling all around a subject, you take the prize." He let the muzzle of the rifle drop toward the ground but did not entirely relax his guard, mindful of the jingle about the French being a funny race, fighting with the feet, swiving with the face. "Why don't you just come out and say you're in desperate need of a fiddler for the ball, but not if he's a desperado?"

The young man responded with an infectious laugh and an invitation he never regretted. "Come with me, mon ami. I think you are just what the ball needs."

"What if you are wrong?"

"Papá will give me hell," said the young man with the extremely pleasant personality. "Come on. We're going to have to hurry. Oh, incidentally, my name is Francis Vallé and I live in Ste. Genevieve. You can stay at our house tonight and tomorrow we'll talk about you and what you are looking for so far from Pennsylvania."

Andrew Henry gave his name but resisted the impulse to follow it with the obvious question.

Merry, observant, young Vallé explained. "You sound just like all the Pennsylvanians who were at school with me. And Walt Fenwick. Maybe you know him?"

"I've heard of the Fenwicks. I understand they were invited to come to Ste. Genevieve, not shanghaied." Henry flashed his own pleasing smile. "Do you know anything about lead mining? or what Moses Austin is doing?"

"I know where all the lead mines are," said Francis. "I know Moses Austin. Come on. He'll be at the ball. Everyone will be."

They were. Those that couldn't squeeze into the commandant's parlor danced in the streets.

Ste. Genevieve, a predominantly French settlement, founded some 60 years earlier when the area belonged to France, was as prosperous and populated as St.Louis by the year 1800, with nearly one thousand people. Everyone of them loved to dance, and did so, on Sunday evenings, holidays and spur-of-the-moment, winter and summer, from dusk to dawn.

They made a stranger welcome, Andrew Henry discovered. With barely time to wash up and change clothes, he and his violin were propelled willy-nilly into the ball, and there was no language barrier as he let his music-making speak for him. Still, when there came a pause in the dancing, he was relieved to hear an inquiry made about Philadelphia in a familiar accent.

"Am I acquainted with Philadelphia?" he repeated, exchanging a firm handshake with the self-introduced Walter Fenwick who gestured for him to put aside his violin and join him. "First and last time I was there was in '96. Got lost trying to deliver a load of hides to the Guy Bryan warehouse. You know the place?"

"I know the Guy Bryans. I was called in when one of their boys had the quinsy. When the Bryans learned I was moving out here, they gave me letters of introduction to their Morrison kin in the Illinois country. The boys wanted to come with me. Whoa, there, Francis," he broke off, "You've been dancing every dance. It's time you took your turn with the musicians and let your guest have a breather."

Meeting Andrew Henry's accusing gaze, Francis shrugged eloquently. "If you'll recall, mon ami, I never said I could *not* play the violin."

"Francis would rather dance than make music," said Walter Fenwick perceptively, "and he'd go to most any lengths to do so."

"He did today," said Andrew Henry dryly, exchanging twanging glances with Francis, who shrugged cheerfully before turning to confer with the musicians.

"Have you met all these good folks?" asked Dr. Walter Fenwick, letting his gaze sweep over the crowded parlor.

"Francis presented me to a pride of Vallés; a slew of others, including the Austins."

"Except for the Austins, it's hard for a newcomer to keep them all straight," said Fenwick sympathetically.

"You think so?" said Andrew Henry, who never had understood how some folks found it difficult to remember names. Eyeing the gathering, and with no intentions of showing off, only to hold up his end of the conversation with the cosmopolitan Fenwick, he enumerated, "There's Papá and Mamán, Oncle Jean and Tante Jeanne, Oncle Charles and Tante Marianne, Souer Marie with Beau-Frere Joseph Pratte and the Patrick Flemings, no kin apparently to Francis, getting ready to dance the reel; Cousin Louis is playing the accordion; the Villars, kinship unspecified, are playing twenty-one with Mr. Austin while Mrs. Austin is tapping her foot; the Grandmères Carpentier and the Mesdames Beauvais are keeping an eye on young Julie Valle and her cousin, the Villars girl, who are longing to join the young people dancing in the street; and your brother Ezekiel who is motioning for us to join him on the porch."

"Gallery," corrected Walter Fenwick absently, leading the way out onto that architectural adjunct where they joined Ezekiel in the ritual of tamping and lighting up their pipes. "My God, Zeke," he said in awe, "you should have heard this man calling the roll of the folks in there."

Ezekiel raised his eyebrows.

Andrew Henry said simply, "I couldn't keep up with Francis' French so it was easy to concentrate on the names. He was also telling folks something that made them laugh a lot. I have a feeling it had something to do with the way Francis and I met."

The brothers exchanged glances. Ezekiel grinned. Walter chuckled. "It certainly did."

"Well?" prompted Andrew.

"Let me put it this way," said Walter thoughtfully. "You couldn't have obtained a better introduction to these folks if you had planned it."

Zeke nodded. "Francis is a master of the droll anecdote. He also knows how to poke fun at himself. The way he describes your encounter, in voluble and colloquial French, is a lot funnier than it probably was in reality — or would be in English."

"The only thing these lighthearted folks like better than a tall tale is an appropriate nickname. With Francis vouching for your ability as a 'sly boots' you now have an unshakable reputation as a superior woodsman," said Walter. "You've got a way with you on that fiddle they like, too."

"Of course, you've still got to prove yourself a 'sly boots' in the minuet, the cotillion and the reel," drawled Zeke leaning against one of the gallery posts, his own expensively booted feet unconsciously echoing the rhythm of the reel.

"Anything else?" said Andrew tranquilly. "Jump through a hoop? over a barrel?"

"Oh, not until the card games."

"One does learn something of one's fellow man over a card table," said Andrew Henry lightly. "But the minuet?"

"One learns that one better put one's best foot forward," said Walter bluntly. "Here, wives are full, if somewhat unobtrusive partners in all business undertakings."

"Including lead mining?"

"Especially lead mining."

"For instance?"

"Your hostess, Madame Valle, who does admire a man who can perform a graceful minuet, invests her chicken-and-egg money in a likely digging every now and then." Walter inclined his head toward the parlor where Marie Carpentier Valle, a short, plump fortyish matron in becoming blue satin wove her way joyfully through the patterns of the reel partnered by her husband of twenty-two years, Francois Valle II, resplendent in an even brighter blue satin coat, decorated in silver braid.

"Madame Fleming, who is tireless at the dance, knows as much about the Mine á Joe operation as Patrick." He indicated a sprightly couple, younger than the Valles, the woman, slender and graceful in an ecru linen frock over French corsets that accented her handspan waistline; the man, in a dark blue serge coat with silver buttons.

"Madame Villars," nodding toward the frivolous taffeta gown of pink that failed to bring color to the sallow complexion of the intent, lined face of the woman at the card table, "who likes to winter in New Orleans among her husband's aristocratic connections there, invested part of her dowry in a keelboat that transports lead ore, and the Villars to that port every fall, and back again in the spring with trade goods - - and the latest tunes, dances and fashions."

"If you are still heeling-and-toeing it at dawn, with elan," said Ezekiel cheerfully, "your stamina and energy will be much admired."

"And?"

"You will be invited to every ball," said Walter Fenwick with a chuckle. He added, with unmistakable precision, "And, very likely, to participate in some profitable enterprises."

They smoked their pipes in companionable silence. Then, Andrew Henry, knocking the dottle from his pipe against the gallery railing, said, "Does Mrs. Austin minuet or reel?"

Again the brothers exchanged glances. Moses Austin, who didn't share the French love of dancing, was circulating, convivially, purposefully. Maria Austin, knowing that Moses and the French hadn't been getting along all that well lately, had been doing her bit all evening, in her charming way, toward mending fences.

"Why don't you ask her?"

When Andrew Henry bowed before Mrs. Austin, she said, "No French, please." She patted the recently vacated space on the bench beside her. "Sit here and say something in English. Anything. So long as I don't have to decide whether to reply with the informal or the formal *you*."

"Who was the best dancing master in Philadelphia?" said Andrew Henry politely.

Surprised, the beginning of a smile held in abeyance, she gave him a searching glance. This was not the typical American frontiersman. "Dancing master?"

Married for fifteen years, a mother who had lost in infancy two out of her four children, she had a pleasant face, lined with thirty-one of living. Descended from Anglican and Quaker first families of New Jersey and Pennsylvania, she had been raised in comfort, schooled in deportment, household management. Motherless at thirteen, she had gone to live with her great-aunt Rebecca, wife of the prosperous merchant, the Anglo-Irish Benjamin Fuller. There, in the handsome Fuller house on Front Street in one of the best section of Philadelphia, in luxurious surroundings, socially graceful, popular, "Polly" as the Fullers called her, she had been like a favored daughter, even having one of the Fuller trading vessels named for her. Wooed and won at seventeen by the smitten Moses Austin, she'd had as fine a wedding as her grandmother and great-grandmother, and in the very same impressive Christ Church, followed by a honeymoon cruise to Richmond.

Her new life, in the fine mansion built and staffed by slaves, had revolved about her beloved husband. It still did. Wherever he went, without demur, so did she. From the amenities of Richmond to the backwoods of Austinville, Virginia. From Virginia to Spanish Louisiana.

It hadn't always been easy, particularly the last move. There had been forty men, women and children in the Austin party that set out to travel by boat to Kaskaskia. After a three month trip, nightmarish with accidents and illness, only seventeen survived, and only two of them strong enough to disembark under their own power.

From October 1798 to June 1799, Maria Austin had enjoyed the civilized comforts of Ste. Genevieve in the house Moses had bought for them near South Gabouri Creek. Not since the summer before, when they had moved the forty miles to Mine á Breton and settled into the handsomely appointed Durham Hall, had there been an occasion for Maria to visit with the friends she had made in Ste. Genevieve.

True to the plain folk side of heritage, she was wearing unadorned Quaker gray, but fashioned out of a splendid, costly brocade that was most becoming to her fair complexion. "A dancing master," she repeated, adding dryly,"For the Plain Folk?" Smiling, Andrew pointed at the black satin slipper, peeping out from beneath the gray brocade, tapping absently in time to the music.

She looked down. "Some folks in Philadelphia have nothing against dancing," she conceded, her eyes twinkling. She gave him a reminiscing smile. "Uncle Benjamin sponsored a dancing master once. The nephew of one of his old friends in Dublin. My best friend caused quite a stir by eloping with that Englishman. He may not have been the best, but for a time he was the most memorable of the dancing masters in Philadelphia."

"An Englishman? From Dublin? In Ireland?"

She nodded. "Fifth generation and still calling himself English. Sad." She looked pensive. "Will my grandchildren harken back like that, calling themselves Pennsylvanians?"

"It's easier to say than 'Ste. Genevevians'."

"Such a mouthful!" Her laughter was a charming, tinkling sound. "Joyous, the people of the Middle Valley. Such pleasant surprise to find that Ste. Genevieve is not the typical bleak frontier village, don't you think?"

"Tell me about it. I'm new here."

"Mr. Austin is really the one you should talk to. He knows more about the area than many of the natives." She gave Andrew Henry a considering look. Her husband had spoken highly of another Mr. Henry, who had made the difficult winter trip from Vincennes to St. Louis with him. This young man, in the way of venturesome families, might be here on the recommendation of a kinsman. He was certainly a gentleman in the American mold, humorous of mind and phrase, able to take care of himself on the frontier in the way Mr. Austin admired.

"When he has time to spare, I would indeed like to talk with Mr. Austin. In the meantime, can you tell me: what is a Commandant?"

"He is," said Maria Austin indicating Francois Vallé II with the high forehead, arching eyebrows over large, deep set eyes. He had an aristocratic nose above a thin-lipped mouth, now relaxed in an indulgent smile as he pousetted gracefully with his light-footed spouse. "The Commandant of Ste. Genevieve. There's no American equivalent, Mr. Austin says."

With selective discretion, she proceeded to tell him more of what Mr. Austin had to say, interspersed with some of her own observations, providing Andrew Henry with information that he would augment and expand in the days to come.

The Vallés, through heritage, interlocking marriages, aptitude and connections spreading from Normandy to New Orleans, were the most prosperous, and powerful, family in the Middle Valley. The first Vallé, a surgeon, had immigrated to Quebec in 1645. His son, Charles La Vallé, hard-working and prolific, added property, experience and ten children to the family assets. Two of those sons, Charles and the first Francois, sought their fortunes in French Kaskaskia, in the Illinois territory, early in the 18th century.

"Francis, the younger brother, was a real go-getter, a trait Mr. Austin admires," said Mrs. Austin, who knew her husband for one, and, sometimes, amidst the upheaval of following a go-getter around, or coping during his absences from home, wondered how it might have been with one or another of her suitors, who stayed firmly put in Philadelphia and still managed to 'get ahead', comfortably. "He was Commandant under both the French and Spanish. 'Papá Vallé.' That's pretty much what a Commandant is, a father to his people, constantly sought out for guidance in all matters, from the cradle to the grave."

In little over a decade the first Francois Valle had gone from working for hire for Monsieur Beauvais to resident-trader, lead-miner and leading citizen of Ste. Genevieve. When the French, giving up Canada to Great Britain, out-foxed them by ceding Louisiana to the Spanish in 1763, the change for the leading Vallé was more titular than actual: 'Don Francisco' continued much as before, presiding over civil and military affairs for nineteen years.

During the Revolution, Papá Vallé, like so many of the French, favored the American cause. When called upon to house American troops, he did so cheerfully, as well as provisioning their garrisons and their Indian allies.

"His son," Maria Austin gestured toward the floor where the reel was coming to a conclusion and Francois II was bowing over his wife's hand, "has been Commandant since 1794. He had two older brothers. The Indians killed Joseph many years ago. Charles died in disgrace in Opelousas just a few years ago. Now the Commandant and the youngest brother are raising Charles's son and daughter."

"The youngest brother?" prompted Andrew Henry. "Francis's 'Oncle Baptiste'?"

"Jean-Baptiste Vallé. He's a go-getter, too," began Maria Austin, then paused to say, "Here's Mr. Austin, looking like he wants to converse with you."

"When I heard 'Mr. Henry' was here, was hoping it was that fine fellow I got to know so well the winter of '96-'97. Looks like he sent out a younger version instead." Mr. Austin, steady eyes below thick brows and the high, intelligent forehead, assessed the newcomer. His wife, rising, put her hand on his arm. She could feel how charged he was with tension, knew better than to ask if he had succeeded in getting the Commandant to set the date for the long over-due survey of his land grant. His temperament was so different from the men he'd been trying to get moving on his survey. Of an optimistic nature, he saw the answer to his problem in action, not submission. Frustrating, tiresome, rolling the same rock up the same hill. He needed distraction from his smoldering preoccupation and, it would seem this nice young man had provided it, as Moses asked, "What's this I've been hearing about your 'sly boots?'"

When Andrew Henry concluded his story of the 'sly boots,' she murmured a suggestion to her chuckling husband, who nodded agreeably. Despite the disparity in status, this newcomer brought with him the fresh air of the outside world, a welcome change of perspective.

"Come sup with us tomorrow," said Moses Austin.

"Tonight," said Maria Austin. "It's past midnight."

"I would be honored, ma'am," said Andrew, sketching a mannerly bow that did his mother proud, letting them both see his pleasure at the invitation.

The Austins departed shortly thereafter, for they were early risers, and Mr. Austin, as he explained to his hostess, had places to go and things to do on the morrow.

Francis appeared at Andrew's elbow to insist that, if his new friend was not going to dance, then he should get back to fiddling, so Francis could. Andrew Henry took up the violin again, spelled considerately by another cousin, who said he was Jean-Baptiste the two-th, so Andrew could squire, in what Mrs. Austin had pointed out were his 'duty dances', the Mesdames Vallé in successive minuets, Madame Beavais in a cotillion, and just-for-fun, Francis's thirteen year old sister, Julie, who was anxious to practice her English, in a reel.

The next day, he was up before his host, strolling about, getting better acquainted with Ste. Genevieve and its people.

The New Town, after the Old Town had succumbed to the advances of the Mississippi, had been relocated rather haphazardly on higher ground between the forks of Gabouri Creek and further from the scrollwork of the River. Along the irregular streets weathered houses, of perpendicular log construction, many of them thatched, occupied large lots enclosed in 7-foot stockade-like cedar-picket fences, flocked over with tangled spring greenery of vine and fruit trees, with a handful of taller buildings, and the benevolent silhouette of the log church in sentinel position.

Roads led out from the center of town in various directions: to the river traffic of the Mississippi at boat landings north and south of town; to the road north to St. Louis; west to Mine á Breton; and south to the Saline through New Bourbon, the twin of Ste. Genevieve founded by French emigres and home to the Royalist school master the polished Augustin-Charles Fremon de Lauriere as well as the Fenwicks.

As Andrew Henry made his way toward the Vital St. Gemme Beauvais house on a bright spring day in April of 1800, he thought about the civilized amenities of Ste. Genevieve. Colorful water jugs. Soap, imported from France. Copper basins for washing and shaving. Featherbeds to sleep on. He paused to doff his hat and bow to Madame Beauvais. The plump cheerful-looking French matron was directing a slave in the round-up of half-a-dozen straying chickens. Clad in workaday dress of patterned red cotton, full skirted, she flapped her enveloping apron of unbleached muslin at a recalcitrant rooster. With expansive gestures, which he understood better than her voluble French, she let him know she had enjoyed the ball, their minuet and his fiddling. Beaming a cordial adieu, she swivelled on moccasin-clad feet to follow the slave and chickens back inside the picket fence, humming "Yankee Doodle."

Last night he had learned she had been the foster mother referred to by the Reverend Craighead. Young Henry Brackenridge at age seven had travelled stoically from Pittsburgh to Ste. Genevieve to be welcomed into the warm embrace of Felicite Janis Beauvais, her household and her church. Schooled in the French language and old world courtesies, the prosaic schoolboy had returned home with good things to tell his father, in rusty English, of the civilized life and friendly, honest folks of Ste. Genevieve.

Like young Brackenridge, Henry was finding these people friendly. And, judging from last night's ball, free of prejudice. Apparently everyone had been invited — slaves, Indians, children, American — and everyone, from Beauvais toddlers to Francis Azor, the Breton nonagenarian, had shown up.

They were hospitable people as demonstrated by Joseph Pratte. Encountering Henry at the corner of Main and Merchant streets, he insisted Andrew join him for breakfast. He and Madame Pratte, Francis' older sister, would enjoy an opportunity to get better acquainted.

"After last night, you might like a little peace and quiet," said Joseph cheerfully. He paused to adjust the fit of one moccasin, settled his blue bandanna on his head before leading Andrew to his home. "You'll seldom find it at my in-laws. Counting the slaves, they must have fifty people in that household." The Commandant's house served as the city hall. Most official business was conducted there. "All the visiting big-wigs from St. Louis to New Orleans lodge there when in town. Even I don't always know who is in residence." He ushered Andrew into his house. "But here I do. Marie, we have company for breakfast."

Vivaciously hospitable in a mixture of English and French, Marie Valle Pratte set out a breakfast of impressive proportions. At twenty-two, wife, mother and busy homemaker, she was again wearing blue. Not the satin of her ball gown but a boldly patterned calico, the full skirt brushing the tops of her ankle-height moccasins. Around her middle was tied a sturdy deerskin apron. Like Joseph, she wore a blue bandanna on her head.

"Lead mining, oui, I do know," Joseph responded to Andrew's query. The French had mined lead for years. Farmers put in a few weeks annually skimming off the top three or four feet of soil to get enough lead to barter for extra supplies, tools and services in Ste. Genevieve. "Industrious Americans," said Joseph with a pleased smile, "like your M'sieu Austin are showing us how to make lead-mining a profitable, full-time business."

Chapter 2

"Stop asking so many questions, Mr. Austin," said Maria Austin, smiling at her husband from her place at the foot of the dining room table set with china, crystal and flatware. The appointments in the Austin house in Ste. Genevieve were in no way equal to those at Durham Hall, but any place Maria Austin presided over, even for two days, would be a well-run household, giving a guest the feeling of a warm home-life and loving family. "Let Mr. Henry enjoy his food."

"I am enjoying it, Ma'am," said Andrew, who had found his host's questions about his background and experience a bit like a job interview. They had found they shared some of the same values and a number of mutual acquaintances, some of whom were already participating in the Austin endeavors at Mine a Breton. "I haven't seen such a variety of good food, or in such abundance, since I was in Philadelphia."

"People in Ste. Genevieve think corn pone and fat hog meat poor fare," said Moses, referring to the staple food of the American frontier.

"I agree, wholeheartedly," said Maria Austin. "It can't begin to compare to the chicken fricassees, omelets, salads, fresh vegetables, and the rich, creamy desserts of Ste. Genevieve."

Five-year old Stephen bounced in his seat. "Everybody has crusty bread, every day," he said approvingly.

"Better make the most of it," said his father, helping himself to another slice of bread. "We'll be returning to Mine a Breton tomorrow. You might like to come - -"

"Dangereux," said Stephen portentously.

"Stephen," said his mother, "remember your manners. You are not to interrupt your elders."

"What is it, son?" asked Moses indulgently. "What's dangerous?" "Mine a Breton. That's what Vitale told me. He says if I go back there the Osage will get me."

His parents exchanged glances. They did make their home in a rambunctious place but they had striven to make it a safe place for their children.

"If I stayed here Vitale and I could play together every day."

"Now that could be dangerous," Moses chuckled.

"Vitale will just have to come visit you at Durham Hall. Then he'll see that your father makes it just as safe a place to live as here," said his mother.

"We live in a mansion," said four-year-old Emily, giving their guest a long look up through her demurely lowered lashes to see if he was impressed. Her mother looked disapproving. "Everybody says so," she went on defensively. "It's named after my father's hometown in Connecticut. It's almost as nice as the one he had in Virginia."

"Will you come see us there?" said Stephen. "It isn't really a dangerous place. Vitale's French, you see — just a scairedy cat."

"Out of the mouth of babes," murmured Moses, while Maria said firmly, "Stephen. Emily. No more interruptions or you'll have to leave the table before dessert is served."

After dessert had been served and the children had been excused, as Maria Austin poured coffee for the men, Andrew Henry said, "What about the Osage? Much of a threat?"

Moses Austin said he considered them mostly a nuisance, particularly in the spring. When migrating through the region at that time, they made off with anything not nailed down. The French had never offered much opposition, preferring to avoid any confrontation by working the Mine á Breton site in late summer and fall when the Osage had wandered elsewhere. Until he arrived, few of them had the gumption to make permanent homes at Mine á Breton. Last year, backed by some good men, experienced Indian fighters, he had shown the Osage they couldn't buffalo Americans like they had the French. At that time the French had stood up to the Indians, too, rallying around the Americans to drive off the Osage attack on the settlement. Since the defeat of the Osage, some of the French, like Basil Vallé, were building substantial homes and businesses, creating a small, but permanent French village, right in the middle of his land grant. This was of more concern to him than the Osage. He wanted an end to the procrastination over his survey, lines drawn and squatters identified and discouraged

He began talking about his settlement, getting totally immersed in the subject, clarifying his own thinking, not seeking an opinion. His wife, recognizing that the sensible young man would make a good sounding board, refilled their coffee cups and quietly withdrew to oversee the packing for the trip back to Mine á Breton on the morrow.

Austin, benefiting from his successful undertakings in Austinville, Virginia, had brought his own experience, knowledge, workmen and their families, to establish, with modifications, improvements, an even more efficient lead mining operation in Missouri. Instead of hiring men or using slaves to dig up the ore, Austin leased mining rights. Making his contracts with care, he limited a miner to one plot at a time, sale subject to Austin's approval. He let the miner pick out the site for his diggings, granted him exclusive rights within a fifty-foot radius of the initial excavation, required all minerals from the diggings to be delivered to the Austin furnace house for smelting.

The advanced smelting process, which Austin used, reduced the ore with hot air instead of direct contact with the fire. This process recovered so much more of the lead than the French log furnaces that independent miners also started bringing their ore to him. In his businesslike way, Austin drew up smelting contracts with these customers, and the production of, and the profits in lead, shot up.

When he had begun negotiations for his land grant, Austin had asked for sixteen leagues, a square of about 70,000 acres centered on the lead mines. He was going to need wood, lots of it to keep the furnaces going, and that would require handy access to acres and acres of trees. The cleared acres could be parcelled out to settlers later for he envisioned developing a self-sufficient community of farmers, millers, and artisans. By the time the land grant was made, Moses was already committed to making his move. He accepted the disappointing award of one league, approximately 4,250 acres. He had figured on getting all the lead mines; instead, he had been whittled down to a third. Still, since he figured he could lay out his league as he saw fit, his grant would take in the richest of the diggings. He had not figured on the difficulties he would have in establishing the exact boundaries to his league. He had finally got officialdom to order a survey over a year ago. Since then, Spanish land laws had been revised. Besides the surveyor and the land owner, the commandant of the district and two neighbors of the land owner must get together to lay out mutually agreeable boundaries. Title to the land could not be obtained until there had been a certified survey.

"They are a likable enough people, the French. Just not hustlers when something needs to be done," said the Connecticut Yankee hustler "Americans here have a phrase for working speedily. 'Get the lead out!' And we certainly have."

Andrew Henry, who had been listening carefully, had an idea that Austin's phenomenal success at getting the lead out might have contributed to his problem of getting full title to the mines and land.

He had shown the French, who had been mining for years, just how profitable it could be to hang onto their diggings.

"Not to worry," Austin said, more to his wife looking in on them, than to his guest, remembering that the friendly surveyor, Soulard, had said flies were not caught with vinegar. "Polite perseverance will eventually get us a survey."

Andrew Henry, thanking his hostess in a courtly manner for the hospitality he had enjoyed, prepared to take his leave. His host held up his departure, saying, "I did all the talking. Never found out what you were interested in. Mining, smelting, farming, milling, distilling, clerking?"

"Like Stephen when offered a choice of dessert," said Andrew Henry with a smile, "I'd like to try a little bit of each."

"A man after my own heart!" Austin clapped him on the shoulder. "The sooner you come to Mine á Breton, and go to work for me, the better."

The next day, entering the Vallé trading post, where rich and poor alike obtained their supplies, primarily through barter, Andrew Henry, the likable American newcomer who had been welcomed into the community life of Ste. Genevieve and had quickly made friends, paused to let his eyes adjust from the brilliance of the sunny morning to the dimmer interior. His nose told him he was close to a stack of fur pelts and not far from a barrel of pickles before he could make out the lithe form and beaming features of the young man advancing toward him.

"The horses are ready and waiting. What mine do you want to visit first?" Francis Vallé said gaily. The scion of the most prosperous and influential French family in the Middle Valley, Francis seemed more American than French. Modestly when asked, the twenty-one-year-old French Creole attributed this to the New Jersey school he had been attending. Henry surmised that when the French, canny wights in their own way, had accepted the Brackenridge boy for schooling, they had negotiated a cultural exchange. The amiable young man leading the way out doors to the horses very likely was benefiting by the association and sponsorship of one of Princeton's outstanding graduates, Judge Brackendridge, in getting that New Jersey education.

"Mine la Motte? Mine Renault?" continued Francis, ticking them off gracefully on his fingers. "Mine á la Plate? Mine á Maneto? Mine á Lany? Mine á Gerbore? Old Mines?"

Andrew grinned at him, warmed by his light-heartedness and cordiality. "How about finding me a brand new mine?"

"Aha! One with a name like Mine á Andre?"

"More like Henry's Diggings. That's about all I could afford, a pick-and-shovel operation."

Francis gazed thoughtfully at Andrew Henry. "I do not think that is what M'sieu Austin has in mind for you."

"I think I'd rather — hey, what's the packhorse for?" Henry broke off his reply, eyeing the animal, skillfully packed with tent, food and supplies for a lengthier outing than he had envisioned when Francis had proposed showing him around the area. "Where are you taking me? Looks like you've outfitted us for a regular expedition!"

"Oh, I know you Americans," Francis said lightly, swinging up on a chestnut gelding and indicating that Henry should mount the sleek brown mare. "No matter what I show you, it'll be, 'What's over that hill? What's around the bend of the river?'

"It is best to be prepared when dealing with a man who has such an inquiring mind and an eye for a distant horizon. Who knows what you will want to see — first the mines, then what-are-the-Chouteaus-doing in St. Louis, maybe even visit your fellow American, M'sieu Boone up on the Missouri, n'est-ce pas?"

Francis, with his heritage of first-hand experience, was well-qualified to show him what was around the next bend and over the next hill clear to Quebec. The French-Canadian Vallés of Ste. Genevieve were the equals of those French-Creoles from New Orleans, the Chouteaus, in fur trading expertise. Francis's uncle, Jean Baptiste Vallé, in his knee breeches, broad-cuffed coat and cocked hat, presided over widespread, interlocking undertakings as a prosperous merchant. As an experienced fur trader, still on the supple side of forty, he participated in the Vallé and Menard ventures, had wide experience and knowledge of the Indians, the trade routes up the Missouri, and the potential of this land, including its lead mines.

At the moment, although intrigued by the offhand, brief descriptions of the fur trading ventures of the Vallés, in which Francis anticipated an active and rewarding future for himself, Andrew Henry was more interested in the potential of the lead mines.

"Dr. Fenwick, Joseph Pratte, and Patrick Fleming are expecting us?" said Andrew Henry as they rode.

"Oui," Francis chuckled, waving his hand toward the packhorse. "But their mines — they are not side-by-side."

Little by little, as they made their tour, Andrew Henry got a feel for an opportunity here, one there. At Mine á Joe, Patrick Fleming was waiting to show them around. Patrick Fleming and Joseph Girard dit Megan were the original owners of Mine á Joe, granted them by Don Manuel Perez in 1790. Associated with them were Joel and Laurent McGayne who did much of the actual mining. The Fleming son, Nicholas, was there, disappointed that Dr. Walter Fenwick was not with them, for he wanted to be a doctor, too, and was more interested in discussing the ailments of lead miners, than their procedures.

From Mine á Joe, Francis oriented Andrew Henry on the trails leading to the various working mines, with frequent recourse to the compass. They travelled over forested hills, amidst close-ranked trees. At a venerable concession, one the Spanish had granted to St.

Gemme Beauvais, Joseph Pratte was expecting them. He discoursed entertainingly on the trials and tribulations of Phillippe Renault, who had come to the area seventy-five years earlier with five-hundred negroes from Santo Domingo and established the potential of the lead mines. He outlined the procedures he and his partners, the two Vallé brothers and St. Gemme Beauvais, were using to extract the rich lead ore. They still followed the practice of hiring others to do the digging, supplying provisions as well as paying wages but were going from a seasonal to year-round operation.

Walter Fenwick put in his promised appearance, suggested they postpone the projected visit to the claim Fenwick shared with the French Canadian, Jean Baptiste Labreek, until the next day.

They settled down for the evening in the one room cabin Joseph used for a combination office and living quarters and shared the venison stew and fresh-baked bread one of the miners wives had prepared for them.

When Joseph brought out a bottle of excellent imported wine and Francis a deck of cards, Andrew Henry said forthrightly that he wasn't sure he had the head for either, and certainly not the purse for vingt-et-tun. Francis showed Andrew how good wine was to be sniffed, sipped and savored. Joseph, suggesting they use markers, produced more of the grape, this time in the form of a package of his own home-grown, sun-dried variety, which worked quite well until the third glass of wine when the dealer, Francis, who had been absently eating his raisins, went broke. Andrew, sipping, said he'd teach them the New Orleans 'poque' that had won him his 'sly boots', if Joseph would stake them to more raisins. By the time they had finished the wine, both Francis and Walter had consumed their winnings, so that, laughingly, Andrew and Joseph agreed to play one last hand, winner take all, which Francis did with a pair of queens, then generously divided his winnings. Munching happily, they all bedded down on pallets for the remainder of the night.

Continuing their tour the next day, Francis and Andrew, accompanied by Walter Fenwick, came to the original Mine á Breton discovery. Francis Azor, a native of Brittany, was not a young man when he made his find about 1773. Born in 1710, he'd been a soldier of France on the Continent, at Braddock's defeat, and finally at Fort de Chartres, before retiring from soldiering to settle in Ste. Genevieve. Azor, as the discoverer of the substantial vein of lead, under Spanish law got title to the mine and an adjacent three acres. When the Fenwicks arrived in Ste. Genevieve, he was beginning to feel the weight of nearly ninety years. Walter Fenwick negotiated a partnership deal with Azor and now took an active interest in the workings of the mine, named for Azor's native province.

After Walter showed them the old workings, and his current undertakings, they headed for Austin's mining camp, passing several diggings and French-Creoles that Andrew Henry suspected were on land claimed by Austin.

When Andrew Henry asked if they were mining for Austin or for themselves, Francis said laconically, "They were here before Austin."

Fenwick nodded agreement. "Austin's been a bit irked about it. He is determined to limit further encroachments. He wants the Spanish to send in their official surveyor so there will be no doubt where his boundaries begin and end," said Fenwick. "Unfortunately, he's finding that Spanish subjects feel they can dig for lead and salt if, when and where it can be found."

"He has a lot of land to police," said Andrew as they approached the mining camp itself. Looking over the layout, where primitive and crude living quarters were crowded in among the sheds containing the various stages of lead processing, he observed, "Rough and tough."

As if to confirm his assessment, there was a lot of shouting from a rough shack serving as a tavern. As they watched, a group of men, in violent conflict, boiled out into the open. One of the men managed to extricate himself, ran toward a hitching rail with several others in pursuit. He leaped on his horse and galloped away before he could be overtaken.

Three men lay sprawled on the ground, one of them with his leg canted at an unnatural angle.

"Nothing like a broken leg to make a doctor feel welcome," said Francis. "Wonder what that was all about?"

"A card game," said Andrew Henry gesturing at the cards and coins scattered about. He dismounted and joined the Doctor beside the injured men.

Taking charge of the horses, Francis drew to one side of the rutted track, and watched in admiration as the Doctor sorted out the injured men, Andrew Henry the uninjured but indignant, all Americans. In no time at all, Henry was addressing the men by name, setting them to turning the ramshackle tavern into a first-aid station, commandeering a door for a stretcher, a couple trestles and another door for an operating table. When the agitated womenfolk of the injured arrived in full cry, he settled them on a bench outside the tavern with a drink of whiskey, also commandeered. Through the empty door, Francis could see Dr. Fenwick busying himself at setting the broken leg, sewing an ear back in place, and patching up an assortment of gashes.

When Austin came hurrying up to investigate the rumpus, the

injured and their comforted womenfolk had been assisted to their respective dwellings. The remainder had turned the door used for an operating table over and were gathered around Henry who was explaining the intricacies of 'poque.'

"Mr. Vallé here," Andrew inclined his head toward Francis who had found a place to leave the horses and was now pulling up a stool to the card table, "says 'poque' is just a French word for 'card game.' Basically, players bet on the value of the cards, usually five, dealt to them. The winner is the one whose hand contains cards of the highest value."

"You sure you're talkin' about the same 'poker' as that slicker was teachin' us? He kept changing the rules as we was playin', gettin' us to throw away good cards, draw poor ones, and he kept scooping up the winnings'," said the miner with a rakish bandage above his shrewd blue eyes.

"Actually, the rules don't change. They just get complicated, depending on the circumstances." Henry monitored the playing of several hands.

"Hey," said bandaged miner looking at his cards, "I think I've got the hang of it." He looked across the table. "Come on, Davey. Dole out those coins I saw you picking up and we can all start over again." As Davey complied, his friend said eagerly, "I'm ready to bet on this hand. What about the rest of you?"

"Looks to me like the rest of you can go ahead with your 'poker' game without Mr. Henry," said Austin. Having been filled in on events by one of his men, he had been watching Henry intently.

Davey looked up. "This ain't a bad place to locate."

"Seen worse." One of the other poker players said encouragingly to Andrew. "Think on it."

"Mr. Henry likely could show you how to turn your hands at more than cards," said Moses Austin. "Need to take him around, though. Let him see for himself that we don't spend all our time raisin' hell."

Andrew Henry grinned at his fellow Americans. "Seen worse."

Following the conducted tour given them by Austin, the three young men, making a leisurely return to Ste. Genevieve, got better acquainted. One day they devoted to stalking the elusive turkey, another day they had better luck in their deer hunting. Fenwick, Vallé and Henry found their liking for each other growing with each passing day, talked more freely of their lives, their future plans. Henry listened more than he talked, absorbed in the growing companionship with minds even more varied than his. Francis, telling of his travels and travails, was a lively, resourceful companion, possessing a shrewd, whimsical sort of mind. Fenwick had the hardihood and self-possessed nature that went with his profession and an open, inquiring mind.

They sounded out Henry regarding his own future, made some helpful contributions toward clarifying his options. They discussed at length how an industrious man, with limited capital, could get a start in a primitive fashion, dig down ten-fifteen feet, then use a windlass to haul the ore to the surface where the spar could be cleaned with a pick, broken into manageable chunks, baked in a brick furnace to get rid of the sulphur. Smelted, the ore would yield about fifty percent lead. Even with such primitive techniques, the profits would be substantial from such rich ore.

On the other hand, as Henry said musingly, "A man could learn a lot more than just the mining of lead from Austin."

"From what Francis has heard about the Don's changing their minds, it might be the best course for you right now," said Fenwick.

When they got back to Ste. Genevieve, it was something of a setback to discover that the rumor Francis had heard was true. The Spanish, in an abrupt about-face, had changed their immigration policy. Worried about the growing American expansion and influence in Upper Louisiana, they had decided to make no more new grants to Americans.

Like other Americans, Andrew Henry found he would have to work in Moses Austin's mines or take his chances squatting on land without a title. He decided he would learn and earn more by casting his lot with the expanding Austin interests.

By the middle of May Andrew Henry was housed with Austin's workmen, getting acquainted with the work and the men who did it. He came to know the manager, Judather Kendal; dependable Austin relatives, Moses and Elias Bates, Donald Phelps; trusted associate from Connecticut, Martin Ruggles, and his older brother, Comfort, of Boston Tea Party fame; miners like John McNeal; farmers like Robert Sloan; the millers, saw amd grist; the distiller; the French blacksmith, Pierre Vial, who had circumvented Austin by latching onto the slag discarded from the inefficient French furnaces but had lacked the know-how to get the remaining lead out; and Joseph Bell, the Austinville miner who mentioned that he had made the trying winter trip of '96-'97 with Austin himself and, on a note of inquiry, another Mr. Henry, possibly kin of some sort. Possibly, agreed Andrew, who hadn't been in touch with any of his kinfolks in years, had only a vague idea who the Mr. Henry might have been carrying a letter of introduction to Lt. Governor Trudeau in St. Louis. Like Moses Austin and Joseph Bell he could only speculate on what became of that Mr. Henry after he stayed on in St. Louis as a guest of Trudeau's. He was his own man and had no intention of trading on a vague relationship however well that Mr. Henry had been regarded.

One morning, near the end of May, Andrew Henry saw Antoine Soulard, the Surveyor General of Louisiana, gather the survey team together in front of Durham Hall, plotting lines on a map. At long last, Austin was to have his boundaries determined officially.

By law, Surveyor Soulard, Commandant Vallé, landowner Austin, and two landowner neighbors, one of them St. Gemme Beauvais, were to mark out the boundaries of Austin's concession. To protect their interests, the French miners sent their own representative.

With five out of the six men on the survey team French, Austin could not expect to have things his own way. The first day there were objections, arguments, with the lines moved, debated again, moved. Despite his friendship with and admiration of the stubborn American, Surveyor Soulard had not been looking forward to this undertaking. He was relieved on the second day when Austin proposed a compromise agreeable to Commandant Vallé that would encompass only one-third of the mines. Soulard completed, forwarded his official return, and Lt. Governor DeLassus accepted the agreed-upon boundaries in June of 1800. Spanish officialdom finally got around to granting Moses Austin title to 7,153 arpents on July 5, 1802.

During that two-year period, Andrew Henry was part of the complexity of action at Mine á Breton, mastering mining techniques, learning about smelting, record keeping, supervising laborers, toning down disputes. Indians came to trade at Austin's stores and the village stores across Breton Creek, Steve Austin and the French children playing with little Shawnees and Delawares. Men came and went with lumbering carts and burdened pack trains, carrying shot and sheet lead to Austin's keelboats on the Mississippi for transport to profitable markets, returning with supplies and trade goods, varying from the necessities such as nails to the exotic, such as ladies silk hose.

Basically, despite the complex spreading out from Durham Hall, Mine á Breton, was still a mining camp, a focal point for Americans wishing to establish themselves west of Ste. Genevieve. The prosperity of the miners attracted opportunists of all kinds. They set up commercial enterprises where the miners could drink, gamble and fornicate, for a price. Crude and turbulent, Austin's mining camp bore little resemblance to genteel Ste. Genevieve.

In 1801 Nicolas Caillot di Lachance's son was named Commissioner of Police at Mine á Breton, bringing an illusion of law and order if not much of the real thing. Raucously, Austin's mining camp, and his various other undertakings, continued to grow.

The French inhabitants of the Middle Valley had never been inclined to come to blows over differences; the Americans did, sometimes maiming and killing their opponents in the process. This disdain for civilized behavior, coupled with Austin's nagging about French squatters within his boundaries, resulted in a thinly veiled resentment, and such petty harassment as logging off some of the handiest wooded areas Austin was counting on to furnish fuel for his furnaces.

The fragile goodwill that had survived was breached when the pleasant days of May and some very unpleasant Osage arrived at Durham House in 1802 determined to kill all Americans there. On other occasions, in particular the one in 1799, many of the small French landholders had hastened to help the Americans repulse the Osage attacks. On May 12, 1802, the French kept their distance.

Many of the Americans, including Andrew Henry, went to fight off diversionary attacks on outlying households where one miner was killed and one woman kidnapped. This left only Moses Austin and nine of his men to stand off thirty Osage, superior warriors all, when they attacked with great vigor and bloodthirsty intent. Outnumbered three to one, the defenders stood firm behind the walls of Durham Hall, decimating the attackers to such a discouraging extent that they never mounted another attack on the Hall.

When it was all over and it was plain the French had provided no assistance, it was the turn of the Americans to feel resentment, and there was nothing mild about it. Commandant Vallé scolded his countrymen for refusing to fight. This did little to allay Austin's bitterness particularly when the Commandant refused to station a detachment of soldiers at Mine á Breton to protect the settlement.

All Austin got from the Commandant was a three-pounder cannon and he had to dig that up out the street where it had been lying unused in Ste. Genevieve for years. The Commandant did agree to stand the cost of putting the cannon in working order. Austin got the dirty field piece shined up and set in place beneath the flagpole in front of Durham Hall. Eyed uneasily by visiting Indians, its use so far had been reserved to sounding as a fire alarm, saluting special occasions such as the Independence Day celebration.

Shortly thereafter, when Andrew Henry learned that Austin was sending a shipment of his lead shot to Nashville, he found he was homesick for the familiar, reassuring, reliable American ways and government. He didn't relish being in a land under the haphazard control of Spain. When making his request to accompany the shipment to Nashville, he told Austin so, adding, "They don't like to see a man get ahead. They've got so damn many taxes it discourages the ordinary man from building a decent house. Chimneys, windows, mirrors, stair treads, beds in the attic, for godssakes, even carvings on the bedstead are taxed."

When he went to Ste. Genevieve to make his farewells, Francis Vallé urged him to return. There was a rumor abroad that Louisiana was being ceded back to France. The prospect didn't appeal to Andrew like it did to Francis. With Napoleon needing money to pursue his conquests, there would be more, not fewer, taxes. For the ordinary man wanting to settle down on his own piece of land, the complexities could be compounded rather than eased.

Andrew Henry didn't tell his friends in Ste. Genevieve he would not be coming back. However, when he got to Nashville, the merchant who took delivery of the shot made him an offer of employment. He decided to remain in Nashville.

"C'est du joli!" said Julie Vallé Fenwick to her husband Walter.

From her tone of voice, he realized she meant the news about Andrew Henry was *not* a fine thing. "Why?"

"I was hoping we'd be dancing at his wedding this year."

"His wedding? To whom, my dear?" said Walter Fenwick curiously.

"I'm not really sure," said Julie. "It's just that Marie and I think Andrew Henry would make a conscientious husband and father. If he'd stayed around a little longer, we'd have found some eligible girl he couldn't resist."

Chapter 3

By the year 1802, the tide in the affairs of men had swamped the 'liberty, equality and fraternity' of the French Reveolution and swept into power a remarkable middle-class Corsican. Napoleon Bonaparte, as First Consul of France for life, was riding the surfboard of ambition with spectacular success. While 29,000 of his soldiers were dying of yellow fever in Santo Domingo, the dictator of France was contemplating an empire and the title to go with it.

In 1803 Ohio became the 17th State. President Jefferson, catching the tide at the right moment, made a deal that would insure there would be states west of the Mississippi instead of a Napoleonic empire.

Andrew Henry rode back into Ste. Genevieve that year, coming this time with buoyant optimism, feeling in his bones that there was an inevitable truth to the rumor that the United States was buying the Louisiana Territory. The diplomatic, secretive decisions in distant capitals that had transferred this territory from Spanish back to French ownership could be of benefit eventually to him, personally.

"M'sieu Henri," came the greetings that February morning as he rode toward the Commandant's house, followed by a chuckling, "Bottes Ruse," now and then, confirming his recognition.

He had scarcely dismounted when "Bottes Ruse!" and an uninhibited bearhug greeted him. "Ol' Sly Boots, you 'ave come back!"

"What the - - Francis, is this really you?" he pounded the shoulders in worn, greasy, and redolent buckskin.

Francis held him at arm length, chuckling as Henry took in the unusual apparel of his young Creole friend. "This time, I look the desperado, ne ce pas? Non, non, you are looking at a successful fur trader returning after months of - - don't do that."

"Don't do what?"

"Sniff, then turn the head. Maman already said I was a stinker."

"Been lookin' forward to a hot bath myself," said Andrew.

"Best we go to Julie's house," said Francis. Lowering his voice, looking over his shoulder, he went on, "The parents need the resting. Mon Mere has been up all night with the littlest one. Mon Pere has the maladie."

"Anything serious?"

"Walter will know."

Dr. Fenwick was not sure. As the Fenwicks made them welcome, he was noncommital. The fever season of late summer and early fall was over; they were coming into the winter fluxions of the chest. His father-in-law, not yet fifty, hadn't snapped back from his annual bout with malaria, slight as it had been this time. Debilitated as he was, with a weak, susceptible chest, Francis II was causing his doctor some anxiety.

"Papa has been like this before. Walter always makes him well," said Julie Fenwick who had her own anxieties. Mamán, after eighteen pregnancies and fourteen children, had finally reached menopause. Worse than being enceinte, she complained, which, Julie, who was, doubted. She still had spells of nausea, particularly when subjected to rank odors. She wrinkled her nose at her brother. "Don't you want to bathe, get out of those stinking clothes?" Both Francis and Henry nodded. "You know here to find the tub and hot water. Soon as you get cleaned up, we can eat."

Looking and smelling considerably better, Francis entertained them as they ate with his fur trading anecdotes. The Fenwicks brought their guests up-to-date on news of mutual acquaintances.

Andrew Henry was itching to talk about the rumors that had brought him here. Out of consideration for Francis, he refrained. Even for someone as Americanized as Francis, there had to be some lingering regrets for what-might-have been. Heir to generations of Frenchmen who had held all this land once, he could not be faulted if he hoped the Corsican upstart would be wise enough to hang onto the vast Louisiana territory.

For Henry, Fenwick and other Americans like them already in Missouri, the immediate satisfactions would be great if Louisiana Territory became part of their nation: the familiar American legal system; separation of church and state; and, once again, available land.

Land, Henry decided, for the moment, was the safest subject. Available for lead mining. Smoothly, he guided the conversation, mentioning that he had encountered a young Virginian, William Ashley, who was interested in a joint venture. No, he told Francis, he didn't think they would be more interested in the fur trade. It would take a bigger stake than they had to invest at the moment. Lead mining would not require much capital, not the way he and Ashley would go about it.

While he was going about it, Andrew Henry, came and went from Ste. Genevieve, looking up old friends, making new one, always welcome in their homes and at their social gatherings. He heard about, but didn't see, the official communique Commandant Vallé posted on the church door June 5, 1803, announcing the transfer of the territory to France. There was no indication Napoleon intended to make any changes in officialdom, which was just as well, for two months later unofficial word arrived of the sale to the United States. The jockeying for power did not cease, merely took a different direction. Americans began arriving, many of them people of substance. Single men and, more significantly, men with families, were hanging out shingles, setting up businesses, until there were more people around speaking English than French. In the French households of Ste. Genevieve life went on in much the same easygoing fashion as it had for over fifty years, the traditional customs unchanged.

Compared to most frontier settlements, the dwellings in Ste. Genevieve were roomy and well furnished. Most families were large so there was not much domestic privacy. In the standard two-room home, even with the additional space provided by the all-encompassing galleries, people ate and slept in the same rooms they used for work, for receiving visitors and for dancing. Much of the casual socializing was done outdoors, on the galleries, in the yards, along the streets, weather permitting.

With the harvest season over, the active social season got underway in November. From Advent Sunday through the celebration of St. Nicholas day on December 6 to reveillon following Christmas Eve midnight mass, it was in full swing, combining a reverent observance of the Christ Child's coming with lighthearted revelry.

"Come," and "See," urged the youngest Vallés when Andrew Henry stopped by one December morning. Three-year-old Charles and two-year-old Audile grasped his hand, tugged him forward to admire the Vallé Nativity Scene. Treasured santons d'argile, the painted clay figures of French villagers, were displayed in a setting resembling a French countryside. "Don't touch," Julie Fenwick cautioned her siblings as she offered seasonal greetings at the same time she put the final touches to the focal point of the Christmas observances that memorialized both the Savior's birth and the Vallé's French homeland.

"On Christmas Eve," said eleven-year-old Emily, joining them, "We put Petit Noel there." She pointed to the straw in the manger.

"Me put, too," said Audile, reaching out, only to be swung up into Andrew Henry's arms. "Then what?" he asked.

"Put out sabots for Petit Noel," said Charles. Julie explained that on the hearth of the fireplace where a huge log burned throughout the Christmas season, the children set out wooden shoes for the Christ Child to fill with sweets, nuts and little gifts.

"Then we tell stories of le Jour de Noel," said thirteen-year-old Catherine. "You know, how the animals spoke out on Christmas

Eve." At his puzzled look, she exclaimed, "Your Mamán never told you? Oh, Julie, can we?"

Julie, nodding permission, approved the way Andrew Henry settled Charles and Audile on his lap, Emilie and Catherine on either side of him. Best of all, she liked his way of treating little ones as persons of consequence. Charles and Audile weren't just 'the Twin' and 'the Baby' to him. Resting her hand on the stirrings in her womb, Julie resolved her baby would have a name all its own. Unlike those of her mother's generation, no matter how many babies she buried, and there were bound to be some, no names would be repeated. Not for her one baby after another, each named Francis, until at last one Francis survived.

"Well?" prompted Henry. Charles crowed like a rooster.

"That's how his favorite story begins," laughed Julie. "The cock crowing 'Christmas Notus Est.' Which means - -?"

"Christ is born," chorused the children. Charles mooed "Ubi?" The children provided the translation, "Where?" Charles baaed "Bethlehem!" then brayed "Eamus" like a donkey. The children chanted the meaning, "Let us go!" "And" concluded Julie, pausing for appropriate sound effects from Charles, "the cock, the ox and the lamb, led by the donkey, went to bow and kneel before the Christ Child."

Andrew Henry applauded. "That's a dandy story. Never heard it before but then my people never made much of Christmas."

"Oh, that isn't all we do," said Catherine. There were weeks of pre-Christmas meals and balls beneath the Christmas chandelier. The candles at the top were for Jesus the light of the world; the evergreen wreath, the symbol of everlasting life. The apples and wafers hung below the wreath represented man's fall and redemption. "We help Mamán make gingerbread men and other good things. After midnight mass we sit down to revillion, a feast of soup, bread, wine, cheese, crullers, turkey, goose and thirteen desserts representing Christ and his twelve apostles and the Buche de Noel."The latter was the frosted cake rolled to represent the Yule log Henry was to learn later. "Then we rest up for La Guignolee."

"I have heard of La Guignolee," said Henry. On New Year's Eve, just as their forefathers had done in Canada, costumed young men of the village went from door-to-door making lyrical demands for food, drink and dance partners via the traditional French folksong of the season, La Guignolee.

"And this year I am the eldest daughter of the household."

"Are you sure the eldest daughter of the household has enough dancing slippers to make it through La Guignolee and the Twelfth Night Ball?" teased Andrew Henry.

"Come and see," said Catherine with a flirtatious toss of her head.

Andrew Henry did intend to do so but when New Year's Eve rolled around, his new partner, William Ashley, preferred celebrating with their fellow Americans at Mine á Breton.There, the talk of transfer was unrestrained, for it was said it would become official soon, probably in March, so never mind the New Year, let's drink to the new era. Henry did, enthusiastically, and what with that and some inclement weather, did not make it back to Ste. Genevieve until shortly after Twelfth Night. Calling at the Commandant's house, he learned that the home of the Commandant had not been the center of festivities this year. Looking at the Commandant, who had gone down hill since he last saw him, he could understand why. He was one sick man.

Once the Commandant had greeted Andrew, Madame Vallé and Francis, looking worn and anxious, had little difficulty in persuading him to be helped into the parental bedroom for an afternoon lie-down. They left Andrew Henry in the parlor explaining that some English words and phrases that were puzzling Catherine and Emilie were not meant for the ears of young ladies and shouldn't be used in polite company. When they returned, the two young ladies were giggling over the bowdlerized words and phrases Andrew had suggested they use instead, little Audile was riding to Banbury Cross on Andrew's foot. Charles, sulking because Catherine had told him he was too big for Banbury Cross, was brightening as Andrew said as soon as Audile got to Banbury Cross, Charles could have a bareback ride.

Madame Vallé retrieved Audile, telling her she was too little for a bareback ride, which set well with Charles, clambering onto Andrew Henry's back. Andrew crawled on hands and knees across the floor, bucking gently with the exuberant Charles until the little boy began to get a trifle shrill, which made his horse collapse in mock weariness. Andrew, gathering Charles to his chest, whispered they must be quiet so the Papa could rest. Madame Vallé, watching Andrew Henry entertain the little ones with some simple magic tricks, said, "M'sieu Henry should take a wife."

Andrew, who had found not being able to speak French very well didn't preclude understanding, said, "Good idea. Whose?"

Francis grinned. Madame Vallé tut-tutted. Andrew Henry said, "On second thought, I think I'll wait - - say, until Odile here grows up."He tousled her hair. "Will you marry me when you grow up?"

Emilie exchanged a disturbed glance with Catherine. "You can't. You're promised."

Francis raised his eyebrows at his younger sister.

"M'sieu Henry promised to marry little Mary Fleming when she grows up. She told me so."

Madame Vallé said, "Did you do that, M'sieu?" Andrew Henry, momentarily at a loss, considered her question. He thought back to his last visit to the Patrick Fleming household when he had carried Patrick's cute little three-year old around on his shoulders. He nodded. Madame Vallé tut-tutted again, told her daughters M'sieu Henry just meant to be jolly, cautioned them that it wasn't just Americans who could be jolly about marriage, and in chiding tones, looking at Francis, sometimes French men were not as serious as they should be about marriage either. Francis changed the subject. Wouldn't everyone like to take a walk, see what was going on down at Oncle 'tiste's? Everyone but Madame Vallé, who was glad of the respite, did.

Oncle 'tiste's house was full. Since his brother had been ailing, J.B. Vallé had been seeing to the civil and military responsiblities of the village. Hospitable as his brother was, he could not sustain the socializing which usually centered on the Commandant's house, hadn't been able to dance more than an hour or two this season, so, J.B. gestured in his own hospitable way, waving them inside, lots of folks were here instead. Looked like there was to be music and dancing and where was M'Sieu Henry's fiddle?

It wasn't quite like old times. Probably never would be again thought Andrew Henry as he did a bit of fiddling, dancing and visiting and rode back toward the new times. The Stars and Stripes were already flying at New Orleans which was to be the capital of the more populous, Orleans, or Lower Louisiana portion of the Purchase; St. Louis would be the capital of the Upper Louisiana portion, largely an unpopulated wilderness.

Before he got back to Ste. Genevieve again, the changeover was made official in St. Louis, with drum rolls, cannon fire and speeches. The Spanish flag was lowered on March 9, 1804, and the American Captain Amos Stoddard took symbolic possession in the name of France. The next day Captain Stoddard, having signed all the necessary papers marking the transfer from France, marched his company of troops through the town, and, as the Stars & Stripes was hoisted to troop and cannon salutes, took charge of the territory for the United States of America.

Stoddard asked the outgoing Spanish commander, Carlos DeLassus, to supply him with a list of those in his employ. DeLassus gave high marks to the ailing Commandant at Ste. Genevieve and his brother, J. B. Vallé, as well as recommending Joseph Pratte as a zealous officer who spoke English. In the militia detachment DeLassus had led to New Madrid the year before, he pointed out that Francois Vallé, Jr., son of the dying commandant, had served with zeal, alacrity and correctness.

As the new era was ushered in, the Vallés of Ste. Genevieve were literally in mourning. Nothing the Doctor prescribed, nor

Madame Vallé tried, had improved the health of the Commandant. They hadn't been able to help little Audile, either, when she started ailing. Audile succumbed one week, the Commandant the next. By the time the bad news reached Andrew Henry, Francis Vallé II and his youngest child had been laid to rest in the village log church.

When he arrived to pay his condolence calls, Andrew learned that Jean-Baptiste Vallé had been confirmed as first American commandant of Ste. Genevieve. Whatever his personal feelings, J.B. was a pragmatic man.

"We are all Americans," he noted when accepting the appointment. "As such, I wish, as I would under any government, to devote my services to the country and to the well being of its citizens."

In the house of mourning, Madame Vallé was holding up quite well. Julie Vallé Fenwick seemed more upset over the loss of her baby sister than her father, rounded on Zeke Fenwick for using that term, spelling out her sister's name a bit hysterically.

"A-u-d-i-l-e?" repeated Andrew Henry. "I always thought it was O-d-i-l-e." He looked around the room, at the family gathered there, Madame Vallé, and the children still at home, Catherine, Emilie, Charles, at Francis, the Prattes, the Fenwicks. "Either way, it suited. Audile was a bright little girl who did a lot of 'oh-ing' and 'aw-ing' while she was in this world. I won't forget her." Julie, patting his hand, thanked him with a great deal of fervor.

"How's everything at Henry's Diggings?" Francis changed the subject.

"Ashley built us a hoist that's really speeded things up," said Henry. Ashley had also tinkered with other machinery, made some improvements, drawing on the skills he had mastered as a mechanic's apprentice back in Virginia.

Henry and Ashley were making a hardscrabble beginning, living and working at the claim known locally as Henry's Diggings, sheltering in primitive accommodations. Of humble, not elite Virginia background, William Ashley was about the same age as Henry. He had even less to say about his birthplace, parentage and early years than Henry. Of medium height, slight of build, noticeable of nose, Ashley had a lot of rough edges, no social polish. He rode and shot well, liked outdoor sports, could hold his own with other frontier types but not always his temper. An ambitious man, he had some formal education, a determination to get ahead. He was more comfortable among the American to be found at Cape Girardeau than the genteel French Creoles of Ste. Genevieve.

Both men were hard workers, knew how to make the most of very little. Working together, making improvements on their claim, the two men found they had complementary skills and abilities. As they made enough to pay $250 for the 640 acres near Little Mine Creek, they laid an enduring groundwork of trust and friendship. Like others in the mining district, however, they were in limbo as far as clear title went, waiting for the American government confirmation of Spanish land grants.

After several successful years living on and working Henry's Diggings, the interests of the two men began to diverge. Ashley found he had more aptitude for marketing their lead than digging it, began developing a transport and marketing service for other mines. While Andrew Henry was taking on civic responsibilities, binding himself personally closer to the Vallés in Ste. Genevieve, Ashley was buying property and slaves in Mine á Breton, courting the daughter of prosperous Yankee in Cape Girardeau. Andrew Henry, who had always wanted his very own mine, began making arrangements to buy out Ashley's share of their operation. Ashley, seeking upward mobility, was one of those men drawn into the orbit of the notorious John Smith T.

John Smith T scared the hell out of a lot of people in his day. His contemporaries found him a violent and devious man, had some harsh things to say about him. Chroniclers, defensive, soft-pedaling, say he killed only three men in duels, not ten or fifteen; and was not, really, involved in the Burr-Wilkinson Conspiracy to form a separate government west of the Mississippi. Footnotes say, that driven by a ruthless territorial imperative, he was a land hog, a claim jumper and a knee-jerk rival of Moses Austin, feuding with him for political control in the mining district, choreographing scenes of discord, pushing folks into taking sides.

Andrew Henry didn't feel called upon to say anything but 'Good luck,' when his friend began making plans to establish the Wm. H. Ashley Company in partnership with Robert Brown and John Smith T. Henry had known the man when he was plain John Smith, scouting out opportunities to be found in the mining district at the turn of the century.

Fifth generation in America, imbued with all the aristocratic traditions of landed Virginia albeit raised on the Georgia frontier, John Smith had attended William and Mary College in Williamsburg, Virginia. Related to the Meriwethers and the Wilkinsons, he had kin active in military and government circles. After he began to make a name for himself in East Tennessee in public office and land acquisitions, John Smith added the distinctive 'T' for 'Tennessee' to his signature. By 1803 he was commuting between his holdings in Tennessee and Missouri. When he moved to the mining district in 1804, he found that getting clear title to land in Missouri was more difficult than in Tennessee. The United States government had no precedent to follow in taking charge of a region with foreign laws and land rules. After cession, there was a period of unsatisfactory caretaker government. Worse yet, Congress declared that all land grants made after October 1800 were null and void. The only exceptions were for a handful of settlers who actually occupied their small tracts before December 20, 1803.

Land values sky-rocketed. There was difficulty separating legitimate land grants from the fraudulent. Bogus, antedated documents claiming Spanish rights, some of them for the best of the lead mines, proliferated. Speculation in, and dispute about land became the order of the day.

To remedy the volatile situation, Congress, in March 1805, created the Territory of Upper Louisiana and a commission to review and validate all claims to land and mineral deposits. President Jefferson appointed a governor and three judges, who would serve as the legislative body, and a territorial secretary. To insure the defense of the new territory against the inroads of the British, Spanish and Indians, James Wilkinson, Brigadier General commanding the US Army of the West, was sent to St. Louis to take office as governor. He was allowed to retain his command. This suited the General's secret agenda.

By 1806 it was obvious John Smith T had the unqualified support of James Wilkinson, Governor and General. Moses Austin was dismissed from positions of authority, Smith elevated. Smith obtained appointments and preferment for men of his selection. Smith opponents were dismissed, replaced. At least one was arrested, another court-martialed, many intimidated.

A significant number refused to be intimidated both in the Ste. Genevieve District and in the capital itself. Charges and countercharges led to litigation. Rumors, innuendo added to factional discord. Political unrest increased, rather than diminished, under Wilkinson's pernicious administration. There was growing opposition to the governor, including but not limited to members of his administration.

And no place suffered from lack of decent government more than the mining district. Hollywood has provided us with a glimpse of the chaos and anarchy concomitant with any bonanza, from the day of Roman finds in Spain to those of modern day in Brazil. Drama in the diamond fields of Africa, comedy in the Klondike, a musical farce in Colorado, or the love triangle of wildcatters in the oil fields of Oklahoma can be entertaining for two hours. Mine á Breton, tough as a cob, had a varied cast struggling with their uncertain roles who found nothing entertaining in having their 1806 Fourth of July celebration spoiled by John Smith T's machinations.

Andrew Henry, on hand for the holiday muster of the militia, found himself caught between a rock and a hard place that day.

Despite the feuding between his old friend, Moses Austin, and John Smith T, the partner of his partner and his commanding officer in the militia, Henry had stayed on good terms with both men.

Andrew Henry had prospered, modestly but steadily, in business. As a man of integrity and good judgment, he had been called upon by his fellow citizens to serve in various responsible civic capacities, including that of school board trustee. Since he was well-acquainted with how an American community was ordered, decisions made and justice administered, he had been selected to serve on the grand jury in December 1804 and appointed justice of the peace in November 1805. In this capacity, on July 4, 1806, Andrew Henry was required to play Solomon when Smith decided to commandeer Austin's cannon.

The scenario is vintage Hollywood: the lawman trying to keep the peace between two powerful protaganists locked in an ongoing struggle involving not only land rights but political, ethical and economic status. The setting is authentic: a frontier village carved out of the wilderness, a-swirl with varied types in a holiday mood, miners, farmers, Indians, rifle-toting militiamen and their respective women and children.

In the early morning hours, Moses Austin, the sturdy Yankee mining developer, emerged from his mansion, backed by his partisans. He had organized the surrounding compound into a defensive system, with ways and means planned for handling disturbances. At his signal, the Stars and Stripes is set flying from his flagpole and his cannon fired in a ceremonial salute to Independence Day.

As folks cheered the cannon salvo, John Smith T, frowning, rode into the settlement, backed by his bravos. Disarmingly soft-spoken, a John Carradine sort of southern gentleman, lean and mean, he wore his usual armament: two pistols in his belt, two others in each side pocket, a dirk under one arm, rifle at his side. Ever alert for means to humble Austin, he urged his horse toward a group of men. "That piece of ordnance is the property of the US government," he declared. "It's rightful place is with the militia. It shouldn't be in the hands of a private citizen."

"Hell's Bells, man, Austin dug that cannon out of the mud himself years ago," snorted John Scott, elbowing his way to the front of the group. "The Dons never paid him for cleaning it up so he didn't let them have it when they pulled out." A lawyer and one of those unintimidated by his fellow Virginian, Scott never hesitated to speak up for or take action in support of his principles. He was a familiar figure in the mining district, entrusted to make collections on debts for an increasing number of clients. "He's not going to give up that cannon on your say-so. No sensible man would expect him to."

The slender Smith T looked down his nose at Scott. As Lt. Colonel Smith T, he was the ranking officer present that day, here to carry out his duties as commander of the county militia. "With three men of my choice," he said, in the ringing tones he reserved for issuing orders, "I could take that piece of ordinance. And," he added in his normal soft voice, his eyes fierce, "have Austin hanged."

"A damn fool notion. Unlawful, too," said Scott, his native Virginian drawl well nigh replaced by the more rapid diction characteristic of a Princeton graduate. Hoisting up his oversize pantaloons, he settled his brace of pistols more comfortably on his hips. "You're supposed to be a justice of the peace. Godamit, act like one."

Right on cue, Smith was presented with an opportunity to do so.

From a nearby house where, as an observer put it with prim understatement 'several persons were in the drinking way', a raucous crowd spilled out into the front yard, making noisy bets, forming an impromptu circle about two men stripping to fight. "M'money's on Tom," shouted one man, "Scott'll scotch 'im."

Almost at the same time, both Johns, the justice of the peace and the lawyer, realized that one of the contenders was John Scott's younger brother.

Commanding the peace, John Smith T elbowed his way through the circle followed closely by John Scott. Recognizing their colonel, those of the militia fell back, quieted; others, recognizing the voice of authority, did the same. The two contenders, intent on each other, exchanged a flurry of blows, and one man went down.

"You, Tom Scott," said John Smith T confronting the man still standing, "are going to jail."

"What the hell for?" said John Scott, collaring John Smith T and yanking him around so they were face to face. "If a drink or two and a friendly fist fight is a crime, then you better be prepared to throw half the folks here today in jail. Not just my brother."

Smith T reached for his dirk. John Scott grasped but did not draw his pistols.

"What jail?" said the bewildered Tom. "I didn't know this place had one."

One of Tom's fellow militiamen chuckled. "You wouldn't like it."

"Helluva place," added another teasing voice. "Reserved for troublemakers."

"Not the place for you," another militiaman spoke up. "You

ain't done nothin'." A murmur of agreement swept around the circle.

Recognizing the tide of opinion was not on his side, the thirty-six-year-old Smith T dropped his gaze from that of the twenty-five-year-old John Scott's, removed his hand from his dirk. Growling that he feared no Scott, he strode out of the yard, tossing over his shoulder a reminder, "It's time all soldiers were at the muster ground."

That's where John Scott found Andrew Henry later in the morning, some distance from Durham Hall. The muster, or assembly of his company, had involved Henry in the roll call, inspection of men and equipment, lining up and parading with the other company of the battalion, and some rumors that were flying about.

John Scott, drawing him aside, confirmed the rumors. "That son-of-a-bitch from Tennessee is set on making trouble."

"Tell me about it," said Andrew Henry, something he would say often as he ad-libbed his way through the tensions of this day.

In his rapid fire way, highlighted by colorful profanity, Scott described how, in an exchange of correspondence, Colonel John Smith T had demanded the surrender of the cannon, Moses Austin had refused, was in the process of hauling the cannon back inside his compound. "Now that damned fool of a reeving colonel is calling for fifteen volunteers to take it by force. Somebody is going to get shot if you don't put a stop to it."

Andrew Henry didn't say anything, eloquently. He was not inclined to be judgmental or overly critical of others. Well-adjusted himself, he could tolerate a wide-range of differences in personal behavior. If it did not hurt or seriously disturb other people, he was not one to impose restrictions.

"You're an honest and fair man. Everybody knows that. You've managed to stay on good terms with both Smith and Austin which is a helluva achievement," John Scott patted Henry on the shoulder. "You'll be hearing from Austin shortly. There's some of us who've remembered you are a justice of peace, too." Beckoning to his brother Tom, he pulled his black cloth cap down more firmly over his eyes, hitched up his pantaloons, and headed toward Durham Hall. Other muttering dissidents, in groups of two's and three's, followed.

Not long after Scott reached Durham Hall a dispatch from Moses Austin was delivered to Andrew Henry:

"I have this moment been Called on by Colo Smyth to give up a three pounder in my possession and as I have been told my House is to be forced to take it from me I pray you make use of your Authority as a piece officer and I demand that protection the laws of my Country give me."

"Smith T," said Andrew Henry, speaking as the Judge of the

Court of Common Pleas of the Ste. Genevieve, and not as a subordinate addressing his commanding officer, a subtlety that did not escape the other man, "This is a helluva note." With an all encompassing gesture, he took in the developing scene of confrontation.

"Let me see what Austin had to say." Smith T read, returned the appeal with a dismissive wave of his hand. A pluralistic society is a frustrating nuisance to would-be tyrants. "Ignore it."

"Can't. It's only natural to have fireworks on the fourth, but a shoot-out over a cannon? Plumb foolish." Andrew Henry said shrewdly. Leaders of men, and Smith was that, have a certain vulnerable self-image. Compromise could add luster, ridicule would leave pit marks on the image. "Wouldn't want to have the battalion end up the laughingstock of the territory."

"What do you intend doing about it?"

Andrew Henry called for pen and paper and began drafting a reply, which he then handed to Smith T. "I'm asking Austin to let the battalion borrow his cannon for the day," he said, stressing 'borrow' and 'his.'

"You are also, on your honor, pledging the return of the field piece?"

"Exactly."

Smith T, who had found Henry to be a man of his word, handed back the document. Five men volunteered to make the delivery to the entrenched Durham Hall. Only one ambled back with Austin's reply, and a laconic, "The sides are gettin' about even."

Henry didn't have to point out to Smith that his supporters were dwindling. Citizens fed up with the trend of their anticipated holiday celebration were speaking out, soldiers unsympathetic to the loose cannon spoiling their muster were deserting, making their way one at a time to Durham Hall and taking up positions within Austin's perimeter of defense.

When Austin indignantly refused to consider the compromise Andrew Henry had proposed, Smith T shrugged. "Let him sweat. There'll be another day." He turned his attention to the final festivities that concluded the muster, the traditional company feasts, hosted by the officers.

As word trickled back that "The Colonel's pulled in his horns," Austin laid on a feast for his supporters who drank to 'life, liberty and the pursuit of happiness.'

Andrew Henry, joining with his company at their festive board in the same traditional toast, was damned glad to see the day come to a peaceful end.

In the months to come, circumstances and inclination distanced him from the ongoing divisive contention and rivalry that kept the mining district in continual foment as Austin and Smith T jockeyed for dominance. He bought Ashley's share in Henry's Diggings, invested in other claims. Andrew became a partner of Walter Fenwick's when Francis Azor dit Breton assigned his grant to them. Since the aging Azor had long been acknowledged the original discoverer of the Mine á Breton tract, the Board of Land Commissioners, going over land grants one by one, found this claim an easy one to settle. Fenwick and Henry were among the first to be granted clear title by the US land commissioners.

All legal business was transacted in St. Genevieve. Andrew Henry, combining various aspects of business with pleasure, was often to be found in that expanding trading center.

He added further cement to his friendship with Francis Vallé. He welcomed arriving Americans, such as Dr. Aaron Elliott, Moses Austin's brother-in-law; the lawyers, John Scott, George Bullit, Nathaniel Pope, Rufus Easton, Edward Hempstead, and Eliott's son-in-law, William C. Carr, laid the groundwork to lasting friendships.

Several of his new friends were members of the Masonic Fraternity, a successful and vigorous institution at the beginning of the nineteenth century. Dr. Elliott had been a senior warden in St. Johns Lodge in Stratford, Connecticut. Rufus Easton was a member of Roman Lodge No. 82, Rome, New York. John Scott had done his degree work in Pennsylvania.

Freemasonry in America had been imported from England about 1740. The chief founders of English Freemasonry in 1715, Reverend James Anderson and Reverend John Theopholis Desuglieres, were learned and influential men, members of the prestigious organization for the promotion of scientific research, the Royal Society of London. They were confidents of men with responsible standards of conduct from both the aristocratic and the middle class, men who were repelled by the venality and corruption to be found in high places. Such men found the notorious "Hell Fire Clubs" particularly repugnant. In these clubs, licentious behavior was encouraged, orthodox religion ridiculed, traditional values belittled. To counteract such decadence, the two clergymen devised a positive alternative, attractive to men of achievement, which would reinforce, not flout, ethical behavior.

Anderson and Desuglieres took the scientific and religious rationale of their day, infused it with Christian ethics, explained it in the pragmatic language of the highly respected building trade of working stonemason operating out of their guild hall or Masonic Lodge. To distinguish it from the still operative guilds, the organization was called speculative Freemasonry. Men with other occupations than that of stonemasons were eligible for membership. By 1721 the non-operative members outnumbered the actual working mason. By 1775 Masonry and its lodges were to be found around the world as well as in Colonial America.

At the outbreak of the Revolutionary War, the Fraternity was officially neutral. Some lodges, however, had a preponderance of Tories and British officers. Other lodges had a number of the opposition, including a growing amount of members active in the Continental military and naval forces. As the tide of war turned and carried the Tories and British out of the country and the lodges, it was the patriots who remained.

The leading patriot was George Washington. He emerged from the conflict the undisputed leader of the country and the venerated leader of American Freemasonry. He was highly praised as exemplifying the Masonic ideal during his life as well as the ideal American citizen. This enhanced the reputation of the Fraternity, gained much public respect from outsiders, attracted leaders of contemporary society into its ranks.

As Blue Lodge Masonry advanced along the frontier and into the back country, it filled vital and long-felt wants for many an unsophisticated backwoods youth. It instilled a respect for learning and for teachers. It brought a sense of order and gave a point and direction for existence to many who had been without either.

Masonry came into Andrew Henry's life at a critical time when he was most in need of direction in his life. In 1805 his Masonic friends in the Ste. Genevieve District got together with other Masons across the river in Illinois to establish a lodge in Kaskaskia.

When Western Star Lodge, No. 107, AF&AM, was formally chartered by the Grand Lodge of Pennsylvania, June 3, 1806, Francis Vallé was one of its charter members. The first to petition for the degrees were his brother-in-law, Walter Fenwick; Fenwick's partner, Andrew Henry; and Henry's friend, the lawyer George Bullit.

On the fluid frontier, lodges such as Western Star provided a measure of cohesion, were vital net-working centers of far-reaching influence. Lodges, per se, did not take direct action. They did, however, offer a forum where members, concerned with preserving the stability of society, could discuss problems freely and reach a consensus of opinion under the protection of the oath of secrecy. These members in turn, knowing their own best interests were best served by promoting peace, order and understanding among the more solid and thoughtful men of their neighborhood, could marshall public opinion on their side. This encouraged potential members to request admittance to the Fraternity.

For, as Andrew Henry had discovered, a man had to ask of his own accord to be considered for membership. Like Fenwick and Bullit, Andrew Henry was given a petition to fill out. The information he provided on his background, beliefs, physical condition, maturity, means of support and freedom from bondage was then thoroughly investigated during a one-month waiting period. The investigating committee gave him a favorable report. The vote for his acceptance into membership was by secret ballot and as required, unanimous.

Once accepted, his initiation and advancement through the three degrees proceeded apace. This required a great deal of concentration, a lot of memory work, and considerable travel to and from Kaskaskia. By the time he passed the third and final stage of proficiency to become a Master Mason, he could vouch that 'to get (or give) the third degree,' involved a very elaborate test of ability. His commitment to this enlightening expansion of his life is reflected in the rapidity with which he achieved proficiency, so that only seven months after Kaskaskia received the charter for Western Star Lodge, he was one of the Master Masons who petitioned the Grand Lodge for a warrant to form a lodge in Ste. Genevieve; within a year of presenting his petition for membership in the Fraternity, he was one of the first officers of the first Masonic Lodge to be established west of the Mississippi.

Despite the good fellowship they found in Kaskaskia, and the fraternal network available there, the Masons often found it difficult to ferry across the Mississippi to meetings, especially at night, during high water or when ice floes dotted the winter surface crossing. With a growing number of the brethren living on the west side of the river, there was need for a handier meeting place.

Louisiana Lodge No. 109 at Ste. Genevieve was instituted July 17, 1807, with Dr. Aaron Elliott as the first master, Andrew Henry as the first senior warden, and Francis Vallé, Walter Fenwick and George Bullitt, among the charter members. As was often the custom, particularly for a new lodge just getting started and not yet able to afford the cost of erecting a building of their own, arrangements were made to hold meetings in the local inn, the Green Tree Tavern.

Originally the home of Nicholas Janis, friend of George Rogers Clark, it had a three-sided fireplace with openings into three rooms but using only one taxable chimney. The triangular design extended down into the earthen cellar where a hiding place had been hollowed out in the center of the foundation. In event of Indian raids or other dangers, this bolt hole could be reached through a false panel in the fireplace in the children's bedroom, was large enough to offer concealment to several children or two or three adults. Since the house was outside the city gates, the front steps were fashioned so they could be pulled up at night to discourage curious Indians and other intruders.

After Nicholas's death, his son Francois Janis made it into a boarding house and tavern. The basement, with an outside entrance under the gallery, was converted into a tavern. The first floor was the family living quarters. The attic was used as sleeping quarters for travellers. According to the English traveler, Thomas Ashe, it was a comfortable haven by 1804. The inn-keeper saw that the latter's horses were looked after in the stables at the rear of the property; the inn-keeper's wife 'made me a cup of coffee with as much perfection as ever I drank at the Palais Royal or at the foot of Pont Neuf.'

As 1807 drew to a close, Andrew Henry was attending meetings regularly at the Green Tree Tavern. Following adjournment, there would be refreshments and the coffee of much perfection and many things to talk about:

The treason charges against Colonel Burr and the leading local Burrites, John Smith T and Henry Dodge. The abilities and achievements of Meriwether Lewis, named to replace Wilkinson as governor, and his orders for all those clearly involved in the Burr scheme to be removed from office. The arrival at the mines of the new teritorial secretary, and acting governor, Francis Bates, to conduct the investigations.

Although the Bates findings were never released, he came down hard on John Smith T., who had resisted arrest. Smith lost his civil and military appointments, and a large measure of his power and influence in the mining district.

Bates did listen more sympathetically to the innocence pleas of some of Smith's supporters, allowed them to retain their posts. He was more than a bit miffed with the way William Ashley called attention to himself.

A practical man, Ashley was not the conspirator type. He was loyal, however, and not one to turn his back on an associate. In protest to Smith's removal as militia colonel, Ashley resigned his captaincy, in an undiplomatic letter. After that, he couldn't expect any favors from the new territorial government he had criticized. Having effectively excluded himself from the circle of men in public office who held power in the district and territory, he concentrated on the business, exclusively in his name now.

From merchants in Ste. Genevieve, Wm. H. Ashley & Co. stocked up on supplies for mining families. In ox carts and on pack animals, tools and household goods were carried the forty miles to the new mines and new settlements opening up around Mine á Breton. There, Ashley traded the supplies to miners for their lead which he transported back to Ste. Genevieve, sold to buyers.

Ashley did give folks something to talk about when he was arrested in Cape Girardeau twice for assault within a five month period. The second time he beat up the same resident, John Gasper, he was jailed and fined $800.

Mary Able, the American girl he had married in 1807, was said to be a good influence on him, polishing up his manners and gentling his temper. His father-in-law, Ezekiel Able, an American of considerable property and influence in Cape Girardeau, was backing him financially; his brother-in-law was arranging for him to acquire extensive holdings on which to recreate the life of comfort and gentility he had admired from afar in Virginia.

While Ashley's stabilized personal life now centered on Cape Girardeau, Andrew Henry still saw him occasionally at the mines or in Ste. Genevieve. Like other friends of Henry's, Ashley avoided the subject of marriage.

Andrew Henry was willing to listen to and talk about many things. The one thing he would not talk about, even with his closest friends, was his failed marriage. Nor would he talk about his pending divorce from Marie Villars, Francis Vallé's cousin.

Chapter 4

The one event in his life that Andrew Henry was reluctant to recall to mind, and blandly reticent about discussing, was his short-lived marriage. When he wed Marie Louise Dubriel Villars, daughter of Marie Louise Vallé and Louis Dubriel Villars, December 16, 1805, in Ste. Genevieve, William Ashley was his best man. When Henry and Marie separated January 3, 1806, eighteen days later, Ashley was one of those who didn't ask any questions. He just nodded his head, when the necessary account was made to him, but not necessarily the full account, that Henry's marriage was to be dissolved.

In the next six months, Henry's friends considered it good therapy that he immersed himself in the expansion of his mining interests, and dubious therapy for him to start up a commercial distillery for the manufacture of whiskey for sale and too often, staggering personal consumption. Fortunately, his first tentative inquiry to Dr. Elliott about Masonic membership resulted in a therapeutic lecture on the sobriety requirement. Henry profited in more ways than one, from the prompt sale of the distillery, and a sober, serious attention to meeting that requirement.

In the intervening months before the divorce proceedings were finalized, he maintained a tersely bleak reserve about his failed marriage with both friends and acquaintances and they, more quickly than he, put it out of their minds. Except one person.

Only one person, and that a child, a resolute bundle of sensibility and common sense, had the temerity to bring up the subject and reduce the burden, lightening it in her inimitable way to manageable proportions.

When Andrew Henry returned to Missouri and renewed his friendship with the Fleming family, he was charmed by their winsome new daughter, a three-year old who delighted in being transported gaily about on his shoulder. As he had acknowledged rather shamefacedly to Madame Vallé, he made the jocular offer to marry her when she grew up. As Catherine and Emilie Vallé had pointed out, little Mary Fleming had accepted.

Shortly after receiving confirmation that his divorce had been finalized October 16, 1807, Henry had business that took him near Mine á Joe. He realized it had been some time since he had talked lead mining with its owner, Patrick Fleming, or heard the medical shop talk of his son, Dr. Nicholas Fleming, so, his business concluded, he made his way to the mining complex where the Flemings spent much of their time annually between April and November.

Hospitably welcomed by Pat and Dr. Nick, his booted legs stretched out before him as he relaxed in a comfortable rocker on the Fleming porch, he made small talk with Nick while Pat went to persuade Mrs. Fleming of their need for some of her refreshing, highly respected wine, made from the secret Bequette formula handed down from her French grandfather.

Listening to Dr. Nick, he was not aware of Mary's approach until she was before him, making a graceful curtsy. He smiled at her, noting absently that she was taller than he remembered, but as always, neatly feminine, with her lustrous curls smoothly brushed into place.

"Miss Mary, you are prettier than ever," he said, making her a sketchy bow without moving from the chair.

Mary's brother halted in mid-sentence, straightened up from his lounging position against a porch support and took a step forward, with a low, admonitory, "Mary, remember what Mamán told you!"

"Come away from those steps or you'll fall down them," the child said in a reasonable tone without turning her gaze from Andrew Henry. "Again."

She clasped her small hands loosely in front of her pink pinafore. "You can sit down over there. It will be all right. Don't worry. I don't have much to say to him."

The Doctor, her senior by more than a decade, sat down abruptly, tossing a beseeching word over his shoulder, "Mamán!"

"Are you unmarried now?" she asked gravely.

For a moment, holding his breath, her brother thought she was going to get the same abrupt, cold dismissal as Henry's other friends who trespassed on his privacy.

But Henry's smile stayed in place as the import of her question registered. "That's right," he said with equal seriousness. "I am no longer married."

"Then why are you still so mis'able?"

"Still so — oh, miserable," Henry interpreted, meeting her unswerving brown eyes. As, awaiting his reply, she folded her arms judiciously over her chest, he found himself bemused by the resemblance of this miniature female to his mother when he had violated her code of conduct.

"Miserable? No, I don't think I am still miserable," he said thoughtfully, then remembering Nick's presence, added firmly, "Not to speak of, anyway."

"You deserved to be mis'able," she said coldly. "You promised to wait and marry me."

"Mary!" Mrs. Fleming was standing in the doorwary in response to the doctor's summons.

"That's what I said. Marry," her daughter said firmly but politely. "I am not quite through with him, Mamán. You can sit down if you like."

A hint of a dimple showed at the corner of her cupid-bow mouth as she continued, her voice softer, although her gaze remained intent. "Now that you are unmarried —" she paused to correct herself, picking up Henry's phrasing, "no longer married, the sitchy-ashun has changed. You must not be mis'able."

Henry's expression became indulgent, a trifle teasing, as he raised a quizzical eyebrow.

"Now, you can wait and marry me like you promised. You won't be mis'able when I am your wife." She curtseyed briefly and made her exit with a final observation, "I will not drive you to drink."

"I'm not so sure about that," her father said with a grin, looking at the speechless trio. He carried a bottle of wine and clinking glasses. He filled one and placed it carefully in Henry's rather limp grasp. "I think she just did."

Mrs. Fleming sank into the nearest chair, fanning the air before her face with one hand, accepting the glass Pat held out with the other.

From hearsay, from long acquaintance with the leading families of Ste. Genevieve, she had pieced together her own scenario of Andrew Henry's marriage. Marie Ann Bequette came from one of the French-Creole families that set the tone of society in the French communities on both sides of the Mississippi. Descended from Jean Bequette and Jeanne Clair Demont, emigrants from their native village on the Sambre River, in Cambrai, France, she had relatives in Cahokia, Kaskaskia, and St. Louis, as well as in Ste. Genevieve.

She knew from personal experience that well-to-do outsiders, like her Patrick, could marry into the group. Dr. Walter Fenwick, a good friend of Andrew's, had become a member of the town's leading lights when he married Julie Vallé in 1801.

It was well known that Francis Vallé held Andrew Henry in high esteem. He was well liked by the Joseph Prattes, was often a guest of both the Fenwicks and Prattes. When Marie DuBreuil De Villars came from New Orleans to visit her Vallé cousins in Ste. Genevieve, Madam Fleming had an idea Julie Fenwick and Marie Villars exercised their propensity for matchmaking. Andrew Henry would have been invited to the dinners, picnics and balls given for their cousin.

Mrs. Fleming didn't know much about Marie herself but she had known her parents. Her mother, Marie Louise Vallé, was the daughter of the founder and first French commandant of Ste. Genevieve, Papá Vallé. Her father, Louis DuBreuil de Villars, one of the patrician French Creoles of New Orleans who entered Spanish service. He had met, married Marie Vallé, while serving as the first Spanish military commandant of Ste. Genevieve. He had been rewarded with a better position in New Orleans, moved his family there. The mother died in 1801, leaving seven children.

Madam Fleming was sure the Vallés would have kept in contact with the children. Marie could have been one of the gaggle of relatives who enjoyed the hospitality of Madame Vallé's household off and on over the years and could have had her eye on Andrew Henry long before reaching nubility. At any rate, possibly with the contrivance of her cousins Julie Fenwick and Marie Pratte, Marie Villars came to the notice of Andrew Henry.

In Marie Fleming's salad days, the winter months were the time of weddings, when the basically agricultural community had more leisure for festivities. She supposed that Andrew Henry, an impatient American, without that sense of tradition, and Marie Villars, an urbane product of New Orleans, choosing to be united in a civil ceremony, didn't know it was bad luck to be married in December.

She had an idea that their basic incompatability was revealed when Andrew Henry took his bride from their honeymoon accommodations to his diggings. Andrew would have been proud of all he had built and accomplished. Marie would have been appalled when she realized she was expected to be chief cook and bottle washer in the primitive backwoods.

Although not often exercised, under the French legal folkways system a wife had the right to renounce the marriage contract and withdraw her share of community goods and property. Since the marriage had been a civil contract, Marie's church would not consider it binding, so she was free to herd her ducks to market again, and probably was doing so, but not in Ste. Genevieve.

In Ste. Genevieve itself, whatever the circumstances that ended in the no-fault divorce, it didn't seem to have made any difference in Henry's standing in the community. Marie's uncles and cousins had been good friends of Andrew Henry before the marriage. They remained good friends after the separation. From what the Flemings had heard, there did not appear to be any indication of misconduct on Andrew Henry's part.

They had heard a great deal about his misconduct from a source much closer to home. Mrs. Fleming winced at the memory. Little Mary had been furious. Andrew Henry had promised to marry her. He had broken his promise. He should be punished. Papa, or brother Nick, must see to it.

Dr. Nick, who had brought the news of Andrew Henry's marriage that gave them such a stormy time of it with Mary, had actually been relieved when he heard the marriage had only lasted eighteen days. Without bothering to learn any of the details, he had hurried home with the news.

Looking back, Mrs. Fleming realized guiltily how little thought they had given to Andrew's feelings. Instead they had been selfishly relieved to have the tears and most of the indignation vanish, to see Mary bright-eyed and cheerful again.

Now, months later, Mrs. Fleming let her gaze rest on a somewhat discomfited Andrew Henry.

"It is not often a middle-aged Mamán has to suffer through the betrothal, jilting and reconciliation of a girl-child before she has lost her milk teeth," she said dryly, her eyes twinkling as she raised her glass of wine to Andrew Henry. "You were not ungallant, M'sieu. Thank you."

Andrew Henry rode away from his afternoon with the Flemings with a sense of well being, more lighthearted than he had been in several years. Partly it was the magic of the Fleming's themselves, partly it was the encouragement they had given him about the undertaking he was just beginning to give serious consideration.

As Patrick had acknowledged in complimentary fashion, Henry's circle of acquaintances in recent years had continued to expand until it included a great many of the enterprising men of achievement in the territory.

Among them were two men, Meriwether Lewis and William Clark, who, in in making a round trip to the Pacific, had taken men's minds off petty, mundane affairs. They and their men had been telling stories that stirred the imaginative, excited the adventuresome and stimulated the ambitious. When Andrew Henry, Francis Vallé, Walter Fenwick and some of their fellow Masons paid a visit to the lodge recently established in St. Louis through the efforts of Meriwether Lewis, they lingered after the closing to hear Lewis and Clark give a brief, factual account of their discoveries.

Through Parfait Dufour, who had his home in Ste. Genevieve, Andrew Henry heard more. Even before the Lewis and Clark expedition, Dufour had been a highly respected scout. He had rendered valuable service during the Revolutionary War by guiding George Rogers Clark, William Clark's older brother, when he ventured forth with his frontiersmen to capture Vincennes and Kaskaskia. He was a forthright man, not given to exaggeration. While Lewis and Clark were at Wood River, preparing for their expedition, he had spent considerable time with them, going over their maps, filling in some of the gaps, telling them what he had seen and knew of the country up the Missouri.

Dufour took an interest in the progress of the expedition. At

Francis Janis's Green Tree Tavern one evening he described in detail to Andrew Henry the contents of the keelboat, and the men who had been sent back downstream while the remainder of the Lewis and Clark expedition took off overland for the Pacific. When the expedition returned and the men from that expedition began looking around for the land granted them in partial payment for their years of service, Dufour welcomed them, showed them around the area. One of those, a George Drouillard, he brought to the tavern. Men lingered late at the tavern that night. Among them, spellbound, were Andrew Henry and Francis Vallé, Walt and Ben Wilkinson, Pierre Menard and William Morrison.

Out there, Drouillard told them, waving his tankard in a sweeping westward direction, was an abundance of game, mighty snow-capped mountains, monstrous bears and fortunes in beaver in every creek bottom.

As he listened to Drouillard, Henry began to realize the real significance of the transfer of the Louisiana Territory to the United States. This man Drouillard, and others like him, had glimpsed a portion of that territory. Inherent in the precise, restrained reports of the leaders, Lewis and Clark, or the saga-like reminiscences of their men, was the revelation that out there lay opportunities far beyond the scope, challenge and profit of any undertaking so far attempted.

In the rising tide of expectations, the prosperous Illinois merchants Pierre Menard and William Morrison gave serious consideration to proposals made to them by Manuel Lisa.

Born in New Orleans, September 8, 1772, Lisa was a Spaniard who moved to St. Louis at an early age. He began trading in a small way, then in 1800 got the Osage-Indian-trading license away from the Chouteaus. He had a knack for dealing with the Indians, monopolized trade with some of the tribes, profited, expanded and was resented accordingly by other traders. He was on the look out for opportunities to expand further, toying with the idea making a trading trip to Sante Fe when Lewis and Clark returned to St. Louis in September of 1806. Electrified by their descriptions of beaver in abundance, Lisa set his sights on expanding his fur trading into the rich area they said could be found at the headwaters of the Missouri.

He latched onto returning Lewis & Clark veterans, Peter Weiser, John Potts, George Drouillard, conferred with Menard and Morrison. In 1807 they entered into a partnership agreement with Lisa that led to a fur trading expedition to the Upper Missouri. George Drouillard was selected by Menard and Morrison to act for them, serve as second in command of the undertaking. He and the other Lewis and Clark veterans guided Lisa's party up the Missouri, down the Yellowstone to the mouth of the Big Horn. There

Lisa established the post he christened Fort Raymond for his only son.

Lisa, returning to St. Louis with an impressive catch, knew that when word of his profits got out, he better brace himself for some cutthroat competition. Fur traders, big and small, would be treading on his heels. The Chouteaus, with their assets and organization, were the most worrisome. The thing was, if they drove him to the wall, they would also be causing problems for one of the Chouteau in-laws, Pierre Menard, which would not set well with the family as a whole. Licking them was out of the question. With Pierre Menard on his side, joining them was not.

The entrepreneur of the upper Missouri fur trade flung himself energetically into persuading the leading fur traders to forget their differences, band together into one organization. Shrewdly, he got to them individually, then collectively. The considerable advantages, fiscal and physical, were not to be ignored.

The government, in the persons of Meriwether Lewis and William Clark, listened courteously, encouragingly. In 1807, the same year Andrew Henry bought out William Ashley, the same year his divorce became final, Meriwether Lewis had been made governor, William Clark, Indian agent and brigadier general of the territorial militia. They had a problem in the person of a Mandan chieftain who wanted to go back to his people. Despite the best of intentions and a lot of careful planning, they had been unable to get him back up the Missouri.

When Lewis and Clark had come down river in 1806, Shehaka, or Big White, and his family had accompanied them as well as Rene Jessaume and his family. The French-Canadian Jessaume, as official interpreter, had been part of the escort that took Shehaka to Washington for an audience with President Jefferson. There had been various sidetrips and meetings with the great and near-great designed for mutual benefit, to impress the Indian on the one hand, and to illustrate in some small measure the achievements of the expedition on the other.

When the junketing Shehaka was returned to St. Louis in 1807, one of the first undertakings of the new governor and his Indian agent was to set up an expedition to return their friend, and figurehead, to his people, as they had promised.

For the ill-fated undertaking, they selected one of the experienced sergeants from their expedition, the dependable Kentuckian, Nathaniel Pyror, now an ensign with the regular army, to command a twenty-five-man military escort.

To beef up the manpower and provide mutual protection, there was Auguste Pierre Chouteau, the eldest son of the one of the leading businessmen of St. Louis. A West Point graduate, young Chouteau had served with General James Wilkinson before leaving the military to go into business with his father. He was bound for the Mandan villages with thirty-two traders and trappers. William Dorion, one of the sons of 'Old' Dorian, the free lance interpreter, by his Sioux woman, was headed for the risky territory of the Yankton Sioux with ten trappers, two interpreters, and Lt. Joseph Kimball and his seven soldiers, escorting home another group of junketing Indians, eighteen men, women and children of the Yankton Sioux.

Somehow, Pryor, young Chouteau, and Frederick Bates, the acting governor of the territory while Lewis was on a trip east, got the idea they could count on, as well, Lisa and the forty-two men who left St. Louis about the same time on the venture he'd worked out with Menard and Morrison.

The unpredictable Lisa, leaving them and a regrettable reputation for breaking his word behind him, got upstream, scot-free, to establish the first fort in Montana. He left a lot of irascible people behind, including the capricious Arikara and the testy Teton Sioux.

Pryor and Chouteau deposited Lt. Kimball and his Yanktons near the James River, keeping William Dorion with them to interpret, in case they met the Teton Sioux. At the Arikara villages they did and learned that Shehaka's Mandans were currently at war with the Tetons and the Arikaras. They had to fight to keep Shehaka from being taken captive.

The unlucky Captain Pryor, blaming Lisa for treacherously setting them up to be victimized by the Indians; Chouteau, blaming the Canadian traders for setting the Indians against Americans; the three dead, blaming no one, the ten wounded, the other reeling survivors, tired and sore with defeat, blaming incompetence in general; all were driven ignominiously back down the river.

Pryor went back to the Bellefontaine Cantonment accompanying another Lewis and Clark veteran, the badly wounded George Shannon. The surgeon at Bellefontaine, Dr. Saugrain, gave George his choice: lose his leg, badly shattered at the knee by shot from an Arikara musket, or die from gangrene. George chose to become Pegleg Shannon. Operating without anaesthesia, Dr. Saugrain, assisted by Dr. Farrar, performed the first thigh operation on record west of the Mississippi. It nearly killed George, was taking him some time to recover.

Shehaka, revising some of his first, favorable impressions, was quartered at Bellefontaine, too. Whatever prestige he had brought to Lewis and Clark, his enforced stay in Missouri was beginning to reflect on the prestige and might of the new government. Somehow, and soon, he must be returned. For many people, including Governor Lewis and Brigadier General Clark, there was a certain ironic justice in putting the onus on Manuel Lisa. The new company Manuel Lisa was promoting could take the responsibility of delivering Shehaka home to his Mandan village before getting on with its primary objective, the development of a flourishing fur trade.

When Lisa got together with Menard and Morrison, Francis Vallé, who had observations to contribute from his own, earlier ventures up the Missouri, was drawn into the discussions. He in turn got Andrew Henry interested.

He found himself dealing with other men with backgrounds much like his own. Many of them, like Henry, were migrants to the area. They were comparatively young, physically active, with varied but similar experiences in border wars, Indian confrontations, the rough-and-tumble of frontier life, and the opportunities for making a living.

Their talks moved from speculation to specifics: the ways and mean of organizing, financing and supplying a unified trading expedition. Andrew Henry, as a partner in the profitable enterprise, would be going not just up the Missouri, but clear to the headwaters of the Missouri in the fabulous land of the Shining Mountains.

By the end of 1808, Henry could see that the company would be made up of men with at least one unifying quality: they were all survivors. A small number had already profited in their endeavors and would eventually become rich men. A slightly larger number of them would achieve precarious short-term affluence. He anticipated that the majority would have their ups and downs and in the end find they had advanced very little, if at all. With typical optimism, Andrew Henry did not see himself among the latter.

When the objectives of the company, its standing, the nature of its financial arrangements were finally hammered out, eleven men signed the articles of agreement: Benjamin Wilkinson, Pierre Chouteau, Sr., Manuel Lisa, Auguste Chouteau, Jr., Reuben Lewis, William Clark and Sylvestre Labbadie, all of St. Louis; Pierre Menard and William Morrison, Kaskaskia, Illinois; Dennis Fitzhugh, Louisville, Kentucky; and Andrew Henry, Louisiana, Missouri.

Henry, as he went about setting his affairs in order, was already giving thought to the recruiting of qualified men. For the contract of the Company, dated February 24, 1809, required the St. Louis Missouri Fur Company to raise an armed force of 125 men, 40 of whom should be Americans and "expert riflemen."

This force, as constituted, would be a part of the Territorial Militia, under command of Pierre Chouteau, Sr., until they had discharged their commitment to return Shehaka and his party safely to the Mandan towns on the Upper Missouri.

Shehaka, who was looking forward to strutting before his people, regaling them with tales of the fabulous world of the white man, achieving secure status, was getting impatient. Not only would it be the responsibility of the St. Louis Missouri Fur Company to insure his safekeeping and transportation, but they also had to accommodate his family and all his fine gifts, Jessaume and his family aboard keelboats for three hazardous months.

The government would pay the Company $7,000 to do so. To further sweeten the pot, Governor Lewis would not authorize any other persons to go above the mouth of the Platte until after the expedition's departure date. This would give them a near monopoly in arranging Indian trade, getting started on the planned establishment of convenient forts, sending out their own bands of trappers.

As a commissioned officer in the Territorial Militia, Andrew Henry would be paid to assist with the return of Shehaka.

As one of the eleven partners in the company, Major Henry would get in on the ground level of the new enterprise and be in a position to capitalize on the investment of his time and money in a challenging personal way.

By the end of April, 1809, the Major had come to an agreement with his friend, fellow migrant and brother Mason, Walter Fenwick, regarding the stewardship of his mining and other properties in his absence. He felt fortunate to be able to leave his affairs in the hands of this competent, provident businessman and physician.

He also felt fortunate with the caliber of the men he had recruited to be with him for three years in the mountains. The nucleus of what would be a larger group, these select men, he was sure, would prove flexible enough to serve as militiamen before embarking upon the more vulnerable life of the trapper. This nucleus consisted of tested men Henry knew had a professional approach to the techniques of travel, trade, craftsmanship and sustenance.

His good friend and brother Mason, Francis Vallé, would be heading up one of the trapping parties. They would have one or two novices of importance to instruct in survival skills. Samuel Morrison, the younger brother of William Morrison, and his cousin, scion of the Bryan merchant family of Philadelphia, would be accompanying them, learning the fur trade business firsthand. For the others, Henry had found, among the Americans scattered through the lead mining district, products of the frontier. There was steady Charles Davis, one of the lanky, sandy-haired Jackson boys, a couple friends vouched for by Jackson, equally young and eager, but already experienced from the kind of life that was imperative for the survival of the second generation west of the Appalachian.

He knew these Americans and their backgrounds well enough to recognize that the ways of survival in the wilderness were deeply ingrained in them. They would not need instruction in the basic skills. In the Rocky Mountains, their purpose, their procedure in Indian intercourse, even their dress and personal equipment would be essentially the same as Davis, Jackson, McBride and Cather had known all their lives, second-nature to them.

Now, he told Francis Vallé, as they packed for the trip to St. Louis to join the expedition, he wanted to swing by the Flemings, partly to see if Doctor Nicholas Fleming had decided to accompany them, partly to make his farewells, as well as leave his violin and most of his books in their safekeeping.

So, the first week in May, 1809, Henry, accompanied by Francis Vallé, rode up to the Fleming holdings located on the Ste. Genevieve property Marie Bequette Fleming had inherited. Little Mary, carrying a jug of milk from the spring house toward the kitchen, was the first to note and intercept his approach, beaming at him as he dismounted.

"You remembered," she exclaimed, her dark eyes dancing with gratification. "I told Mamán you would. Please come up on the porch and make yourself comfortable. You, too, M'sieu Francis." Gesturing at the two slightly older boys who came running up with broad grins, "My cousins, Augustin and Henri, will see to your horses. This one is Cousin Augustin. That one is Cousin Henri." The boys, representative of the children of other, more prolific Bequettes, to be found in varying numbers in their Tante's household, nodded. "Excuse me while I tell Mamán you have arrived."

She whisked herself off in a flutter of blue ruffles, calling, "Mamán! Papa! The Major is here. He did remember my birthday."

"Did you?" Francis asked him in an undertone as they turned away from a mutually friendly exchange with the boys who were now leading the horses away.

The Major, dressed in linen breeches and boots and a worn, but well-tailored riding jacket of rich brown corduroy that reflected the color of his hair, brought forth from the inside breast pocket of the jacket a package. "A rainbow of hair ribbons. Will these be adequate, do you think?"

More than adequate, Francis thought, watching the little girl accept the ribbons with shy pleasure, then persuade Mrs. Fleming to tie the blue one that matched her birthday frock in her curls. They sat at ease on the porch, with Patrick and Dr. Nicholas Fleming joining them, with the cousins that bridged the gap between Nick and Mary breaking off from their domestic tasks to greet them cordially, all of them friendly and lighthearted, giving the day a festive air as they indulgently made an occasion of Mary's eighth birthday.

"Major," they said in speaking to and of Andrew Henry, "Major." Americans, Francis thought wryly, for all their vaunted democratic disdain of titles, took pride in one. He had observed in his travels to other territories and states, how a high-militia office was considered an honor, much sought after, regardless of the salary or the position itself. Until superseded by a loftier commission, the inherent splendor of the military title, no matter how long or short the militia service, seemed to be irrevocable. His friend would be the "Major" for the rest of his life.

He roused from his reverie to catch the Major's answer to a question he had missed.

"— not before June," the Major was saying in his pleasant voice. "And, no, I'm not sure we have all the good men we need. We certainly have more than I expected. However, out of 300 men, there's bound to be some who will change their minds. We stopped by to let you know there's still a place for you, Nick, if you're still inclined."

"I am so inclined," said the Doctor. "I've looked over all the reports and maps you loaned me. I've gone into the scope of the proposed chain of fortified points and it fires the imagination. You obviously learned all there was to know about the route and the resources before you put your name to the company agreement. You are already an expert on a virgin land."

"Give Francis credit for supplying me with much of that material. He's been in that virgin land."

"Only part way," said Francis. "Much of it will be new to me, too."

"We have a Dr. Thomas going with us. Ever heard of him?"

"The former army surgeon? I'd like to meet him."

"But?" the Major raised an expressive eyebrow.

"Hank Brackenridge. He wants me to join him on a trip up the river. However, he won't be able to leave Pennsylvania in time for us to go with you. He's coming out as soon as he can. We'll be following you to the Upper Missouri, be there before you get all those trading posts in place."

Patrick leaned forward to knock his pipe out against the edge of porch. "How many of the other partners will be going up river with you?"

"All of them except Clark, Morrison and Fitzhugh, last I heard. According to the company articles, Clark doesn't have to go up river but all the other partners have to go or send substitutes, alternates, acceptable to the other partners," said the Major. "William Morrison is sending his brother Samuel and his Uncle Guy Bryan's boy to represent the Bryan-Morrison interests."

Doctor Nick nodded his head. "The company, when you stop to think about it, is a shrewd amalgamation of interests. You are talking about men close-knit by friendship as well as commerce, amd linked by intermarriage as well as by kinship of blood. They command respect," he said, "except for — "

Madam Fleming interrupted to get them all moving inside to gather around the laden dining-room table. As Francis held the chair for Mary to seat herself gracefully then took the place next to her as she had indicated, with the Major on her right, he realized the Flemings were sincerely interested in this undertaking, eliciting and providing footnotes to his running commentary, that was put into momentary abeyance as everyone was seated.

"I do hope you will like the fricasseed chicken," Mary said to Francis, graciously exercising her budding social talents in unconscious imitation of her mother, an excellent role model, in Francis's opinion. "We do know it is one of the Major's favorite dishes." Francis murmured a courteous response and Mary said, "It's mine, too."

The Doctor recaptured the conversation with, "As I was saying, the company and their first-line recruits," with a nod to Francis, "is made up of men of good repute and well-earned respect with one exception," and Francis found himself caught up in the lively verbal vivisection of Manuel Lisa.

The Major listened to the exchanges, smiling once when Mrs. Fleming contributing her bit, capped it firmly with, "And your own Presbyterian minister deplored it!" Finally, he gathered up the strands firmly, but lightly, with, "Lisa does lead an unorthodox life — but who can say there is a man who does not, out in the field. Granted, he may be a bit of a tyrant — "

"A bit?" Patrick snorted. "He's going to have trouble with those free-willed Americans of yours, Major. They won't let him push them around any more than what's-his-name — Rose — did."

Francis chuckled. Dr. Nick looked at him in anticipation. They shared a free-running sense of humor and a pleasant streak of individualism that made them both favorites wherever they went.

"Patrick, you would have been a trifle put out with Rose yourself," said Francis. "He gave away all those trade goods Lisa entrusted to him. Said it made him a big man with the Crows. It didn't do a thing for Lisa. Besides, Rose had no sense of timing. Imagine, showing up to make his boastful but unprofitable report just as Manuel was getting into the keelboat to return to St. Louis, already a bit testy over the lean pickings from other bands of Indians."

"Wasn't there a fight?" prompted the Doctor.

"A fierce one, with Rose winning, until Potts pulled them apart and hustled Lisa onto the keelboat.Then Rose ran to one of Fort Raymond's cannons and tried to blow Lisa and the keelboat out of the water. Failing to do that, Rose turned around and headed back to the Crows."

"If he has survived, I might look him up," the Major said cheerfully. "Rose may be able to handle the Crows better than he does a cannon."

Following the spontaneous burst of laughter, he went on thoughtfully. "Manuel Lisa may be all that hearsay claims. Ruthless, unorthodox, unable to remonstrate wisely, he still has one thing going for him that counts most of all: he seems to be lucky."

"Thinking in one language, communicating in another," said Francis dryly, "can lead to misunderstandings as I well know."

The Major nodded. Lisa probably did organize his thoughts, make his plans in Spanish. When he put them into voyageur French or fractured English, something was lost in translation. As a result there were misunderstandings, accusations and notoriety for not being a man of his word. "He's been teaching me Indian sign language. Maybe that will be the best way for us to communicate. Anyway, I'll know Manuel Lisa much better after I spend some time in the mountains with him."

"His lack of fluency in English is no reflection on his abilities," said Dr. Nick. "He succeeded in persuading ten, eleven men, reasonable men for the most part, but still men used to defining and making the most of the market on their own, a number of them his rivals in the trade who needed careful handling, and he not only got them interested in his proposal to work together as a company, but committed. Now, you take the Chouteaus — "

And the adults at the table did just that. As they polished off the fricasseed chicken, the platters of vegetables, hot biscuits and fresh butter, they polished up their recollections of Chouteau history.

Mary, in an undertone, inquired innocently of the Major, "You know the Chouteau brothers? Are they both bastards?"

There was a lull in the conversation so that Mary's inquiry rang out more clearly than intended. Mary felt her Mamán's eyes on her and realized she made a faux pas. Henry covered her discomfort by answering easily, "I couldn't say. I don't know either of them that well."

The men laughed. Mamán, with a Gallic shrug, said smoothly, "Cheri, Madame Chouteau was most unfortunate in her first marriage. Her husband mistreated her. Some say he deserted her and their son, Auguste Pierre. They would have starved had it not been for good friends, among them Pierre Laclede Liguest. Her friends supported her decision to contract a civil marriage with M'sieu Laclede. However, all of their children, Jean Pierre, Pelagie, Marie Louise and Victoria could not call themselves by their Papa's name. By French law, they had to be known as Chouteaus."

Mary was thoughtful. "That doesn't seem fair."

LaClede's son, Jean Pierre Chouteau, was now fifty-one.

He was one of the territory's most successful businessmen, experienced and influential through his profitable enterprises based on the Indian trade. As specified in the company contract, Pierre had the command and responsibility during the initial military phase of the expedition and would discharge his responsibilities by overcoming any obstacles to the safe delivery of Shehaka.

"Young Chouteau," said Patrick Fleming, referring to Auguste Pierre Chouteau, Jr., the twenty-three-year old son of Jean Pierre, "didn't he and Louis Vallé graduate from West Point together?"

"He and cousin Louis were among the first appointees President Jefferson made to the military academy," said Francis. "Neither one of them seem inclined to make the military a career."

"Still, young Chouteau has both military credentials and frontier experience. Labbadie has been very successful in his undertakings and has ties with Chouteau family. Doesn't really seem a frontier type to me, though."

"He's been helpful in the matter of Drouillard," said the Major. Sylvestre Labbadie, at thirty, had a quiet, restraining strength about him that was proving helpful in the preliminary preparations, working out the niggling little details with the recruits, smoothly circumventing pointless arguments. "You haven't heard about Drouillard?"

"Pierre Drouillard's boy by his Indian woman? The one Simon Kenton trained?" Patrick asked.

"And one of the best scouts Lewis and Clark had with them on their expedition. He has that route etched in his mind, mile-by-mile, clear to the Three Forks of the Missouri."

The table was cleared and the wine glasses refilled, with everyone lingering at the table, listening now to Patrick reminiscing about the visit Simon Kenton had paid to the territory over a decade ago.

When he finished, Dr. Nick said, "What about Drouillard? Menard and Morrison let him represent them in the field in that partnership they went into with Lisa."

Francis looked up from his dessert of flaky, rich chocolate eclair. At a nod from the Major, he took up the tale.

"This all happened in the spring of 1807 when Lisa was starting out. Near the Osage River, Antoine Bisonette deserted. Lisa sent George to bring him back. He did, more dead than alive. Bisonette died of his wounds.

"A murder charge was filed but not acted on until George Drouillard got back in reach of the authorities. The trial has interfered more with his plans than ours. He was hoping to get back to Detroit and visit all his Drouillard relatives before heading into the wilderness again. He hasn't been back since he headed out with Lewis and Clark.

"However, Lisa says he has a good man available up the river who was with Lewis and Clark, too. He's already made a foray into the country we're interested in. Name of Colter."

The Major saw that the sun was well advanced in the afternoon sky. He thought of the other company men and the divergent topics that had not yet been touched on, but would be, if he didn't take measures to bring this occasion to a courteous close so he and Francis could be on their way.

There was Benjamin Wilkinson, a respected businessman, but whose relationship to the notorious Jamie would lead to a discussion of the Burr trial; Reuben Lewis, brother of the Governor, would remind them of the complaints against Meriwether that were beginning to surface and, it was said, would have him heading soon for Washington City to refute them. That left Dennis Fitzhugh and William Clark. Fitzhugh, a respected Kentucky judge and third husband of the twice-widowed Fanny Clark, William's sister, didn't seem to have much interest in the expedition, except as an investment. William Clark, everyone would agree at more length than he and Francis could spare that day, was a conscientious Indian agent and military commander.

The Major inserted himself unobtrusively into the conversation, guiding the talk, leading them into relaxing with his infectious laughter, and, now, into a toast to Mary, saying, "I will think of you next year on this day when I am in the mountains."

Mary acknowledged the toast gracefully, then told the Major firmly, "I hope you don't have any adventures there."

There was a course of disclaimers from her cousins. The Major patted her hand. "Mary is talking good sense. An experienced traveler takes pains not to have adventures." He smiled. "Oh, there's bound to be a hazard or two to overcome that I can spin into an exciting tale for you when I return. To my mind, however, the successful journey is the dull journey. Therefore, no adventures."

"Let's all drink to that!" proposed the Doctor. "To a dull journey."

The toast drunk, the Major and Francis exchanged the necessary courtesies that placed them five minutes later outside on the porch. While the boys went to bring the horses and pack animals around, the Major handed Mary his cased violin. "Keep it tuned for me."

She took it out of the case with respectful care. "I wish I could play like you do. The voyageur's song, that's what I'd play for you now." She hummed a measure or two. The Major took the violin, softly began to accompany her so that she took confidence, sang the words clearly, sweetly, "Joy to thee, my brave canoe, there's no wing so swift as you." The others joined in, happily rendering the song of their French-Canadian heritage, when the rhythms of the paddles sent the sleek canoes out from Quebec into the wilderness, generation after generation. "Gently, now, my brave canoe, keep your footing sure and true . . . "

When the song ended, there was a long silence. Briskly, the Major broke the melancholy aftermath with a short, bouncy tune, completed with a flourish of violin and bow overhead.

"What tune was that?" asked Mary.

"The American theme song," said Francis. In his pleasant baritone, he gave her the words, "The bear went over the mountain, the bear went over the mountain, the bear went over the mountain to see what he could see!"

Mary clapped her hands. "That's just what the Major is going to do. The Major is going over the mountain to see what he can see!"

As they rode away, the Major humming under his breath, Francis realized no one had asked them how long they would be gone.

Two years later, as the year 1811 advanced from spring to summer, the Flemings were not the only ones asking, "How long is the Major to be in the mountains?"

Francis, who had been there and back, had mastered his outward, if not his inward shudder, reminded of the hazards, the grizzly as well as grisly he had faced in those mountains, knew when the question was put to him that they were asking more than that.

Would the Major return? So many good men had not.

Chapter 5

"It was much like any other trip up the river," Francis told the Flemings shortly after his return from the mountains, late in the summer of 1810.

All of May and a large part of June of 1809 had been spent in turning the original lists of men and supplies into actuality. The lists turned out to be inadequate as the roster swelled. The inventory of supplies, the number of barges for transport, grew accordingly, in an atmosphere of intense, concentrated, continuing adjustments.

The Major and Francis, in company with the other partners, and alone, toiled through the lengthening spring days. They came to know all the frontier village of St. Louis that tilted up from the scattered log huts, warehouses and docks strung along the river's edge.

In Manuel Lisa's house on Second Street they reviewed the lists of work done and still to be done. They assessed the man power, the weak and the strong, backgrounds and boasts. Over good wine they listened attentively to Lisa's acute dissertation on the notional people of the Upper Missouri who had no money, no roads, only vague territorial lines and a number of different languages, and the need of the swivel cannon to speak to all of them.

Along with the good wine, Lisa presented them to the bearer, the neat, self-effacing Mrs. Lisa, and the combed and tidied Ramon, reminding them and his son that Fort Raymond on the Yellowstone had been named in his honor.

After leaving their host, the energetic, enthusiastic Manuel, keelboatman, Indian trader and proud family man, the Major seemed thoughtful. Francis asked the reason.

"There's something about Mrs. Lisa," the Major said slowly. "My Mother said the only vessel for the frontier was an iron vessel. Some vessels are too fragile. Some vessels are flawed. The frontier is no place for either. I think Mrs. Lisa is an iron vessel, but dented by life on the frontier."

"How much wine did you drink?" demanded Francis. "There's nothing wrong with Mrs. Lisa that I could see."

"That's what I said. She's one of the iron vessels. Sometime or another, I'll wager she saw Indians at their goriest."

Francis, stepping over a maudlin trapper who had staggered out of a bar and folded up in the dusty street, searched his memory for details about Polly Charles Chew, the widow with an infant daughter that Manuel Lisa had married when he had a frontier store in Vincennes over a decade earlier. "She and her baby were the only ones of her family who weren't killed in an Indian attack. Seems to me she was a captive of the Kick-a-Poos for a short time. Hmm. She doesn't like talking about Indians. At any rate, she left us rather abruptly when Lisa started on the subject. Is that what made you curious?"

"That. And her eyes." Andrew Henry had seen other survivors, particularly the women, with that same haunted look.

They took the time and steps on the hilly street to Main and Pine Street to locate the Spanish house that had been the home of Benito Vasquez, Lisa's fellow Spaniard and second-in-command at Fort Raymond, who was to meet the expedition at the Mandan villages on the Upper Missouri.

Now it housed the unassuming William Clark. They were introduced to his fair patrician bride, Julia Hancock, and her new piano that the Major found irresistible until Clark, striking an even more responsive chord with his mention of a map, led them into his Indian museum, a small wooden building adjoining his gleaming white one-story home.

There, amidst walls lined with Indian regalia and the Indian derring-do recorded on tanned hides, Clark brought out his map.

"George Drouillard has filled in some of the empty spaces that we never reached. We did view the spot you have in mind," said Clark, his forefinger pointing to the location of the strip of wooded grassland between the Jefferson and Madison Rivers where the Major planned to erect his fort.

Francis, as they continued on from the Clarks, said cheerfully, "There's nothing haunted about Mrs. Clark's bright eyes. Agreed?

Then why are you shaking your head?'

"Because William Clark's 'Miss Judy' has the bright eyes and rosy cheeks of a likely consumptive," said the Major regretfully.

Entering one of the more raucous streets, they encountered the men who had signed up for the expedition, whiling away their time before departure.

French and Canadian voyageurs, coming out of a shop, would greet them loudly, gaily, but respectfully. The American riflemen, lean, laconic and libertarian, pausing to look in at a noisy bar where a gambling game was in progress on a buffalo robe spread on the dirt floor, would greet them with barely perceptible nods. The Delaware and Shawnee Indians, attending to their barter in the open air market, acknowledged them with aloof hand motions.

The Major responded appropriately to each culture. Affably with his eyes, hands, atrocious accent and first name to the French, "Marie. St. John. Baptiste."

With expressionless face, no gestures, and surnames to the Americans, "Dougherty. Cheek. James. McDaniel."

With an impassive face and guttural sounds, "Luthecaw. Placota," for the Indians.

Impressed, Francis asked, "What did you do? Memorize the roster?"

"Something I got from my mother, I guess." The Major shrugged. "She could remember the name and describe in detail everything about anyone she'd ever met, years after. Just a knack. She said it came from seeing so few people in the early days on the Pennsylvania frontier that each one was memorable."

"Is that the reason, on any given day, you are able to give a rundown on the status of everything — men, boats, supplies? You carry all that around in your head? Then why the hell can't you speak better French?"

"Lack the knack," grinned the Major, taking Francis's arm and drawing him back and around a sudden scuffle of Indian filles de joie disputing over a drunken coureur de bois who was being yanked back and forth by grasping claimants. "Watch your step. This street is hard on the roster. We need two replacements since yesterday's knifing here. But that can wait until the Chouteaus decide how much tobacco and powder they can buy with that extra $500 they got from Governor Lewis."

They were closeted with the head of the Chouteau enterprises up in his little balcony office at the heart of his busy trading post. The broad store building with two galleries was located on the corner of First and Washington, warehouses on three sides, and out front, a split-log sign in white birch and a dozen horses at the hitching post.

Jean Pierre Chouteau, Sr., commissioned commanding colonel of the militia on special service, Osage Indian agent, and not unaware that it was said, "To make a name or a fortune in St. Louis, it's best to be born a Chouteau. For second best, marry one," wore one of his velvet coats and a businesslike mien.

From the privacy of the family quarters on the second floor, shaded by the green draperies of tall fruit trees of apple and pear, emerged Auguste Pierre, of the youthful military bearing and practical merchant mind, who still smarted from the criticism of the aborted 1808 Mandan-bound undertaking, and his urbane and versatile cousin, Sylvestre Labbadie, to join them in conducting and sustaining the business at hand.

Francis, used to assessing those in authority, could feel the strength of the Major's presence among these vigorous, masterful men. They did not invite anyone to work with them but those who were capable of it. Rich, by flair, by luck and hard work, they savored their prosperity. By practical negotiation, the wise selection of supplies, men and material, and careful deployment, they insured their investment with great efficiency.

They quickly determined the suitable selection, stowage and protection of the gifts for safe-conduct, the tobacco and gun powder to pay the toll for up-river good-will along the way. These would not reduce the company's $40,000 capital any further. Instead they were to be paid by the $500 draft Governor Lewis had drawn on the government.

Francis wondered if, as the $500 bought them good will up-river, it would be buying Frederick Bates, the Secretary of State of the Missouri Territory, already at odds with the governor, greater leverage to discredit Lewis, down river. Francis noted, also, that these hard-headed men of business did not mention such a possibility.

Instead, there was, as at Lisa's house, the subject of the Indian gauntlet facing them, sprinkled with some illustrative anecdotes, and, mellowed by even better wine than Lisa's, a philosophical excursion into the consequences of overdoing either the gifts or the cannon, and a reaffirmation that without hard work and vigilance, they wouldn't get Shehaka home, this time, either.

As they headed for their lodgings with a French family, friends and business associates of the Vallé's, "Now, I suppose you are going to surprise me with some acute observation about Madame Chouteau," said Francis sardonically. "You did get a glimpse of her?"

"An impression, rather," said the Major amiably. "Matronly serenity. Impeccable French, like her sister, Madame Menard. And a pleasant, chastening soprano coping capably with some unauthorized bedlam. She does have a clutch of healthy, energetic sons."

"They're not all hers. The Colonel was married before. To Joseph Taillon's granddaughter, Pelagie Kiersereau. She had four children, three boys and a girl. You met the oldest, Auguste Pierre," said Francis matching step with the Major as they turned a corner to take a short cut to their lodgings. "You'll probably get to meet the Colonel's namesake, the one they call the Cadet, before we leave. He's young, not more than twenty but his father considers him able enough to be left in charge of the Chouteau business while he and Auguste are up river .. and that's a real vote of confidence."

"Nepotism," observed the Major wryly, slowing his stride as they approached a cluster of dusty children playing in the street, "is rather prevalent in the fur trade, isn't it?"

"In any French family, it's well-nigh compulsory. In fact, the prolific Madame Chouteaus of this world make it practically mandatory." Briefly, Francis explained that the Colonel, after the death of his first wife in 1793, had married Brigitte Saucier. The Colonel now had nine sons to absorb into the business.

"There's the in-laws, too, Papin, Gratiot, Labbadie, Menard –" The Major interrupted him. "Near forgot — we're to meet Francois Ride at the Grove Tavern. You know, the one Jim Audrain has started up in the old stone house of Cerre's."

"Then we should turn here," said Francis, suiting action to his words.

"Wasn't Pierre Audrain a partner of Pierre Menard's at one time?"

"Oui. In New Madrid. Shortly after Audrain helped transplant a number of his dissatisfied fellow emigres from Gallipolis to New Bourbon," said Francis.

They were welcomed into the Grove Tavern by James Audrain, the naturalized Frenchman, most recently of Kentucky. Audrain, showing them to a table, also showed a keen interest in their venture, making passing reference to the potential to be found at Fort Osage.

Francois Ride, awaiting them impatiently in the crowded taproom, told him shortly to come along and see Fort Osage for himself. With a genial smile, Audrain said he'd take their orders first and did.

Over generous platters of crisp fried catfish washed down with strong beer, and tasteful civilities, they got to the matter of victualling the expedition.

Francois Ride, the Frenchman of the stubborn chin and no great height who was in charge of the provision barge, began the evening with a barely concealed air of reservation. As he digested the meat of the suggestions the Major put forward, and his unqualified acknowledgment of Ride's own abilities, the little man's reserve melted into hearty cooperation. They finished up the evening defining needs and distribution in mutual accord.

There would be barrels of pork, dried and lyed corn, dried navy beans, tins of hardtack, sugar, tea and coffee, the basic fare of the voyageurs and the riflemen, to be augmented by fresh game supplied by the latter, and the kegs of liquor allowed, ostensibly, to supply the crewmen with their traditional, daily allotment at the end of the day.

The partners swept the embargo-stricken shelves of St. Louis clean of supplies. Men pushed through the doors of shops and trading posts, came and went from warehouse to warehouse, with wagons loading out front. On the docks, the strenuous work of unloading onto the barges, interspersed with some full scale cursing, brought the embarkation date closer.

The partners got Shehaka, also known as Big White because of his light hair, eyes and complexion, garrulous and a trifle corpulent from inactivity and white man's food, and his woman, Yellow Corn, his youngest son, White Painted Horse, and his black frock coat that was getting rather snug, along with a strutting rooster and all his other gifts from the Great White Father loaded for this second attempt to get him back to the Five Villages of the Upper Missouri.

Jessaume, favoring the leg wounded in the first, ill-fated attempt to get Shehaka home, went on board, followed by his woman, Broken Tooth, a flatiron in each hand, and her two children, Touissant and Jeanette, who may, or may not, have been the interpreter's. Jessaume was notorious for wagering, when he had exhausted all other available coin in the heat of his gambling fever, an assignation with the complaisant Broken Tooth.

"Flatirons?" murmured the Major to Francis. One of the voyageurs on the boat, grinning, gave him a clue in the French patois. The Major turned it over on his tongue slowly, put it questioningly into English. "Dog food?"

Grimacing, Francis said, "Puppy mashers. Possibly. Probably."

They had more than one farewell drink with the militia surgeon, Dr. Thomas, and got him and his medical supplies, as well as the militiamen he would be doctoring, to the assigned boats.

Dr. Thomas and the militiamen, along with voyageurs, trappers, Shawnees and Delawares assigned to the Chouteau contingent were on the keel and Mackinaw boats and on their way by the middle of May. Under the watchful eyes of the grimly determined Colonel Chouteau and his son, Auguste, who was beginning to prefer the initials A.P. to distinguish himself from his uncle, the eldest of the Chouteau clan, they were the vanguard of St. Louis Missouri Fur Company expedition.

In succeeding days, while May gave way to June, the Major and Francis were on hand for the departure, one section at a time, of nearly as many more men, mostly hunters, with the lead, the ammunition, the woolen pants, the blankets and the beads carefully stowed away.

While Lisa made sure of the worthiness of the transport for the remainder of the expedition, the Major quartered the town, garnering and assessing the latest official and unofficial news. His intelligence sources supplied unedited tid-bits on the embargo, Tecumseh and the Prophet, duels, lethal and ludicrous, Astor and his American Fur Company, Sir Alexander Mackenzie and his North West Company, Lord Selkirk and his Hudson Bay Company, law suits, likely and unlikely, liaisons, prosaic and promiscuous, and the Russians, at Sitka, bludgeoning the sea otter and Aleuts, indiscriminately.

"We need more traps," said the Major, leading the way into the store of Bartholomew Berthold, the well-educated gentleman who had emigrated from the Italian Tyrol in 1798 and was now a successful St. Louis businessman. "The princely, ancient ornament of furs . . ."

". . . sable . . . ermine. . all else is mundane and middle class," said Berthold in his gentle voice, coming forward to greet his brother Masons cordially. "Would you gentlemen be interested to know that the beaver trap and Beau Brummel were conceived roughly at the same time?"

"Roughly? Are you sure?" asked Francis, shaking hands with the bright-eyed, dapper citizen. "Poor Madame Brummel."

Berthold chuckled delightedly. "Say, rather, poor Madame Beaver. It is her children who are being sacrificed on the altar of fashion because Madame Brummel's son looks better in a beaver hat than a tricorn. And likes beaver trimming on his dressing gowns. Yes, gentlemen, you could say Beau Brummel and beaver go together like — "

"Snap and trap? or trap and horse collar?" said the Major, shaking hands with the proprietor in turn.

"At last! a gentleman who grasps the broader picture. Trap and horse collar. Indeed. Both inventors unknown and unsung. But the ripple effect — awesome," said Berthold enthusiastically.

"Traps," said Francis firmly. "Never mind the horse collars."

"Ah, gentlemen," sighed Berthold. "Horse collars we have." He also had some ox yokes and bows, he said, deploring the French custom of fastening five-foot stakes with leather straps to the oxen horns, requiring their teams to pull with their heads. "But traps?" he shrugged eloquently. "Maybe Hunt and Hankinson — "

"— have squirreled away any they might have. McClellan and Crooks will get those, plus whatever that enterprising young Scot can get out of Machilimackinac," said the Major positively.

"For the use of the Indians, of course," said Berthold. He was needling them about the gentleman's agreement that maintained the polite fiction that, in accordance with the US licensing act of 1802, only Indians trapped for beaver or other furs on Indian land. "You gentlemen, when you get into the Stony Mountains, will be demonstrating to those untutored Indians, who prefer to hunt buffalo, how to trap the beaver? As an example to follow, naturally."

Francis ignored the rhetorical question. They would be illegal as hell trapping beaver at Three Forks.

"The Major thinks the rejoicing here over the ending of the embargo maybe be premature. Anyway, traps on order are not traps in the field. Have you any idea who might have a spare trap or two they'd part with?"

The only idea Berthold could come up with, an impoverished small-time trader whose idea of getting a license had fallen through when he was reluctant to give up his British citizenship and swear allegiance to the US, yielded only three traps, battered ones at that.

The Major did find that Berthold had an overlooked, aged bolt of strouding, the twenty-five-yards of coarse woolen cloth the Indians fashioned into clothing, and some falconry bells. After trying to pick out a tune with them, he noted plaintively that middle C was missing. Francis told him he'd never known an Indian who could have played "Yankee Doodle" with or without middle C. If the Major found he wanted to make music with some Indian belle, these were good for peal, after peal, and peeling was all that some of them thought of anyway.

Light-heartedly they transported their gleanings to the pier, and found places for them in the cargo space of Lisa's well-designed keelboat, as well as places for Berthold's parting gift, a case of excellent French brandy, and the personal supplies of the partners, wines and whiskey, tinned foods, the tents, the cigars and the playing cards, medical supplies, and the ledgers for the bookkeeping chores.

By the middle of June preparations were well enough in hand for them to round up the last of the men engaged earlier that year. Some of them had already frittered away the advance they had received on account. Naturally, they were having some second thoughts, and, therefore, harder, but not impossible to locate.

On a Saturday, half-past June in 1809, they were ready to depart. Reuben Lewis, forehead wrinkled in concern, waved the Major and Francis over to where he, Samuel Morrison and William Bryan, stood beside the Lewis barge, and its steersman, Thomas James.

Reuben had found the Major knowledgeable about the recruits, particularly helpful in dealing with the Americans such as James. "We've had guards on these boats for the past week but James, here, thinks there may have been some pilfering."

"What do you think is missing?" asked the Major.

Thomas James, square of brow and jaw, twenty-seven and unmarried, with a mother, father, brother and a piece of ground in Florissant to maintain and no money to speak of, was, however, speaking up often for the Americans.

"Whatever it is, you can probably negotiate a loan from Shehaka when we catch up with the Chouteaus. The Mandans are going to think he sacked St. Louis single-handed, as it is," said Francis blithely. "Do you suppose it will give them any wrong ideas?"

"Damned if I care what the Mandans think," said James curtly, his black hair and thick, frowning brows over intense blue eyes reflecting his Welsh heritage. "We can't find the tobacco. I don't want any booshways getting wrong ideas about my men and blaming them. About tobacco or anything else."

There was a clarion shout from the barge, loudly proclaiming that the tobacco had been located. Cheek just forgot to mention he'd found a safer place for it, never mind bothering the Major. The unbothered Major made a remark that was received with knee-slapping hilarity aboard, and allowed the red-faced, stiff-necked James to get back on board, unobtrusively.

"I don't really think they could have negotiated a loan of tobacco from Shehaka." The irrepressible Francis had found literal-minded Reuben Lewis easy to tease.

"Certainly not. Shehaka has to give everything away when he gets home. That's the Mandan way," said Reuben. He had been appointed sub-agent of all the Western tribes at the same time Clark was made Indian agent. "You already know that."

"I didn't," said young Bryan from Pennsylvania. "No one told me they had such a communal attitude toward property. Or is it just expected of a headman? The Indian way of buying votes?"

"F'heaven sakes, Will," said his Morrison cousin, "it isn't costing him anything. It was all free in the first place — a gift from the Great White Father — which means the taxpayer foots the bill in the long run."

"His return isn't costing him any thing either," said Bryan thoughtfully.

"He doesn't even have to take his turn at rowing," said Francis.

"Too bad," said Sam. "Might slim him down some."

"Speaking of rowing," said Reuben Lewis, turning to the Major, "James does take his responsibilities as barge captain seriously."

The men moved along the dock to Lisa's keelboat, keeping an eye on activities about them. The Major, who had verified James was a seasoned frontiersman before he signed up, waited for Lewis go on.

"We've got mostly Americans on board. That big fellow from Tennessee is already telling them that rowing is the work of mangeurs de lard. That Cheek is — "

"— well named?" said the Major. "Rueben, you've handled cheeky bastards before. Don't let this one get under your hide."

"I was thinking that if James put the crew on their mettle, like rowing further, faster and longer than the French and Canadians, Cheek and the others would like the idea of showing what Americans can do. He's been heard to say that one American is worth ten of the manguers de lard."

"You do that, Reuben," said Francis equably, "and my voyageurs will set such a pace we'll catch up with Shehaka before Cheek misplaces the tobacco again."

"Good for you, Vallé!" said Samuel Morrison. It wasn't only the Tennessean who was a cheeky bastard. Francis was too polite to say so. When dealing with other races, most Americans had the same attitude of superiority.

Manuel Lisa went by, moving quickly, giving some last minute orders. Morrison registered the fact that an air of superiority wasn't just limited to Americans but Manuel's was already resented by James and his Americans.

"Those voyageurs of yours, Francis, they're products of the frontier, just like Cheek, and for a longer time," said Rueben. "Nearly two hundred years. Never hear them complain. James and his bunch never stop. Why so different?"

"Selective breeding," said Francis bluntly. As the Major turned his level gaze on him to make sure he was serious, he added, "I mean it. You can see it right on my barge. Our old French houses, the families that have been in the Indian trade for generations, developed a strain of dependents with very definite characteristics.

"The French have the independent hunter of the woods, the courier de bois, who are the hivernants, the winterers, who take their chances in the wilderness where the pays sauvage is to be found. The backbone of the French houses is the boatman, the submissive, cheerful toiler, who crosses himself at the mere mention of the pays sauvage.

"My family, and others, brought their methods and their dependents down here when it was still French territory. When the French lost Canada to the English, many French fur traders and their families came here, preferring the lackadaisical Spanish to the competitive English.

"The men on my barge are representative. They come from a long line of men who have always expected to serve with the Vallés. Even the Shawnees and Delawares in my group have known a form of limited service with the Vallés. Granpére Vallé welcomed their fathers and grandfathers when the tribes were resettled near us and encouraged them to act as a buffer between Ste. Genevieve and meandering Osages.

"The voyageurs expect me to be the decision maker. If anything out of the ordinary comes up, anything that cannot be handled in the traditional way, they want their patron to tell them what to do. They not only don't want to make independent decisions, they don't know how any more. It's been bred out of them."

"Selective breeding? By God, you've got something there, Francis," said Morrison reflectively, noting there was still time to pursue the subject to the enlightenment of his cousin. "That's what I've been trying to tell you, William. Circumstances have made Americans cocky and assured."

Circumstances encouraged the development of certain types in Canada. Circumstances had much to do with it south of the border. From the beginning, the Americans were on their own, with no patriarchal system to coddle them. The independent and self-sufficient survived, bred up sons of like kind, accustomed to making their own decisions. "This could be an interesting trip," said young Bryan. "Two different cultures on a collision course."

Reuben Lewis winced. Smiling, Francis offered specious comfort. "Maybe all the troublemakers will desert."

"The Americans will do great in the set-up we have in mind for Three Forks," said the Major positively. "As for now, they've all had experience on the Ohio, some on the Mississippi, and they aren't afraid of hard work. They'll get your boat up river, Reuben. So let's get under way."

"How many will this make, Major?" young Bryan asked. "Not just Americans. The entire expedition?"

"Chouteau set out with one-hundred-and-sixty, we've loaded up one-hundred-and-ten more, and with luck we'll get underway with eighty today. At least three-hundred-and-fifty men," said the Major, giving a total none of them felt certain enough to dispute, then, noting a splash, some catcalls and the French boatman being helped back on board Francis's barge, soberer, qualified his statement with, "Give or take a few. And, unless they've stove in, or set fire to another one of them, thirteen boats. And Lisa's damned canoe."

From the burgeoning polyglot town of St. Louis, where it rose from the rock-strewn banks of the Mississippi toward a high terrace, the last section of the company flotilla set out on June 17, 1809.

The boat in charge of Rueben Lewis, with Thomas James as the steersman, or captain, was typical. Sixteen feet wide at the beam, nearly sixty feet long, steadied by the heavy keel running from bow to stern, it was shallow of draft, with a sharp prow, a mast with a square sail, and a long heavy oar with the side blade attached to the stern and moved on a pivot that served as the rudder. Narrow gunwales ran along each side, with the area between covered over, providing a squat, square housing, with the flat roof serving as the deck. To augment the storage space of the shallow holds, there were cargo boxes at each end of the boat, rising four feet above the deck, the near one serving as a platform for the steersman. There was room for twenty-five men, provisions and assorted supplies for the expedition. With a man on the bow with a long pole to fend off all the Missouri would fling at them, they would be able to buck the current going upstream and avoid obstacles coming down.

As they started up the Mississippi to the mouth of the Missouri, the sun was high in the sky, shining on the limestone bluffs behind the village of St. Louis, brightening the aging Spanish towers, the forts that former regime had erected for protection against the British and Indians. The least dilapidated of the towers now served the Americans as a jail. Looking at it from the deck of Lisa's keelboat, the Major wondered idly if George Drouillard, exonerated along with Lisa for the death of deserter, Bissonnette, was looking forward to seeing the Three Forks.

Lisa, who liked his own craft to have a sturdy keel, a responsive rudder, a main and topsail on an oaken thirty-foot mast, and a swivel gun, also had a cabin of respectable size between the gangways. None of the partners aboard — the Major, Menard, Labbadie, Morrison or Bryan — had to duck his head on entering or leaving.

Each of the partners, or one of their designated representatives, was on this expedition because the company articles demanded their presence. Some held strategic positions in the flotilla, such as Reuben Lewis with James and his Americans; Francis Vallé, with his French and Indian crew; while the Chouteaus and Dr. Thomas, with Shehaka and the main body of the militia, awaited them upstream at Cote sans Dessein.

Pierre Menard, bleak and drawn from his leavetaking with his beloved Angelique and their good, their civilized life, came to stand beside the Major. In silence they watched Lisa's boatmen.

On the narrow gunwales on each side of the keelboat, the men were in single file, with faces toward the stern, heads bent low, planting poles in the river bottom pointing downstream. As the boat moved ahead they walked toward the stern. As the one in front reached the end of the gunwale, he would turn about, pass the other and take his position at the rear.

The men labored at poling up the Mississippi. As they encountered deeper water, they took to the oars. Lisa considered putting up the sail but the wind was not right.

There was the horseshoe bend to negotiate and then there was no mistaking the dingy-yellow water of the Missouri, the 3000-mile long river, whose headwaters they planned to cap with a fur trading post. Where the two rivers joined, the waters stretched out on either side of the flotilla like a small sea.

"Look at that," said young Bryan. Unlike Menard, he was looking forward with youthful eagerness to this voyage. "It's a full-size tree."

Lisa chuckled. "The Missouri welcome," and shouted encouragement to the man on the prow, fending off a smaller tree.

Lisa set a strenuous, remorseless pace. The long days in the summer heat blistered tender, fair skin, and turned the rest vermillion and russet and sable. The sudden thunderstorms, with the wind and the drenching rain, left them sodden and chafed. The Frenchmen sang as they pulled on the oars, less so as they set the poles, or 'bush-whacked' their way along, grabbing limbs and brush to lever the boat along; the Americans did not; and neither had the breath for it on the cordelle.

The cordelle, literally the little rope, was secured to the top of the mast, then passed through a ring to be fastened by a stout rope to the bow of the craft. When the time came for its use, the men would throw the tow rope over their shoulders and walk in stooping position along the shore, pulling the craft, while the mast attachment swung the rope clear of the brush on the bank of the river, and the ring on the bow assisted in guiding the boat.

In the shallow places where the bottom dragged, they fastened a rope from the boat to a tree on the bank, dragging it slowly ahead by means of pulleys, warping the vessel along at a snail's pace from tree to tree. When the wind was right, which was seldom, the sail was put up, but the man on the bow to fend off the drift and the steersman at the rudder had to stay alert.

Lisa, former mariner, master of Missouri navigation, vivid, black-haired and muscular, brought order to the upstream progress, and skill, shouts and laughter to accompany the brilliant improvisations with which he met the challenges of the river. As they moved upstream, they overtook one section after another of the trappers dispatched days before. Lisa incorporated these men and their transports into his flotilla and, they grumbled, demanded excessive and unrelenting labor while providing lean fare.

Lisa had them up and on their way each day at dawn, allowed a half-hour break for the crews to breakfast on dried corn or hominy; another at mid-day for fat pork and biscuits; and, when the long day was done, a pot of mush with a dollop of tallow melted in it for supper, and the daily liquor allowance. The hunters brought in fresh meat, never quite enough to stop the Americans from grumbling.

Lisa selected the daily stopping places with care: the boats tied up close together at night, no straggler allowed; and, with guards posted, the men slept on shore or on the boats, in buffalo robes and blankets. For the partners and the men in charge of the other boats, such as Reuben Lewis and Francis Vallé, there were briefings in the mornings, fellowship in the evenings.

Attuned to the Americans, the Major had expected a certain amount of grousing and contention and had dealt with them in his capable fashion. He felt vindicated as he watched Harris, Jackson, Cather, McBride and the other men he had recruited personally buckle down to the challenges of the river trip in more amiable fashion than most, particularly those under the thumb of Thomas James.

Morning, noon and night, the Major made his way from one group to another, welding bonds of shared experiences, learning to know the trustworthy, the competent, and the malcontent. He set them to guffawing with droll words of encouragement, to treating cuts and lacerations, to using poling tricks to conserve strength, and to wearing protective strips of leather on hands raw from the cordelle. His resourcefulness spelled security, even as his advice and his attendance to their well-being kept them working like dogs.

He listened to Thomas James when the exhausting work on the cordelle made James's barge late catching up with the rest of the boats the night they neared Cote sans Dessein. James's black Welsh brows were as lowering as the stormy sky as he watched his men flop down wearily by the cooking fire. Their morose mood contrasted sharply with their earlier high spirits at the beginning of the journey when they had come in victorious for several nights in a row from cheerful, noisy races with Vallé's crew.

"We should have pulled up and camped two hours ago. I had the devil's own time getting my crew to come on in," said James grumpily. "How come we have to camp where that damned Eesaw says?"

"Why fuss at the Major? I heerd you say it your ownself, time 'n again." Cheek, handing a bowl of food to James, hunkering down beside the Major with the other, quoted dispassionately. "We're under government contract until we get Shehaka to his Mandan town and have 'to do and perform . . . all lawful and reasonable orders given us by our employers.'"

The Major could see that James, who usually found the gratuitous support of his self-elected lieutenant gratifying, was inexplicably annoyed with him for interrupting.

"Get over by the fire and dry out, man. You're in and out of that river more often than any mangeur de lard! Can't swim a lick either." said James petulantly.

A man of limited education but unlimited ambition, Thomas James had signed his contract March 29, 1809, following his enlistment as a rifleman in the expedition. He was very conscious of his status as boat captain, was looking forward, once the military aspect of the expedition had been accomplished, to continuing on as a leader of a band of trappers. James and his trappers were to be employed by the company for three years, furnished with certain equipment, and compensated for the performance of such services as might be required by agents of the company.

The Major, from the occasions when he had spelled Reuben Lewis in listening to the complaints of Thomas James, had concluded that James's long-term hope of betterment made current discomforts bearable, if frequently verbalized, had his attention drawn back to Cheek, who said, guilelessly, "I told you my grannie said I'd never hang. Or drown."

The large, shallow eyes of the big man met the Major's as he lifted a large bony hand to rub his craggy face, flicking water from wet shirt over James, who made an impatient exclamation, and abruptly got up and walked away from both of them.

"The men in our family ain't got the sight. Not until the very last," said Cheek almost dreamily for the practical frontiersman, given more to confrontation than tact. "Then it's gey fey and away with him. There's something about this here country we be bound for —"

"— makes a man feel he's shrunk whether he's been dunked in the river or not?" the Major offered as Cheek paused, uncertain how to verbalize his uneasiness.

Cheek nodded, mutely, unable, fey or not, to articulate the feeling of being vulnerable, unprotected, and, compared to the world opening up, spreading about them, small.

So, relaxed on a bank beside the Missouri River, the Major heard the story of Cheek, who came from a family of warriors, on a frontier where a man could hardly be anything else: a good, honest fighting machine struggling for survival in the shadows of alien cruelty, given to spontaneous anger, whose grannie had said he would die bravely, without a gray hair on his head.

"When you are old and bald, you mean?" suggested the Major.

"I never thought of it that way," said Cheek, brightening. "I thought she meant I'd be scalped." And, squishing slightly, moved off to steam beside the camp fire while the Major rejoined the partners on Lisa's boat.

Thereafter, when the partners met, the Major, more than any of the others, seemed to have already anticipated the objections men like Cheek might have to something new, or tiresome, in the routine. He made, accordingly, some unorthodox suggestions that, disconcertingly, worked. No one, except perhaps Francis understood that, unlike Ride, who angered Cheek when he went to draw provisions by offering him a bear's head and a belittling comment, the Major's suggestions came from an understanding of how a big man could suffer distress, when made to feel small by man or nature.

The days and miles added up. Twenty-one miles from St. Louis to the village of St. Charles where the black and white cows were grazing on river banks and most of the villagers involved in a farewell party for those of their number waiting to join the expedition. Firmly, Lisa kept the other boatmen from joining in the festivities, and got the men under contract, two Baptistes and a Jean, separated from their well-wishers and to the assigned places, poling.

Sixty miles and they were passing Femme Osage, the developing settlement established by Daniel Boone, his sons and several friends, upon land granted the former by the Spanish governor, Don Trudeau, in 1795. They went on past Point Labbadie, named for Sylvestre's father. Every so often, on each side of the river, they glimpsed clearings: a few acres with a small log cabin, stables for horses, outbuildings for hogs and cattle, a straggling fence enclosing plantings of corn, pumpkins, potatoes and turnips. The settlement at Charette, where they didn't stop, had about thirty families, supported by hunting and small fields of corn.

Cote sans Dessein, in sight of the Osage River, had the beauty and fertility of prairie mixed with woodland, and about a dozen French families, a couple of Indian ones, handsome fields, and the Chouteaus, père and fils waiting, with half as many men as they had started out with the middle of May.

Immediately, company management had to attend to a festering personnel problem.

"There have been some desertions," said Colonel Chouteau, which was an understatement. "Mostly from the militia."

Compared to Lisa's contingent, the Chouteau section of the expedition had a very leisurely trip to Cote sans Dessein. No one, militia or hunters, had been press-ganged against his will, no one released from jail or servitude in return for enlistment; and no one promised plunder. Typically, they were boisterous, headstrong, hard-drinking volunteers, and in the free-wheeling American tradition believed they had every right to change their minds. A good many of them did so during the weeks they awaited Lisa's arrival at the idyllic location.

"It's been a very pleasant time," Dr. Thomas, the company surgeon, told the Major and Reuben Lewis in all sincerity. "I had the leisure to do some exploring. Got in some very good hunting until John Stout blew up my gun." John, one of the American hunters, had also blown off his thumb and lacerated his hand, requiring the Doctor's services. "A shakedown cruise is a shakedown cruise. Bound to get some complaints. I've doctored the most serious ones."

The Major asked for details. Pleurisy. Dyspepsia. Cuts, abrasions, strained muscles, a hernia or two, cracked ribs and some venereal disease.

"Pleasant time!" snorted Reuben Lewis as they left the Doctor organizing his medical supplies and personal effects for transfer to the James barge where he would share quarters with Rueben for the remainder of the voyage. He matched stride with the Major as they strode down the meandering path that served as a village street to the dwelling a French family had made available to

Colonel Chouteau for his headquarters. "Captain Menard is hearing a different tale."

Pierre Menard, a man with a reputation for rectitude and a measure of benevolence in supervising personnel, had been exercising a great deal of forbearance amidst the rancorous confusion. A sympathetic listener, he had been dealing with labor unrest from the moment he stepped ashore.

The American hunters waiting at Cote san Dessein, soured and discontented, wanted some changes made in their job descriptions. The militia, now formed and drilled for the rigors ahead, couldn't expect much of a change in theirs.

"The militia we have will do," said the former Army officer, A.P. Chouteau, with assurance.

The Major, observing the partners gathered around the rough, hand-hewn table in the main room of the cabin, reviewed the principles of a military viewpoint. Strength, objective, simplicity, strategy, timing and unity of command. There was something to be said for using those same concepts in the civilian aspects of this expedition as well. The strength was there, the Major decided, as their military commander, Colonel Chouteau, agreed with his son that those who had gone AWOL were no great loss. The expedition still had sufficient men and arms to make the Indians think twice before attacking.

"It's not the loss of the militia that's costing the company money," said Pierre Chouteau, with some asperity, as he switched hats, from military commander to that of company executive, envisioning the bottom line of the company profit and lost statement. "It's the American hunters who have drawn on the company stores for supplies and equipment."

Pierre Menard, who had more of a civilian mind than military, sighed. He hadn't heard of Murphy's Law but the depressing evidence of its operation had made him somber. The objective was taking longer to reach than expected. And, unless some of the complaints of the men were taken seriously, the expedition could fail.

"We need to keep the infection from spreading," said Reuben Lewis, thinking of Thomas James and his Americans. Those rustic frontiersmen were able, but not particularly willing to work with those from another socio-economic background and be tolerant of their attitudes and life styles.

"We need to make new arrangements with them," said Menard. He envisioned a frank and forthright overhaul of the management cycle of planning, directing, coordinating and controlling the work force. Unfortunately, the unity of command was not his, and as the other partners followed Colonel Chouteau's lead in making it a committee effort, he found it stressful and unsatisfactory.

The Major, recognizing there were pitfalls to avoid in group-decision making, had taken some prudent measures and smoothed some hackles. Meeting with his own American recruits, he got their input. They were acquainted with many of the disaffected Americans grousing at Cote sans Dessein, personally or by repute, and they soon revealed an aptitude for identifying individual knowledge, abilities, goals and objectives. The provisioning and the work schedules were areas that would require some affirmative action.

"There are some we should make an effort to keep," said the Major. "We will need men to double as blacksmiths, farriers, carpenters and cooks," and he named them.

Lisa, who usually found American hunters badly disposed anyway, had been this way often enough to know any job description would have to include long, often irregular work hours, in adverse weather conditions and exposure to hazards. However, he was satisfied with the size of the expedition, and preferred no further reduction, for economic and defensive reasons. Large or heavily armed parties on the river were usually safe from Indian attacks, and, despite the desertions, the company was still both. If the Americans needed some form of reassurance, so be it.

Management and disaffected personnel sought and found a basis of accommodation. They reached an understanding of sorts, with lingering reservations on both sides.

On June 28, 1809, as the St. Louis Missouri Fur Company expedition loaded up its military and civilian force to take leave of Cote sans Dessein, the Major said to Francis, "We have 172 men, not counting the militia."

"We really should, you know. Count on the militia," Francis said lightly. "Although I'm not sure Shehaka thinks he can."

Shehaka, who had found the stay at Cote sans Dessein a pleasant interlude and the basic training of the militia, hilarious, didn't confide his misgivings, if any. He did make sure his many gifts, including the strutting rooster, were secure.

Chapter 6

"A dirty, mean river, the Missouri," said the men who knew it best, proudly. Over there, today. Here, tomorrow. Wash your camp right out from under you in the middle of the night. "Full of snags, all out to get you."

The same could be said of the fur trade. Before he had ever committed himself to this venture, the Major had decided the fur trade, like the Missouri, had its embarras, its planter and its sneaky twin, the sleeper, and most worrisome of all, the sawyer. Familiar with the more infrequent but similar navigational obstructions on other rivers, Andrew Henry applied himself to learning how to maneuver around the numerous and malevolent obstacles on the Missouri.

On the first day of July, not as far above the Little Osage as Lisa had intended, they had a favorable wind and an hour's respite under sail, moving easily up the winding river, finding favor in the scenery for the moment, the succession of islands, the changing view of the tree-lined banks. Then the winding river took them into the wind, which was dying away, and up against a succession of embarras, which they got around, only to find facing them, the worst of the embarras encountered in two hundred seventy miles.

The river, since Lisa had come this way last, had undercut the bank, dropping a venerable hundred-foot cottonwood tree into the water. Bobbing like a raft from its tether of roots, the huge tree had been bombarded by a fast-moving cedar, a couple of willows, but the roots held, and the drift piled up tighter and tighter against the tenacious cottonwood, snaring in turn, more floating trees, some rolling logs, a dead buffalo or two. The force of the current had beat against the barrier, matting it tighter and tighter, flinging more debris against it, plastering mud onto it, cementing it deeper, wider, firmer. When the flotilla reached it, a little past mid-day, the sun high in the sky and hot as damnation, they found this grandaddy of an embarras angling down toward them. They paused for their second meal of the day, eaten in near silence, except for an occasional 'Merde,' 'Hell' and 'Dios,' as the respective cultures estimated its proportions. The barrier reached fifty yards downstream from the undercut bank, half again as deep, nearly as broad.

The current foamed and spumed noisily against this solidifying diversion dam, forcing the frustrated waters into a narrow spillway, to charge past the point of the embarras in a raging torrent, and the crews had to take to the tow line and the bank.

Tediously, they inched one boat after another past the embarras, the partners laboring along with the men. As the sun was setting, and a sudden, gusting wind came at them head on, they began repeating the exhausting maneuvers with the last, the barge steered by Thomas James.

No one, not even Cheek, who could not swim, knew exactly how it happened. One moment he was on the slippery, crumbling bank, his back and all his tremendous strength bent into the tow line. The next, he was flailing helplessly in deep water.

No one on the tow line noticed at first. The Major, who could swim and had taken notice, was suddenly and not by accident in the water, too. As the alerting shouts went up, they were both swept out of sight.

There was a moment or two there, the Major was to acknowledge later, just before he was able to give the frantic Cheek a hard blow to the head, when he felt the Missouri was out to get him.

Then with a spiteful, roiling thrust that put them both under water to the limit of the Major's breath, the river relented and flung them toward shore. The Major, gulping in air, struck out strongly, towing Cheek behind him. He got both of them out of the water and up on the bank, far downstream. With some firm prodding, he got Cheek to spew out his share of the Missouri, and at length, back into his place on the towline, putting an end to his gasps of gratitude.

"That was a fool thing to do," Francis Vallé said reprovingly, exasperated relief barely concealed in his voice, when the reappearance of the two men put an end to an anxious search along the river bank. "You could've drowned."

"Cheek damn near did," said the sodden Major, wringing water from his shirt abstractedly, his attention given to the towline, tightening as the boat was warped and winched with blistering slowness upstream a few more feet. "How could I make a liar out of his granny? She told him he'd never die by drowneding."

"Dammit, she didn't tell you that," said Francis sharply, viewing him critically for signs of damage. The Major, his stance alert, didn't reply. He was peering intently through the deepening dusk of the evening, turning his head to eye the progress of the boat, sensing more than seeing something amiss.

Following the Major's gaze, Francis shouted abruptly to those in charge of the towline, "Hold it! Right there!"

The subject was put aside, in the immediate demands of the moment: the heaving, and the hoisting, skillfully done, as Francis called out directions to steady the boat, now swinging back and forth dangerously as the steersman, Thomas James, fought for control. Finally, just as night descended, the unrelenting, disciplined labor got it successfully past the awesome embarras.

The wind died down as the barge edged into the bank to join the rest of the flotilla in the strategic location Lisa had chosen. For a moment, the cheer that went up seemed to be for James and his crew, then word quickly went around. Lisa had decided to lay over until noon the next day to check the boats for damages. There would be an extra ration of liquor for all hands tonight.

"What a cheering thought," said Pierre Menard approvingly as the Major joined him aboard Lisa's keelboat, in the lukewarm darkness under the vast, glittering stars. "Not to be embroiled in back-breaking work for half a day. Some of the men are so tired they would be a hazard to others and themselves if we set out at dawn tomorrow. I'm glad to see that Brown was able to bag several deer. The Americans will have something besides complaints to go with their mush tonight."

The partners, too, enjoyed a thoroughly satisfying meal in their quarters. While it was digesting, they took their coffee and a bottle of Berthold's French brandy on deck. Leaning on the rail, watching Dr. Thomas light up one of his after dinner cigar, the Major listened to them comparing notes on the events of the day, and his elective swim in particular.

"This river and the fur trade are full of snags, all out to get you," the Major put his earlier conclusions into words, seeking to put his praised rescue of Cheek in proper proportion, without being churlish. "Both have their embarras, planter, sleeper and sawyer."

"Hmm," said Menard, holding out his cup to the Major for another generous dollop of brandy. "That embarras today. I don't believe I've ever seen a worse one. What would you say was its equivalent in the fur trade?"

The Major, clean, dry and tidy, in cotton shirt and homespun linsey breeches tucked into moccasins snugged below his knees, all in shades of brown, like his sun-bleached hair, caught at the nape of his neck with a rawhide thong, rubbed his cheek. He savored a welcome realization. Tomorrow, all of the partners, meticulously and routinely clean-shaven men, would have enough hot water, and time, and elbow room, to shave in a leisurely, comparatively civilized fashion, including himself.

"First, shouldn't you define embarras?" said young Bryan in his light tenor, with school boy overtones, clearing his throat self-consciously when Labbadie shot him a quizzical look. "Well, I'm here as a student to learn the trade," he continued shyly, with endearing youthful earnestness. "Father said I'd find no better instructors any where than the partners in this company."

"All right, Major," said Dr. Thomas genially, offering the Major one of his cigars. "Instruct our eager young Marco Polo."

"On the Missouri," said the Major, feeling his way into one of those philosophical exchanges his companions, with their sharp, unsentimental brains, found both relaxing and stimulating, "the embarras is a barrier thrown up by the river itself. It makes the current mean, oars and poles useless. You've got to change your way of doing things to get past the embarras. You can't make any headway against the current until you do."

While Thomas lighted the Major's cigar from his glowing tip, Reuben Lewis and Francis Vallé came aboard, and the coffee, the brandy and the cigars were passed out to them.

As the two men were getting their cigars lit, Menard said, "The Major thinks the fur trade and the Missouri are alike. Both have their embarras, planter, sleeper and sawyer, he says. Can you think of an embarras in the fur trade?"

"Lots," said Reuben. Francis nodded agreement. "But you first, Major."

"Alexander Henry. Peter Pond," said the Major, referring to the time, when, along with losing Canada to the British in 1763, the French abruptly lost their monopoly of its fur trade. The first of the invading opportunists swept into Quebec and Montreal like logs in high water. "And the Scots."

"Of course. The 'Pedlars'," exclaimed Menard, slapping the rail for emphasis, sending sparks of his cigar flying. "One beeg embarras. Sandy Mackenzie's making it a bigger one. Lord Selkirk has been known to call him and his lot worse names, especially now Mackenzie's been made a 'Sir.'"

"You're talking about the Northwest Fur Company, aren't you?" said young Bryan, standing beside Lewis with the tin coffee pot he had unobtrusively fetched anticipating the customary refills. "I thought they'd always been in the trade."

"Hudson's Bay Company has. That's Lord Selkirk's company," said Reuben, unconsciously taking the right note of the veteran with the novice, instructive without being patronizing."They have been throwing a monkey wrench into things for the Americans since the War."

"HBC, sure," nodded Bryan, refilling Morrison's proferred tin cup. "They've always had that easy route down into the Athabaskan country."

"They've got a route everywhere, out in the field and back in the trade marts of Europe," said Reuben dryly. "But you're right. Out in the field, they've never had all the portages and varied waterways to buck to get to the tribes the Northwesters and the traders from Albany have had."

"How about it, Captain?" Francis asked Menard. "You came from Quebec. Do you remember the problems created when the 'Pedlars' dropped into the fur trade stream and became an embarras for others to get around?"

"Mon Dieu, how old do you think I am?" protested Captain Menard good-naturedly, taking a sip of his coffee. "That was in the '60's."

"The Major's right, Pierre," said Reuben. "Many of the French got around the embarras by moving south to the Mississippi."

"Oui," agreed Menard reflectively, murmuring something in French that made Francis throw back his head and laugh. "The old granpères when they got together used to cackle gleefully about how the American colonials and men from Scotland troubled the fur trade waters for those arrogant Hudson Bay English milords."

The Major shook the last drops from the brandy bottle into Menard's cup, while Francis, continuing the analogy mentally could see what the Major meant. The venerable Hudson's Bay Company at first, from their position of ascendancy, did not even concede the Northwest Company more than the status of a planter in the Missouri River, one of those trees whose earth-laden roots caught in the river bottom and left the top protruding like the tilted mast of a sunken derelict, easily spotted and avoided with only minor navigational adjustments.

The two American colonials, the tenacious Alexander Henry from New Jersey and the rambunctious Peter Pond of Connecticut, who made their way to Canada and the taking of Quebec as military men with Jeffrey Amherst's army, stayed on after the end of the French and Indian War. They pioneered a fluctuating amalgamation of fur traders they named the North West Company, headquartered in Montreal.

As rivals of the long-enduring Hudson's Bay Company, with its international tentacles reaching out from a London base, they were mere planters in the current. For the smaller fur traders, they constituted an embarras from the beginning, making it difficult for them to make any headway in the trade. Alexander Mackenzie, another American, an expatriate loyalist, a generation younger, was one of those who found them an embarras for his small company, but a unique opportunity for his own flamboyant genius.

The adroit Alexander Mackenzie, who was to carve out an impressive reputation as one of the North West Company directors, came of American loyalist stock. Schooled in Canada, where his father, a judge in New Jersey, had sent him at the outset of the Revolutionary War, he was associated with a small company absorbed by the North West Company. Such was Mackenzie's recognized stature, although only twenty-three years old, that he was made a director of the expanded company. In the intervening years he had bent every effort to building the North West Company into a barrier of durability and dimensions that altered the current for the Hudson's Bay Company.

By 1793 the doughty Mackenzie had crossed Canada by land to the Pacific Coast. Knighted by the king, lionized in London salons, deferred to and sought out by shrewd London investors, he was a power to reckon with, an embarras, and he and his company wholeheartedly detested by Lord Selkirk and his. Mackenzie had already petitioned the crown for permission to erect a chain of posts across Canada, to corral the sea otter trade on the Pacific coast, and drive the Yankee upstarts, forever a stench in the nostrils of the exiled American loyalists, out of the market place.

Now Francis's reverie ended as Lisa, who had come from sending the last of the crew to their blankets and the guards to their posts, finding the brandy all gone, tossed the bottle to splash in the gleaming waters, and dispatched young Bryan for a fresh one, while Menard reminded Reuben Lewis, "You said you could think of lots of embarras in the fur trade. Name one, Reuben."

"The embargo," said Reuben promptly. "When we left St. Louis, the latest news was good. It was said that ships were preparing to sail from all the main Atlantic ports. Suppose they don't? We swept the shelves clean in St. Louis. Unless those ships are allowed to go out and trade, and soon, there won't be any new trade goods."

"I've got one," said young Bryan, hurrying up with the brandy, which Lisa took from him. "It goes along with the embargo. Napoleon. He's bound to rub the British the wrong way again before long. Then the British will start impressing our seamen faster than ever to man their navy for more battles with the French."

"Tecumseh. And the Prophet," said Morrison dispassionately. "Big Indian troubles."

Lisa, pouring brandy into his cup, shook his head. "Never mind those ol' embarras." He added a generous amount to the other cups, except for the Major, who waved the brandy away, murmuring that he wanted to be sure to have a steady hand in the morning so as to enjoy his shave.

"We've maneuvered around all of those ol' ones in times past," Lisa continued with pragmatic conviction, sipping from his cup, half-sitting on the rail, his gaze beyond them, his head cocked to the sound of the river. "It's the new ones we've got to watch out for. The ol' ones we know about and get ready for when we reach that stretch of water. What's building up around the bend? That's what I need to know."

"Astor," said the Major succinctly. At the half-hearted protests, he held up his hand. "I know. Still rumors when we left St. Louis. There has to be a base to those rumors. Astor did get to President Jefferson. The letter he wrote to your brother, Reuben, is proof of that. Jefferson was impressed with Astor's international view of the fur trade, something he can identify with. After that missive, Governor Lewis couldn't ignore a man who has Jefferson as a partisan."

"Astor's had his eye on St. Louis for a long time," said Menard. "Do you remember, Manuel, how the Chouteaus turned him down nine-ten years ago when he wanted to team up with them? Since then he's become a very wealthy man with influence in European capitals and Washington."

"Little German pipsqueak's got a hankering to control all the US fur trade," said Lisa scathingly. "President Jefferson should never have listened to him."

Morrison, thoughtfully recapitulating the good news that had reached St. Louis while they were readying the expedition for departure, said, "When we left, the embargo, seemingly, was at an end. President Jefferson had signed the bill repealing the general embargo before he left office. It seemed likely the British would do the same with the orders in council that led to the non-importation decrees against England in the first place. We got word that President Madison had acted on that assumption, proclaimed that free trade with Great Britain would be resumed June 10."

"Just so. What you're getting at, I think," said Menard astutely, "is that, with the embargo ended, Astor won't have much chance to buy in with the Canadians. Now, by paying ordinary duties, they can do business in their own right. They don't need him. They can once more take their goods anywhere in the USA east of the Mississippi."

"But not on the Missouri," said Lisa with satisfaction. "Only Americans are granted licenses to trade here."

"I thought Governor Lewis promised not to license anyone else but us," said Bryan, his voice showing his continuing interest.

"Not to license anyone else until the last day fixed for our departure," corrected Sylvestre Labbadie mildly. "I have an idea he granted a license or two after we left. I'll bet it was to Astor men."

"Whatever reservations Meri has, and he does have some," said Governor Lewis's brother, Reuben, "as Governor, it wouldn't be politically wise to deny licenses to Astor's men. We know Astor was already making overtures to experienced men. If those men are American citizens, they could have petitioned and got their licenses to trade on the Upper Missouri by now."

"Well, Manuel," said the Major cheerfully to Lisa, "We may have a sawyer or two to contend with before long. Do you suppose it will be McClellan? or Crooks? or both?"

"Damned sawyers, both of them," snorted Lisa disparagingly. "Worst thing on the river. Can upset a boat without warning."

It was neither McClellan nor Crooks, however, but deserters, who upset Lisa next.

Following the half-day spent checking the boats, they had progressed past one vexation after another, with irksome slowness. The Fourth of July was spent in pitilessly brutal labor to get past a ripple created by a sandbar. The men bedded down, the French boatmen, cheerfully, as was their wont, the Americans, grimly, and in tight-lipped silence, which was not.

Earlier than usual, the Major, from the fogged sleep of fatigue, was routed out by a furious uproar. Lisa, who could swear fluently in four languages and obscenely in several Indian dialects, was doing so.

Hastily pulling on his pants, the Major, carrying his socks and footwear, padded out on deck to find Lisa pacing up and down, fulminating with gestures to Rueben Lewis.

Looking at Reuben Lewis, who had been bearing the brunt of the American disgruntlement and insubordination, he deduced that Lewis had delivered some bad new to Lisa. Lewis, standing there, was smiling. From that, he assumed correctly the crisis demanded no immediate action so sat down on the deck and pulled on his socks and boots.

"What's he yelling about? His canoe?" asked Menard, wriggling into his shirt as he joined them, followed by Labbadie, Dr. Thomas, Morrison and Bryan.

"Someone borrowed it without his permission," said the Major gravely, sitting cross-legged, his eyes beginning to twinkle. "Again."

"Hell, I thought that was the whole idea when we brought the damned thing along. To be used by the hunters to go out and get game," said Morrison sharply. "Some of them are to take it every day - -"

"But not take off in it. Downstream," said Lewis cheerfully. "That takes care of whose turn it is to use the damned thing, thank God. We got rid of the damned canoe and three trouble makers. All in the same night."

"Dammit, this isn't my shirt," said Morrison.

"You grabbed the Major's. They're the same color," said Bryan handing over another shirt to Morrison. "Here's yours."

While Morrison and the Major donned their flannel shirts, the original blue color faded and streaked from sun and weather, Menard looked bleak. "What does it add up to now, Major?"

"An expensive total. Incompetents dismissed, ten; disabilities, two; deserters to date, thirty-four. As of now the Company is out $3700 for their advance drafts."

"That'll make Colonel Chouteau swear, too," said Bryan, with youthful insouciance.

He did, too, but only in two languages, when he joined them.

"This is costing us."

"$3700 and a very good canoe," Lisa emphasized with feeling, his dark eyes snapping with angry lights.

"That's your loss, not the Company's," retorted Pierre Chouteau, his expression not unfriendly. With frowning concern, he decided it must be determined which would be a case for litigation, which for manual force. Captain Menard, perturbed at the failure of the accommodations he had labored over at Cote san Dessein to dissipate the animosities of the intransigent, allowed his brother-in-law to lead him off to the paperwork that would give lawyers back in St. Louis employment and the deserters, at the very least, troublesome notoriety.

"Those Chouteaus act like we've got all the time in the world to get upriver," said Lisa without rancor, looking after the stiffly erect back of the Colonel as he headed for the disgruntling clerical tasks of recording losses instead of profits. "They can't expect to put those soldiers ashore every day for exercise and drill, or we'll be another three days creeping up on Fort Osage."

"Nobody creeps up on Fort Osage," said Reuben Lewis, who had built it. "General Clark has an eye for a strategic location."

"Fort Osage can see us from a long ways off," said Sylvestre Labbadie who had helped build it. "Gives Captain Clemson time to get his soldier boys looking neat."

From the triangle of the fort, on a bluff handsome as a Tiffany setting, clasped and embellished by the golden, sweeping scrollwork of the river, there was a panoramic view of the amber-jewel tones of the prairie in summer and all approaching traffic.

When the guns of the flotilla saluted the Fort, not quite two days later, the men sweating lightly in the noon-day sun of July 8, 1809, the guns of the fort replied politely. An interested and motley audience had assembled at the landing in anticipation of an exchange of news and conviviality and back-slapping reunions.

The men from the fort and the factory and the sutler's watched with a sprinkling of jocular comments; Indians, Osage, Pawnee, Otto and Kansas, from encampments outside the fort, some of whom had appeared at dawn to keep pace with the boats along the river bank, stood to one side, breech-clouted or coarsely shirted or robed in skins, and watched from dark-skinned and taciturn faces as A. P. Chouteau saw to the disembarkment, smartly executed, of his drill teams.

While they marched, mostly in step, to flank left and stand at attention with rifles at present arms; while the partners exchanged greetings with the commanding officers, Captain Clemson and Lieutenant Brownson and with the youthful sutler, George Sibley; while the voyageurs scrambled cheerfully to get the boats tied up so they could get on with their accustomed and highly anticipated

R&R; the American hunters, good humoredly and aptly, sharpened their wits on one and all, before leaping lightly ashore.

Colonel Chouteau tended to the military aspect of the expedition by having the entire detachment, militia and American rifles, parade for Captain Clemson. Following his inspection, and some complimentary comments, Colonel Chouteau gave his attention to an Indian delegation waiting with complaints about the dearth of merchants and merchandise.

Drawing the Major away from the other partners before he, too, could be caught up in the civilities of the gentlemen of the garrison, Reuben Lewis took him on a tour of the frontier outpost, as promised.

Reuben, said to take after his more personable mother and thus bearing only a passing resemblance to his better-known brother, was an able man in his own right.

The Major had found, as they had shared, philosophically, the experiences of demanding and unpleasant travel, and made, often caustically, the best of it, they were of a kind and could speak of many things of common interest. They had agreed, ranging over the many subjects that stimulate the minds of well-read and well-informed men, that the future of whole communities could be steered or reshaped, improved or jeopardized, by a handful of people.

They mentioned, in passing, the negative examples, James Wilkinson and Aaron Burr, and that bogeyman, Napoleon. Then Reuben, with unusual fervency in such a sensibly matter-of-fact man, waxed lyrical over a positive example.

They were here, Lewis said, advancing the interests of their country, because of the vision and hardihood of one man who had given his country unexpected substance and form when it was at its lowest ebb. The Major expected him to name the friend and neighbor of the influential Meriwether and landed Lewis families, Thomas Jefferson. Instead, the man he was talking about turned out to be George Rogers Clark: his star had rocketed high over the Illinois and Kentucky lands a generation earlier and, it was said, fizzed out in a whiskey bottle.

The Major, tentatively, offered the achievements of his brother, not certain just how much Reuben felt over-shadowed by them.

Reuben, who felt more concerned about his moody brother's future than his past, said briefly that Meri could not have succeeded, and he knew it well, without the heartening presence of his best friend, William Clark. William, the student and partisan of his much-elder brother, had all the vision and hardihood and none of the shortcomings of George.

It was not only William, but the extended family of the Rogers and the Clarks and the Lewis's who had made substantial achievements for their time and place on the frontier, in communities that would never have existed but for George Rogers Clark. Now, in turn, General William Clark was the example and sponsor of the multiplying O'Fallons, Fitzhughs, and the ubiquitous Rogers and Clarks.

"And I had the temerity to chide Francis about the rampant nepotism of the French families," the Major said, ruefully.

"If a man can't count on the abilities and performance of the members of his family, what can he count on?" said Reuben.

The Major, who never touched on the reasons he lacked such strengthening ties, sighed, and said, under his breath, "Himself."

Speaking of practical things, Reuben, the government sub-agent to the Osages, took the Major on a tour of the fort. It wasn't a very large fort, Reuben pointed out, but sufficient for the company of men stationed there and it had gone up quickly.

To most men of their era, a frontier fort was too familiar for comment, with blockhouses at each corner, the parade ground, barns and corrals, sentry gate and an arrangement of log buildings inside the palisade all protected by firing posts and apertures.

They and their fathers and their father's fathers had been erecting forts at key sites of fords or crossroads or the narrows of a pass for time out of mind. The Major was qualified to make comparisons, from Fort Pitt, rich in its rivers, with its glum frontier village, to Reuben's more recent construction. He did so now with a mind trained to observe, analyze and digest, thinking ahead to those same practical things he would require at Three Forks.

"It's utilitarian," Reuben Lewis said of the fort, sometimes called Fort Clark, for the man who had first seen the defensive site when he and Reuben's brother passed through this idyllic stretch of land called Fire Prairie back in 1804; more frequently for the people it was designed to serve and police, the Osage. "And not quite a year old."

Reuben Lewis had come up river in August of 1808 with six boats loaded with eighty-one soldiers to build the fort. General William Clark, who had travelled overland with eighty mounted militia, enlisted to protect the fort builders during their work, had met Reuben Lewis on schedule.

"We got started on the fort September 5," said Reuben, his deep-set gray eyes so like his brother's sparkling as he led the Major over the layout, through doors and up steps, gesturing at the arrangements designed to make outside assault a difficult proposition.

"Ten days later General Clark sent his scout Nathan Boone to bring in the Osage and Kansa headmen for a treaty-making council. He was sick as a dog at both ends. But he's got such strength of will and purpose. I've never seen the like. Musta been weak as newborn kitten. Still managed to get through all the folderol of treaty-making for the land. With Indians, you can't get away without giving them a chance to make speeches. The General is pretty plain spoken. I think he made some of them understand it was for them the government was putting up a fort and factory. You never know, with Indians. They'll put up with a lot of rigamarole to get free gifts. The General gave those out himself and was on his way back home to St. Louis a couple days later."

There were, Reuben went on to say, some things he would do differently when building his next fort, the one to be erected near the Five Villages of the Mandans. He pointed them out to the Major as they went along, so he, too, would not make the same mistakes at Three Forks.

"Syl was here, too, you know. He likes his comforts, Syl does. You got to watch him or he'd have things fancier'n the Labbadie mansion. Syl isn't much for rough livin'.

"As for the infirmary, Dr. Thomas has had some harsh things to say about the tendency to use any old hole-in-the-wall for sick men. He likes cross ventilation and a location that's easy to heat in the winter, gets the afternoon shade in the summer," said Reuben, opening the infirmary door and walking into a room like a blast furnace from the afternoon sun and an impromptu medical consultation between the Doctor and a young soldier, red-faced, but not entirely by the heat of the room. "Sorry, Doctor. Didn't know there were any patients in here."

"Oh, I'm finding there are some candidates. The company surgeon is with a patrol out on the prairie and won't be available for a few days. But I won't be putting any of them in this bake oven," said the Doctor, affably conducting the soldier to the door, and giving him a dismissive pat on the shoulder with orders to report for sick call line-up at the keelboat, where it would be cooler and more convenient, first thing tomorrow, and to pass the word to his mates. "I gather Reuben is showing off his spartan erection to you, Major."

There was a guffaw, hastily smothered by the soldier as he hurried off fastening his pants.

"Callow youth. He's bearing the penalty for his," the Doctor shrugged. Taking out his linen handkerchief, he mopped his brow. "Let's get out of this hell-hole. I wouldn't put a sick dog in here. Really, Reuben, you should give serious thought to turning this into a drying room for parching corn. Even the kitchen is cooler. And it smells much better. The cook is baking bread for the dinner the commandant is having for us tonight."

As they crossed the parade ground toward the kitchen, which was shaded by the afternoon sun, and approached the outdoor baking ovens, giving off shimmering waves of heat and the appetizing aroma of baking bread, the Major, hearing a familiar, domestic sound not associated with isolated posts, halted in midstride. Reaching into the stack of firewood near the ovens, he said "Somebody's lost a kitten." Dr. Thomas and Reuben drew nearer, watching as with a neat, economical gesture and a number of soothing sounds, he extricated a small and lamenting calico kitten.

"Where did it come from?" he said curiously, gently unhooking the miniature scrabbling claws digging for anchorage on his hand and sleeve, then cradled it against his chest, stroking it reassuringly. "It's not big enough to leave its mother."

"Here comes Momma. And the owner of both, I'll wager," said the Doctor, looking toward the kitchen entrance.

Approaching them, anxiety giving way to a broad grin of relief, was a soldier of sorts, his globular middle swathed in a rough sacking apron streaked with flour, his impressive lack of military bearing not enhanced by the lean, nursing calico cat making him stumble as she twined in-and-out between his feet, complaining.

The Major repeated his question as the cook removed the kitten appreciatively, but carefully, from his arms. Talking all the time, the cook gestured for them to follow, and led them into his surprisingly neat, clean and well-organized kitchen. While Dr. Thomas and Reuben made their way, digestive juices surging, to the table spread with loaves of crusty French bread set out to cool, the Major squatted before a crate lined with what appeared to be the cook's shirt and a litter of kittens in an assortment of colors making awkward attempts to climb out, mewing plaintively.

"There's four of them, you see," the cook said proudly, replacing the rescued kitten in the crate. The mother cat followed quickly, settling herself with throaty feline croonings that quieted down the kittens except for smacking sounds of satisfaction. "Two calico. A black-and-white. An orange — a tom, I'm a thinkin'. Worthless, except for makin' more cats."

"Female cats are worth more than beaver," explained Reuben eyeing some flakes of bread that lay on the table with a bemused expression. He licked the tip of one forefinger and touched a fallen flaky bit of crust carefully and put it in his mouth. "Everybody wants one. When you move in any where, the mice and rodents move in with you, and ruin what supplies they don't eat. You could sell cats to every settler on the river."

"Nary a mouse in this kitchen," pointed out the private with great satisfaction. "That kitten you found is the best of the lot. Gonna be as good as the mother cat. I don't know how I can thank you for findin' her so quick like."

The Doctor cleared his throat and looked meaningfully at the

Major. The Major smiled, said persuasively, "A slice of your bread, perhaps? For each of us?"

"My bread and butter?" said the soldier, stiffening.

"Butter?" breathed Reuben in tones of awe.

"That French feller swapped the mother cat for me receipt for French bread. You'd think a Frenchee would know how to make French bread but he said not like mine. For keeping 'em supplied with milk and me with butter, he's to get the orange one when it's old enough. He was making his bread like in the old country and it was terrible. It's the attitude, you see."

There was a silence, slightly puzzled and with a touch of tension in the air as the soldier considered the Major's request.

"Don't get me wrong. I'm that grateful to you," he said rather apologetically. "It's me rule, you understand, that makes me pause."

"No food for favors?" murmured the Major with understanding and regret.

"As a reward?" Reuben suggested almost beseechingly.

"I'm a fair man. Made that rule me ownself. You did find me kitten. I was lookin' all around for her, inside. If you hadn't come along, one of them sneaky Indian curs mighta got her." The Major supposed he was referring to the dogs, but wasn't sure.

The soldier cook looked long at the Major. "So," he said decisively, "Fair's fair." He reached for a butcher knife with one hand and a loaf of bread with the other. "Sit over at that table. Now, you gotta recollect, when you leave here, no talkin' up me bread and butter — leastways, not until everybody else does at the dinner tonight."

Solemnly, avidly eyeing the bread he was slicing deftly and slathering with butter, half-melted by the heat of the July day, Dr. Thomas and Reuben assured him he could count on their discretion, and the Major nodded bemused agreement. While the cook placed the slices neatly on a china platter and set out china plates and cups and saucers and cutlery, they re-affirmed that no one, absolutely no one, would learn from them that he had broken his hard and fast rule.

Bread and butter were only for special occasions and worth a beaver plew, each slice, if he was of a mind to go in for that underhanded sort of thing.

"You must be in the right business, Private - -?" said the Major to their generous host. "I didn't realize cats and bread could be so profitable."

"Cook's me name. An' cookin' for sojers is me business," said the private, his tone gently rebuking.

As they made their way through not only one but two loaves of bread, and the cook brought out more butter, and offered them some cream, just on the turn, for the freshly brewed coffee, which they declined, he also served up more than a glimpse of his history. From hard, lean beginnings on a hill farm to the even harder life of an inept soldier, he had blundered awkwardly through each day made miserable by peers and superiors alike, until an astute commanding officer ascertained that his preoccupation with food included not only gargantuan ingestion but, given the opportunity, a dedicated interest in its careful selection, meticulous storage and most adept preparation.

"It's ben me life ever since. Cookin' fer sojers," he concluded gravely. "Sojers have to stomach a lot. I make sure it ain't bad food. So, I make it plain to one 'n all. I won't part with me kittens for no beaver plews. Fair's fair. Four barrels of white flour. A block of good, clean sugar. A sack of raisins. A crate of dried apples."

"Each?" said Reuben in disbelief, aware of the costliness of such provender.

"Each," Private Cook said firmly. "Then won't me sojers be surprised when they find raisins in their mush on Sundays. And get apple pies come Christmas."

Replete, they took polite leave of the staunch little frontier gourmand. He assured them they would enjoy more of his fare that night at the commandant's dinner, and the next night at the sutler's, but he cautioned them not to expect the same quality at the Chouteau's, the Frenchie they had cooking for them poured too much wine into his sauces and himself.

They strolled from one point of the fort to another, discussing what they could see from the top of the bluff: the foreshortened figures of their own riflemen engaging the experts from the garrison in a marksmanship contest, and winning; the frontiersmen from the James boat cheering on Cheek, stripped down to his breeches, and involved with an unidentifiable number of lithe, bare-torsoed and muscular hunters from the other boats, in some kind of knockabout physical contest; three red wavering toques marking the progress, faintly musical, of a group of French voyageurs straggling toward the Osage encampment and a routine assignation with some of the women there, waiting, jabbering and gesturing, coarsely; a canoe, low in the water, coasting into the landing; Lisa, identifiable by his red neckerchief and characteristically vigorous gait, hastening from his keelboat toward the agile newcomer swinging about from tethering his canoe; the aesthetically impressive view of the river and the prairie, free at the moment of all discernible traffic, except for a vaguely defined large animal moving about in the general vicinity of the putative plantation of the Audrains that could be one of their prized oxen.

There wasn't much daylight left and the heat was abating but not the humidity, so they moved leisurely, perspiring, to tour the group of buildings forming the factory, past the house of the sutler, and were approaching the quarters of the Osage Indian sub-agent when Francis Vallé and Sylvestre Labbadie overtook them.

"Where have you been? We just witnessed an interesting confrontation," Francis began, then paused to reach out delicately to remove a gleam of butter from Reuben's chin, sniff it, then flicked several cat's hairs from the Major's sleeve and eyed the scratches on his hand. "Butter? Cats? Here?"

"The altitude can't have anything to do with it," Dr. Thomas mused aloud, pursuing an anomaly that had been nagging at the back of his mind since they left the kitchen. "We're not that much above sea level."

"About seven-hundred feet. Not quite double that of St. Louis," said the Major, supplying the statistics, readily, that the Doctor was seeking, indirectly. "It's not enough to affect bread or much else. Maybe 'attitude' is correct."

"Attitude?" repeated Francis and waited, mystified, for an explanation that never came.

Instead, the calm of the dwindling day was shattered by a cry of keenest anguish. It came from the Indian encampment. So sustained and piercing was it, hurtful to the ears, they all spun around to gape at the source, one of the fifty or so lodges set up within rifle shot, and to the regret of the inhabitants, within smell of the fort.

The unedifying village, on the verge of reaching the littered and odorous high that would soon impel the Osage themselves to seek out a fresh camp spot further out on the prairie, was made up of structures primitive in concept and construction. Skewed rectangles sided up with palings, covered with loosely woven mats of coarse reeds, with a smoke hole in the roof above the shallow fire hole dug into the dirt floor, they were portable units certain to provide plenty of cross ventilation in a limited and claustrophobic living space, and to leak like a sieve.

"My God," exclaimed the Doctor, "One of the women must have changed her mind."

"Sounds more like the town crier. Poor ol' No Name gets a bit addled after one of his frequent naps. Thinks it's morning," said Sylvestre Labbadie. He pointing out a stooped, elderly Osage, only his loins clothed, standing before the smallest and nearest of the lodges.

As they watched, the old Osage threw his head back, his thin, tangled locks of graying hair swaying across his naked shoulders, his scrawny neck working as he lifted his ropy arms and his wavering cry toward the sky again.

Reuben shrugged. "If you're around the Osage for any length

of time, you get used to the custom. See, the fort regulars aren't paying any attention."

"Some mournful Osage custom?" said the Major, wincing, as the cry was taken up by other voices.

"More a morning mourning custom. Usually doesn't hit them this late in the day," said Reuben, grimacing, for now the dogs were protesting against the painful impact upon their eardrums. "Generally hits one of them when he first wakes up in the morning and remembers that one or more of his relatives is dead. Or some friend. Or even his dog. Then the whole village joins in, including the dogs."

With mutual and unspoken agreement, they were putting as much distance as possible between them and the keening.

"There goes somebody with an authoritarian stride to tell the poor old man to save it for morning," said Francis hopefully. As No Name's keening cut off abruptly, and the other voices died away slowly, and sticks were thrown at the dogs, "Thank God."

Reuben, leading them to his agency quarters which they were to share during the stopover, said, "Syl and I got kinda used to it when we built the fort."

Labbadie grinned. "The bugler got in the habit of sleeping in, counting on the Osage to sound the wake-up call for him every morning."

In answer to an inquiry about the bereft No Name, Reuben gave a thumb-nail history of his wards.

A semi-nomadic people, speaking a Siouan dialect, with more or less permanent abodes in western Missouri, the Osage had proved troublesome to the eastern settlements throughout the Spanish regime. Not much given to killing, they would sneak into a settlement on a dark night and carry off anything they could find; or remove, with much incivility and gross indignities, horses, supplies, armament and wearing apparel from an unwary traveller.

The Major, thinking of the sorry specimens he had seen here today, wondered what had happened to all those muscular warriors, the superbly fit and fighting horde, seemingly six feet tall and fierce as Vikings, that had besieged and would have overrun them at Austin's Mine a Breton but for the resolute opposition of the American frontiersmen there almost a decade earlier.

"The pox — chicken, small and the venereal kind — has taken its toll, I imagine," said the Doctor as if he had read his mind.

"Also, according to No Name, who once had quite a reputation as a warrior, the American immigrants," said Labbadie baldly. "He mourns for the good old days of the Dons almost as much as for the departed. They had a gran' time looting eastern Missouri when he was a young buck."

"Especially in Ste. Genevieve," said Francis emphatically.

"Killed your Oncle Joseph," said Labbadie.

Francis nodded. "Even after Papá Vallé persuaded the Spanish it would be a good idea to have the resettled Shawnees and Delawares actively discourage their meandering raids, the Osage kept coming back for our livestock. They liked the peaceful, restrained attitude of the people of Ste. Genevieve almost as much as they liked our horses."

"Well, they sure didn't find the attitude of the American immigrants peaceful or restrained. No Name gets rather bitter over the discouraging ways of the American riflemen around Mine á Breton," said Reuben, escorting them into a plain building, no flourishes without or within, but compared to the cramped quarters of the keelboat, spacious and comfortable. "He's always warning the young bucks to avoid them. Says they look upon the shooting of Indians as being akin to squirrel hunting. He shows them the bullet groove in the top of his head where he got 'barked' as proof."

Reuben got them settled into the unusual, civilized luxury of chairs in the front room, a combination office and living room, that had a table with a scattering of well-thumbed books, counters and the walls lined with rough shelving, and a fireplace. The back room, where they would all sleep, had double puncheon floors like the front room, one small window, and double bunks attached to the walls spread with straw ticks, and their personal belongings brought up earlier from the keelboat by some of the enlisted men.

"Well, as we had pointed out to us so fortuitously, 'fair's fair,' " said the Doctor, with a smothered belch, as he settled his stocky self with his usual ponderous dignity into the unusual comfort of a chair and folded his hands that he kept meticulously clean over his faded but not-so-clean shirt. "If the Osage enriched themselves in their fashion in eastern Missouri, at the same time there were white men enriching themselves on the Osage trade. The Chouteaus certainly did all right. I'm not sure Lisa had time to recover what it cost him to get the monopoly away from them. The Louisiana Purchase put stop on so many of the transactions with the Dons."

"The Chouteaus have always dealt fairly with the Indians," said Syl, who should know. "A lot of traders didn't. One thing I'll say about Lisa, he keeps his word to Indians."

Reuben looked solemn. "Prospering fairly is one thing, but cheating the Indian is something else again. The Dons, as long as they got their cut, didn't seem to care. There's been a lot of changes in the way things are done now the US took charge."

"Oh, I don't know about that," said Francis lightly. "The Chouteaus have the Osage trade just like they used to, but as agents of the US government instead of as Spanish petitioners. Speaking of changes in the fur trade, that reminds me. Major, just as you predicted, that sawyer has bobbed up, here."

"The man in the canoe," said the Major without hesitation. "Crooks? or McClellan?"

"Crooks," said Francis. "Looks innocuous at first glance, like all sawyers."

"What did Lisa do?" Reuben asked anxiously.

"Invited him to dine with all of us at the commandant's tonight," said Francis delightedly. "His cook does him proud, they say. Dotes on formal dinners. So, gentlemen, dig out your best bib-and-tucker and let's away. Think of the entertainment that awaits!"

Chapter 7

They were at Fort Osage for three days and four nights. The Major and his colleagues were in frequent conference in and around the warehouses. The barges were subjected to much overhauling and refitting. The cargoes, particularly the supply of the blue beads, depleted by advances made to the French boatmen who used them in turn to make successful advances to the Indian women, were picked over, rearranged and repacked.

Those not involved, like young Bryan, ate rather well, had more time and space to move about in, to take in the limited amenities of the outpost and splash in the river and look into the ways of the people here by chance and by choice.

With some forethought, and the appreciation of his responsible, rather phlegmatic cousin, Samuel Morrison, who sometimes found the breathless eagerness of his young charge wearing, the Major paired Bryan successfully with the slightly younger wilderness-wise Kentuckian, Len Cather. Both Morrison and the Major were relieved when another Kentuckian from the James boat, John Dougherty, who was a sober young man of restraint, befitting his Methodist upbringing, volunteered to keep them under observation, discreetly.

To Bryan it was all stimulating to his appetite, like the delicious food the commander's superb, but slightly eccentric cook, laid out on the glistening white cloth night after night.

Bryan had been a trifle disappointed the first night to arrive at Reuben's quarters, bubbling over with all the interesting things to share with them, to be bundled through a quick wash and into the clothes Francis had ready for him. The latest mode in Philadelphia, in advance of the fashion in St. Louis, he was uncomfortably certain they were out of place in Fort Osage. He was relieved when he looked over the gathering at the commandant's and the surprising sartorial achievements on display, to find that Francis had known what he was about and, relaxed, prepared to enjoy himself here, too.

When he wrote to his mother, which he should do before they left here, he would tell her that Senor Lisa looked liked an elegant Spanish grandee, all in black; the Colonel, dignified as always, in another velvet jacket he hadn't seen before, a rich Prussian blue, of impeccable tailoring; Francis, downright dashing in an outfit as fashionable as Bryan's; the Major, his usual neat and well-groomed self, in the militia uniform he had been wearing when Bryan had first taken to him back in St. Louis, his boots brightly, and voluntarily polished by the enlisted man the cook had sent to remind them of the approaching dinner hour; the other partners, Menard, Morrison, Labbadie and Lewis, in their militia outfits, too, and creditably comparable to the turn-out of Captain Clemson and Lieutenant Brownson. The latter had campaigned with A.P. apparently, to judge by their deceptively prudent reminiscences about their one-time senior officer, General James Wilkinson.

The Doctor, in dark broadcloth and gleaming shirt front, snorted something about aphrodisiacs in reply to something said about poxy squaws by the sutler, Mr. Sibley, whose jacket and breeches of brown were considerably less old-fashioned than those of the aristocratic M. Audrain but lacked the expensive French splendor of material and design.

Just introduced, a young man with the firm handshake and pleasant Scotch burr, moving to a seat further down the table, next to Lisa, where Bryan, curious, could watch him unobserved. The most outstanding thing about him seemed to be his bright trousers which had the Major murmuring, "Clan MacDonald breeks." As they all seated themselves in the places indicated by Captain Clemson, the breeks, snug over muscular shanks, were placed out of sight under the table so all that showed above was a ruffled white shirt and a worn and rusty looking black velvet jacket.

Except when he smiled, his teeth flashing engagingly at something Senor Lisa had said, there was nothing memorable about the smooth, unlined face and nondescript hair of Ramsay Crooks, Bryan decided, mentally composing his letter. Then, as he watched, the profile, briefly presented, reminded Bryan of an engraving he had found intriguing in one of the history books back home.

The Major must have seen the engraving, too, for he said quietly to Francis, on his other side, "Put an iron helm on him and you've got the classic Scot border reaver off to harry the Sassenachs."

Francis, evidently unfamiliar with Sassenachs, only raised his eyebrows. Reuben Lewis, whose background gave him more insight, picked up on the comparison, and leaning forward, pointed out with a smile, "Sassenachs? I thought Clan MacDonald breeks were for going after hairy-legged Campbells. Any body here Campbell clan?"

While Bryan was giving some thought to that exchange, a chubby soldier looked in, caught Captain Clemson's eye meaningfully. The commander broke off in mid-sentence, then began mumbling, just like Bryan's father at his mother's nod, now-we-will-hear-grace, and everyone bowed their heads briefly for his further mumble. With the 'amens' a pair of enlisted men began serving the food deftly and Bryan, who enjoyed eating, could begin.

His mother, who prided herself on being a successful hostess, would be pleasantly surprised to learn she could not have faulted the table setting, the food or the service. Because it was an informed and intelligent gathering, the kind she and his father preferred, the conversation wasn't monopolized either but moved easily from topic to topic of concern to them all.

Bryan, remembering his father's admonitions, listened and saved up his questions. It's more important to be observant and get the facts right than to be able to interpret them, the older Bryan was fond of telling him. If you have observed enough of them accurately, you won't have to interpret them. They will explain themselves. He must remember to tell his father that Len Cather, giving him his first lesson in tracking today, had said pretty much the same thing.

That night, and succeeding nights, there was civilized conversation, and the reminiscences of men who had a wide variety of experiences, including many humorous, and, as Bryan was discovering, there is nothing like a good laugh over the disasters of others to make the current group feel superior.

They talked easily of their trade, for it was something all of them knew and enjoyed, whether fur or military. They were all professionals, and one professional recognized and looked up to another.

So, taking keen enjoyment in his food, Bryan listened that first night as the Major determined that Crook had no recent news about the embargo; exchanged with M. Audrain news of mutual acquaintances in Pennsylvania and the French enclave of Old Regime refugee aristocrats in their New Bourbon settlement near St. Genevieve, in which Francis joined. M. Audrain and Francis dropped comfortably into idiomatic French, to which Captain Menard and the Colonel contributed, and sometimes Labbadie, and which the Major, keeping to English, seemed to be able to follow, chuckling. Bryan decided his French wasn't as good as he'd told his mother. Cousin Sam's wasn't either. He looked glum. Bryan determined to get some tutoring from Francis so as not to miss out on anything amusing.

Then, in giving attention to generous second helpings, he lost the thread of the conversation in English, too. While the anecdotes built up, he was unable to identify the near-legendary hero they were talking about. The fellow leaped over spans of oxen, eight-foot high quartermaster wagons, outran, out-foxed and out-fought Indians and rescued comely captive maidens, not necessarily in that order. Bryan was surprised to learn it was Ramsay Crook's partner, the other sawyer, Robert McClellan, waiting for Crooks up near Council Bluffs. Idly, Bryan wondered why Lisa hadn't recruited McClellan to join their expedition, then remembered hearing, coming up river, Menard remind Morrison that McClellan, who had absorbed wilderness ways so completely he even talked and looked like an Indian, bore a grudge against Lisa. They had been involved in some kind of a dispute and a lawsuit a couple years before and McClellan had to pay out a tidy sum. Ever since, like an Indian, McClellan was more determined to get even than to make a profit.

Then Lieutenant Brownson drew him out about recent cultural activities in Philadelphia and waxed nostalgic about the civilized amenities he had enjoyed on his last visit there, and made Bryan aware that out here, men were thrown on their own resources more than ever before. For audience, for entertainment, for sympathy, and sometimes, to their detriment, for the heightening and intensification of differences, they had only themselves.

Later, when they were getting ready for bed in Reuben's quarters, and he'd finally been able to tell them about his day and heard in his turn about the cook having kittens, he got them to tell him about Ramsay Crooks, pointing out with a shade of disbelief that such a young man, certainly not much older than he was, should not be a worry to a veteran like Senor Lisa.

"Oh, but he is much, much older than you in the ways of the fur trade," said the Major gently.

"Is that a fact?" Bryan was still murmuring, much later, sleepily, and a trifle overwhelmed.

The facts were, as Bryan was to confirm in subsequent and friendly contacts with the young man himself, not unusual. Ramsay Crooks was a product of the near-universal education system of Scotland that, in an era when illiteracy was more the norm than the exception for the general population of the world, saw to it that the Scotch youth were taught, along with the tenets of a rigid Calvinistic code, to read and write and cipher with exemplary honesty. Employers, all over the world, were in need of clerical help who had mastered such basics. Able and ambitious young Scots, finding opportunities limited at home, were fanning out, all over Europe, the Orient, as well as North and South America, their common-school training giving them a leg up in the marts of trade. From a lowly clerical job, more than one young Scot was pulling himself up by his bootstraps.

Appropriately enough, Ramsay, the youngest son of a shoemaker, was a connoisseur of boots and, if possible, always included a selection of sturdy footwear, profitably, in his stock of trade supplies. From his own experience, as a novice, he had learned that the novelty of wearing moccasins wore off as quickly as the moccasins wore out, usually in the first experience of picking a way through, and then picking out, cactus. Experienced hands and such Indians as could afford the luxury of boots became repeat customers.

Born and raised in Greenock, a thriving seaport town beside the busy Firth of Clyde, the comings and goings of ships from all over the world beckoned Ramsay to wider horizons as they had his older brothers, already settled in Niagara, Canada. When his father died, Ramsay's widowed mother promptly packed up her teen-age son, young daughter and all their belongings and joined the brothers, the same year as the Louisiana Purchase, in 1803.

In the succeeding six years, Ramsay Crooks, in his way had made leaps the equal of his partner, Robert McClellan. Leaving the rest of his family in Niagara, he had gone to Montreal and found a clerking job, learned enough by the time he was eighteen to become a trader himself, ranging far: Michilimackinac, the Great Lakes, the Mississippi, the Wisconsin, the Illinois and the Missouri. After several seasons as a durable Canadian 'winterer', he had brought a load of furs to St. Louis, became an American citizen and had been grubstaked by no less than Sylvestre Labbadie Sr. and Rene August Chouteau; and more recently, as a partner of the irascible McClellan, had been shunted up into ol' Joe Robidoux's territory by Pierre Chouteau's Indian agency.

He had a grasp of the value of swift communications and the world-wide ramifications of the fur trade. Astor, who knew the critical importance of keeping in touch with Leipzig and London and Paris and Washington and Montreal and St. Louis would value a man who could put it all together with the scattered Indian villages of the far West. And Ramsay Crooks was only twenty-two years old.

"The younger generation," said Francis. "Like Bryan here."

"No. Bryan is a romantic. He'd pack a mandarin robe," said the Major. "Yon Scot is more like Pierre Chouteau's namesake."

"The Cadet. Umm. A hard-headed, pragmatic generation, then."

"Certainly not a romantic," said Reuben blowing out the candle and settling into his bunk. "Anyway, the romance has all gone out of western ventures. The age of realism is here."

Bryan roused himself. "A mandarin robe?'

Yawning, the Major explained. The legendary Henry Hudson, and his venturesome peers, were reputed to have sailed into the unknown with just such exotic apparel packed carefully away, ready for the day when they would meet and treat with the Chinese.

"Chinese red silk embroidered with the imperial five-toed flying dragon, I suppose?" scoffed the Doctor, turning over and settling himself comfortably in the bunk below Bryan. "Now, what would a Mohawk chieftain make of that?"

"A toga," said Bryan who was beginning to get the hang of their exchanges and felt suitably rewarded by their answering chuckles for everyone knew Mohawk chieftains bore a surprising resemblance to the statues of those old Roman senators.

During the days, speaking straightforwardly of mundane matters and enthusiastically about the ways of wilderness survival with Len Cather, he found some things to mull over from their conversations, too, particularly when John Dougherty joined them from time to time.

He was more relieved than he let on, when John bobbed up at the Indian encampment just as the strange old Osage, after showing them his scarred head, started yelling and making threatening gestures. John had steered them safely out of that smelly place and told them where they could bag some fat geese, which they did.

When he and Len came back, loaded with geese, and would have lingered with the Americans who were taking their ease with the pleasant-talking Mr. Crooks, John Dougherty hiked them off to a shady spot on the river to pick and dress out the geese, tediously, and then, not the least bit tediously, to try their luck at catching catfish.

"He's making them promises, isn't he?" Len said indignantly, in a low tone, as they left the Americans.

John Dougherty said dismissively, "He's a promisin' fellow."

Bryan, so they wouldn't think he was eavesdropping on a private conversation, told them about the mandarin robe.

John, who Bryan was discovering had a better than average education and was ambitious, said with a grin, "I hope we get established on the Pacific coast before we'll be needing Cossack hats."

Bryan grinned back. "The Chinese robe does sound more civilized."

However, John didn't sound so civilized when he enlightened Bryan, grimly about what the Campbells had done to the MacDonalds, and vice versa. So Bryan didn't tell him about the breeks, in case Crooks was one, and John, the other. From the undercurrents at the sutler's table the second night, he was beginning to suspect there were enough hard feelings over recent disputes, without bringing up old feuds.

Instead, he summarized the interesting new information he had gleaned from dinner table discourse on traps at Mr. Sibley's.

"Traps are a new invention?" said Len doubtfully. "I don't remember a time when there weren't any traps."

"Old timers like Captain Menard do. Before then, nobody,

especially the Indians bothered much with beaver. They're still scarce. And expensive. Spring steel traps."

Before Bryan had a chance to get bored, the last day arrived. The Major, who had discovered that Len Cather not only could read and write and cipher but liked to, set him to work on some letters and calculations. His friend McBride came looking for him and despite some grumblings, sat down to share in the work. Their companion, the tall slender Jackson came in quietly and taking out his sketch book, began working on a likeness of the Major.

Bryan penned a letter to his parents, shorter than he'd planned at first, but carefully reassuring. When he finished the Major sent him on an errand to the cook. Playing with the kittens one last time, Bryan was given some interesting tid-bits by the cook, some tasty items he ate immediately, and some curious ones he saved for the Major to digest later.

When he returned he found an extemporaneous geography and economics class in session. The Major had spread out a map on the counter in the front room, and using one of his long, slender forefingers, the almond nail trimmed short and kept clean like his other fingers, was pointing the route supplies came out from, and furs returned to, London.

Gathered around him were the young recruits, Jackson and McBride that Bryan was coming to know and like, and who were nearly as good in the wilderness as Len Cather and John Dougherty, who were also at the Major's elbow. Francis Valle and Charles Davis came in just as the Major got from London to Montreal, and were attentive, even if it was an old story to them.

A long time went by, the Major was saying, between the ordering of goods and the realizing of a profit. Bryan nodded his head, having heard his father deplore his own dependency on the importation of manufactured goods from European markets. He looked at the roundabout route the Major was tracing to get the trade goods to St. Louis. From London to Montreal and to the Great Lakes and then down to St. Louis seemed a long way around. But, as his father grumbled on more than one occasion, he had to send goods over the Allegheny Mountains or clear around the country to New Orleans and then up the Mississippi. When the furs, coming back over the same route, arrived in Mackilmackinac, the fellows there were lucky to have the cooler weather. Furs did not keep well in the humid heat during the months it took them to get from St. Louis to Philadelphia. His father often did a lot of swearing, even at home, over the arrival of worthless, worm-eaten pelts.

Bryan put his finger on the key spot of the Great Lakes and said, "Joseph Miller. He was one soldier Private Cook said he wouldn't allow in his kitchen, let alone cook for."

The Major nodded, exchanging glances with Francis, and went on without pausing to explain that goods ordered in London this year would not be at Mackilmackinac until the summer of 1810, and would not get out into the field until sometime in 1811. The furs to pay for those goods would not get to Montreal until late in 1811 and would not arrive in London for sale until 1812. Then the cost of the original goods could be paid.

Line of credit had to be financed for as long as three years. Many a trader had gone broke trying to stay afloat that long.

"Hell's Fire," said Jackson indignantly, "We should be getting our supplies from Americans instead of the British."

"Some day we will," said Charles Davis, a sturdy man who had been with the Major in those early days at Mine á Breton. "Now, though, we're in real trouble when we can't get goods through by the route the Major showed you. The supplies we'll be needing next summer haven't left London yet. We'll be lucky if they get to St. Louis in time for Lisa to bring them up the river to us in 1811."

Dr. Thomas came in then and suggested everybody go for a swim. They all made their way to the river, with Charlie Davis protesting he was getting to the point where even the coldest water wasn't going to make any difference. The Doctor said dryly that he realized that propinquity was a universal aphrodisiac and his supply of mercury was far from exhausted, at which Charlie groaned and dived into the water.

Bryan, who had only recently learned what an aphrodisiac was, enlightened the other young men as they ventured further downstream.

"I ain't seen a pretty squaw yet," said Jackson, wrinkling his nose. "Let's go explore that there island over yonder."

Bryan, Cather, Jackson and McBride, leaving the others to frolic in the shallower water, swam to the island and stretched out on its bank.

"Drouillard says 'there be some' among the Sioux," Len returned to the intriguing subject. "Anyway, while we been here, Captain James wouldn't let even Cheek have any blue beads."

"You're lucky," muttered McBride. The others looked at him, speculatively.

"Bryan," said Len, "tell Mac that one about the mercury."

"You mean, one night with Venus and six months with Mercury?" said Bryan.

"Hell's Fire!" said Jackson, very thoughtfully. Instead of elaborating, he shrugged, and asked Bryan what his first name was.

"My first name?" repeated Bryan absently, wondering if Jackson had his own private supply of blue beads, or had stumbled upon an equally acceptable item of barter.

"Would you believe mine was Belthazzar?"

"Really? How come?"

Drawing his knees up to his chest and hugging them, as a slight breeze came up, cooling their wet bodies, refreshingly, Jackson said, "Ma named the whole slew of us for folks out of the Bible. I don't think it mattered much to her what the feller had done as long as the name rolled out in a way she liked. Anyway, I'm on the rolls as B. Jackson. Most folks, if they think about it at all, figger I was named for my Uncle Benjamin. He's supposed to be somewhere up river."

"Up river? Are you sure, Belthazzar?" said Len.

Belthazzar frowned. "I don't answer to that. M'folks call me Belt." He persisted. "Everybody calls you young Bryan from Philadelphia. You must have some other name."

"I was christened William P. Bryan. If I'd been named for both grandfathers as they wished, that's what my name would have been though: Young Guy Bryan."

"Oh, you poor guy!" said Belthazzar.

All four of them fell back laughing. McBride, who was sensitive about his first name, was relieved when a shout from the river bank called them back to the rest of the bathing party. Mac was an easy handle for most people, his mother wasn't around to insist on Pet, and P. McBride did for a signature. Still he was just as glad to see them forget about first names as Bryan parted from them to go get ready for the dinner with the Chouteaus.

The linen and the table setting were same, also the guests, except for Crooks who had departed in his canoe after a lengthy conference with Lisa. The room was rather more luxurious than any Bryan had seen at Fort Osage, and, he felt, Frenchified, and reflecting the Chouteau affluence, a room reserved just for eating in. When the same enlisted men started serving after the Colonel was reminded to say grace by a familiar figure nodding from the doorway, Francis said in an undertone, "I thought the Chouteaus had a French cook."

Bryan, who was pleased to recognize the catfish and the geese among the food being offered, was able to tell them about the accident. The French cook, to no one's surprise, except his, had fallen in the river, claiming he had been pushed, in hysterical French, which the bored Americans who pulled him out, slowly, chuckling, didn't understand.

A.P. Chouteau said the commander's cook had been kind enough to volunteer his services, and he certainly was an original, wasn't he?

M. Audrain, sighing, said that original would have had a great career as a chef in Paris, and less costly for everyone hereabouts. The commander, ruefully, that he was a shrewd negotiator, putting together what he considered the necessities for presenting food properly, including the valuable linen and place settings they saw here. His former commander was after him to join him, but fortunately, he had been able to obtain his promise, just today, that he wouldn't leave until after Christmas.

"My God," Dr. Thomas said to Reuben. "He is getting the raisins and the apples."

"And the sugar and the flour?" said Reuben, looking across the table with surmise at the Major. "You know?"

"I put forward a suggestion or two," said the Major pleasantly and noncommittally. "Up here, where there's little or no cash available, the barter system can get very complicated."

"Speaking of cooks," said George Sibley, who had found his niche at twenty-seven in the government's Indian store, "No Name tells me he regrets his Osage patron has not bestirred himself to offer hospitality to the visiting white men. He was looking forward to preparing a feast in your honor."

"No Name, the town crier?" said Francis incredulously.

"He's that, too —"

"— yes, indeed —" agreed Francis.

"But he's not too bad a cook. I have feasted daintily on his acorns and buffalo grease. Didn't taste half bad after two days on lean rations," said Sibley. Born in Massachusetts, he had been raised in North Carolina, where his father, Dr. John Sibley, the Revolutionary War veteran, had moved when he left the army. As the newly appointed government store clerk, he had accompanied Reuben and the troops to Fire Prairie two years before and took pride in the growth of the establishment at Fort Osage.

"Actually," said Reuben, "you could do worse than their favorite dishes: sweet corn boiled in buffalo grease; or boiled meat and pumpkins."

"His patron would probably have wanted him to serve tea. With boiled meat and crullers," said Sibley.

"Tea?" said Francis, a note of incredulity in his voice.

"Tea," said Sibley smiling. "His patron came back from a trip to the United States enamored with the white man's custom of serving tea."

"Isn't that an awful come-down for a warrior to end up as a cook?" the Major asked.

"Not if it's by choice," explained Sibley, who had come to appreciate many of the customs of his charges. "Cook and town crier are honorable alternatives for warriors past their prime. Particularly when, like No Name, they've lost their sons in war and their womenfolk to disease. Walking Rain, the great warrior and brave man, had no reason to go on living. As No Name, the cook and town crier, he did."

Bryan found his attention wandering when Sibley began describing the meals he and his clerk took. At nine in the morning they had coffee and unbuttered toast; beef, pork or venison with milk and hominy at two in the afternoon; and a dish of tea, milk and hominy in the evening, no set time.

Senor Lisa and Captain Menard were talking about where to store the $500 worth of salt pork purchased from Dr. John Hamilton Robinson to replace the inroads on the provisions and take care of any possibility of running short.

A.P., Syl, Rueben and Sam were comparing notes about the way Crooks had made himself especially agreeable to the Americans, spending considerable time with Thomas James and his men, and being generous with a jug. To Lisa, and the table at large, Labbadie said Manuel should be congratulated for the way he had handled a sticky situation.

Bryan thought the partners seemed relieved not to have Crooks with them. They were speaking out more freely than had been their custom on preceding evenings, speculating about the former military man turned trader, Joseph Miller, who was supposed to follow Crooks with a keelboat and a load of supplies. Lisa doubted Miller would obtain much in the way of supplies, considering the bare shelves the expedition had left behind in St. Louis.

"Michilimackinac," the Major said gently. Lisa, who had been smiling smugly, looked nonplussed.

He and Crooks had come to an agreement, Lisa reminded the table. Crooks was to await them at McClellan's camp, not venture upriver ahead of them. He was going right now, if the gentlemen would excuse him, and put that agreement in writing and dispatch it to General Clark, so the General would understand if, later on, Lisa found Crooks in violation, and had to take measures.

Senor Lisa was in a fetching, Bryan decided, falling back on his mother's terminology when, his father, much less often than Senor Lisa, thank goodness, became visibly agitated in a fashion deplored by his mother. Like his mother, the partners were wise not to keep him around, for he would just have spoiled the last nice, civilized evening they would have for a long time.

Reuben Lewis, who may or may not have been the agency representative who had given Crooks and McClellan license to try their luck, unsuccessfully in Roubidoux territory last year, grinned at the Major. "Our own Billie Goat Gruff."

Bryan, who had come to appreciate that Reuben did have a classical education like the Governor's, was disappointed to hear him talking about a mere fairy tale. He was glad when M. Audrain drew him into a conversation that included Francis. Both encouraged him to make use of his French, correcting his grammatical errors and accent gently.

They all lingered late, seemingly reluctant to have the evening end, talking desultorily. Yawning, Bryan congratulated himself that he could keep up with all the threads woven into the conversation. When they left the Chouteau's, after Private Cook had been escorted in and given three cheers, Francis said, "Billie Goat Gruff?"

Briefly, the Major gave him the gist of the fairy tale, known as the Three Billy Goats Gruff.

"Oh, my," said Francis with a rueful shake of his head. "The poor trolls."

Bryan, recalling the things he had been hearing about Senor Lisa, felt the sympathy was misplaced. When he slept that night, Middle-Sized Billie Goat Gruff lingered somewhere in his subconscious. He dreamed that Senor Lisa trit-trotted successfully over the bridge. When Mr. Crooks, looking very nice in his McDonald breeks, came trit-trotting along sometime later, he got tossed about by a troll that looked and sounded just like poor ol' No Name, only much bigger and fiercer.

The next morning Bryan was able to recognize, if not name, everyone who came to see them off. This included poor ol' No Name, who had buried his name with the last of his kin folks. Bryan also suspected he was the one who had set off the dawn caterwauling from the Osage camp that had brought him straight out of a sound sleep, swearing, with the Major saying, sleepily, "My goodness, you have been augmenting your vocabulary."

They got away from Fort Osage smoothly and without incident on a bright and clear day with the sky an unclouded blue and, according to Lisa's report to General Clark, with "153 men, all armed, Burgeois, Indians, Engages & Mullatoes."

Business correspondence, letters home, the last touch with civilization, were all put behind. The river once more dominated their lives.

Lisa exhorted, bantered encouragingly and led the boatmen in their cheerful songs. He succeeded in keeping the French-Canadians from dwelling on the lonesomeness around and in store for them. The Americans, who did not like his patronizing air, eyed him critically but worked willingly enough. Lisa suspected that it was also done calculatingly as they estimated how far they had yet to go to reach the camp of the promising Ramsay Crooks.

The river narrowed above Vincent's Island where they met a large party of traders, floating buffalo robes down from the Yankton Sioux country. They exchanged news. Near the Kansas

River they shared their camp on a large, crescent shaped sand bar, with four hunters heading upriver in a canoe.

The four men, experienced hunters, were considering taking the Major up on his suggestion they join the expedition. While giving the matter due consideration, they watched A.P. Chouteau wasting valuable travelling time drilling the militia on the smooth, hard sand. Shaking their heads, they pulled out ahead of the flotilla, after the Major had ascertained that they did know where they were going, had been there before, and they certainly would bring their furs to him when he got that fort built at Three Forks.

The flotilla passed the Kansas and the Little Platte, in turn. The river was generally narrow, with lots of deer and turkey to be seen and taken, even by the most inexperienced. The roasting spits were turning every evening and the men ate their fill with only an occasional American noting that he'd have preferred a buffalo steak.

There was an undercurrent among the American hunters, particularly noticeable on the James boat, Lewis confided to the partners. He had a feeling they were just biding their time until reaching Crook's camp.

Dr. Thomas was furious with Cheek by then, Lewis resigned and James defensive.

"When we stopped for breakfast and the men scattered to gather wood, that damned Cheek tolled that big, witless Irishman out of sight and sound and beat the hell out of him. For 'sassin' Captain James, of all things!" Dr. Thomas told the partners indignantly. "That puffed-up James took it as a tribute, the stupid man. Now he's a hand short. That Irishman won't be able to do a lick of work for a week."

To no one's surprise, before the week was up, James was grumbling to Lewis about being short-handed because of malingering Irish help. Unobtrusively, the Major guided the Irishman, whose eyes were nearly swollen shut, limping, to Francis's boat. There, in a happier and bigot-free atmosphere, he added his pleasant Irish tenor to the French songs of the boatman, and worked with a will, albeit, as Francis said wryly, "Never eptly."

Just as they came abreast the remains of an abandoned village of the Kansas Indians, they ran into thunder and lightning from the skies and the management. Colonel Chouteau, in a towering fury, with lightning flashing behind him, dismissed two of the militia caught stealing whiskey. They were set ashore, without any whiskey, and all their company equipment, which included their rifles, confiscated.

At a nod from the Major, the reliable John Dougherty, a veteran at making his way alone through the wilderness, escorted them out of the Colonel's sight. As the thunder and lightning receded and the sun came out once more, he took a stick and drew a rough map in the dirt. If they moved right along, taking these overland shortcuts, they just might overtake the men rafting the buffalo robes downstream and hitch a ride with them.

As they voyaged toward the end of July and closer to the junction with the Platte, they found Crooks and McClellan. As agreed, they were still on their assigned side of the river, camping a little above the mouth of the Oto, and trading with the Otos living there.

When the flotilla tied up, the partners, with seeming casualness made some purposeful moves. There was no hint of any other feeling than that of relaxation and good fellowship to greet Crooks when he came to Lisa's boat accompanied by several of his men. The Major dickered with him over some supplies Crooks was seeking while Menard and Morrison, keeping at Lisa's elbow, drew him off to take a look at some of the buffalo hides the Otos had brought in from their summer hunt.

Bryan, waiting for Dr. Thomas, who wanted him to accompany him upon a call on the legendary McClellan, stood off to one side, as the Major directed the unloading of the supplies for Crooks. He watched, a little enviously, as Len Cather with his other young friends, came by for a word with the Major, before quartering the camp, and the Major, touching John lightly on the shoulder, told him to watch out for traps.

Some of the Americans, with James in the lead, came purposefully toward Crooks, who looked a trifle uncomfortable standing there with the supplies he'd just obtained, which included two kegs of whiskey. The Major suggest that James and his men give Crook's men a hand in getting the supplies and the whiskey to his camp, as long as they were headed that way. Bryan heard him tell John Dougherty, too, quietly, to watch out for traps.

"Och, man, they'll be disappointed," Crooks flashed his infectious grin at the Major. "You got second sight?"

"Nope. Had a gypsy tell my fortune once, though. Was on the road to Fort Pitt and there was this rickety old wagon and poor ol' nag mired in a mud hole. Got my fortune told for pullin' them out. I was very young. Had never seen a gypsy before. Wasn't much impressed," said the Major idly. He hadn't been impressed by her words, either, telling him he had wisdom and that's all he'd ever have. Or need. Something in Crook's expression made him ask, "What did your gypsy tell you?"

"That I'd never see Scotland again," said Crooks uncomfortably. "How'd you know about my gypsy?"

"Heard they always recognize a man of destiny," said the Major, drawing the conversation out, keeping Crooks lingering while James and his men moved off. He felt impelled to add, "You are destined to make trails. And have trials. And be a leader of men."

Crooks took a deep breath, his gaze a trifle awed, then with a shrug, said dismissively, "The same drivel they tell all impressionable young men, aye?"

Dr. Thomas arrived just then, carrying a jug of whiskey. Bryan went off with him, forgetting about gypsies as he pondered the wisdom of asking about the whiskey. Just in time, he remembered his father reiteration to keep his eyes open, his mouth shut, and he might learn something.

The first thing he noticed was how pleased Mr. McClellan was to get the whiskey. As time wore on, he decided the intense little man had to be pulling Dr. Thomas's leg with his long-winded yarns. Gradually it dawned on him that Dr. Thomas was making the visit last as long as possible. There must be some reason, such as keeping McClellan at a distance from Senor Lisa.

Bryan became more helpful, a trifle more naive, leaning forward intensely at the right moments as Mr. McClellan acted out some of his adventures. One part of his mind was able to go back to thinking about the whiskey.

The traders licensed by the government to trade with the Indians were limited by the intercourse laws in the matter of alcoholic spirits. Bryan hadn't really thought about it before. Now he realized the expedition was allowed a whiskey ration for the workmen, the personal use of the partners and to meet the needs in running the fort they were to establish. He was used to the fact that a whiskey ration was included in any workman's hire, three pint cups of whiskey each day.

While it was accepted that hands and laborers were to be furnished a given amount, the government tried to discourage giving liquor to the Indians. Everyone knew it was custom to give an Indian one cup of watered whiskey at the conclusion of a trade. He expected it and would not have traded without it.

He decided he had a glimmering of what the Major was doing.

He leaned forward, prompting McClellan as he paused at the climax of one of his tales. McClellan and Crooks really need those supplies Joseph Miller is supposed to be bringing.

The Major has made sure all the men who have been toying with the idea of leaving the expedition and joining up with Crooks know that they are running out of whiskey. Nor do they have any traps.

Dr. Thomas left the depleted jug with McClellan who stood up when they were making their farewells and looked out over the camp. He could see James and his men concluding some kind of conference with Lisa, Menard and Morrison before making their way back to their boat.

"Lisa has been his ol' persuasive self, I see," said McClellan smiling grimly. "He fools a lot of people. Not me. Not ever again."

Bryan realized that he and Dr. Thomas hadn't fooled him either. Flashing his own bright smile, showing his admiration as he met and held McClellan shrewd gaze, he was able to tell the older man, and mean it, that he had learned a lot this day. His father would be pleased to know he had made the acquaintance of a man of Mr. McClellan's caliber.

"Likewise," said Mr. McClellan. "Guy Bryan has a worthy son."

Bryan was gratified to find that Len and his friends, in turn, had been envious of his activities that day. He was pleased he was able to remember all Mr. McClellan's tall tales and pass them on straight-faced and impress his friends.

That was later. The urgency of the moment was to find out what had happened during his absence. For a while, as the flotilla took advantage of the remaining daylight to row several miles up river before making camp, it seemed as if nothing had happened. Not until he overhead Francis joshing with the Major.

"Well, mon ami, you did it again," said Francis, clapping the Major on the shoulder as he joined the partners around the camp fire after the evening meal. "Your Americans are quite jolly over their liquor ration tonight. For a wonder, we don't have any mosquitoes to speak of tonight, either. Did you arrange that, too?"

"You don't 'arrange' anything with Americans. You have to let them see for themselves," said the Major easily. "And make their own decisions."

"Your young recruits were helpful," said Labaddie. "Of course, they'd never seen a summer camp before. Probably didn't realize it wasn't necessary to have better quarters, that lean-tos and leafy bowers are sufficient in the summer."

"They did report that the men were disgruntled with Crooks and McClellan over running out of tobacco," said Francis cheerfully. "Young Cather told James that Crooks' men were having a lean time of it, having to live off the hunting, and didn't have much to do."

"Dougherty clinched it," said Reuben, "when he told James how few of McClellan and Crook's men had any traps."

"James did all right, too," said the Major. The others nodded, acknowledging the dignity with which James had conducted the conference with the partners, allowing the men to save face by listening to Lisa reiterate the terms of the contract and get a trifle lyrical about the haul they could expect to make in the mountains.

Even Cheek had made his contributions. "Better the Devil you know," he had grinned, looking right at Lisa and getting a chuckle from his cronies.

"We know our men pretty well by now. I'd say we have some good ones with us," said the Major. "Including our newest recruits. Ayres, Marie and St. John."

A.P. exchanged a glance with Syl that was intercepted by Menard.

Alexis Doza had passed on the word that the American Ayres and a couple of his French-Canadians would not need much persuasion to leave Crooks and McClellan. A.P. and Syl had acted promptly. "Doza is one of our best hunters," said Menard. Self-satisfied chuckles swept the group.

"On this next stretch of the river, the men will start thinking about the Platte ritual," said Rueben with his quality of tough-minded tranquility which sometimes seemed stolid but more often served as deliberate balm. "They look forward to that. And the brandy Lisa serves."

"It puts the men in good humor, planning and carrying out the initiation," agreed Francis. "You should have seen me. Even the Indians had to laugh at my new coiffure. It's one way they can spot the newcomers on the river."

"Who originated the custom?" the Major asked.

"I think it's something Lisa brought to the Missouri from his days at sea," said Menard. "Similar to the Neptune ritual for those crossing the equator for the first time."

"Rites of passage into an exclusive fraternity," said Dr. Thomas. "It would serve to establish a certain esprit de corp."

Chapter 8

As they began their approach to the mouth of the Platte, the days became almost idyllic, with a steady strong wind that wafted them upstream, almost effortlessly. The nightly encampments were pleasant, free of mosquitoes and gnats, in green and verdant settings of beauty, with relaxed camaraderie about the evening fire, everyone well-fed on the variety of game the hunters were able to bag easily. Conversation quickened and sparkled.

At the mouth of the Platte after the Major, Bryan and all the other uninitiated either paid a forfeit or submitted, sometimes after some good-natured rough-housing to an inept barbering ceremony, the Major, running his hand over his head, said, "Mohawk is in fashion this year, I feel. It is rather becoming to Bryan and Cheek. I'm not sure you have propitiated either the river deities or Cheek. All you left him was his ears." He made a coarse joke which sent his barbers into thigh-slapping laughter.

Turning to Lisa, the Major asked for more details about how the initiation ceremony had been transplanted and adapted from an oceanic to a landlocked equator.

Lisa, who had been passing out tin cups of liquor to all hands, filled one for the Major from the bottle of Napoleon brandy he was carrying and pondered a moment.

"Truly, I cannot say when it began. With Clamorgan, maybe," said Lisa. "Or that Mandan-loving man from Wales, Evans. It was an old custom when I came. I did not start it," he insisted. "I do not know who did. I think it has been going on since white men began going up and down the river. So it could have begun long, long ago."

He was probably right, the Major thought. White men had been going up the river much longer than most men realized. Francis had told him about a French aristocrat and his sons who had been in the area where they were going long before any of the men here had been born. They had claimed the territory for France.

It was very likely there even had been men venturing across the continent before Lewis and Clark made their famous trip. It was not something that had been bruited about but knowledge guarded carefully, used to advantage by French families in St. Louis.

While their arrival at the mouth of the Platte was marked with ceremony, its arrival and entrance into the Missouri was scarcely perceptible, the color of its water indistinguishable from that of the Missouri, with numerous sandbars and islands and more than one channel. The change that was perceptible, the great, open plains, the ground gently rising and spreading out forever, without any close woods to be seen, reinforced the feeling that the expedition had indeed crossed a demarcation line, an equator that divided the lower from the upper Missouri.

As if to prove they had crossed a demarcation line, the wind now was always against them. They were beset with rain, hail, sudden awesome thunderstorms full of riveting lightning, with the cantankerous river throwing up sandbars for them to zigzag around, sawyers to fend off, and dams of driftwood to curse, breathing hard.

August proved an acrimonious month. Men worked grimly, eyes bloodshot, lips chapped and skin opened raw from the weather. The French boatmen complained of pleurisy, mild fevers and the toothache; the Americans, in a baleful humor, about everything else, including the French boatmen. They were scornful of the submissiveness displayed by the boatmen in the unrelenting toil on short rations.

Ride, in charge of the provision boat, cautioned Reuben Lewis about James's prodigality with the allotted provisions for his crew. He warned that their current rate of consumption necessitated some modified rationing. Otherwise Lewis could expect them to exhaust their share of provisions long before the trip was completed.

Early in August, as the barge captained by Thomas James pulled in behind the others for the noon stop, Reuben Lewis, wincing, almost automatically, heard once again from the querulous James about his crew seething over their lean fare.

Uncompromising, uncomplicated, personally likable, and sorely, repeatedly tried, Lewis was short and negative with him over the tentative proposal to broach one of the thirty barrel of pork carried aboard.

"Brown and Dougherty have been after you all week to be allowed to go out and get some meat. Let them go hunting this afternoon and you leave that pork alone. It belongs to the Company. The agreement with the Company doesn't include providing you and your crew with any of that pork," Lewis told James firmly.

Glad to escape from the unspoken rancour aboard, Lewis moved off, leaving James irresolute behind him. The welcome respite of a noon meal shared with the other partners aboard Lisa's barge, and the relaxation of their ongoing poker game, would, he felt, this day, serve the Company better than tossing James and his petulant, dwindling rebuttal into the river.

Sometime later and several barges away, Francis Valle and

Alexis Doza, holding up the departure of their barges as they waited for Lisa's boat to take the usual lead, became aware of some stridency emanating from the James' barge. At a quiet word from Francis, their steersman, Baptiste, joined them to move quietly along the riverbank to investigate. They halted, warily, on the edge of a palpable, altered atmosphere of impending violence.

Center stage, in the small clearing where the men had begun preparations for their noon meal, the unexpected tableau held James, obdurate jaw outthrust, arms folded and legs braced apart, glaring. A shouting Lisa, carrying a matched pair of pistols, was advancing upon him.

Behind James, lined up on the deck of the barge, the American riflemen stood with their guns at the ready, while Cheek trundled a barrel of pork forward. Waving an axe truculently over the barrel, he bellowed at James, "Give me the word, Captain. Give me the word!"

The other partners, experienced men, were spreading out to back up Lisa. Menard was moving to his right, the Chouteaus to his left, Labbadie and the others bringing up to the rear, when a voice cut through the confusion.

Although Francis could not make out all that was said, it was a voice he recognized, but with a deliberate power in it he had heard only rarely. Clear and cold and savage, it was a voice that controlled men, commanded their immediate attention, and reduced the shouting to a rumble.

Watching, still too far away to make out all that was being said, Francis saw the Major striding forward, taking his place between James and Lisa, with deliberate calculation. In that vulnerable moment, he took an action so irrelevant that all of those watching, braced for aggressive action, found themselves unexpectedly diverted, turned in a new direction, one at odds with the preliminary scenario.

The Major, lifting his right hand up high, smoothly fanned out the cards he held in a flamboyant one-handed gesture designed to rivet all eyes. He shook them first under James' nose, then under Lisa's. His words, in a strong, steady voice, cut the air of tension around him into fluttering ribbons of puzzled curiosity.

The Major had pitched his voice just so. They had not only listened to him but he made them believe what he said was important, Francis realized. What had the Major said? Unobtrusively he moved closer.

Lisa, with an exclamation of disbelief, holstered his pistols. He took the cards and riffled through them, while James stood gaping.

"By God, he does have a royal flush. In diamonds. Look there!" Lisa thrust the cards at James.

Disconcerted, James took a step backwards, waving the

proferred cards away. Cheek, flummoxed and thrown off-balance by the sudden change in the script, from drama to farce, lowered his axe. The riflemen, leaning forward attentively, also lowered their rifles. Lisa returned the cards to the Major, clapping him on the shoulder and laughing uproariously.

"You heard the Major," Lisa, still chuckling, told James dismissively. "If your men want to be 'mangeurs de lard,' he says go ahead. But, by damn, just don't ever interrupt his poker game, not ever again!"

Francis saw James, frowning, gathering his resources, attempting belatedly to regain command of the situation, direct Cheek to open the barrel of pork. The partners were gathering about the Major, passing the cards from hand to hand as they all headed back to the lead barge.

"My, my, but the Major was a tad testy," remarked Cather to Brown, one of the hunters on the James boat, who replied, "I knew a man once who won three farms with just a plain ol' flush."

"I ain't even held a plain ol' flush, ever," said Miller, one of the riflemen at Brown's elbow, plaintively. "Imagine, holding a royal flush. Jeez-uz, he could've taken' them booshway for a cleanin'. No wonder he gave us hell!"

Brown, spitting a stream of tobacco juice and 'mangeurs de lard' in the direction of Cheek and James, said, "That Major. He's somethin'."

To James, seeing Cheek produce the first of the pork with a smirk of triumph, it didn't really feel like a moment of triumph, particularly when Brown said flatly, "I'm goin' huntin'. I ain't no pork eater. I'll see you-all up river, later on."

To Francis, as they made a slight detour so as not to intersect with Brown's course, Alexis Doza echoed the American hunter's assessment of the Major at greater length, "Mon Dieu, he even had me believing it was a great crime, breaking up that poker game!"

The two Frenchmen were overcome with mirth. Still laughing, Alexis made an admiring prediction. "The Americans will laugh, too. They'll make one of their funny tales out of it, the kind they like, that makes them the butt of the joke. Lisa, now, he never does much for their tempers. He understands us French. But the Major understands the Americans."

On Lisa's barge, Reuben Lewis was, in his turn, admiring the way the Major played out the remainder of the scene.

"You can bet I'm entitled to the pot," the Major told Lisa, who still chuckling, was shoving the markers across the table to him. "Goddamn it, man, that hand could've won a helluva lot more. If it hadn't been for that damned Cheek I would have had all of you pledging your shares until I'da owned half the Company!"

Reuben Lewis, watching the long fingers of a musician's hand dexterously gather up the markers, reserved his greatest admiration for the quick mind that had guided those fingers. A formidable poker play himself, Lewis remembered calculating the value of his pair of kings, one of them the king of diamonds, just before they were all caught up in Lisa's tempestuous rush from the cabin into the pork barrel battle. In his mind's eye he could see the cards, suddenly tossed down, scattered over the table, while the owner of that quick mind and long, nimble fingers paused long enough over the card table for the deft selection of the cards he needed. Sweeping them up, he had swooped down on the seething clearing to effect a brilliant, improvised, and, increasingly droll, resolution of a charged situation.

Pierre Chouteau, tapping his fingers irritably on the table, cleared his throat. "We should never have put that pork on your boat, Lewis. We should have put the pork on Labbadie's and the lead on yours."

The Major caught Reuben's gaze, held it. "Remember, you were telling me that James was fussing because the boat needed a good cleaning. Well?"

So, even as Pierre Chouteau continued to grumble, his merchant mind preoccupied with his profit-and loss, "I would not have allowed that Cheek even one barrel of pork," Lewis, Labbadie and Lisa put their heads together, and came up smiling.

A couple days further up river, the barges were ordered tied up for an afternoon so that some necessary repairs could be made. Since this required the shifting of some supplies, James put his men to washing down their barge, and other steersmen followed suit on their vessels.

The French-Canadians, who had cheerfully unloaded the boats, just as cheerfully re-loaded them, in darkness lit only by campfires. It was several days before James pointed out to Lewis the stupid mistake of the 'mangeurs de lard' who couldn't tell a barrel of lead from a barrel of pork: they had not got the original cargo back on the original boats.

Lisa, in his urgency for a swift, safe passage, pushed them on toward their goal. His efficiency and judgment of what his French boatmen could or could not bear was seldom at fault. His instructions and the manner of their delivery to the Americans often were. Following some plain-speaking by the Major and Pierre Menard, the orders and the rations dealt out to the hard-working American became slightly more palatable.

Bright, sun-browned and charged with bountiful vigor, the Major moved from boat to boat, going out with one hunter and then another after the many kinds of game, storing up information on the daily changes in flora, fauna, soil and geological formations; and on the men, brash and outspoken; the meditative; the wary; the dogged.

Lisa pointed out Council Bluffs and the fact they still had another thousand miles to go. The high, clean meadows on the left side of the river had been selected by Lewis and Clark for a council with the Oto and Missouri Indians when they were outward bound on their journey to the Pacific, thus the name.

The Major found the meeting location a restful sight, the ground rising gently, with a grassy cover and slender trees or shrubs in the hollows. The river, however, was not restful. It turned crooked and narrow, treacherous with driftwood and sawyers. They camped at the beginning of a great bend of the river, twelve miles around, but the Major was able to pace the distance across the bend in three hundred of his long strides.

A few days later, as the Missouri took them back and forth before the Blackbird hills for nearly thirty river miles, Colonel Chouteau told him, with a certain grudging admiration, of the Omaha chieftain buried there by his own edict, in barbaric splendor, on horseback, on the pinnacle.

A redskin Borgia, the Colonel termed Blackbird, sardonically. Shrewdly selective in his dispensing of arsenic, a helpful secret he had from some trader, Blackbird found it even better than cajolery in dealing with any incipient opposition. An achiever, by deed and daring he extended and maintained his tyrannical control over his Omahas and became a power to reckon with over a wide area with many of the adjacent tribes deferring to him.

Born with an innate aptitude for sizing up people, red and white alike, he was adroitly arbitrary with the traders, deftly despotic with the tribes, and complacently ruthless about getting his own way.

When it came to playing one white trader against another, he proved as artful as a Machiavellian prince. Among other nefarious activities, he held up the Spanish sponsored Mackay-Evans expedition in 1795, and maneuvered Mackay into building a crude, short-lived post, called Fort Charles, for Blackbird's trading convenience.

Colonel Chouteau, drawing on his memories of that period under Spain, reminisced about James Mackay. The venturesome Scot, one-time British trader, and, eventually, by naturalization, a Spaniard, Mackay led one of the most ambitious thrusts upriver when Spain, in a spasm of brief, feverish optimism, was striving to forestall the encroachments of the British.

With Mackay was the fantasizing Welshman, John Thomas Evans, of the Cardogian Society. A trifle eccentric, but so dedicated in his quest of the legendary, lost colony of Wales postulated by the Society, he had turned fur trader in order to seek out descendants. He had been drawn to the Upper Missouri by reports of the light-skinned Mandans who paddled about in round skin boats said to be strikingly similar to the Welsh cuirrachs.

Blackbird did, eventually, let Evans and a small party take off on foot, getting as far as the Sioux before being turned back. On a second try, in canoes, Evans made it to the Mandans. He came to the disillusioning conclusion that the Mandans, even allowing for a considerable passage of time and intermarriage with native tribes, were no relation to his wandering Welshmen. He also reported, indignantly, that the British already had a man there ahead of them, Rene Jessaume, at that time employed by the Northwest Fur Company, and that no-good Jessaume had tried to kill him.

For John Mackay, Blackbird proved excessively expensive. Looking down his nose, he took all the gifts proffered, and a great many items that weren't, including the nubile maiden bearing a peace pipe from some beleaguered Poncas. He also made some supercilious observations on the superiority of British goods and British generosity over that of the Spanish.

"Sounds like a ruddy terror," said the Major with a grin. "How did Manuel handle such a troll?"

"Smallpox got to Blackbird before Lisa did," said Chouteau almost regretfully. "The survivors didn't stay around. From time-to-time, offerings, mostly food, are left at Blackbird's grave. Mostly to placate the old devil, I suspect."

"Tell me," said the Major reflectively, "How many white men, to your knowledge, made it to the Mandan villages before Lewis and Clark?"

"The Verendryes, maybe. They certainly made their way over a lot of the area when they came down from Canada in 1742. Clamorgan. Truteau."

The Colonel found he was enjoying himself. Rarely had he known an American who could look at the tapestry of the fur trade and see beyond the surface picture and overlaying embroidery of time and distance to the warp and woof, the subtle threads that linked it all together. He told the Major what he knew, and sometimes, what he had extrapolated, speaking now in French, and pleased to find the younger man following him easily, even catching the play on words, and making his responses, if not fluently, at least with a much-improved accent.

Neither France nor the Verendryes realized any profit from their explorations and the British conquerors never got to see their reports or maps. Certainly Spain did not, when France handed them territory by treaty that the British hadn't taken over.

There had been a period there, under Spain, almost as exciting for the traders of St. Louis as the present era. Jacques D'Eglise, visited the Mandans in 1792, brought back disturbing news. The Northwest Company had managed to get representatives overland from the Assiniboine River in Canada to trade on the Upper Missouri.

Spain and Britain were already seriously at odds over the rewarding sea otter trade off Vancouver Island on the Pacific coast. Always a trifle paranoid about the British, the Spanish government, vague about the real geography, saw Hudson Bay as dangerously close to the tempting silver mines of northern Mexico, and fretted accordingly.

In 1794, the Spanish government chartered the Commercial Company for the Discovery of the Nations of the Upper Missouri. It was to forestall the British from Canada, to find if possible a way to the Pacific, and to repay its membership for these efforts by collecting, under franchise, whatever furs the Indians offered. One lackluster expedition after another went out and came trailing back, glumly.

Traders from St. Louis did get to the Mandan villages. Jean Baptiste Truteau; D'Eglise; James Mackay; Jacques Clamorgan. Pierre-Antoine Tabeau, who concluded the Indians there would never take to trapping. John Thomas Evans, preoccupied with the fate of Prince Madoc, legendary son of the actual Welsh King Gwain Gyneed, who sailed off toward America in 1170 with three hundred colonists in ten ships, didn't really care whether it was white men or Indians who trapped the furs as long as the British didn't profit from it.

"Truteau's, Mackay's and Evan's journals and their maps filled in a lot of gaps for Thomas Jefferson," said the Major "Their efforts were helpful, after all."

"To the Americans, oui," said the Colonel, resisting the impulse to mention some journals and maps that had not made their way into Jefferson's hands. After all, in this business, a man didn't tell all he knew. This likable young man might not always be a partner of the Chouteaus and would then be no more, no less, rapacious, than other competitors.

"There are whites and half-whites wandering around up there now," said the Major, marshaling his speculations. "They will be able to fill in some of the gaps on our maps."

"Some of them are men Lisa has sent out," said Chouteau with selective candor. Some, as he was well aware, no one else knew about. They would bring their trade, and any of the Indians who had befriended them, to the Major's fort at Three Forks. When that happened, there would be profits for the Chouteaus. Until it did, a wise head in this business must take care not to be seduced into indiscreet garrulousness by formidably intelligent young men. "I think there will be rejoicing from the Shining Mountains to

Washington when it is known you have built your American fort. And interesting reverberations in other national capitals when they realize the Americans are there to stay."

The next day, August 11, there was rejoicing among the people of the Omaha village as the expedition arrived. Dr. Thomas, who was keeping a journal, wrote:

"It is situate on a prairie on the south side, 4 miles from the river, resembling at a distance, the stack yard of an extensive farmer, having their huts in the form of a cone, about 15 feet high. Their council house is built in the centre, large enough to contain 300 men; the materials consists of split sticks and pieces of tim(b)er; covered with earth.

"Here we were served the first dish of dog meat, it is esteemed delicate, and none partake of it but those they wish to honour.

"These people are very filthy in their dress and food: the former consi(s)ts of skins, and the latter of the flesh of animals of that country, with corn, pumpkin, &c.

"They had a skirmish with the Sioux a few days before we arrived in which they lost several warriors; this nation contains only 4 or 500 men able to bear arms, and are in danger of being exterminated by the Sioux, who boast they are able to muster 15,000 men. . . .

"On our arrival, Shehekeh expressed a wish to visit the village, being invited by the principal chiefs. Having put on an elegant full dress suit of regimentals, with his horse covered with the most showey ornaments, he set out accompanied by thirty Mahaz chiefs on horse back, in their best dress.

"The whole nation were lost in astonishment at the (s)plended figure of the Mandan, so much superior to any thing their chiefs could display. Before dinner a council was held with Mr. Chouteau for the purpose of requesting a trader to reside among them, and to beg presents, in which the Mandan preserved the dignity of the superior; indeed Shehekeh's manner would grace any circle; he took great pains to copy the manner of the first characters of the United States whom he was acquainted with.

"On the 13th we left the village and a few miles up we met with 3 Soux, who informed us that a party of their nation were waiting for us about 80 miles up the river. Twelve miles further we passed Floyd's river, called after one of the followers of Lewis and Clark, who is buried on an eminence in its neighborhood; the Indians had mounted a flag over his grave." They had also placed the body of a chief's son beside that of Sergeant Charles Floyd.

The Major noted how James and his Americans viewed respectfully the last resting place of the only casualty of the Lewis and Clark expedition.

"Bilious colic," said Dr. Thomas dispassionately, a term

which covered all sorts of gastro-intestinal upsets, including the probable cause of Floyd's death, a ruptured appendix. "Nothing heroic about it. Yet, as you can see, the Americans are already viewing the last resting place of the young sergeant as something of a shrine. Serves as a tribute to your brother and the General, losing only one man."

"Nat Pryor figured they didn't lose any of their expedition," said Reuben stoutly. "He felt the real trip started and ended at the Mandan villages. Charles Floyd was his cousin so Nat wasn't belittling him in any way."

Len, who had edged closer to them at the rail, hoping to hear more about the brave young man buried on the bluff, did hear, to his surprise, that not all the men of the expedition had gone on to the Pacific. By the time Lewis and Clark had reached the Mandan villages, they had accumulated so much information and so many specimens of flora and fauna, they spent part of the winter sorting it all out. When spring came, just before they headed west, they dispatched Corporal Warfington and a small party with Joseph Gravelin as interpreter and river pilot to return east with the crates, bags, notes and reports destined for Jefferson back in Washington.

"Floyd was only one of a number of men who participated in the preliminary part of the expedition," concluded Reuben, adding, "Did you know Nat's descended from Pocahantos on his mother's side?"

"What's that got to do with it?" wondered Len, but to himself. He hadn't had Bryan's experience in making the mental leaps necessary to keep up with these men.

"Acceptable," said the Doctor reflectively. "And respectable."

"Rolfe got away with it because he was an aristocrat," said the Major.

"No need to concern himself with middle class mores?" said the Doctor.

"She died young. An exotic, legendary and romantic heroine," replied the Major.

"I thought Pocahantas was an Indian princess," blurted Len. He flushed when the men turned to look at him. "Well, wasn't she?"

"Offhand, I can't think of any other," said the Major agreeably, lifting a quizzical eyebrow at Len. "Too bad, isn't it?

Len gave it some significant consideration. "An Indian princess might just be tol'able," he said finally after running an imaginary scenario through his mind's eyes, with special attention to the fact that he had no doubts how the womenfolks he knew felt about acknowledging such a mesalliance. "Maybe."

"The French have a more civilized approach," said Dr. Thomas tolerantly. "In a sort of grand seignorial way, they fold the children into the embrace of their faith through baptism and inculcate them into their culture, acknowledged members of their extended family."

"A home and a French wife in St. Louis. An Indian wife or two and a home-away-from-home," said the Major lightly. "Firms up all sorts of tribal ties. And, at an early age, weaves kinship ties to strengthen the dynasty."

Unfortunately, such kinship ties had not been established to smooth their way with the Sioux, although the Colonel had established some favorable ties with some of the leading men who had enjoyed his hospitality on visits to the United States.

They made their approach to the Yankton encampment with due care and dropped anchor with some trepidation, as fifty warriors spread out along the shore and discharged their guns in a salute, aiming their pieces so the balls fell into the water just slightly ahead of the bows. For two days they threaded a wary path through the intricacies of Yankton Sioux officialdom.

The Major, following a stint with young August P. Chouteau and the militia, was with the latter on the Chouteau boat when the first encounter was made, downstream from the encampment.

"One has earned his chevrons, the other his bars," said A. P. of the two Sioux, covered with a mixture of charcoal dust and grease and little else on this August day. They were shunted to the James boat and the experienced diplomacy of Reuben Lewis, while the third Sioux departed as a messenger to alert the summer encampment near the James River.

"If they knew their own strength, nothing could stand in their way," A.P. said. The Major supposed he was thinking of the difficulties the Sioux had made for him and Pryor two years earlier.

Auguste Pierre, taller than most Frenchmen, slender, with dark flashing eyes, at twenty-five was an ornament to any society, with the manners of a prince, the palate of a gourmet, and the morals of a grand siegneur. He was comfortable in military circles, among traders and knowledgeable about the Indian tribes.

Ambition was there, the Major could see, the ambition that had made A.P.'s house great, turning out men that were the amalgam of the military, the diplomat and the businessman. There was also an ironic sense of humor that had been delighted with the Major's inspired poker bluff and moved the young man, who had shared bachelor quarters with Meriwether Lewis, to further his acquaintance with this American, too.

"They are to be cultivated as the hawk is to be cultivated," A.P. went on. "They don't make dependable hunting hawks, much to the despair of their British friends. They are pro-British but can't be turned into British puppets. They have no development or feeling for majority rule."

"Democratic chaos?" suggested the Major.

"Absolute," nodded A.P. The Major, prepossessing and rude, a masterful combination, had surprised him with his knowledge and grasp of affairs. "The ones who want to do something, do so. Those who don't, they stay put or pack up and leave, to wander on their own, or join up with another group pursuing a course more appealing to them."

The vanguard of their Sioux escort could be seen and heard, firing their guns into the air, and, frequently, into the water, just ahead of the lead boat. By the time the selected boats were maneuvering into the landing, with the others, as planned, finding safer anchorage in midstream, or, as in the case of the one bearing Shehaka, a defensible island, the numbers and the noise had the Major murmuring, "Where's the riot squad?"

"There, right on cue," said A.P. gesturing. "The ones with the crow feathers on the head."

When they were rowed ashore from the mid-stream anchorage of the Chouteau boat, the Major could see that a squad of Sioux had indeed taken charge of the James boat. The whistle and noise makers backed off as more law-and-order types moved in to mount guard on each boat that pulled up to the bank. The curious, sternly, were not allowed to board.

"Chevrons. Stripes. Bars," A. P. murmured, indicating the appropriate example with a lift of his chin so that the Major was soon able to recognize the difference between the military, the civil and the law enforcement. "Don't see any equivalent of a marshal's baton. Any of those will be held in dignified reserve to receive Lisa and my father. Along with a sort of mayor and his council."

"And the rest, the sans culotte?" said the Major for the bare, blackened bodies all around them were without breeches and the scene one of disorder and incipient anarchy.

"Unpredictable. Ah, here's my coach and four. No. Six. And yours," said A.P. as a dozen muscular young braves hurried up to them and began unrolling a pair of buffalo hides.

The buffalo robe the Major saw was a work of art, expertly tanned, and painted on it in bright colors, a fast-moving buffalo hunt. He seated himself on the robe, crossing his legs, holding his rifle across his lap. The braves, three on a side, stooped and got firm grips on the edges of the hide with both hands and lifted.

As they started off, following A.P. being transported in similar fashion, the Major looked around. He could see the spread of the tipis, covered with the portable sewn hides decorated with painted symbols similar to those on his palanquin. Without really having to put his mind to it, his inherent mental calculator told him the population of this immediate encampment far outnumbered those of the expedition.

"The labor force," said A.P., pitching his voice to carry over his shoulder as his bearers labored past women coming and going with loads of wood and kettles of water.

The women of polygamous tribes were raised to please men on the marriage cot or off it, the Major thought idly, keeping his face expressionless, using his peripheral vision. Here they doubled as the cheering section; overseers of slaves and the nursery; the bane of captives; tailors; profitable rental units on a short-term basis.

No wonder his bearers were huffing and puffing at a task that four of his Americans could handle effortlessly. They spent all of their time on themselves, taking excellent care of their stocky, short-limbed bodies. They were passing one now, vain as a Regency rake, touching up his black body make-up. While one of his women held up a trade mirror, another was dressing his hair, weaving horse hair into the braids to give it more body and length, while a third was preparing his food, and a very young girl, possibly an Omaha slave, was putting down her armful of wood, unobtrusively.

"The bank account," said A.P., stepping off the palanquin as another carefully groomed brave riding a pony with beribboned mane and tail and leading two other horses eyed in passing the unusual sight of his tribesman bearing a burden. "Transport backup and alternate commissary," kicking aside one of the snarling yellow curs that darted in too close. "Of course, the buffalo is the mainstay. Nothing in this lunatic country matters as much as the hunt."

While their bearers rolled up the buffalo hides and trotted off, they looked back the way they had come. The Major could see other palanquins, including one bearing Thomas James, proud as any nabob, and wondered at him leaving the boat. As James came closer he realized the man was at his ease, his self-esteem salved with this momentary promotion to equality with the partners.

He looked for his recruits and spotted them on the landing talking with Cheek. Lisa, who was continuously taking the pulse of these people, had felt that there was no immediate animosity. The more pragmatic of the Indian leaders had wrestled it into submission. The Major had advised his recruits on procedures and precautions suggested by Lisa.

Putting one of the precautions he carried with him casually across his arms, he let A.P. guide him through the interminable proceedings and introduce him to all the amenities. Blithely, A.P., whose feelings toward these people were not particularly generous or just or wholesome, made it all intelligible, with uncanny, often caustic, parallels from their own world.

There were welcoming ceremonies. The passing of a variety of peace pipes. Food and more food, some of it identifiable because of the puppy foot garnish. A great deal of boastful talk embroidered with sign language. And an increasing amount of abstracted scratching.

On the third day, sated in more ways than one, they were able to leave the Yankton Sioux. Lisa, a master of the art of Indian negotiation, had been florid in describing the eminence, the experience and the trustworthiness of the expedition. With the support of Colonel Chouteau and well-presented appeals, protestations, gifts and careful exercise of forbearance, Lisa had obtained not only safe passage but also qualified agreement to the emplacement of a trading establishment.

Colonel Chouteau, however, was unable to recruit an auxiliary force to cooperate with the detachment against the Arikara. He settled for a peace delegation of six Sioux and got them settled comfortably on one of the barges for the upstream trip.

Eight days later they met with the Teton Sioux and got a sense of deja vu from a repetition of procedures. They left a group of traders on Cedar Island, at Regis Loisel's old post, and hoped they would fare better trading with the Tetons than Loisel had in 1804.

Not until they were well away, safely beyond these tribes that might and had murdered travellers and destroyed the tenuous pathways of trade, did Manuel Lisa allow a brief pause for recuperation and recapitulation.

They had tied up at a safe anchorage on an island in midstream and spent a restful night. There was an air of congratulations and cheerful relief among the partners as they lingered over a leisurely breakfast on the campsite warmed by the September sun.

To Francis Valle, joining them, the encouraging status report went well with the fresh coffee brewed over the campfire. He settled himself comfortably on a driftwood log beside the Major, listening to the partners exchanging their impressions of the recent encounters.

"Yes, I heard that James and some of his men persuaded the Sioux to haul down the British flag," Reuben Lewis was saying to Pierre Menard. "What I'd like to know is how James managed to find a friendly Sioux to take him in and feed him buffalo meat instead of dog."

"Probably had some kind of service in mind for him," said Menard blandly. "He is an impressive figure of a man."

"From the jaunty look of him today," A.P. offered, flashing his teeth in a perceptive smile, "He satisfied more than one appetite while visiting his 'friendly Tetons'."

"They are selective," said Dr. Thomas with a sigh, then grinned good-naturedly in turn at the ripple of laughter. "I'd swear I saw one youngster who was a miniature of York."

"We'll probably see more," laughed Reuben. "That black rascal was very popular with the ladies all along the route of the Lewis and Clark expedition."

"What about Seaman?" asked the Major referring to Meriwether Lewis's black Newfoundland dog named for his love of boating and swimming that had accompanied him.

"That'd be even more noticeable," said Reuben.

"Mon ami, I haven't seen you since the first day when you unobtrusively upset your bowl of canine stew," said Francis who had spent much of his time fending off such gastronomical offerings and council cramps and offending his men by putting a cramp in their fraternizing style which could have left them with their throats cut. "I trust Chouteau fils was selective in introducing you to certain customs of our red brothers."

"Ah, yes, Major, I have been meaning to ask you," drawled A.P. "It would seem something went awry with one of the amenities. Mon dieu, what's that?"

Suddenly, a wriggling brown body was in their midst, trailing a frayed rope, and waggling his tail ecstatically as he tried to get all of his solid twenty pounds into the Major's lap.

"One of Seaman's mementoes, several generations removed," said the Major, taking a moment to welcome the cavorting newcomer before directing him to sit at his feet. "He must have got away from Cather."

"I'm sorry, Major," said Cather, trotting up, the other end of the rope in his hand. "There was no holding him when he heard your voice."

"What a nice change," said Francis, leaning forward for a better look. "A live dog."

Reuben Lewis, coming closer, looked over the well-proportioned, bright-eyed pup. He pointed out that the introduction of the Indian mongrel bloodlines had blurred resemblance to the original Newfoundland. Francis, in another time and place, after he saw his first Chesapeake retriever, would realize he had been right that afternoon, saying idly, "With his luck, the Major is the discoverer of a new kind of dog."

The new kind of dog, half rising every now and then to wag his tail, then looking up at the Major with a beatific expression, leaning closer against his master's long legs, accepted their overtures, as A.P. chuckled.

"I didn't misunderstand after all. Even when she was indignantly showing her bite marks to her father, I assumed something was being lost in the translation. You do have an impertinent black dog that goes around biting black swans."

"He is only a puppy. Dark brown. And she was no black swan," the Major corrected him temperately. "He doesn't bite virgins."

"You don't say!" exclaimed A.P. delightedly, moving closer and settling down cross-legged on the ground at the Major's feet. "Now, tell me how you know this for a fact. It will be even more interesting than how you came by such a unicorn."

"Oh, he traded Cheek for him," said Cather matter-of-factly, then gave a start. "Sorry. I almost forgot what I came for. There's been some kind of a hullabaloo over Cheek. The Colonel stopped me when I was out walking the pup and told me to fetch the Doctor and Mr. Lewis."

"I'd better get my bag," said the Doctor, getting to his feet.

Looking up at Cather with anticipation, Francis patted a spot next to his on the ground. "Sit down and tell us all about the discovery of the new kind of a dog."

"Well, we were all goin' along, mindin' our own business, just like the Major told us to, when we came up on this little boy trying to save his pup from the cooking pot. The ugliest squaw you ever saw was whipping a big iron spoon about, trying to mash in the pup's head. So Cheek handed his rifle to me and just scooped the kid and the pup up, one in each of his big hands, and held them out of her reach, fending her off with his foot, and her screeching like a wildcat. The next thing I knew we were hemmed in by a lot of scolding squaws. A bunch of their menfolk gathered around, glaring at us. I was sure glad to see the Major arrive when he did," said Cather. His voice trailed off as he glanced at the Major. "He can tell you about the rest of it."

The Doctor had returned with his bag. He took Cather firmly by the arm, indicating he was to guide him to the scene of the carnage, and joined by Reuben, they moved off quickly.

"Wait," said Francis belatedly. "Damn," he said, settling back with a look of chagrin, "now the Doctor will get all the firsthand details."

"So you might as well tell us your version, Andy," said Menard, while Morrison, Labbadie, and Bryan made seconding sounds of agreement.

The Major sat forward on the log, putting his elbows on his knees, now and then rubbing an itching spot behind the pup's ear, smiling.

He hadn't been surprised to find Cheek at the center of the commotion. Cheek always was. Even as the Major ordered his companion, one of the interpreters from the council who had invited him to partake of the hospitality of his lodge, to get them a

Solomon to adjudicate the dispute, and quickly, he was noting that the little boy resembled York and the pup put him in mind of Seaman.

With Cather and Jackson guarding their backs, they had been led by the interpreter to the tipi of one of the chieftains, escorted by a growing audience of Teton men, women, children and dogs.

"Remember the fine-looking Teton on your father's right that you said held the equivalent office of Marshal of France?" he asked A.P., who nodded. "Apparently he's the boy's grandfather. He was sitting out in front of a fine tipi when we arrived. He held up his hand, palm outward, solemn as any judge, and everyone quieted down. Cheek put the boy down and set the pup in his arms. The kid ran to Grandpa and clambered into his lap, talking a mile-a-minute.

"Grandpa listened, then he set him and the pup down in front of him and motioned for the squaw to come forward. He talked to her, then he talked to the kid again. From what the interpreter could make out, the pup belonged to the squaw but the kid had been allowed to treat it as his pet.

"You could see Grandpa giving it some thought. He would've liked to let his grandson keep the pup. But the crowd was on the side of the squaw — at least the other squaws were. The men were looking for something to brighten their dull day and anything that embarrassed the white man would please them.

"Grandpa came up with an interesting solution. The kid could not keep the pup. He could pick out a new owner for him. The new owner had to pay the squaw for the pup.

"The little boy, he couldn't have been much over four years old, picked up the pup slowly, patted him once and headed for Cheek. You could hear the crowd hiss indignantly. But he marched right by Cheek and shoved the pup at me, his lower lip quivering just a trifle. So, I had been given a pup I now had to buy.

"The little boy went back to stand with his arms folded by his Grandpa, trying to look as if he didn't care. The squaw stood there stony-faced. Grandpa said something sharp to her and she gave grumpy assent then began to look pleased as it dawned on her greedy soul that she could set the price for the pup beyond our means.

"Cather and Jackson and McBride spread out all the trade goods they had with them. The interpreter kept making suggestions, like my knife, my belt, and so on. Dougherty happened along and added his shirt to all the stuff laid out for her. No sale.

"Then Cheek indicated his new shirt, a bright red one he said some of the squaws had been fingering in an admiring way earlier in the day. The squaw stepped up to Cheek and stroked his chest thoughtfully, then ran her hands over his shoulders and down the sleeves. When he made to remove the shirt, she shook her head.

"Now, you've got to see her, definitely past her prime, five-by-five, with a homely, flat face, wrinkled skin, and a cast in one eye. I was considering having Jackson put in that old musket of his when there was some sort of suggestion put forth from the crowd. All the squaws tittered.

"The Chief, I suspect, has a rude and lewd sense of humor. He said something to her. She repeated it slowly. The interpreter began to grin but before he could translate, she nodded eagerly, and gathered up the blanket and all our offerings in a bundle in one hand.

"You should have seen the look on Cheek's face when she reached out with the other hand and grabbed him by the shirt front and began hauling him off. He struggled to get out of the shirt until she grabbed him lower down and made it plain she wanted," he paused with mock delicacy, "all of him."

When the laughter died away, Francis leaned over and ran his hand down the pup's brown back, lifted one of his feet, noting the webs between the toes of the swimmer, said, "A born swimmer. What do you call him?"

"Priceless," said A.P. with a chuckle.

"The men are already calling him 'Cheeky'," said the Major. "I think I'll go along with that."

"Cheek," said Menard thoughtfully. "Did I understand he was in some kind of trouble again? Too much ribbing from the men?"

"Not at all," said the Major. "To hear him tell it, the others don't know what they missed and, if anything, are a bit envious. He's been strutting around looking as self-satisfied as James. And he still has his red shirt!"

"He does attract trouble like a lodestone," said Francis. "What do you suppose it is this time?"

"Stupid catamite. Damned sodomite," said Dr. Thomas striding huffily into the campsite. Gathering up a pan and pouring some water into it from the kettle heating on the fire, he began washing his blood-stained hands and arms. "Cheek wasn't any where around but he seems to be getting the blame. I told the Colonel not to pay any attention to that pair of trouble makers."

"It wouldn't be that pretty little engage," said A.P., "and his brawny, but not brainy, companion?"

"The one that was sashaying around Cheek down at Fort Osage?" asked the Major. "I thought Cheek showed his disinterest when he back-handed the pretty boy. Of course, the protector was made to look ridiculous when he attacked Cheek with his knife. Cheek twisted it away casually and booted his backside out of sight. So they both may have been nursing a grudge against Cheek."

"The Colonel, my father, he does not like to acknowledge these things," said A.P. with a shrug. "There was some trouble, earlier, until the pretty boy settled on who was to be his protector. But was he satisfied with a strong, faithful protector? No. He must keep his protector off-balance. A flirt here. A flirt there."

"No one will call him a pretty boy ever again. The other bastard slashed his face into ribbons. Got his own hands chopped up considerable while he was at it, a couple fingers and part of one thumb gone entirely," said Dr. Thomas grimly. "When I left they were wailing over each other and taking great satisfaction in making the Colonel believe it was all Cheek's fault."

"I told father some time ago that we should dismiss those two," said A.P. getting to his feet. "But he would not see what was there."

"From what I heard the Colonel telling Reuben, he wants Cheek dismissed," said the Doctor, drying his hands upon a piece of toweling.

"I'd better have a talk with my father," said A.P. heading for the Chouteau boat.

The Major didn't say anything, just got up and started strolling toward the James boat, the puppy at his heels. Francis and Bryan, with an exchange of glances, followed. All the Major said, handing the frayed rope to Bryan as they neared the James boat, was, "Stay here and hang onto the pup. Don't release him until I snap my fingers."

There was an alertness about the men on the James boat, Francis saw as he followed the Major aboard, but it had none of the tension of the confrontation over the pork. He supposed many of the men were still relaxed from the hospitality they had enjoyed among the Tetons.

Even James was restrained and dignified, as he stood talking to Lewis.

"Tain't right to set a man adrift in this wilderness, 1400 miles from home," James was saying sturdily.

"Oh, I don't mind," said Cheek, managing to swagger as he leaned indolently on his rifle. "I know where I can find a good friend. And it ain't 1400 miles from here. She didn't want me to leave."

Lewis gestured toward Cheek's rifle, a reminder that it was company property and would have to be left behind.

"No, sir," said James instantly. "If he must go, he must have the rifle. How else can a man eat or protect himself?"

"Rifle?" said the Major pitching his voice so all could hear him as Francis had heard him do once before. This time, he was just as sharply perceptive, displaying an almost intuitive knowledge of what the men might find diverting. "Cheek's friend wouldn't be interested in polishing his rifle."

Cheek let out a tremendous guffaw and slapped Brown so hard on the back he staggered a couple steps before getting his balance. Others took up the anatomical theme with coarse good humor.

"He's right, you know. James, I mean," Reuben said in an undertone to the Major. "If he'll just come down off his high horse, I'll tell him so."

James, getting a trifle carried away with his own rhetoric, did not realize he was left with an audience of one. Francis, since he could not get past him without shoving, listened politely. So caught up in his tilting, windmilling his arms fiercely, that he did not seem to realize the men were not heeding him, James reiterated at length the cruelty of dismissal and pointed out vehemently that the men were backing him up with their arms. As far as Francis could tell, the men were drowneding him out with their uninhibited laughter. Furthermore, Francis thought he said, somebody else, and again Francis wasn't sure whether he said Lewis or Chouteau, or both, would have to take away that rifle, personal, for he, Captain William James, would not.

"You're right," said Francis.

"Quite right," said Reuben.

"Huh?" said James. "I can't hear you."

"Forget it," said the Major, snapping his fingers. "By now, A.P. has convinced the Colonel to do the same."

His last words were followed by a scrabble of puppy feet and puppy whuffing as Cheeky hurled himself aboard, followed by a grinning Bryan. Cheeky bowled two of the riflemen aside, went between Cheek's legs like a brown streak and flung himself at the Major. Patting him approvingly, the Major told him he was a good dog and he should now sit. The puppy did so in a sprawling fashion, looking about him with his tongue lolling out in a caricature of the grins he saw about him. When he caught sight of Cheek, he perked up his ears and wagged his tail with such vigor he beat a tatoo on the deck. As the laughter was dying away into light chuckles over the last, and weakest, of the ribald comments, the sound of the beating tail drew Cheek's attention.

"Look at that pup, will ya! He remembers me," exclaimed Cheek delightedly. "Hey, all of you. See. Over there. Now, maybe you'll believe me. There's the pup I got for the Major."

The big Tennessean came forward, a pleased grin on his broad face as the pup welcomed him with a little bounce. With a word, the Major released the pup from his sitting command. Cheeky raced around Cheek exuberantly, twice, then flung himself on him, overbalancing Cheek so that he half-sprawled on the deck with the pup swiping away happily at his face with his moist tongue.

Cheek cradled the pup in his arms, glowing with the guileless affection a good dog aroused in the heart of all but the most dubious of Americans, and carried him into the circle of like-minded men. They passed Cheeky from hand-to-hand with proprietary affection, expounding on his likely heritage, and waxing nostalgic about the dogs they had left behind them.

The Major, with an easy manner that indicated any lingering resentment would be a waste of time, turned his attention to the cross-grained captain of the boat. Lightly questioning, commenting, he drew William James smoothly into a discussion about the next stage of their journey, the approach to the Arikara villages. James found himself diverted into describing some of his frontier experiences, and considerably mollified as he was encouraged to expound on how hazards bested could be the basis for preparing to overcome those ahead.

There was a tutelage underway here, unconscious or otherwise, Francis thought, and James was responding in a positive way. For the Major to guide a man to develop his potential without laying down explicit instructions for behavior modification took a great deal of skill. Following the Major's lead, Francis contributed a stroke or two of his own.

Thomas James, it seemed to Francis, took himself too seriously. Still, he was a conscientious man who took pride in living up to certain taut standards he had set for himself. And a man of pride, once he developed a sense of proportion, and set greater value on solutions instead of confrontations, would be an asset not a liability.

Unfortunately, he would always be impervious to the humor of a disconcerting situation, but he would bring a certain stolid common sense with him, assisting where he could, when he could.

The Major's purpose was to strengthen, not to weaken, a dependable man. Thomas James could be one of the dependable sort the Major seemed to be grooming for the undertaking at Three Forks.

As they left, a relaxed Cheeky tucked under the Major's arm, Thomas James was proposing to Reuben the steps that should be taken to augment the provisions that were again running low. The next few days could be best for a couple of hunters to go out, Lewis agreed, now the expedition was safely away from the Sioux, and still had some ways to go before entering Arikara territory.

Cheeky's rescuer was acting out, entertainingly, the rescue itself. Showing an unexpected talent for mimicry, Cheek was playing, first, the part of the skirmishing little boy, snatching the pup from beneath the descending bludgeon wielded by the unprepossessing squaw; then, the belligerent pup, yipping, yapping, dodging and biting; and then, with a roar and a pounce, himself, as he unexpectedly scooped up two surprised riflemen and hoisted them shoulder high, while fending off the imaginary, wrathful squaw with one foot.

Francis, walking along the bank, between Bryan and the Major, reached over and gave Cheeky an affectionate pat on the head. "I take it all back. Cheek is not entirely an albatross."

Chapter 9

"Until you have smoked out this den of vipers, you can do no good anywhere."

Bryan looked over at Colonel Chouteau. On this bright September morning with the rising sun dissipating the mists from the river, the Colonel was sharing the command post on Lisa's keelboat as it coasted under sail at the head of the flotilla on a cautious approach to the Arikara villages.

In his princely manner, the Jean Pierre Chouteau was voicing his frustration with the Arikara. In private conversation and semi-official correspondence, the Colonel had emphasized the universal mercantile viewpoint: the need to neutralize anyone or anything that interfered with the successful pursuit of trade. Usually in the language favored by diplomats, French.

His son, the West Pointer, commanding the guard on the boat that concealed Shehaka and the six-man Sioux peace delegation, was skeptical, in military language. Not about the need, nor the satisfaction, after last year's mauling, of military chastisement. About the chances of succeeding.

Lisa, gesturing now toward the bank where the Major and Menard were disembarking an advance guard of the militia, wanted the Arikara trade. The trader's trader, he would try to find a way to milk them of their venom, then sell the venom. In the trader's lexicon, the man who provides a service that benefits all, even those at a temporary disadvantage, is a good businessman.

There was silence on the keelboat. Bryan could see some rises in the distance. The Arikara had watchers there, at all times, it was said. On the look out for buffalo. Or enemies.

"The remains of seventeen different tribes." He had spoken aloud, softly, for Sam patted his shoulder, reassuringly.

"They're nothing to write home about. So don't. Your mother would be appalled," his cousin said seriously. "You'll see. They have no secret vices. They do everything out in the open. Publicly."

Just out of sight, self-engrossed, neither afraid nor foolish, the Arikara would be awakening.

Lisa spoke, quietly. The steersman nodded. The boatmen manned the oars. Over Bryan and Cheeky, the sail fluttered slightly as it was lowered. Cheeky, left in Bryan's charge, leaned against his leg, looked toward the river bank and made a faint, plaintive sound.

"It's all right. The Major's got things under control," Bryan whispered, rubbing Cheeky's head, a trifle plaintive himself at being left behind with the cannon detail instead of accompanying the Major.

The Major, leading a handpicked advance guard, most of them the expert American riflemen, paralleled the flotilla along the river bank. Menard was with him, sparing him a glance now and then, feeling both puzzled and vindicated.

To look at the Major, only mildly dishevelled, you wouldn't know he had just chastised, physically and severely, two men. One of them marched cheerfully, with aching ribs and sore jaw, beside Len Cather. The other, a notorious malcontent, dismissed. Confiscating the company rifle, Cheek and Charles Davis had delivered him to the pirogue heading down river with the discharged and disgraced convalescing pair of *vice contre naturs* from the Chouteau contingent.

Time and again, on this trip, Menard had felt vindicated in having recognized the significant contribution this man could make if brought into the partnership. He had known Andrew Henry for nearly a decade. A man who could drink and not show it; quick to laugh; slow to anger; and, in a fight, fit and fast. What made him valuable, when he did give an order, was the quiet, understated expectation of the immediate execution of a reasonable order. Or else.

Time and again, he had been puzzled, as now. How did the Major, in dealing with these Americans, know when it was time to laugh? to ridicule? to be supportive? or to knock the hell out of a man?

Technically, these were militia. American militia, whether made up of frontiersmen or clerks, had a reputation for being undisciplined, wilful, irksome and irresponsible unless kept under tight control. They wouldn't follow a leader who was not a fighter. When necessary, the Major could and did serve up punishment suited to the culprit.

He only did it to make a point. He could turn a man's psychic back to bloody ribbons with his tongue. Some men needed that. Some men had to be beaten down and stomped. He could do that. Some men writhed under ridicule. It was all one. The tools of an effective leader.

Here, in a group commitment, were hunters, carpenters, farmers, clerks and frontiersmen. Already, he had seen how they chafed against restrictive rules; indulged in aggression more related to status than to hate or fear. How, in contrast to their reaction when Cheek was under threat of dismissal, banishment appeared to be acceptable if it reflected the consensus of opinion. Likewise, punishment for speaking out of turn. He had to admire the skill with which the Major had brought it about.

"That," the Major had said, after knocking Miller down for the third time, "was for thinking out loud."

Miller, a garrulous man, nearly as big as Cheek, had sat up slowly, reviewing, as Menard was, what he had blurted out. Looking up at the Major, he had taken a tentative breath and felt his ribs, then had waggled his jaw experimentally with one hand.

"Damme, Major," he had said in an exaggerated stage whisper, "I'm thinkin' you're right." With the help of Cather, he had gotten to his feet and rejoined his fellows.

And that, evidently, was what the Americans wanted. The Major's timing had coincided with the desires of the group. The Americans had wanted to be rid of the one man. And they had felt Miller needed disciplining.

Now they moved along without a trace of resentment. Their minds were on the job at hand, taking reassurance from being led by a man who could and did exercise control, with disconcerting, penetrating insight.

Blue, gray, hazel and some brown eyes scanned a landscape that had all the wretchedness of an agoraphobic's nightmare. The enormity of the all encompassing space was disconcerting, distorting to the senses. Distance and depth perception deceived, unsettled. Dry grasses crackled underfoot, continuing on wearisomely to infinity, open country, monotonous to eyes accustomed to the restful variety of a forested landscape.

Round-topped on the prairie above the west bank, the two Arikara villages, with a beaten corridor and a small stream between, were about two-dozen keelboat lengths apart. The dwellings, mounds of prairie-colored earth, like great overturned bowls, were lined inside with poles and posts, camouflaged outside by the ubiquitous prairie grasses growing on them. Only the occasional streamer of gray smoke from a smoke hole, rising into the clear sky, indicated this was not an over-sized prairie-dog town on a benchland but a primitive example of limited-access architecture behind an equally primitive city wall giving a clear view of the bottoms and fringe of cottonwoods and willows.

Kicking their way through a sudden eruption of grasshoppers, the only sign of life encountered in their show of strength, the advance guard halted a half mile from the lower village. Speedily, a perimeter of defense was set up, with the cannon the focal point, the expert riflemen placed strategically.

"Here they come," someone said tensely.

He wasn't the only one remembering the debacle of the year before when an alliance of the villagers and Teton Sioux, six-hundred-fifty strong, at war with the Mandans, had demanded the surrender of Shehaka. Some of their enmity at that time stemmed from the fact that Shehaka had survived his sojourn in the white man's land and the Sioux and Arikara chieftains had not. In the wake of the Lewis and Clark expedition, Pierre Chouteau had taken on the reluctant role of travel agent for Arikara and Sioux representatives. His reservations about their resistance to white men's disease, unfortunately, had been correct. Shortly before Pryor and A.P. arrived at the Arikara village last year, unofficial word had preceded them, the unsettling news that their admired Chief Ankedoucharo was dead, along with several Sioux subchiefs, of white men's ailments.

In the flare up of hostility last year, Rene Jessaume had been hurt. Three white men had been killed, ten wounded, one of whom died later, and Pryor and A.P. and their bedraggled men, turned back in disheartening retreat. Today, Jessaume, his thigh and shoulder giving him painful twinges still, needed no encouragement to stay out of sight.

"They think it's a party," the Major said, pitching his voice so as to reassure the men watching the approaching Arikara.

A mixed bag, mostly pedestrians, dark skins in animal skins, grimy and gabbling. The curious, the thoughtless, greedy and envious, they were eager for distraction, reacting exuberantly to the possibility of carnival abandon after a long, dull summer. "Ah," his voice deep and steady, quirking up with amusement, "That fellow doesn't agree. He thinks it's a funeral."

Riding flat out, a figure of authority was rapidly overtaking the heedless villagers. The Arikara sent his dun pony ruthlessly into the van, bowling over the leading figures, galloping back and forth before the milling edge, haranguing them, pointing at the cannon.

"He hasn't forgotten what happened last year anyway. He expects some kind of reprisal," said Menard as they watched the chieftain bring the Arikara, slowly, reluctantly to a halt. "This year they don't have all those Teton Sioux to fight for them."

The chieftain snapped his rawhide whip at one recalcitrant, then another, shouting. One, then another apprehensive horseman joined him, and the last of the stragglers was herded back into the village.

The frontiersmen settled back, alert, observant but no longer tense. The Arikara, caught off balance, uncertain, would parley, probing for clues to the white man's intentions. Experienced in the tedium of negotiations imposed by the Indian predilection for oligarchical republicanism, the men made themselves comfortable.

Bryan, while his cousin Sam was distracted with Lisa's arrangements for erecting an awning and setting out the inviting trappings of hospitality, told the steersman he was taking Cheeky for a walk. For the greater part of two days, he did walk Cheeky about.

Settling down unobtrusively on one fringe after another, idly tossing a stick for Cheeky to fetch, he picked up an item of information here, a tid-bit there. He sorted out his dubious accumulation, adding to his knowledge, stimulating his imagination, and, mindful of Sam Morrison's warning, sifted out some items to write home about, circumspectly.

He observed the arrival of, not the Arikara headmen, but the twenty-man peace delegation of the Mandans who had been re-establishing friendly relations with last year's enemies and, incidentally, smoothing the way for the safe passage of Shehaka and the expedition. Chouteau, coming out of a huddle with the Mandans and the six-man Sioux peace party he had persuaded to accompany the expedition, sent the resident interpreter to invite the Arikara leaders to his camp.

The interpreter, a dark little man of mixed heritage, with two decades, several wives and a couple children with the Arikaras, rode off on a spotted pony with Chouteau's message. The Arikara hedged, while they sent their women and children and old men into hiding.

The partners and their men ate in relays, lounged about, making desultory conversation. Four representatives of the Arikara put in appearance. Chouteau smoked a pipe with them and shared meat with them and sounded them out, dissatisfied with the meager representation.

The other chieftains, they said, didn't like the cannon and the rifles. They didn't think the white men had good intentions toward them. "Mon Dieu," the Colonel said, "Of course we don't," but not so the Indians heard him.

The Colonel, in his dignified aristocratic fashion, was a master of the courtesies and rituals of Indian diplomacy. Every formality was observed. Patient, subtle, attuned by hard years of experience to the Indian mind, he was aware that the expedition's unexpected arrival had precipitated some rightful alarm.

Lisa was concluding a parley with other representatives of the uneasy Arikara.

Lisa, watching the interpreter's roving gaze return greedily, again and again, to the goods stacked under the awning, casually mentioned an item or two they had brought as gifts for their good friends, the Arikara. The interpreter said the chiefs wanted the riflemen disarmed and the cannon turned in the opposite direction. Lisa said they could turn the cannon around.

The Colonel said they would reduce the number of men on guard. However, he desired a greater representation of Arikara before a council was held. And during the council meeting, there would be men on guard, and arms.

It was getting on to evening by then. The four Arikara, dismissed, left, with the interpreter who said he'd see what he could do with those terms but not to expect an answer until the next day.

Menard, who had been first introduced to Arikara ways by that Indian expert, George Drouillard, told the Major they displayed a certain primitive shrewdness in maintaining their sovereignty over this stretch of the river. Constantly adjusting to the shifting attitudes of their neighbors, allies of the Sioux and enemies of the Mandans one year, the reverse next year, they were also subjected to the inexplicable, cold war contention between the Americans and the British for their trade.

They had a reasonably stable way of life, albeit a loutish physical one. They raised and stored a variety of vegetables, trading the surplus to their neighbors and the occasional traders; did well with their horsetrading; and because of their sedentary way of life were in the market for a greater variety of goods than a nomadic tribe.

Dr. Thomas asked if there was any truth to what he'd heard, that both young and old of either sex were tainted with venereal disease.

Menard thought so. Also, that the disease probably had something to do with their birth rate, much lower than that of the whites.

"We are a prolific lot, aren't we?" said the Major. "What would you say was an average size family, back home, Doctor?"

"Ten children," said the Doctor. "Although fifteen is not unusual."

Menard murmured that the Arikara considered the white man oversexed. Indignantly, the Doctor said they should talk, the incestuous bastards. The Major said most civilized seaports thought the same about the white men.

Still indignant, the Doctor said he understood it was customary, every evening, for the Arikara men to lead their wives, sisters and daughters to a trader's camp and barter for their favors. He'd certainly never seen the like in any civilized seaport. The Major said perhaps that was because the seaport had the facilities to provide a measure of privacy for the consummation of such transactions.

Bryan heard a great deal about the Arikara and their notorious ways, too.

Miller, who had been here before, said they were great horsemen for a sedentary tribe. They had a lot of horses. They also had the pox, goiter, a great deal of blindness, and very loose morals.

Cheek said that reminded him of a story he'd heard of some folks back home, living out of the way, up in the hill country.

There was this big family headed by a real bossy, patriarchal type. He was very particular about the women his sons and grandsons picked out for wives.

One day, his favorite grandson, without consulting the patriarch beforehand, brought home a bride. The patriarch wasn't pleased with this display of independence but the bride was young and very attractive. He permitted the other men in his family to persuade him into acceptance of the match and allowed the womenfolk to organize the usual party. Despite his maintenance of grumpy forbearance, he ate and drank, danced and drank, chivareed and drank.

He was late rousing the next morning and his white-lightning headache made him extremely short tempered. When the groom came to him and confided that he had already packed up his bride and her belongings and sent her back to her people, "What the hell did you do that for?" he roared.

"Because she was a virgin," explained the grandson, shamefaced and apologetic.

"Because she was a virgin?" repeated Len Cather in surprise and disbelief.

"Yup," said Cheek. "Seems their outlook was much like that of these here 'Rees."

The ol' man says, "Grandson, you done the right thing. If she ain't fitten' fer her own kin, then she ain't fitten' fer our'n."

There was a long considering silence.

"That ain't funny!" Thomas James burst out indignantly frowning in anger and disgust.

"Didn't mean it to be funny. More parable-like," said Cheek gravely. "Now, if you want funny — " and he proceeded with the ribald story of the Ol' Log Inn which even James, as the guffaws rang out, seemed to find funny, for he did smile, with his lips.

By then Bryan had heard that the Arikara relished long-dead buffalo meat. Also dog meat. The towns were filthy. Offal lay wherever tossed. The men raised and cured a sad excuse for tobacco. The women, with their gardening expertise, would have done better probably but they were considered too unclean to handle anything as intimately connected with male ritual as tobacco.

Lisa had kept most of the men and property on an island in midriver, for the sake of defense in the event the negotiations broke down. His own keelboat was in midstream, with the swivel gun ready to be swung about, if need be, and Lisa's ancient spy glass which confirmed the report brought back by the scouts.

Several hundred Arikara were rounding up their war parties and arming themselves.

Forewarned, the Major and Menard and the other militia officers made the professional, the defensive preparations, and did not get much sleep, reviewing the probabilities in the long watches of the night.

Morning came. But no Arikara, for war or for council.

Colonel Pierre Chouteau, containing his impatience, selected from the expedition's pool of interpreters, the most trustworthy to remind yesterday's chieftains of their promise to meet with him. Some time elapsed before the interpreter returned with a grudging answer. They wanted hostages. They got four and immediately eight of their headmen came to hear what the white man had to say.

Bryan, who had been spotted by his cousin and told in no uncertain terms to get back on Lisa's keelboat and stay there, did. With Cheeky still at heel, he watched the proceedings through the spy glass.

After all he had been hearing, he was rather impressed by the appearance of the delegation. Faces: composed; unreadable; forceful; aquiline; taciturn. Demeanor: grave; haughty; formal.

Colonel Chouteau raked them over the coals for their behavior of the year before. The Great White Father was very angry with them for their unprovoked and reprehensible attack on Shehaka's escort, preventing his return home. The Great White Father was determined that this expedition would succeed in conducting the Mandan chief to his village.

"I have orders to destroy your nation," Chouteau told them bluntly.

The impassive councilors, sitting like graven images, were not entirely unreadable to that keen student of the Indian mind. Like all representative officials, when confronted with the consequences, the advocates of the condemned actions were being judged by their peers. There was a subtle, unconscious re-alignment of power, the taut consciences, uneasy; the clear consciences, expectant, anticipating the percentages to be realized out of the elevation of the peace maker.

"But," the Colonel continued gravely, indicating the other Indians sitting in council with them, "the chiefs of the Sioux and the chiefs of the Mandan nation have united together and interceded for your pardon."

The fans, of eagle tail and turkey feather, rustled in the hands of several of the councilors, and waved away a portion of the palpable tension.

"At their particular request, I shall ground my arms until new orders can be received from your Great White Father," said the Colonel, allowing his body language to reveal a certain reluctance. "He alone can pardon. Or destroy you."

Alexis Doza, taking in every masterly nuance with the appreciation of the professional, knew better. With minimal encouragement, and the critical acumen of a long-time student on Indian behavior, he told the Major so.

Young John Dougherty hunkered down beside them, taking it all in. He had an ear for languages. Doza, Menard's man from Kaskaskia, understood a great many Indian dialects, was a skilled communicator in sign language, and held in high regard by his patron. An eighteen-year-old Kentuckian who would like to be an Indian agent some day could learn much from him. Most men here, however, were novices compared to the Colonel and Lisa when it came to dealing with the Indians.

One dignitary, then another, rose to make reply. Dougherty, grinning, said they sounded like a bunch of Congressmen, caught out in an error of judgment, all sincerity and solemnity, assigning, but not accepting blame.

Doza gave them a running commentary. The hawk-like Ree says it's all the fault of some Frenchman. The Frenchie told them Lt. Pryor was cheating when he gave them only medals, that Pryor's barges were full of assorted goodies sent to the Arikara by the Great White Father himself. The Frenchie told them to take those goods away from Pryor. Now, the Colonel is demanding they produce this culprit. They are quite agreeable. However, he lives with another tribe, fifty miles away.

His insistence is making them uncomfortable. They're telling him they'll see if they can't get a party of their young men to escort a detachment of the Colonel's to go after the Frenchman and bring him back. Nothing will come of that idea.

Now, the grave-faced fellow, shaking Shehaka's hand, and promising him safe passage, says everybody was most unhappy over Chief Ankedoucharo's death while visiting the US of A. Besides, when they fired on Shehaka the first time, it was because the principal chief of the nation was absent. Doesn't seem to make much sense to Shehaka, either, but he's being agreeable about it.

Dr. Thomas admired the style and demeanor Shehaka gave the proceedings. The Mandan handed the calumet around the council with all the gravity of a statesman and warrior.

However, the doctor was slightly taken aback when Doza translated what the Arikara had to say, to the grave faces of the Sioux, about them, publicly. Notorious treaty breakers, said the Arikara, these Sioux were on hand only for the presents, the smokes and Arikara horses.

For many years the Arikara had held sway on these river ramparts. In their view, as with most primitive people, they were the center of the universe. Dark, strong-boned faces. Tufted black brows. Some looked fiercer than others. Excellent hearing. Retentive memories.

They called upon those memories to deliver some very frank

and unflattering character summaries of the Sioux sitting in council with them. They knew these individuals better than the white man did. They provided some unflattering specifics. If the white man wanted to be taken in by them, that was his look out. The Arikara weren't accepting any dubious credentials.

These Sioux were opportunists who had come along for the outing and the gifts. Their recommendations might, or might not, carry weight with their fellow tribesmen. The Arikara, realists, knew they couldn't speak for all the Sioux, any more than they could speak for all the Arikara.

The cannon was real to the Arikara. The Great White Father was not. The Mandan and the Sioux were very real. At the moment, neither was a help nor a hindrance. Besides, there were customs, inhibitions, rivalries and uncertainties among them, too.

Lisa, who could think like an Arikara when he put his mind to it, remembering who was prudent, who was obstructive, who was shallow, who was transitory, and how to make the most of it, spoke to them.

Sitting gravely crosslegged, they heard him present blunt terms in a pleasant voice, augmented with definitive, expository sign language. Behind their facade of gravity and wisdom, he knew they were influenced by subtleties quite beyond translation. Spirits and magic all around. Air, rocks, trees, brush, clouds, water. War is a game; counting coup, adolescent tag. Obligations to family, duty to the band, to the spirits. Feelings, erratic, contradictory, fleeting.

Lisa, one with the Arikara, sorting out their self-centered reactions, brought the council to a mutually acceptable conclusion.

There would be gifts. A two-bit item for this one; a four-bit item for that one; and for the hawk-like fellow, the one his peers deferred to, whose stock was the highest at the moment, a six-bit item.

For the hoi-polloi, whose cupidity could and did sway their representatives, there would be some trade, but not much. This in its way was reprisal. No bacchanalia. Which, as Lisa knew and Doza recognized, as did the Arikara, was uncivil, but a trifle compared to the incivility of the cannon.

Before the undercurrent of anxiety among the men of the expedition had ebbed entirely, and before the engages could feel safe enough to undertake their usual convivial fraternization, Lisa had the vegetables and meat taken in trade loaded on the barges, and the horses placed in charge of the returning Mandan delegation, and the expedition on the move, into the final stretch of the long voyage.

Bryan, watching the boatmen taking their places in single file on the narrow gunwale to began poling upstream, realized they were no longer strangers, and their version of French was no longer a foreign language. They were obliging and cheerful at their labors, all for thirty cents a day. He could now understand their light-hearted jokes and sometimes joined in their sing-alongs, in a pleasant tenor.

"A penny - -?" said the Major cheerfully, at Bryan's elbow, Cheeky following closely.

"Galley slaves," said Bryan, smiling. "Steamboats. Balloons."

"Steamboats," said Dr. Thomas, emerging from the cabin where he had been jotting down his impressions of the Arikara and a critique of the theories and procedures of their medical practitioner.

"Balloons," said the Major firmly. "To rise above it all and get it in true perspective."

They were rising, in altitude and latitude. The days were noticeably shorter, cooler; the nights longer, and cold. The Doctor wrote in his journal that they had charming weather, so he went ashore several places, preferring the fertile limits of the low ground along the river to the dun-colored bleakness beyond, where, he had been told, the grizzly bear was to be seen.

They made good time along the edge of meadows, with fewer navigational hazards than usual, and could see clearly all the hills, animated with buffalo.

Bryan wrote home about his first buffalo, the one he killed easily, taking aim along with all the other rifles at the shaggy beasts, easy targets as the boat rounded a willow-lined point crowded with them. He roasted the liver on a stick, sampled the tongue, and ate his fill of hump steak, which, he told his mother, was most tender, with fat and lean tastefully mixed.

Thomas James, who did not write down his impressions but dictated them for publication thirty-five years later, had been out for seven days with the able hunter, Brown. Set ashore to hunt game, they had killed and dressed out an elk by evening and settled down to await the rendezvousing canoe that was crossing from the boat anchored on the opposite shore. An ill wind whipped up the water nearly swamping the canoe. They opted to send the elk across on the first trip. There was no second trip that evening. Nor the next morning.

Still blowing fiercely the second day, the wind thrust the boats rapidly ahead. James and Brown, laboring overland, with many a detour, spent the next six days overtaking them.

Gaunt, they ate the last of the second elk they killed on the fourth day; anxious, for they ran out of ammunition on the fifth day; limping, for their moccasins were in shreds from the rough going; and sore, from the prickly pear spines; and James, at least, at the 'booshway' for not waiting up for them.

"Wasn't that much of a muchness," Brown dismissed it matter-of-factly in reply to a query from John Dougherty in Bryan's hearing. "Cap'n James, he larned a thing or two. He won't be so wasteful with his lead — and more keerful where he sets down his feet — next time."

"When he gets hold of an ax," summarized John, companionably, "He shore does like to grind it — 'specially on the 'booshways'."

Shortly thereafter, James sallied forth on his own, embarking on a redeeming hunting excursion.

The attitude of stalwarts like Brown and Dougherty, who could not work up much pity for a grown man who did not know how to survive, had brought home to him that a successful frontiersman must master conditions, in forest or on the plains. Making certain of an ample supply of ammunition this time, he made his way overland, in a very able fashion, and arrived at the Five Villages of the Upper Missouri several days before the rest of the company.

All five villages, the two Mandan on the Missouri itself, the two Minnetaree and the one Weterson, on the Knife River, had an informal and often indecisive form of democratic rule. Their headmen only reflected, very seldom imposed, the currently acceptable policies and procedures.

Upon first hearing the Mandan villages named, Matootonah and Rooptahee, Bryan said they sounded like cheerful toots on a willow whistle. Matootonah, Shehaka's native village, generally acknowledged the leadership of a chieftain known as Coal. The upper village, Rooptahee, had Black Cat as the nominal head. While Wolf, with an insecure hold on the office inherited from his father, was considered chief of all the Mandans.

At the mouth of the Knife River was the village of the Wetersons, called by the British, the Anaway; by the French, the Soulier Noir; and by the Minnetaree, cousin. West along the same river were the two villages of the Minnetaree, called by James and other Americans, the Gros Ventre, with harsh, barking sorts of names: the lower, Metaharta; the upper, Hidatsa.

The latter had a yapping, one-eyed chieftain, with a cunningly cruel bite, reputed to be both nefarious and influential. A long time friend of the British, pimp and panderer to their representatives, he was known to have an odd and variable temper. He was called LeBourgne, One-Eye, Kakoakis, and worse.

The people of the Gros Ventre villages were more closely related to each other and the other Sioux, than to the Mandan, although all spoke languages with an original Siouan base. The Minnetaree ranged further afield than the Mandans as witness their western raid on the Shoshoni people that netted them the young captive, Sacajawea, who guided Lewis and Clark back to the land of her people.

All of them had promoted the buffalo into ascendancy over the corn-tasselled god of their eastern cousins. The Mandans in particular were inclined to let all things come to them, leaving the growing things to the women, making sympathetic magic to bring the buffalo each season, and depending upon the spring fair for meat, fur and bounty. In 1790 smallpox decimated the population, reducing the number of Mandan villages from nine to two, the current, viable number.

On September 21, thirty miles down river from the main Mandan villages, the expedition came across the half-hearted beginning of another village. These secessionist Mandans were not averse to allowing Shehaka to persuade them to return upriver.

On the next day at latitude 47 degrees 13' N, they reached Shehaka's village, Matootonah, along with a gale force wind.

Thomas James, watching their arrival, saw nothing symbolical in the fury of the wind, and nothing admirable in the Mandans.

Despite the hurricane winds and prodigious waves, jubilant Mandans flung themselves exuberantly into their round hide boats and paddled across the turbulent river, where Lisa's swivel gun fired a salute and the American flag was raised. On the opposite shore, other Mandans raced back and forth, returning the salute, generally with discharges from ancient muskets.

The Mandans welcoming Shehaka, approximately the thirteenth, and, therefore, symbolically, the most vulnerable generation to reside on these river banks, were smugly certain of their place in the center of the universe. The river, in its sweeping fashion, kept them supplied with the necessities of life. Floating timbers, live and dead buffalo, ablutions, recreation, boating, fishing. And keenly competitive traders.

From what James could see, bracing himself stolidly against the buffeting of the wind, the Mandans, piling onto the barge bearing Shehaka, crowding around him and his party and craning to see what loot he had brought back with him, paid little attention to their white visitors.

The partners got Shehaka, swiftly as the turbulence of his welcome would permit, ashore. Raising voices to outbattle the wind, they unloaded Yellow Corn, her dark face animated, and White Painted Horse, two years older and several inches taller than when they left, and the wind-ruffled rooster. Jessaume limped after, with a garrulous Broken Tooth, her two children and the flatirons, close behind.

As the wind blew itself out, the partners made preparations for the next day's pow-wows at the upper towns.

Shehaka's brother was hospitable. A muscular man of middle

years, with the streaked Mandan hair, he presided over a medium-sized household whose womenfolk served up a mid-day meal of stewed meat and vegetables that Dr. Thomas, in attendance with the gentlemen of the expedition, considered very palatable.

"Well, the booshways got their fat ol' Coyote delivered at last," James said to Cheek when he rejoined his companions on the barge and gave them an account of his recent activities. "You can call him Big White if you want to. In the Mandan tongue, he's Coyote."

"He's purty fat fer a coyote," said Cheek of Shehaka, snug in his full dress uniform, mounting the fine horse presented to him by his tribesmen. "An' he really ain't the Big Cheese them booshways thought he was."

Ashore, Dr. Thomas, disillusioned, echoed Cheek. "He's not really chief of all the Mandans," he said to the Major, as they and Francis and Bryan and others of the expedition joined the cavalcade of riders bound for the gathering at Rooptahee.

"He never claimed he was," said the Major, not surprised to find that the American publicity releases did not reflect the reality of the Mandan world. "But he has learned to put on a good show."

"He is a one-man parade by himself," agreed Francis, amused. "Not only is he resplendent as an emperor but he's decked that horse out with a king's ransom in scarlet and gold laced housings, fancy bridle and saddle."

"I wonder who he'll give all that to," said Bryan. "Somehow, I get the feeling all this jubilee over his return is anticipation of the big give-away."

"And, somehow," grinned Francis, "I get the feeling that Shehaka has been too long among white folks. He made sure all his plunder was separated from the other goods for distribution and squirreled away in a safe place. He doesn't intend to give away anything."

Colonel Pierre Chouteau was chagrined to discover that Francis was correct. Ceremoniously, he addressed the assembly of the Mandans, Minnetarees and Wetersons.

With a flourish, he presented Shehaka and his family to them, and told the gathering more than they really wanted to know of the causes for the delayed return. He got a big hand, the first time Shehaka figured in the ceremony, and 'greatest demonstration of Joy ...'

The second time, when he turned to Shehaka and directed him to proceed with the distribution of the presents he had brought back, he got hullabaloo. The Mandans weren't happy with Chief One Eye, who had killed one of their principal men in a quarrel a few days before. They were not agreeable to sharing presents with the Hidatsa tyrant.

Shehaka was not agreeable about sharing his property with any one. He refused, point blank, to do so.

Diplomatically, the Colonel shifted gears. He distracted them from resentments, rivalries and jealousies by focusing their attention on the company largesse. With the distribution underway of sixty pounds of powder, and one hundred and twenty pounds of ball, stocked originally for use against the Arikara, a measure of harmony was restored.

As a token of friendship from the United States to the Minnetaree, Chief One-Eye was presented a large medal and the American flag in the name of the Great White Father, President Madison.

They left Shehaka, still in possession of his valuables, including the rooster, who was starting to crow again, to the judgment of his peers. He never regained the popularity he revelled in that windy September day. His credibility, when he insisted his tall tales of the white man's world were for true and not for entertainment, were undermined deliberately and disdainfully by more than one rival chieftain.

On the last Thursday in September of 1809, the twenty-fourth, a little over four months from St. Louis, and 1640 river miles from the mouth of the Missouri River, Lisa got the expedition to the site chosen for the company fort.

They were fifteen miles above the Mandan villages, twenty-one miles from the Gros Ventre. They were in an enviable location, the area of the redman's annual spring rendezvous.

It was no mean achievement. The acceptance of the American presence at this trading crossroad was a tribute to the perseverance and perspicacity of Manuel Lisa, the skilled Indian negotiator.

With characteristic shrewdness and remarkable understanding of the Indian democratic process, Lisa had, the year before, after interminable meetings, persuaded the people of the Five Villages to allow the Americans to establish themselves within reach of the locale where thousands of tribal representatives traditionally gathered each June for a peaceful spring fair.

Regularly, spring after spring for uncounted years, a variety of bounty had come to the Five Villages. Directly and indirectly, goods came to the high prairie, along with intriguing clues to a distant origin.

Sea shells and walrus ivory with a beached Kanaka. Obsidian from the cliffs of Western Oregon with the Kanaka's barrel-chested traveling companion, a Pannakwate who bartered shrewdly for a horse.

Sand and salt from the Great Salt Lake packed into animal horns by a party of Utes who traded them to some Ojibwas for copper tools and ornaments.

Dried salmon from the Columbia exchanged by a Cayuse for the medicinal plants and herbs of the Crees. Reindeer hides from the far north, passing through many hands to arrive with an Oglala Sioux who lost them in a game of hand to a Hidatsu.

Pipestone, of uncertain origin, which everyone wanted, and which a Yankton Sioux traded to Chief One-Eye for a fine Shoshone stallion, stolen. And a couple of small, sky-blue stones, that a squat little man from the far southwest kept because no one had a musket they would give up.

In time for the June gathering, it had been the custom for the merchants of Canada to send their representatives with cloth and tin and steel, manufactured into blankets and capotes, kettles, knives, spoons, awls and hatchets, to barter. They bought fur. What once lived and breathed and played with its young in northern snowfields. White bear, weasel and Arctic fox. What once moved lithely over the prairie and in and out of the mountain streams. Cougar and wolf. Marten and otter. And, whenever possible, the beaver.

The people of the Five Villages traded to one and all, handsome worked skins of deer, elk and buffalo; glass beads and marbles; the produce of their fields, the dried corn, the beans, the squash, the pumpkin and the gourds.

The St. Louis Missouri Company fur-trading expedition had arrived too late for this year's fair. Next year the Company should do well even though it was going to take time to get the Indians accustomed to harvesting furs. The Indians of the prairies, unlike those of the forest, had no interest in, nor aptitude for, trapping. There was no dash and challenge to it, like the buffalo hunt. It was downright hard, cold and time-consuming; a great deal of labor best done at the coldest time of the year to get the thickest, sleekest pelts. As any sensible man recognized, it was also the time to stay close to a snug lodge warmed by a good fire.

What furs did come in would be theirs. It would seem that the St. Louis Missouri Fur Company would encounter no on-site opposition from the British. With the arrival of the Americans, the three men of the Northwest Company, who had been whooping it up with Chief One-Eye, ignored a dispatch from Colonel Chouteau to meet with him, and were observed by John Colter taking their leave, heading north, probably for Fort Pine, without any furs.

"Now maybe we can get down to business," Thomas James snorted to his cronies on the September day that saw their voyage completed, "and make us some money out of trapping."

The partners, mindful of the same goal, wasted no time. The men were kept busy, unloading the barges, snaking out timbers, cutting, sawing, adzing, hammering. Reuben Lewis had the fort laid out and the palisade going up before the end of September.

On hand with a report for Lisa was Benito Vasquez, the fellow Spaniard he had left in command of Fort Raymond. Vasquez had battened things down at the fort at the mouth of the Bighorn, caching all equipment, and brought comparatively encouraging news.

Charles Sanguinet and Jean Baptiste Beauvais had a party trapping the Green River. Jean Baptiste Champlain and Peter Wiser had spent some time travelling up the Madison, crossing an easy pass to a tributary stream of the Snake River. They had followed the Snake River down onto a plain which, they reported, would be a good location for a fort.

Champlain, currently trading with the Crows, who had learned trapping from Francois Laroque and itinerant Nor'west men and practiced it in desultory fashion, was supposed to have about four packs of beaver and scattered hunters due to bring in more.

Rumor had Charles Courtin befriended by the Flatheads. A French Canadian from Machilimackinac who had become an American citizen about the same time as Ramsay Crooks, and for the same reason, so he could trade on the Upper Missouri, he had done some trading with the Omahas. It was said that several veterans from the Lewis and Clark expedition had turned up at his camp there. Seizing the opportunity to capitalize on their firsthand knowledge, he had employed them to guide him to Flathead country and a successful harvest of furs.

David Thompson, map maker and astronomer for the North West Company, was building Kullyspell House on Lake Pend Oreille for trade with the Kootenai who had promised many beaver for the guns they needed to defend themselves from the Blackfeet. Like Courtin, he was also interested in trade with the Flatheads, who were not flat-headed and certainly not pin-heads, for they were willing to trap beaver, too, to get more firepower. Vasquez, himself, who had been trying without success to get the Indians interested in trapping, had only fifteen beaver pelts and ten buffalo robes.

The stars in their courses wheeled overhead. The Moon When the Calves Grow Hair was past and gone. They were a quarter past the Moon of Changing Seasons. Soon it would be the Moon of Falling Leaves. In no time at all it would be the Moon of Frost in the Tipi.

Chapter 10

"The stars incline," said Francis sententiously, in lieu of any greeting. "They do not compel."

Sitting tailor fashion on the roughly adzed counter, he was at ease in the front room of the blockhouse that, under Reuben Lewis's direction, was being fashioned into a trading post. With a stack of trade goods on one side, a scattering of pelts on the other, he was leafing through a battered, leather-bound volume.

Fresh from the bright outdoors and a great deal of concentrated and varied activity, the Major and his companions, Bryan and Dr. Thomas, paused in the doorway. The Major moved to one side, leaning against the wall, closing his eyes to allow the pupils to adjust to the dimmer interior. Bryan followed his example. The Doctor, peering vainly, tried opening the door in order to see better, letting in more noise than light.

In a cacophony of construction, Fort Manuel Lisa, a.k.a. Fort Mandan and the Company Fort, was nearing completion. A compact and triangular bastion located a couple hundred yards from the bank of the river, enclosed in a 15' high palisade of upright cottonwood logs that doubled as the back walls for the log quarters, storehouses, smithy, harness shop and stables, it had a large heavy gate to bar the entrance. A busy place, it was lively and noisy with the job-related activities of carpenters and their assistants, farriers, blacksmiths, horsemen and clerks.

Rising above the nearly flat, sodded roofs of the other structures, and also nearing completion, was the square, two-story company blockhouse overlooking the river approaches and the surrounding countryside.

Even as the palisade was going up, hectically, the barges had been unloaded and the goods placed under cover. For all members of the expedition, the tone had been one of severe efficiency, brisk as the early days of October.

Inside the lower story of the blockhouse, Francis, his teeth flashing white in the dimness, addressed Andrew Henry with mock seriousness. "You, sir," he said, "are the possessor of a complex personality. As a business partner, you are reliable but unsympathetic. Just, but not generous. And accurate to the last detail."

Overhead, in the second story, carpenters were hammering out sleeping quarters for the partner destined to winter here, the ambivalent Sylvestre Labbadie; for the ambitious hunter, Ayres, that

Labbadie and A.P. Chouteau had tolled away from Crooks and McClelland, already being equipped at company expense to hunt on shares; and for any other company men, yet to be determined.

In a barrel chair drawn up to a rough table near the light from the fireplace, Pierre Menard, on his forty-third natal day, was not celebrating. A scrupulous man, undemanding and unaffected, whose first loves were honesty and fair dealing, he had, once again, found a measure of stress-reduction in unburdening himself in a long letter to his friend and business steward, Adrien Langlois.

The reliable husband and father, whose well-run enterprises provided him and his growing family with a living of comfort and grace, he vented his homesickness in neatly scribed, idiomatic French. The man of affairs, disillusioned with some of the management and their personnel policies, he made his points, discretely, for absolute candor can be the most costly of all attributes. The man of purpose, level-headed, he laid out the material prospects, the human resources related to specific business objectives, stoically, realistically.

This voyage on the Missouri had been his duty, even though, as he confided to Adrien with grim distaste, he wished had never undertaken it. It had unravelled the expedition, disheartening him, revealing all that was stupid and petty and high handed about these traders. He thanked God, keeping in mind that all He'd had to work with was chaos, too, that the voyage was at an end.

This was what, in a lesser degree, he and William Morrison had delegated last year to Manuel Lisa. Toughened and coarsened by endless, tough competition, Lisa had made it profitable for them. This was what, after this year, God willing, he would delegate again, for times change as do conditions, and untrammeled, he could get on with his real interests, back in Illinois.

Now, his constancy bolstering the crumbling edges of the united front of the partnership, the coming journey to Fort Raymond was also his duty. A.P. would get Dr. Thomas and the militia started on the quick run back to St. Louis. The Colonel and Lisa would be leaving shortly, touching base with their traders at the Arikaras, the Tetons, the Yanktons and the Omahas as they rode the current downstream. Back in St. Louis, they would have to plunge into the national and international currents, immediately, to be sure of obtaining the supplies needed to keep the men in the field next year.

He was to take fifty of those men and some boats and get to Fort Raymond ahead of the ice, while the Major, with forty men, would travel overland by horseback. Next June 15, as he had written to Adrien, he was heading home, a time he wished was already here. At any rate, God willing, he would celebrate his forty-fourth birthday with his Cher Papone in their fine, new mansion on the Illinois bluffs overlooking the Mississippi, close by Fort Kaskaskia.

"And you, sir," continued Francis, swivelling his triangular grin toward Menard, "are gentle and amiable, with great mathematical ability. In public affairs, sound and conservative."

Menard, square and muscular, with a skin like barked hide after the days of exposure to wind and sun on the long voyage, bowed ironically. Aware of the other partners coming and going busily, he had conscientiously lent support as it was needed, keeping abreast of the bartering, the planning, the concomitant by-play. It was somewhat akin to the good doctor's way of taking a man's pulse.

Today, the company pulse was beating smoothly. Francis Vallé, in his inimitable fashion, was preparing the new arrivals for some bad news. His diversionary tactics were intriguing and good for the blood pressure. "What about our other Pierre?" suggested Menard, easing back in his chair, cocking one booted foot upon his knee, shoving his thumbs into his belt.

"The Colonel?" Francis flipped some pages. "The Lion. Magnetic. Happy in responsibility. Likes danger and adventure."

"What's he maundering about?" demanded Dr. Thomas, starting to close the door after Sylvestre Labbadie entered until a peremptory bark made him pause, permitting Cheeky to stalk past him.

"As for 'Ee-saw' — hmm. No wonder you get on well with Manuel, Major. Virgo is one of your best companions," Francis went on. "The 'work sign.' Makes the best of any circumstances but — now remember this — breaks off friendships if there are differing opinions. Does have an orderly mind — "

"Books! He's got a stack of books," exclaimed Bryan, pouncing on the assortment in happy anticipation, stumbling over a sawed-off board end in the process, coming up hard against the counter.

"Books?" repeated Sylvestre Labbadie, a well-built young man of good family and good taste, with fluent command of several languages and wide, first hand experience in dealing with finances and people, profitably. He was not looking forward to his winter's exile far from good books, fine food and literate conversation. "What kind of books?"

"This is in Latin," Bryan said, disappointed, one brief glance enough to show him that getting through Gaul with Caesar was not sufficient preparation.

"So's this," said Francis equably.

Labbadie, well educated and a bit of a bibliophile, took the book from Bryan, carried it back to the door, which he pushed fully open so as to examine it in the sunlight.

"It's all stained," the Doctor said disparagingly, looking over Labbadie's shoulder at the maltreated volume.

"So is this one," said Bryan. "And the pages are stuck together."

"Blood," said Francis.

"And guts," said the Doctor with the precision of the medical mind, running his fingers over one of the stains.

"Courtin's," said John Colter bleakly, rising from behind the counter. "Charlie Courtin's. Or one of his men."

Menard, taking one hand out of his belt to rub the head Cheeky had laid on his knee, glanced at his sealed letter, wherein he had written "...one cannot imagine the quantity of beaver — but there is the difficulty of the savage Blackfeet who plunder often and kept our men during the last spring from making a fortune..."

"Happy Birthday," said the Major, pulling up another barrel chair and settling next to the sturdy, unpretentious man he admired. He was cognizant that Menard, truly gentle and amiable, had taken much to heart all the trials and tribulations with the hunters and the engages, conscientiously striving to keep relationships on even keel, despite the rankling manipulations and face-saving mendacities he'd had to tolerate, without condoning. "I've rounded up nearly enough horses and —"

"Anybody here seen Cheek?" demanded Thomas James thrusting his way past Labbadie to peer inside. "No? Well, then —" he spun on his heel, the coyote tail on his fur-skin cap flapping, and he was gone.

"Francis," said the Major dryly, seeing Menard put both feet on the floor, and, leaving off scratching Cheeky's ears, placed both hands on the table, as if bracing himself. "Look under 'Scorpion'."

There was silence while Francis leafed through his book, skimmed through the Latin, and smoothly as a prize scholar, summarized, in English, "Strong will power. Direct to the point. Selfish. Critical. Skeptical. Uncompromising. Turns everything to his own account. Powerful and eloquent speaker." He exchanged an amused glance with the Major. "You'd think the author, whoever he might have been —"

"John Dee? or Nostradamus?" suggested Dr. Thomas. "The book looks that old."

"It is a bit archaic," agreed Francis, "but, like I was saying, you'd think the author had spent four months with Thomas James, too. On the positive side, the horoscope says he's fond of outdoor sports. Is strictly honest. But makes a poor business partner."

"Best companions?" prompted the Major.

"Nobody here," said Francis sardonically.

"There, you see? You couldn't please him if you tried," the Major said to Menard. "God knows you've tried. Been tried. Will be tried. He's agitating for his traps and all his fixin's. And the men he says were promised to him."

"Traps and fixin's?" said Menard warily, an edge of impatience in his voice, his accent slipping slightly, "I 'ave told M'sieu James — plainly, in English — first the fort. Then, in good order, we will equip our ninety men. Then, him and his Americans. We cannot get on with that, I pointed out, until they," tilting his head toward the inventory-taking in the back room, "get done in there."

"Traps an' fixin's?" John Colter raised his white eyebrows. "I have Mr. James's note here," patting the breast of his hunting shirt, "for a set of beaver traps. Powder. And a gun."

"Then what is he waiting for?" Menard asked wearily.

"I thought you knew, Pierre," spoke up Sylvestre Labbaddie, briskly healthy, full of confidence and self-esteem, closing the door and crossing to the table, exchanging the book in hand for one in better condition. "Four 'Frenchies' skilled at trapping beaver to be under his command for three years. Doza, for instance. And three others."

"My Alexis Doza? The best hunter of all? C'est imposible!" Menard slapped the table with the flat of his hand, aghast. "Doza will have none of him. Nor any of my other young men from Kaskaskia."

"All the troubles of the soul, after all," Francis read with seeming innocence from his book, "are merely lines upon a horoscope chart."

"Stuff and nonsense," snorted Dr. Thomas, picking up another of the books. "We're living in the Age of Reason."

"Ours? or the Blackfeet's?" Bryan said reflectively, flicking a spot of dried blood off another book, this one, at last, in English, but barely recognizable as something of Shakespeare's. He wondered regretfully, who Courtin was, and decided not to ask, on the assumption the news was on the order of Donne's tolling bell.

"They have their reasons," said Colter, dispassionately, and didn't elaborate. Good and ill both exist. Sometimes one outweighs the other but both must be accepted and dealt with to the best of ones's ability. At the Hidatsa village, after the hasty departure of the Northwest men the day the expedition arrived, Colter had been offered in barter, by the wily Chief One-Eye, the abandoned bundle of peltries. He had found, shoved in with some prime beaver, the loot taken from some late unfortunate. Some careful inquiries augmented by his own deductive skills had pretty much established how the loot had passed from bloody Piegan hands to the Hidatsa. He had not been entirely surprised since he did know who Courtin was, an opportunistic, nominal American, disturbing the Blackfeet patterned way of life. "You want that book?"

Bryan, who couldn't see any entertainment in a well-nigh indecipherable book, shoved it back across the counter to Colter. The ethics of bargaining over dead men's effects, as Francis apparently had done, and Labbadie, shrewdly, was doing now, seemingly took second place to satisfying the educated man's hunger for reading material.

"I've always been partial to the Age of Enlightenment," the Major said to Dr. Thomas. He smiled at Menard. "What about you? Wouldn't you like to turn your face toward enlightenment, Brother?"

Menard looked up at the man about whom he had written in a positive vein to Langlois ". . . I have a lot of confidence in Monsieur Henry. He fits in very well not only because of his humor but because of his honesty and frank manner and general behavior."

To Henry, "Any time. Any time," Menard said fervently. He sighed. "But before I can turn my face toward the East —"

"The Major is getting us ready to face the West," Bryan broke in eagerly, approaching the table. "When we heard about Mr. Colter's race, we got up this contest and — "

He broke off self-consciously as Mr. Colter himself turned those keen blue eyes on him, raising the light eyebrows, startling against the bronzed skin, that had inspired the name he was known by among the Indians of the Five Villages, Seehkeeda or White Eyebrows.

"— and we came to see," finished the Major smoothly, meeting Colter's gaze, "if the man himself would judge the contest."

Menard found himself accompanying the Major and John Colter, trailed by Francis questioning Bryan about the contest. Labbadie remained behind, not so much to tend the store, more to fend off the incursion of inquisitive Indians satisfying their curiosity. Dr. Thomas lingered, leafing through Sylvestre's acquisition, a collection of Montaigne's Essays.

Making their way through the fort compound, they passed Michael Immel, setting up a tack room, helped by Archibald Pelton, Thomas James's favorite comic from Connecticut. Gil Hull, one of Menard's reliable Kentuckians, was checking the hooves of the horses. William Weir, a large, powerful man, was giving the farrier a hand with a recalcitrant Indian pony. The anvil was in place, the kit of farrier tools set out, the portable blow forge glowing, with the bell-like tones of the shoeing hammer an accompaniment to the proceedings.

At the blacksmith shop, Rucker and Fleehart were working with the smith on minor repairs to the portable hide press. The capable Alexis Doza, whose three-year contract with it favorable terms reflected Menard's high regard for his abilities, and the

Shawnee, Luthecaw, were carrying an assortment, broken traps, an ancient musket, an iron kettle, inside for repairs.

There were, as there had been from the day they set foot ashore, Indians hovering, indolent sidewalk superintendents. From a society with no concept of teamwork as practiced by the white man, and no sense of urgency and no great concern for efficiency, the Indians found such behavior curious. They trekked from the Five Villages to the fort, men, women and children, often bringing guesting Crees or Ojibways or Assiniboins, to share in the most popular spectator sport around, watching white men hard at work.

For the white man, it was one of the occupational hazards of frontier trading, being watched by the Indians, openly or secretly, defensively or enviously, to see what could be realized for sport, for plunder, for power or for self-aggrandizement.

The dark faces, solemn over the passing pipe, or intent over a game of chance played with pebbles or sticks, or, in the case of the women, stitching on leatherwork, found Fort Mandan an interesting place, good for idling away the time until something important came up, like a buffalo hunt or a promising raid.

As they were exiting the gate, Francis, having obtained the details of the race as envisioned by Bryan and his fellow contestants, said, "We're going to need some 'Blackfeet'."

Francis left them and headed for John Dougherty. He found him brushing down the hair upon the back of a recently acquired Indian pony, checking for scratches, wounds or abrasions, smoothing out any lump of twisted hair that could cause chafing if not removed.

The Major led the others to a spot within hailing distance of his tent where they found Cather and McBride just finishing setting up a peeled post. With hatchet and knife throwing, they casually demonstrated its purpose. Charles Davis was laying out a rifle range. James Cheek was discussing gunsmithing with Jackson.

Dr. Thomas, remembering his journal, came hurrying up, to get the factual firsthand details from the man who had inspired the contest. Menard gave close attention to the terse, matter-of-fact account Colter provided as other hunters drifted closer to listen.

While making their way up the Jefferson River after beaver, Colter and John Potts were surprised by a sizable war party of Blackfeet, who ordered them ashore. Colter, choosing between certain death from the firearms levelled upon him and, he hoped, merely robbery and some roughing up, complied.

Potts, from the canoe in midstream, his rifle lying alongside his feet, just out of reach, watched them seize, disarm and strip Colter naked. He, too, was a veteran of the Lewis and Clark expedition, inclined to corpulence, afflicted with a stutter, who could jig like a professional, and under the influence of rum or excitement, spoke with a thick Dutch accent.

In a level voice, Colter pointed out that if Potts didn't come ashore promptly, one of the itchy-fingered braves was going to shoot him.

Potts, preferring a quick death to being man-handled, and, very likely, tortured by the notorious Blackfeet, said so, shaking his head. One of the Indians shot him in the hip, knocking him down into the canoe, from which he pushed up his stocky body, rifle in hand.

"Yes, I'm hurt," he replied to Colter's question, his voice firm and entirely free of either the stutter or Dutch accent. "Too much so to escape. If you can get away, do so. I'll get at least one of them."

He levelled his rifle and shot and killed one of the braves holding Colter. Angry, barking guns riddled Potts body with bullets; angry, yelling Blackfeet plunged into the stream, yanked the canoe ashore, hacked up the sprawled body, throwing heart, lungs and entrails into Colter's face.

Relatives of the dead Indian, tomahawks in hand, were restrained with difficulty from killing him then and there.

Wearing an ice-cool face of disdainful detachment, Colter affected to have no interest in the hasty council called to decide his fate. Inwardly, he was sure it was going to be death by torture, slow, lingering and agonizing.

When one of the headmen, with motions and the Crow words, "Go — go away," led him out from the group, he supposed they intended to shoot him. Instead, the Indian urged him to "Go — faster — faster!:" Looking back, he saw young braves throwing off all encumbrances, as if for a race.

With an eighty to one hundred yard lead, he started running. Whooping and yelling pursuers, armed with spears, raced after him. Five miles ahead was the Madison River. Halfway there, he began to stagger. Blood vessels in his nose ruptured from his abnormal exertion.

He stopped, wiping ineffectually at the blood streaming from his nose, waiting for his blurred vision to clear. He looked over his shoulder.

Only one Indian was anywhere near to overtaking him. He was coming on, not too easily, either, a spear in his right hand.

In the interval, Colter turned to face his pursuer, taking deep, steadying breaths, eyeing the spear, wiping his hands along his thighs. As the Indian closed the distance, Colter stood stockstill, even when he could see the gleam of victory in the black eyes intent upon him.

When the brave lunged at him, Colter sidestepped, seized the spear in both hands, yanking the Indian off balance and breaking off the head of the spear. There was time to see incredulity replace the victory gleam before he used the broken-off blade to dispatch the Indian.

Colter made it to the river, where he lay submerged until his other pursuers gave up the hunt. After dark, he crept out. Nine days of travel later he came upon some Gros Ventre and joined their party. Two days later he arrived back at Fort Raymond, limping, after a journey of three hundred miles, carrying the same spear and wearing a Gros Ventre Indian blanket.

Someone, Menard wasn't sure who, for Francis and a number of other hunters had joined them to hear the tale, told without brag or swagger, asked guilelessly, "How many Blackfeet were there?"

Dr. Thomas frowned. It seemed unlikely that even a man of Colter's caliber would be making a head count at such a time. Menard looked for Colter to make a withering reply.

Instead, straightfaced, Colter said, "Eight hundred and three and a half."

"A half?"

"One of them was part Crow."

Menard chuckled. Dr. Thomas laughed aloud. As the current of risibility swept through the rest of the audience, Menard found his day was being lightened. On subsequent birthdays, he would reminisce about his forty-third, bright and carefree and full of fun.

Francis, who had taken charge of casting, said, "Will eight and a half do?" With a wave of his hand, he indicated Dougherty and the men he had helped recruit, Weir, Hull, Pelton, Rucker, Fleehart, Doza and Luthecaw. "Dougherty here is good with Indian dialects. You can teach him the Crow words and he can handle the start of the race."

Thus Colter found himself the adviser and consultant. Menard, Dr. Thomas and Charles Davis, debating seriously with Bryan and the other contestants whether the half-mile course they had laid out to the river would be a true test of strength, found themselves made judges. With Colter, they looked over the terrain, made some slight alterations in the course, which, not until it was too late, did the 'Colters' and 'the Blackfeet' discover included patches of prickly pear.

The 'Blackfeet' jibed at having to pursue the contestants one at a time. They were upheld by the judges. The contestants, loudly, fended off 'the Blackfeet' bent on stripping them to the skin, and appealed to the judges who in turn deferred to Colter.

Grinning wryly, Colter said it would have suited him better, too, so they were allowed to keep on their breeches. Dr. Thomas, tutt-tutting, tossed away the straws they had stashed for breathing underwater. The judges, the adviser and the casting director ruled out weapons of any kind.

The four, Bryan, Cather, McBride and Jackson, ran well, coming abreast of the post they had set up earlier almost together, where the Major waited. They tugged the axes out of his grip in a token struggle, cast them into the post and raced on.

Bryan, who would dine out frequently back in Philadelphia on his Western adventures, hit the prickly pear first. He yelled a warning, then, gritting his teeth, and divorcing himself from his barefeet, kept going.

McBride, warned, leaped over one patch, landed in another. Jackson, imitating him, stumbled into him just as Hull and Weir overtook them. All of them went down, cursing, with Jackson somersaulting to his feet and running on.

The audience, which had been growing as word of the contest spread, was augmented by three curious Indian youths on ponies, who were now paralleling the course. Seeing the fiasco in the prickly pear, Archibald Pelton leaped up behind one youth and urged him on. Just short of the river, he made a flying tackle from the pony and brought Jackson down.

Another youth raced alongside Cather and gleefully pointed out the hiding spot he had found in the river to Rucker and Fleehart who jumped in and 'captured' him.

Bryan, following his hero's example, made it to the river far enough in advance of the pursuit that no one noted his hiding place, a fortuitous accumulation of driftwood near a bed of reeds. Home free, he settled himself underwater and was breathing carefully through the straw Dr. Thomas had overlooked, when an exuberant Cheeky splashed out to his hiding place and tried to sit on his head.

"Dammit," he said, sprawled on the river with the other captives and their captors, all of them, except Pelton, picking thorns out of their feet and other parts of their anatomy. "The Blackfeet chasing Colter didn't have a dog."

"Or horses," said Cather.

"Thank God," said Colter, handing out their moccasins.

By the time they got back to the starting site, they found that all sorts of contests had developed spontaneously. Francis, atop one of the Indian ponies, was doing trick riding turns that the Indian youths were admiring, then topping with some of their own. Several of the hunters were at the throwing post, betting on their skills with axe and knife. Tom James was winning all bets from challengers in the standing broad jump. Cheek was at the rifle range turning in a perfect score. The Major and Menard and Luthecaw were trying out a bow and arrow while the Mandan owner gave them instructions. Other Indians stood around. The same faces that had watched them leave the fort compound were here, eyeing the white men, providers of wonders and curiosities.

Menard, having hit the target squarely with his first try, decided to rest on his laurels. The Major, after hitting the target three times in a row, said, "It's not as convenient as a rifle but it's just as lethal. It's as quiet as a knife or hatchet — sometimes, you need a long-range, quiet weapon." He handed the silent weapon to Luthecaw who began instructing Len Cather in its use.

Menard, spotting Michael Immel, the former US Army officer, observing the activity with a professional air, strolled up beside him, said idly, "Looks like a training field, doesn't it?"

Immel looked over at the Major who was now at the rifle range conferring with Charles Davis and James Cheek. "Planned that way, wasn't it?" said Immel with characteristic dry intelligence.

Menard, intrigued, turned his attention to the Major. He was moving with seeming casualness from group to group, where men were recovering skills blunted in the long weeks of travelling, honing their physical coordination, and listening, imitating, learning from men who were emerging as expert, unofficial instructors.

Belatedly, Menard, who was no inexperienced youth like Bryan, recognized Bryan had been speaking factually when he said the Major was getting them ready to face the West. This assembly of men, none of them strangers to danger and to hard work, was no sudden, spontaneous form of recreation. The organization involved, the assembly of equipment, the physical layout before him was in no way haphazard.

There was Francis Vallé, an expert in horsemanship, and Archibald Pelton, an expert on horseflesh, putting men and Indian ponies through their paces in an atmosphere of fun and games, and coming up with a good idea of the skills and abilities of both, all of it taking place in an area most convenient for such activities.

There was James Cheek, shooting with astonishing perfection, displaying the art of a lifetime, then taking charge of Bryan and his rifle, making sure it was carefully fitted to the firing habits of the man who shot it.

Colter was there, with George Drouillard, where Pet McBride had laid out his gunsmithing tools and was working on Weir's rifle. The habits of each man, the peculiarities of his gun were being analyzed. There were experiments in powder charges, patches, and proof by trial, and careful readjustment of trigger pull. Every man had his own bullet mould and Charles Davis was making preparations to oversee the casting and paring of bullets to best suit Bryan's rifle.

There was his own Alexis Doza showing John Dougherty the best way to make up a blanket backpack, square, rather long or oblong, depending on whether it was for the back of a man or a horse. When he ventured out on foot, Alexis liked his to contain a tinder box with flint and steel, an awl, a packet of needles and thread, a small sack of corn meal, salt, a slab of bacon, and a thin iron plate, bowl and horn spoon, the whole bundle slung over the left shoulder. He also carried an extra powder horn, a few flints, small gun parts, a pipe, and a fine-tooth comb.

Menard, who had come from a harsh northern province, where the schooling was hard as any to be found, was impressed. The men out there, brash, jaunty, and professionally enthralled weren't here for adventure or to be heroes. They came to get something to sell, to make a living. As they shot and wrestled and ran and jumped, learned the use and practice and assembly and repair of assorted weapons, bestrode horses and discussed their peculiarities and maintenance, they were being welded into a unit that would absorb trapping strategy, peltry care, pressing of pelts. A small world, with a high standard of efficiency, bonded by skill and courage, it could move out under its own power and defend itself, not easily daunted in the pursuit of profit.

As October 7, 1809, drew to a close, the man who had started out the day in a disheartened mood, found himself bouncing up and down on his toes, elated, heartened and enlightened. There was more to come.

"A Henry rifle," said Immel now, nodding to where the Major was demonstrating his ability to fire at a target, move swiftly to another location, loading as he ran, and firing from another location, prone, and getting a bull's eye each time. "Is he one of those Henry's?"

"Colonel Henry was a Moravian," said Menard, repeating the answer he had overheard the Major give to that same question early in their acquaintance. Colonel Henry, another Pennsylvanian, had founded a line of famous Lancaster gunsmiths. "M'sieu Henry is a Presbyterian."

"He is very good," said Immel. He wasn't referring to religious affiliations. "Seven! By God, he just could belong to another branch of the Henry's. McClelland would know. He was on the Western Road himself."

Menard waited for an explanation. Immel pointed out the seven, a number of special significance to him. Bryan, Cather, McBride, Jackson, Weir, Dougherty and Cheek. The Major did not compete. When the need arose, he would demonstrate, and the selected men seemed to find his skills worth emulating. And the Major did seem to be sorting the other men into groups of seven.

Why seven? There was a frontier tale of a remarkable seven, Immel told him, who patrolled and protected the western road in the constant petty but merciless warfare thereabouts, taking the offensive, harassing the enemy, making them wary. Seven expert, carefully trained assistants could move over a far-flung spread of territory and live off the land, unobserved. Add a few more, and they would have to carry or cache supplies and move much more slowly.

The activities today had rubbed away any layer of pretense and revealed the real men underneath. If they didn't know how to hurl an ax, use a knife, handle a gun, make, set and shoot bullets, and fork and ride a mount, they were expected to learn. If they didn't, it would be taken into account, too, in assessing the varied abilities, experience, and degree of probable competence and dependability.

Bemused, Menard was not aware of Francis's presence until he spoke.

"All that's been has led us here," said Francis cheerfully, sliding off an Indian pony to stand beside them. "All that's here must lead us on."

"Oui," said Menard seriously. "It will be done."

In the shortening days of October, it was. In the boatyard, he was particular about the repairs, the caulking, the ropes. He gave particular attention to the supplies needed for his fifty men and even more attention to who did, and who didn't, participate in the unofficial and ongoing lessons at the Major's training field.

His men, in their way, he was pleased to see, were as able as those who would go with the Major. Inevitably, his were the men who didn't have a way with horses.

The Major's men did. Outstanding among them was Archibald Pelton, who continued to amuse Thomas James with his songs, sermons, and mock trials of sinful offenders in a caricature of self-righteous New England. Pelton had an affinity for horses that impressed both Francis and Michael Immel, able horseman themselves.

More than one of the Indian ponies whuffled a greeting whenever he appeared. There was one, a gray with reddish freckles on the hindquarters, unless restrained, that followed him around like a pet.

"My heart aches for their poor damn horses," Pelton said, of the Indian ponies. "It's sinful, the way most Indians treat them."

He took charge of the horse herd to the mutual benefit of all, except a foolhardy Minnetaree who tried to stampede the herd one night, got unseated and lost his own pony in the melee. Once the pony made Pelton's acquaintance, it stayed close to him.

The Major continued to work with his other thirty-eight horsemen. Saddles and bridles, saddle bags, water bottles, food wallets were seen to. The men were equipped with warm clothing, boots and bed rolls. The blacksmith made repairs, giving special attention to the precious traps. Rope was precious, too. So were linen and cotton thread. No scrap of hard metal was wasted or tossed aside.

They had fine autumn weather, with good, clear, starry nights. The partners made the most of it.

Following the policies and procedures laid out for the Company, they held regular meetings. Their decisions were duly noted in the book of proceedings, as were the weekly reckonings and the monthly balance sheets, and the necessary adherence to government regulations.

This information, and other collected intelligence, summarized, would be passed on to the President of the Company, General William Clark, in correspondence, and, eventually, in person by Lisa and Colonel Chouteau.

Compensation. Personnel policies. Management staffing and succession planning. Training and development. Employee relations. Work force management. In every area, there were vexations. So far, there had been no flagrant breach of regulation regarding quarreling and fighting, despite the intransigence of Thomas James.

James, hardworking, certain that every American was as good as anyone else, and better than most, was disinclined to reconcile his sweeping assumptions with reality.

The Company had paid for his journey. He resented having to surrender the company-furnished arms and ammunition at the end of that journey. He didn't like the looks of the traps offered to him.

The fort complete, there was no employment for him.

While Henry and Menard were outfitting their men, James seethed, buying goods on Company credit and bartering them to the Indians for his needs, according to his appetite of the moment.

He was also in debt to Colter for $146, or thirty-five beaver pelts, for traps, a gun and a pound and half of powder.

"You were right, Francis," Menard said sitting down on a bench outside the tack shed where Francis, the Major and Dr. Thomas were relaxing. "He is a poor business man."

Menard had just come from a meeting that the partners, the inventory completed and the company men outfitted, had held with the Americans. He had been pleased that their supply of goods had proved sufficient so they could outfit another dozen or so men with half-a-dozen new traps, good guns and ammunition apiece, and on terms he considered fair.

Unlike the others, James was disdainful of the offer. He took satisfaction in telling the partners, Lisa in particular, that he had equipped himself.

"If I remember rightly," said Francis, tapping the horoscope book tucked inside his shirt, "the description was 'makes a poor business partner.'"

"That remains to be seen," the Major said. "He has teamed up with Miller and McDaniel. Those two, with some forethought, came equipped with their own six traps, two guns and ammunition. The three of them have made themselves a dugout canoe and are heading upriver tomorrow."

"That partnership won't last," predicted Francis. "What about Cheek? Hasn't he been staying with them in their tent?"

"Cheek has made an ass of himself and has Colonel Chouteau down on him again," said Dr. Thomas. "He did his best to pick a fight with Francois Ride this morning. Even struck him. Ride got away to one of the boats and Cheek beat a retreat when he saw the reinforcements Ride mustered."

"There is a certain uniformity to Cheek's actions," sighed Menard.

"Particularly after some exposure to James and his litany of grievances," said Francis tartly. "Isn't there some way we can keep our best rifle instructor out of trouble a little longer? We're due to take off in all directions — literally — in only a couple of days."

"Wine, women and song?" suggested the Major lightly.

"Wine, yes," said Dr. Thomas seriously. "He's already been in two fights over women. And he can't carry a tune."

"Keep him off hard liquor and away from James and he's a fairly reasonable man," said Francis.

"Wine it is," said the Major.

So it was. Wine and a congenial card game did keep Cheek in the Major's snug tent warmed by a portable charcoal stove throughout the evening until an agitated Thomas James arrived and persuaded him to return to the James tent.

All their efforts were for naught, they discovered the next morning.

When Cheek left the Major's tent he had been of a mind to let bygones be bygones. By the time James had completed his description of Ride, a trifle high on drink, with an armed company, beating the bushes about the James' tent in search of Cheek, he was provoked all over again. The availability of hard liquor at James' tent did not improve his choleric outlook.

Shortly after sunrise, Cheek accosted Ride in front of the fort. Ride, sober this morning and mindful of the regulations against fighting, strongly enforced in the environs of the fort, was not in a quarrelsome mood, and told him so.

As Ride turned away, Cheek struck him and knocked him to the ground.

Colonel Chouteau, who had been leaving the fort with a number of armed men, witnessed Cheek's violent behavior. Angrily, he ordered Cheek seized and put in irons.

Cheek, unarmed, picked up the blanket he had dropped when

he launched himself on Ride, and retreated to the bank of the river where James, McDaniel, and Miller, armed, watchful, offered protection.

"Shoot the sons-of-bitches," shouted the Colonel, first in French, then in English.

Alerted by a hasty messenger, the Major, Menard, Morrison, A.P., Labbadie and Vallé arrived, cancelled the order. With difficulty, they persuaded the Colonel to return to the fort.

"Let the Blackfeet have at them, Papa," A.P. said soothingly, leading his father to the blockhouse and pouring him a glass of brandy.

"Ah. Oui," said the Colonel. There was nothing kindly in his smile or his toast as he tossed back the brandy. "Cheek! I consign you to the Blackfeet!"

Chapter 11

As October came to a close, with autumn winds whipping all around the compass, combined with sudden drenching storms of rain and sleet, they did, as Francis had predicted, literally take off in all directions of that compass, west, north, south and east.

The Major had forty men and an equal number of horses and hopes of trading for more when they reached Crow territory. With Colter to lay out their route, and Benito Vasquez, anxious to retrieve his cached supplies and secure Fort Raymond for the long winter, urging them on, they made good time.

The business of arrival at the campsite selected by Colter, the unloading and disposition of animals and packs and setting up camp was efficient, orderly and routine. The men were expected to see to their horses before seeing to themselves. Archie Pelton made sure of that before his selected helpers led the horses to water and grass.

Rucker and Freehart fetched such firewood as could be found while others gathered up the ubiquitous buffalo chips and got camp fires going. Bryan set the coffeepot to boil then left the cook, one of Francis's 'Frenchies' that Thomas James had coveted, preparing the meal and went to help Cather, McBride and Jackson set up tents.

The Major posted guards. After nightfall, the men kept watch, four at a time, except for Pelton, who bedded down with the horses.

It was no plodding sentry-go as Bryan and Cather and Jackson and McBride discovered under Colter's tutelage. He expected them to make use of all five senses with vigilance, constantly. With his example to emulate, scouting every direction through the surrounding darkness, and waking the relief when the time came, noiselessly, became an art in itself.

At dawn, the striking of the camp went swiftly, with the same efficient distribution of the workload and attention to detail. None of the Indian ponies, short-necked, sturdy, durable, escaped Archie Pelton's narrow-eyed review at loading time in the morning, either.

"Don't kick that horse in the belly, you cursed sinner," he shrilled one morning half-way through their first week of travel, advancing on William Weir as he was trying to cinch up his saddle, "or I'll do the same to you."

The big Kentuckian, twice Archie's size, was elbowed aside.

"On this one, you use your thumb. Right here. Like this," he said, demonstrating, as he deftly deflated the pony and tightened the cinch.

"Mon Dieu, he is a strange one," Francis said mildly to the Major. "Those horses have become his religion."

"His sermons have an admirable constancy of purpose, however," replied the Major. He had backed up Pelton's edict that Luthecaw couldn't ride until his pony's sore back healed from inept packing. The Shawnee had promptly retrieved a salve of his own manufacture from his pack that, smeared on the raw spot, had healed the pony's back overnight. Archie, impressed, not only allowed Luthecaw to bestride the pony again, but recruited him to search out and treat similar chafing on man and beast. "No one forgets his message."

They watched Bryan, who had been on the receiving end of one of Pelton's biting sermons regarding the care and consideration of his mount, proving, as Archie had told him, that it didn't take any longer to pack a horse properly than to do it improperly.

Bryan, accepting with eager intelligence the physical gaiety of action that has nothing to do with mind or emotion, felt that, of the two groups which parted company for the trip to Fort Raymond, Pierre Menard's had the more uncomfortable journey. To begin with, he considered it hard dull work, poling northwest up the Missouri to the mouth of the Yellowstone, then heading south and west, breaking ice as they pushed their way against the current of the Yellowstone to its junction with the Big Horn.

Menard did have George Drouillard, hard as nails with a will of iron, as able in his own way as John Colter. Bryan, who was getting quite adept at interpreting nuances of behavior, got the feeling that Drouillard would get on well with Alexis Doza, scouting the stream banks, hunting and communicating on a similar cultural and hereditary level. He did not share the same background or rapport with John Colter.

It was said they had started disagreeing under Lewis and Clark, going so far as to quarrel openly until brought into line by the leaders. Since then, representative of their different cultures, they had gone their separate ways in this strange, new land, successfully, never denigrating each other, but maintaining a careful distance. Even Lisa, who had recruited both of them to work for him, never tried to work them in tandem.

Operating in their own distinctive fashions, Drouillard and Colter scouted the two different approaches for Menard and the Major. Drouillard, long and lean and saturnine, reflected some of the characteristics of the river route.

Colter was more like the plains. The land looks flat and unremarkable. It isn't. The smooth even look is deceptive, concealing surprising depths. Even though the prairie growth is seldom higher than the waist, there is a respectable amount of cover, and it conceals more than it reveals.

As the year edged into November, both parties arrived at Fort Raymond. On a wooded point at the junction of the two river, the Big Horn and the Yellowstone, it was an oasis set down in the relative safety of the Crow neighborhood.

The Crows, like the Swiss, were adept at maintaining their sovereignty. The Indian middle man of the plains, with a similar neutral attitude, the Crow was amicable in an astringent fashion, given more to lifting the horses, instead of the scalps, of travellers.

About the same time, Dr. Thomas, along with A.P. Chouteau and the returning militia, travelling speedily south on the Missouri current, was on hand for the courtesy call Lisa and the Chouteau's made at the Arikara villages. They found the Arikara keening over their slain and howling for a retaliatory strike against the culprits, the peace-breaking Sioux.

With the hawks in ascendancy again, verbally sharpening vengeful talons on a muddle of truths and half-truths linking the white traders with the depredations of their pro-tem, perfidious allies, somebody was due to get hurt.

"Well, they told us so," said A.P. tartly, giving some thought to the boiling cauldron of Arikara hostility, the hawks stoking the fire. "They did predict the Sioux would not keep the peace." He was getting a trifle weary of finding himself cast, willy-nilly, into the same scenario, culpable by association. "No shore leave for the hands. Everybody stays on board tonight."

In the dark of night, he gave orders for the boat to slip downstream. He got all on board safely past the Arikara, the boat gliding silently downstream, taking them swiftly out of reach, forestalling an inimical confrontation.

At daybreak, when it was discovered that two men had flouted orders to go ashore, and were now missing from roll call, Dr. Thomas said, "Judas Priest!"

"No," A.P. said grimly, "Shadrach, Meshach, Abednego."

"I heard it was that carnally inclined Aaron Whitney and another fellow from Massachusetts," said Dr. Thomas. "Now they'll have another bout with the clap, the dam fools."

"If they are turned over to the squaws, they'll catch worse than the clap this time," said A.P. bleakly.

"I don't suppose there's any chance — " Dr. Thomas raised his eyebrows questioningly.

" — of rescuing them from the fiery furnace? Mon Dieu, I'm no angel," replied A.P., hitting the rail angrily with his fists. A man may not suffer fools gladly. Still, he knew that primitive nature fired by primitive emotion could be brutal. He did not relish the thought of what those fools might be suffering.

The missing hands were mentioned, briefly, as 'left behind,' in Dr. Thomas's journal, the first installment appearing in Joseph Charles's November 30, 1809, issue of the Missouri Gazette.

He didn't mention the other stops, the Cedar Island assignment for A.P., or Lisa catching hell from Robert McClellan.

Lisa and Pierre Chouteau, Senior, floating on downriver with rewarding halts to collect the furs and optimistic reports from the traders established at profitable locations on the upriver trip, had been congratulating themselves on the success of their undertaking by the time they reached the retreat of the Astor men near Council Bluffs.

They received no congratulations from the aggrieved Crooks, McClellan and Miller.

Instead, the three angry men were critical to the point of libel, attributing their recent dismaying interception by the Teton Sioux to some subtle trickery of Lisa's. Little Billy Goat Gruff. Middle-sized Billy Goat Gruff. And the river trolls.

Colonel Chouteau, exercising all his inherent tact, got the outlines of their misfortune from the more composed, resilient Crooks. Some time after the company had visited Crooks and McClellan near the Oto River, the new partner, Joseph Miller, had arrived with a keelboat of supplies and forty men. Elated, they took off upriver, nearly a month behind Lisa's flotilla. They found the volatile Sioux waiting for them near the mouth of James River and were forced ashore.

No matter what their claims, the Sioux were comparative newcomers to the Dakota area. Up until the 1500's, their ancestors were more agricultural than nomadic, a sedentary people living in North Carolina, who raised corn, potatoes, squash as well as tobacco. For various reasons, individuals, families, kinship groups began to migrate toward the northwest. Some of them were pushed out by other, expanding tribes; some of them developed a taste for the bigger game to be found to the westward; all of them had incipient nomadic traits. On foot, or better yet, in dugout canoes, they began moving along the waterways leading to the Ohio, the Mississippi, and the western Great Lakes.

About the time Jamestown was founded near their original homeland, the Sioux were living high up the Mississippi River in present-day Minnesota. By this time, the early 1600's, their language had evolved into three separate dialects, Santee, Yankton and Teton. They called themselves Dakota in the Santee dialect, Nakota in the Yankton, and Lakota in the Teton.

They weren't the only Indians attracted to the region. Chippewa, Cree, Ottawa, Sac-Fox-Potawatomie, alone and in varying alliances, were ambivalent about the Sioux.

A northern sub-band of the Yankton made a Pact of friendship with their neighbors, the Cree, intermarried with them, developed strong ties. A generation or two later, when the southern Yanktons went to war with the Cree, they expected but didn't get any help from their Sioux kinsmen. The southern Yanktons won out over the Cree, pushing them northward, and at the same time dished out punishment to their northern kin, who never forgave them.

From that time on, this evolving tribe, called Assiniboin in Cree, earned, in hate-filled and unrelenting warfare, their Sioux name, Hohe, the enemy. About 1689, the Assiniboin and the Crees got firearms, teamed up and drove the Yanktons southwestward. This put pressure on the Teton Sioux who gradually moved out of Minnesota. Early in the 1700's, they got horses from the tribes along the Missouri, began developing, adapting and perfecting their nomadic way of life. By 1750 the Yankton and Teton Sioux controlled the eastern part of the Dakotas. A generation later, groupings of Sioux — Oglala, Sicangus, Saones, Minnecanjous, Hunkpapa, Sihasapa, Oohenunpa, Sans Arc — were pushing across the Missouri in various places, moving in the general direction of the Black Hills, shoving the Arikara northward, thrusting aside other tribes in a westward expansion of epic proportions. The Yankton and the branch of the Teton Sioux known as the Lower Brules held onto present-day eastern South Dakota, keeping an eye on the Missouri River traffic and the traders venturing into their territory.

It was these Teton Sioux who interrupted the upstream journey of the Astor men. They were already in a testy mood. The American government had prevented the usual British traders from reaching them but had promised them other traders. Lisa had slipped past them. The Sioux had run out of patience and were in no mood to let another keelboat filled with trade goods row past them. Arrogantly, they directed Crooks and McClellan and Miller to build a trading post for their convenience.

McClellan, inclined to attribute most anything to Lisa but principles, concluded that this high-handed interruption of their voyage was no coincidence. Like Nat Pryor before them, the Astor men, aghast and furious, made some skeptical deductions based on mortification and insufficient data. They decided Lisa, with malice aforethought, had let the Sioux know they would be following him upriver.

As the shortening days of autumn found them in a precarious position far short of their goal, Crooks and McClellan, carefully concealing all doubts and anxieties, presented a facade of brisk confidence to the Indians. They would build the trading post the Sioux demanded.

The Sioux, who derived a certain primitive amusement out of the game of up-manship, kept close watch over the French-Canadian voyagers sweating in fear, the trappers with glum efficiency, as they went about felling trees and erecting a cabin to serve as a trading post.

The leaders of the Astor men mulled over some devious measures of their own to out-maneuver the Indians. The completion of the cabin was the first step. If all went as planned, that would lead to a relaxation of the constraining surveillance.

"We're ready to trade," said Ramsay Crooks at last, in strong forceful tones to the Sioux, who were getting a trifle bored and restless. When the Indians, assuming they now had these traders where they wanted them, leaped astride their ponies and galloped off, shouting triumphantly, on the twenty-mile trip to their village to bundle up their furs, leaving only a handful of guards, he said, "Now?'

"Now!" said McClellan, stretching his muscular frame, his eyes gleaming at the prospect of body-contact sport. The guards were overpowered, tied up.

Crooks, careful to keep out of sight of the captives, got the trappers and their winter supplies into dug-out canoes and headed up-river. In sight of the captives, the remainder of the party loaded up the keelboat. With insulting messages, demeaning remarks and derisive gestures, they concentrated on leaving the Sioux with the impression all of their party were retreating down river.

Now they were back at square one, in the neighborhood of Council Bluffs, decidedly peevish and looking for a scapegoat.

In early November of 1810, when Lisa and Chouteau, looking satisfied, appeared, Crooks, who had the cooler head, didn't lose his temper. McClellan did.

Lisa, whose autocratic airs grated on McClellan as it did on many of the Americans, was a trifle condescending in refuting their charges. Patronizingly, he pointed out that everyone knew the Sioux were unpredictable and piratical. He swore they neither needed nor received any coaching from him. McClellan, unconvinced, swore at him.

"God damn your lying soul to Hell," said Robert McClellan fiercely, "If I ever catch you away from your bully boys, I swear I'll shoot you daid!"

Chouteau, who believed him, bowed frostily. Taking Lisa by the arm, with their backs protected by the armed men McClellan referred to, he led the way out of the embittered camp. As they re-embarked and were poling away, "Rose. Cheek. Now, Mc-

Clellan," said Chouteau, his lips pursed. "Who else wants to kill you?"

"Men? or women?" replied Lisa seriously. "French, English, American or Chinese?"

"Chinese?" repeated Chouteau in surprise.

Lisa touched a long, thin scar on his neck, partly hidden by the faded red bandanna he wore, smiled fiercely, and changed the subject.

Little Mary Fleming, visiting relatives in St. Louis, was one of the first to hear of Senor Lisa and M'sieu Chouteau's return. She had been there, during part of October and most of the month of November, 1809, with her mother and brother, satisfying her curiosity about a great many things in the adult world, including how to balance a tea cup while eating a piece of cake.

Dr. Nicholas Fleming had some business affairs needing attention. Madam Fleming had weddings, christenings, an expiring great-aunt and a lengthy shopping list in need of her attention.

When his mother reported indignantly of her inability to obtain or place orders for many of the items on her list, Dr. Nicholas said it was because international waters were getting muddier than the Missouri.

Napoleon was extending himself on the continent. The British were extending themselves on the high seas and had repudiated the semi-official promises of the British minister to the US, Erskine, to rescind the hateful orders in council against American shipping.

On August 9, 1809, therefore, President Madison had reinstated the non-intercourse decrees against any trade with England. As a result, few goods would be imported into the country, and very few of those would reach St. Louis.

"Men!" said Madam Fleming to her son. To her daughter, "Don't be too disappointed, petite. We'll find someone who can bring you some slippers from Canada."

Mary, who really wanted a pair of Indian moccasins with lots of beadwork, wasn't as disappointed as her mother who had to make do with her old corset.

There were too many new, and absorbing, experiences to evaluate.

An observant realist, she became privy to the life-style of a variety of households, exercising an inherently discrete mixture of curiosity and sympathy. With an open mind, she absorbed much more than her brother and mother realized about the problems, rituals, the fashions, the pleasures and the taboos.

St. Louis at long last was larger than Ste. Genevieve but not so much so that it was intimidating, particularly when your mother was related to so many of the original villagers, and your brother was on good terms with so many of the newcomers.

They were hospitably received and entertained in one household after another, French, American, Indian and Spanish.

Mary, blessed with restful friendliness and a warm, uninhibited outlook, found no single, pervasive, uniform way of life. She perceived the cultural differences, storing away data as she went, to mull over later.

She visited her favorite Bequette cousins, who introduced her to their cousins, and the latter to theirs. She cuddled the new babies affectionately, sang to toddlers, and captivated her contemporaries. In more than one French household of affluence, she and the French children matter-of-factly accepted the presence of the Indian half-sisters and half-brothers.

As had been the French custom for generation, and not unknown in Ste. Genevieve, these children were being raised in their Papa's household and his own Catholic faith, their own Oto, Osage or Maha mother remaining with their respective Indian tribes.

Mary, like her mother, felt an instinctive need to make every creature, two- or four-legged, who entered her gravitational field, happy and comfortable, from the man she adored to the kittens and puppies. She spent considerable time on more than one occasion comforting homesick newcomers.

After giving some thought to the circumstances that put the half-breed Indian children in need of comfort, and making some private, personal projections of her own, Mary asked her brother, "Would the Major's Indian woman be an Oto like little Marie's Mamán?"

Dr. Nick looked away from the candid, intent gaze of his precocious little sister. He considered several replies. He discarded those smacking of an uncharacteristic moral tone.

"Wouldn't be any advantage in taking up with an Oto woman," he pointed out with the easy naturalness that endeared him to Mary. "Andy won't be trading with the Otos."

"Who, then?" persisted Mary. "If they aren't Oto or Maha, what will they be — the children Major Henry will bring back for his wife to raise?"

Lord above, a bright, perceptive — and imaginative child — could confound a man. Still, he felt a sense of personal responsibility for preparing her for the adult world where geography, occupation and religion make the different kinds of societies.

"The Major isn't French, cherie. He's an American," he said in a cool, academic voice. "Besides he's a Presbyterian." And, he added to himself, knowing Mary wouldn't consider it germane, the Major divorced his wife two years ago.

Mary considered his answer. Her brother was a nice person, one who inspired confidence. She could see he had given her an explanation of sorts and hoped to bring the matter to a close.

"We're Americans, too," she said slowly. "That's what you told me. 'American by paternal, French by maternal heritage.' And you said for me to always remember that 'Human nature is human nature regardless.'"

"So I did," he smiled appreciatively, the instructor in him pleased. "Regardless of race, nationality, politics or sex — and few men and women seem able to understand that it is true."

He believed strongly that the purpose of education of the young was to strengthen, not weaken. A way out for him, while continuing her education had just occurred to him. "If you'd like to know more about the country and the people where the Major is, I think I know just the person who can tell you."

Thus it came about that Dr. Nick took his mother and his sister to call on the General and Mrs. William Clark. William Clark and his Miss Judy had been married for nearly two years and were settled into comfortable domesticity with an infant son, named Lewis, for the Governor. The General, a good, sturdy, patient and selfless man, was away from home often, on business.

Miss Judy, friendly and warmhearted, got lonely for feminine companionship. She was taken with the Fleming ladies. Mary became a frequent, welcome visitor.

Dr. Nick recognized that he could not have selected a better example of an American household for Mary to compare with those of the leading French citizens. A conscientious, able man, with good social connections, and substantial political influence, William Clark had a well-dowered wife of grace, accomplishments and good family.

Mrs. William Clark, who had known from the time she was twelve-year old Julia Hancock of Virginia, bidding God-speed to the big fellow heading for the Pacific Ocean, that she would marry him, could identify with another young girl's interest in a grown man, off somewhere following a map her William had drawn for him.

She had a classical education, an inquiring mind, and a hospitable nature. She took an interest in all manner of people and things, particularly those that impinged upon the well-being of her William. When she had occasion to visit the Charbonneau wives to deliver some lengths of promised calico, she invited Mary to accompany her.

"The General says Janey can tell me more than he can about the mountain tribes," Mary told her mother persuasively. "Janey used to live there, you know. She was stolen from her people and carried far away when she wasn't much older'n me. She and her baby went clear to the Pacific Ocean and back with the General and the Governor. She helped them find their way there."

Madam Fleming considered the invitation. She had no qualms

about leaving her daughter at the Clark household while attending to several errands, but she had some reservations about exposing her to a half-breed's household, particularly Charbonneau's. From what she had heard, this Baptiste Charbonneau was a braggart and a coward, with a primitive carnal appetite for barely nubile young girls. Under no circumstance did she intend her daughter to be exposed to his black-eyed, lewd gaze.

"Janey keeps a neat house. I've never been there when she and her little Pomp were not shining clean," Miss Judy told Madam Fleming reassuringly. "She's a bright little thing. Much more adaptable than Charbonneau's other wife. And much more intelligent than anyone else in that household. It isn't far and this is a good time to visit her. Her husband is away on a hunting trip."

Madame Fleming gave a Gallic shrug and her permission. She'd send Dr. Nick to collect Mary before the end of the day.

"Why didn't Janey stay with her people?" Mary asked Miss Judy, as, escorted by one of the Clark negroes carrying the selections of calico, they made their way afoot to the Clark log cabin where the General, from time-to-time, quartered visiting trappers and hunters. "Wouldn't Charbonneau let her?"

"Perhaps she didn't want to. It's a very hard life. She seems happy enough here. She is especially anxious to have her little boy educated here. William is already sending Touissant, Charbonneau's other son to school and will do the same for Pomp when he is old enough.

"William is giving Charbonneau some farm land. Congress granted each of the enlisted men on the expedition three-hundred-twenty acres of land. William says Janey's service should be rewarded, too, and this farm land is one way of doing it. She was a great help to the Corps of Discovery."

While Miss Judy and the Charbonneau women conferred over the calico, exchanging news of the day, Mary played with the effervescent four-year old, Jean Baptiste Charbonneau, known as Pomp. Miss Judy, skillfully, involved Otter Woman in procedure for making her a dress from the calico, drawing her off to one side so that Mary had a measure of privacy in which to put her questions to Janey.

Mary listened to Janey's soft voice as she began diffidently to talk about her home and people. As Mary's unequivocal sincerity came through, she went on, with an eagerness touched with nostalgia, to outlining kinship relationships and values. Before they left, Mary had even mastered the syllables of Janey's Indian name, Sa-ca-ja-wea, and the fact it was not her Shoshone name, but one given her by her captors, the Minnetarees.

At the end of the day, after Dr. Nick had settled his sister in the carriage and clucked to the horse, she gave him a blithe report.

"Oh, I do hope the Major finds someone like Janey. It would be too bad if he got someone like Otter Woman. She is lazy — and she doesn't seem very smart," Mary told him. "Mamán would not care for their house even though it does have a wooden floor. Janey wants her husband to build one just like it on their land. She says it is so much better than any place she ever lived in before."

"I can believe it," said Dr. Nick, dryly.

"Janey is the sister to a chief," Mary went on. "Among her people, her brother is a more important man than her husband."

"I don't doubt that, not one bit," said Dr. Nick. "Her husband doesn't amount to much."

"I don't think that's what she meant," Mary said slowly, striving with the concept of status. "The oldest brother is important in a different way among the brothers and sisters than with us. Among her people, the brothers and sisters are close to each other and their mother, and the papa is close to his sisters and mother and brothers. Grandmothers count for a lot. A funny thing though — if they lived with her people, Charbonneau would not be allowed to speak to her mother."

"I've heard of that mother-in-law taboo," her brother said, impressed with Mary's exposition, and subduing a momentary impulse to joke about the subject. "What else did she tell you?"

Mary skipped Sacajawea's forthright exposition of matrilineal policies and procedures and brought forth the kernel of information she considered to have some bearing on her own aspirations. "She said it all depended on whether the mother was a Blackfeet, a Crow or a Shoshone."

When Dr. Nick looked blank, she went on with innocent candor, "You know, whether the Major will be able to bring his Indian children back here for his wife to raise."

Dr. Nick was beginning to get a rather clear picture of the scenario his imaginative little sister was weaving about herself. "Have you ever considered," he said firmly, deciding it was time to point out the possibilities of her script being revised in a way she might find upsetting, "that there would be no impediment to the Major bringing an Indian wife back home with him to raise their children?"

The sharp intake of breath indicated she was taken aback as she realized there could be unsettling permutations to her scenario. After a long silence, she sought further clarification.

"Impediment?" she repeated. "Does that mean he could marry the Indian lady? Actually make her Mrs. Andrew Henry?"

Her brother nodded. He awaited further questions. Instead, he got a surprising assessment, reflecting that a lively imagination did not preclude facing up to reality.

"I do not think," said Mary at last in firm, very adult tones, "I do not think that Mamán, Madame Clark — or other ladies of good family — would be as nice to a white man's Indian wife as they would a white wife." Although she had found it an effort to grasp the matrilineal concepts Sacajawea took for granted, she had absorbed the matriarchal standards of her own society so well her response was automatic and assured.

"I agree," said her brother. He persisted relentlessly. "What about you? How would you feel?"

"I would feel sorry for her," she said, her brown eyes desolate. "The Major should know better. If he does not —"

She paused then, and her intelligent gaze was downcast as she mulled over the possibilities. Her brother was saying that the Major was free to take another wife at any time. She lifted her chin, met his gaze firmly and gravely, nodded her head in understanding.

After a brief pause, she surprised him with an impish grin.

"I'll do like Mamán says," she assured him, giving a humorous touch to her response, as she answered the implications of his questions with implications of her own. "I'll monogram my linens with a plain ol' 'F' for Fleming. Mamán says an 'H' would not only be unseemly, it would limit my options."

Dr. Nick laughed delightedly. "Thank God for a hard-headed realist. Don't ever 'limit your options'!" He gave her a quick hug. "Anyway, the Major would be highly indignant if he knew we were speculating about his extra-curricular activities."

Mary nodded. "He has gone to the mountains to bring back beaver."

"And that's all I expect him to bring back. The Major, too, is a realist," said Dr. Nick. "Speaking of beaver, I'm supposed to spend some time with cousin Michael in the morning. Want to come along and try on hats?"

"You mean the cousin Michael who makes hats out of beaver? Oh, yes, please. All the ladies say his chapeau have that chic Parisienne touch."

The next morning, early, they visited the Fleming cousin.

A dapper, middle-aged man with her father's bright, penetrating eye and appreciation of beauty, he exclaimed, "Jolie a corquer!" as he bowed over Mary's hand with old-fashioned courtliness, and "Not for that dainty little nose!" touching it lightly, when she spoke of taking a tour of his establishment. Instead, moving with good-natured briskness, he settled her before a mirror with a selection of his finished products.

Beaming with benign good-will, he placed chairs nearby for himself and Dr. Nick.

"The news is not all good for the businessman," he told Dr. Nick, pouring glasses of wine for each of them. "But it is always good to see a little lady interested in the fashions that enhance." He lifted his glass to her in a silent toast. "As she models the chapeau, she will gladden our hearts — no matter how it saddens us to look ahead and see why business will not be good — perhaps for years."

"You old fraud," said Dr. Nick good-naturedly. "You have been saying that business will not be good ever since you went into the hat business."

"Non! Non! Only since your Papa decided to become a lead miner instead of a hatter and got involved in that Mine á Joe. Now, I ask you — what can possibly be aesthetic about lead?"

"The profits?" suggested Dr. Nick amicably.

"There are always profits. Troublesome times make it harder for some, easier for other to profit," said Michael pensively. "Troubles are coming, you know, sure as Halley's Comet."

Sipping the wine, they considered the future. One could not expect the uneasy peace between the British and Napoleon to last. Of more immediate concern to the frontier was Tecumseh, said to be in the Mohawk Valley to persuade the Iroquois to support his confederation. Already hundreds of tribesmen were joining his settlement, intrigued by the unusual concept he was promulgating, the establishment of a great Indian nation. They were staying, fired up by the passionate harangues of his brother, Tenskwatawa, the Prophet, who was promising the more immediate joys of raiding, looting and best of all, ridding their lands of the white man. The British would not mind if Tecumseh and his supporters made war on the Americans. In fact, they would not mind making war on them either. Tecumseh saw the contentions between the two Great White Fathers as a great opportunity — while they wrangled, he went about consolidating his influence and gathering allies.

This was a troublesome time, too, for the Governor of Louisiana Territory. People didn't want their leaders to have problems or show confusion. Poor Meriwether Lewis. He had friends in high places. He also had more than his share of powerful enemies busy with political intrigues and subterfuges. With Madison now president, instead of Jefferson, he had found his procedures questioned, attacked.

Actually, they had an absentee Governor, said Michael. He had departed for Washington, D.C., in September to defend himself against the intrigues of his enemies. He had not been heard from since.

"You know about the pills and patent medicines?" said Michael.

"I've heard," said Dr. Nick thoughtfully. "I know, however, that Lewis has a good basic knowledge of pharmacopeia. It isn't unknown for a man of his education and experience to prescribe for himself."

"What of the melancholia?" prompted Michael. Dr. Nick just

shook his head without commenting. "He was not so moody while he had his jolly friend, the young Chouteau, to share his company and quarters, see that he dined and danced and stayed socially lively. It was not good for him when A.P. went upriver and left him to himself again," Michael went on with placid regret. "He was not so moody until then — but what man would not be upset when politicians hack away at him and try to discredit him at every turn?"

"The mental attitude often reflects, or is even influenced by, the physical," said Dr. Nick sententiously. "He has been known to suffer from bouts of malaria."

"How sad that a man of such rectitude was not politically adept. Governor Lewis is not one who can be bought, cajoled, flattered, or frightened into doing less than his duty. The same can be said of General William Clark, of course. But he has such a way with him, a warmth of personality that turns aside malice and hostility with a smoothness Lewis has never mastered," said Michael dispassionately. "Still, it was only sensible that, before political and financial waters closed over his head, the Governor decided to go to the Capitol and straighten out his muddle of affairs."

Mary could see them watching her in the mirror. She tried on another hat, took it off and examined it carefully, set it aside. Michael raised his eyebrows. "It is too old for me," she told him. "But it would be most becoming for Mamán."

Dr. Nick sighed expressively. "Expensive, too, I'll wager."

"Non! a bargain," said Michael. "You will see shortly. The price of everything will skyrocket. Trade is at a standstill, same as under the general embargo. This will be hard on the fur traders."

Shaking his head dolefully, Michael went on fitting the pieces into a coherent pattern on his futures board. If American government meant to enforce the importation restrictions, it would cripple the fur traders, close their avenues to the trade goods and supplies they required to carry on their business in the field. Always before, despite the embargo, United States citizens had been able to move a measure of trade goods across the Canadian border.

"It is bad enough to see so little coin. Barter, barter, always barter," said Michael. "Now it will be smuggle, smuggle, smuggle."

"Maybe you could work out something with those balloonists," suggested Dr. Nick lightly. "You know, those gentlemen, A.R. Hawley and August Post, who are planning to travel through the air from St. Louis to Canada."

"You think it can be done?" said Michael seriously. "Could they return the same way?"

Dr. Nick shook his head. "Hawley says there are air currents flowing west to east. These will carry them from here to their destination but there's no convenient currents for a return trip. So, cousin, forget about getting your supplies from Canada an easy way."

Mary swivelled around to face the two men. "A list — you could give Mr. Post and Mr. Hawley a list — "

"Ah, out of the mouth of babes!" exclaimed Michael. "An order could be placed for them to deliver to someone reliable who knows how to get across the border — oh, yes, indeed, it does have possibilities!"

Dr. Nick eyed his little sister thoughtfully. "Just what did you have in mind to head that list?"

"At least one brand new corset. It would mean a great deal to Mamán," said Mary eagerly. "I don't think she would mind if it couldn't come back right away by balloon — just so it was coming."

The two men looked at Mary, her oval face framed in a very plain but superbly cut beaver bonnet.

"That's it! That's it!" Michael clapped his hands and leaped up to circle around her, inspecting the tilt and fit of the bonnet.

Dr. Nick shook his head in mock despair. "This outing is getting out of hand. First you find a hat for Mamán, then you encourage dealing in smuggled goods, and now you've found a bonnet made for you — "

Mary showed her dimples. Michael took her part.

"The young lady only makes suggestions on behalf of her incommoded Mamán. She has not so much as hinted for a bonnet. In fact, I will not consider payment. These shall be gifts, such hats as will make your Papa remember our days together." He bustled about with hat boxes. "Please understand, however, the item which will head my list will not be a gift."

"Hah," snorted Dr. Nick. "Corsets will be out of style before you get one here. I'll wager double the cost — not double your charges, you old rascal — that you'll never get one from Canada."

"Done!" chortled Michael, moving to refill their glasses. Dr. Nick waved aside the refill, indicating it was time he and Mary were on their way.

Madame Fleming was delighted with her chapeau. It was a charming choice, as was Mary's bonnet. Preoccupied with other matters, she did not inquire the cost, saying only that she would decide later whether it would be suitable, at this time, for either to be worn.

Great-aunt Pelagie had taken a turn for the worse and died during the night. The deceased octogenarian, contemporary of LaClede, the founder of St. Louis, and his consort, Madame Chouteau, had been highly respected, of good family, substantial property and a certain unexpected obstinacy about the disposal of a coveted heirloom.

However, the redoubtable old lady was not the main topic of conversation at her own funeral.

Word had reached St. Louis that the Governor was dead. No one could say for sure, then or later, whether it had been suicide or murder.

On October 11, 1809, at an infamous establishment known as Grinder's Stand on the Natchez Trace, Meriwether Lewis, travelling alone, was found dead, at age thirty-five. There was no end to the speculations or the rumors and ramifications.

In the burnished mansion of Tante Pelagie, as the leading citizens of Missouri Territory gathered to pay their last respects, one of the deceased was mentioned more often than the other.

The Flemings heard the Governor's career recapitulated from various standpoints. Born to William Lewis and Lucy Meriwether just before the Revolutionary War, Meriwether Lewis, by the time he was twenty was the head of the family, responsible for his twice-widowed mother and her offspring.

Blessed with a respected Virginia heritage, he had received an excellent education, had a varied and honorable stint as a military officer, and spent two years as secretary to President Thomas Jefferson. His service with Jefferson led directly to the apogee of his career, the successful round-trip to the Pacific Coast.

Ever since President Jefferson rewarded him with the appointment to the governorship of Louisiana Territory, Meriwether Lewis had found life difficult. Some of it was caused by the self-serving, the envious; some of it was of his own making.

He had played into the hands of his enemies with the $500 draft drawn to provide Pierre Chouteau tobacco and powder for Indian presents to smooth Shehaka's return. The Secretary of War had refused to honor the draft.

That was the last straw. Lewis, intelligent, but not always politically astute, was finally aware that affairs and the men in charge under President Madison were not the same as under his old mentor and patron, Thomas Jefferson. He felt obliged to go directly to the source of power and present his case.

"One really can't say he had a presentiment, can one? It was just sensible before undertaking a long journey to make out a will. He left everything to his half-sister, Lucy Meriwether, you know. He left William Clark much cast down by the loss, to administer his estate."

"I say he should not have been travelling alone."

"He should have identified himself at that place. Might have made a difference. Travellers who disappear on the Natchez Trace, have been unknowns, seldom influential, or of standing or renown, n'est-ce pas?"

"As for any suicidal bent, who knows?" Psychological breakdown was not unknown. A combination of high stress, excessive demands of responsibility and the unforeseen effects of the lonesome wilderness environment could make a man behave strangely.

"He wasn't thinking about suicide when he told his good friend Amos Stoddard to forward his mail to Washington, D.C., up until the last of December. After that he expected to be back in St. Louis. You can scarcely believe a man who did that was considering suicide."

The talk swirled around Madame Fleming who was viewing the gathering with an abstracted air.

As Auguste Chouteau, Sr., one of the many who had joined the mourning family for refreshments following the final rites for Tante Pelagie, bowed over her hand, Madame Fleming made her contribution to the subject. "The Governor was a fine looking man," she said, "on a horse."

"Oui," agreed the eldest, and the only true Chouteau with a twinkle in his shrewd eyes. "His legs were made for a horse."

"When he wore his tricorn hat, one didn't really notice his ears," said Madam Fleming.

"That's right. He was jug-eared as well as bow-legged," said the blunt-spoken gentleman with Chouteau. Joseph Charless, editor of the Louisiana Gazette bowed over Madame Fleming's hand. "A melancholy sort, particularly when he had been drinking."

"You Americans all drink," said Madame Fleming tartly. "Then you go out and shoot some one in a duel."

Dr. Nick, coming up beside his mother, said gently, "That isn't considered suicide."

"That's debatable," said Madame Fleming sadly, while her glance moved about the room.

"Good men do die," said Charless, mentally at work on the Meriwether Lewis obituary. "The Governor left his affairs in a muddle."

"His brother Reuben is up in those mountains with Major Henry. Poor man. It will be months before he learns the sad news."

Dr. Nick took his mother firmly by the elbow and, while the gentlemen continued their conversation, led her through Tante Pelagie's house until he found an unoccupied room.

He did not think her mind was on the demise of Meriwether Lewis. She had been so fully occupied in the past week that there had not been an occasion, if she had desired, to confide in him.

"Qua'a vez vous?" he asked his mother. "What ails you?"

He settled Madame Fleming in a comfortable armchair next to the warmth of the fireplace. "Something to do with our much-married Tante Pelagie? I'm sure the old lady expected to hold everyone's attention for a day or two. She did have an interesting past."

Born into an aristocratic family in New Orleans, Pelagie had a zest for life and a courageous, nonconformist approach that overcame all obstacles, which included, but had not been limited to, coping with a mixed progeny. She had been married and widowed five times, the last of her spouses a Bequette, related to Madame Fleming's father. To distinguish her from another aunt of the same name, the Patrick Fleming family referred to her as their 'marrying Tante Pelagie,' something Madame Fleming, who was her goddaughter, frowned upon, just as she was doing now.

Dr. Nick was aware that his mother considered her godmother something of a tyrant and, while treating her with courtesy and consideration, had refused to be intimidated. At the old lady's uncharacteristically meek request, she had extended her stay in St. Louis, and spent hours each day at the old lady's bedside, treating her confidences with tact, delicacy and discretion.

The formidable matriarch of an extended family, Tante Pelagie had substantial property, and an inherent obstinacy about its disposal, which kept her family attentive to her slightest wish to the very end.

Reluctantly, Madame Fleming had accepted the old lady's designation of her, not as beneficiary, but as her trustworthy agent. A coveted heirloom said to have a most romantic history dating back to the Sun King himself, must go to a beneficiary who met certain criteria. Madame Fleming could not argue with the criteria or the fact that the beneficiary met them. She did argue that the old lady must make commensurate bequests for each of those who had hoped to get the heirloom.

Those hours with Tante Pelagie had not been all sweetness and light. She had been firm with her godmother. At the end, the priest summoned, Madame Fleming also had in writing some other, more intrinsically consequential and therefore soothing bequests she felt were necessary to keep peace in the family.

"Just what did our late marrying aunt get you involved in, Mamán?" asked Doctor Nick with gentle perseverance.

"Mamán has been smoothing ruffled feathers," said Mary appearing unexpectedly in the doorway. She skipped lightly to her mother's side, gave her a hug and an envelope, slid a footstool under her mother's daintily slippered feet. "That's what Cousin Francois told Cousin Michael. Cousin Baptiste said thank God, he didn't want that damned monstrosity in his house."

"Don't swear, cheri," said Madame Fleming. She smiled at her son's impatient movements as he pulled a chair up next to her. "Oui, Tante Pelagie did present me with a problem. She insisted on giving away the armoire-with-the miroiri before she died. She refused to let Father Lamar administer the last rites until it was carted away to the beneficiary. However, she was amenable about bequests to Cousin Philomena, Selina, and Alida who each felt she had been promised the heirloom. From what Mary says," she patted her daughter's hand, "I do believe there will be no hard feelings in the family. The bequests were selected carefully so as to make the loss of the heirloom bearable."

Dr. Nick, his brows rising sharply, said indignantly, "So that's what has been worrying you. A family feud over a few trinkets."

Madame Fleming, turning over the envelope Mary had given her, felt pleased that neither her son nor daughter were concerned with what, if anything, Tante Pelagie had left to her goddaughter. She hadn't raised greedy, grasping children, thank God. She bestowed a smile of approval upon her children.

She opened the envelope and read the note it contained. Her smile broadened. Here was confirmation that the armoire had been carted without incident to the home of the surprised and surprising beneficiary. She looked up from note.

"We have been invited to tea tomorrow with —" she consulted the signature on the note, "with Polly Charles Chew Lisa."

"Who is invited?" said Mary.

"Why?" said Dr. Nick.

"You and I are, petite, and our hostess. By Madame Lisa. She wants me to tell her about the armoire. And why on earth Tante Pelagie gave it to her."

"The hell she did!" exclaimed Dr. Nick. "I thought cousin Alida — or maybe Selina — would get it."

"Alida is a business woman like her mother. She gets a Mississippi keelboat. Selina is the frivolous daughter. She gets the Bequette pearls. Philomena gets the house in St. Charles," said Madame Fleming with satisfaction. "The armoire goes to a woman of great courage. That is the tradition. Tante Pelagie never said for sure but I believe it was a gift to Pelagie from Madame Chouteau. When Pelagie's first husband died with LaClede, Pelagie was under a great deal of pressure from her family to return to the civilized life of New Orleans. Instead, she took over running the business herself and remained in St. Louis."

Dr. Nick looked thoughtful. "I suppose someone made a gift of it to Madame Chouteau when she took off into the wilds with LaClede?"

"Does it really have a lucky looking glass?" said Mary who had spent a boring afternoon listening to a pair of sub-teens weigh the benefits of their mother's bequests against that of the armoire. "How does it work?"

"Depends on the owner, cheri," said Madame Fleming a trifle sardonically. "Some people, when handed a lemon, can turn it into refreshing lemonade."

She said as much to the new owner. The story she told Polly Charles Chew Lisa had details only another woman could appreciate, with encouraging examples that had more to do with determination and perseverance than good luck. She wound up admonishing her, as instructed, in the words of the long-gone, first owner.

"Don't tell your troubles to other people. Half of them aren't interested. The other half are secretly pleased to know you are getting what's coming to you. Tell all your troubles to the mirror."

So that was how Mary Fleming came to be taking tea at the Lisa house, wondering how Senor Lisa had made sure the dainty china had travelled safely, so far, when the runner came from Hyacinte Engliz.

She was one of the first to hear of Manuel Lisa and Pierre Chouteau's return from the mountains on a Saturday, November 20, in 1809.

Chapter 12

Donna Lisa did not like surprises. After one smarting experience, Hyacinte Engliz, Don Lisa's dependable agent, kept that fact in mind. Hy had a great deal of respect for this woman. He had found her reserved, with lots of dignity, and, in a very ladylike manner, plain-spoken, with no beating about the bush.

The instant he received word, Hy sent a messenger to Donna Lisa. That high-toned Frenchman and Don Lisa had reached St. Charles.

The messenger, questioned, could only tell Donna Lisa that her husband was safe and well. Following orders, he hadn't lingered for details. For all he knew, Don Lisa might be galloping right on his heels overland from St. Charles; or, as he sometimes did, Don Lisa could be continuing by keelboat all the way to St. Louis.

Donna Lisa, if you want the truth without molasses, was a mite peckish over Hy's timing. Just this once he would not have been in Dutch if he had procrastinated a trifle.

The news, despite its inexact nature, played hob with her plans and the small, intimate tea party at the Lisa house. The messenger had arrived just after the new baby had been handed around, cooed over, and returned to the beaming negro nursemaid, just when everyone was ready to settle down to a satisfying, feminine afternoon. Instead of relaxing in the hospitable atmosphere, the ladies on her carefully selected guest list, Mrs. William Clark, Mrs. Francois Bequette and her house guest, Mrs. Patrick Fleming, made the moves all ladies do when the man of the house is expected, unexpectedly, to cut short their visit.

The hostess, who sometimes thought of herself as the late Polly Charles, tried to stay them.

"We know how it is," said Mrs. Clark in her light, girlish fashion, as cheerful as her becoming crimson wool dress. "When the man of the house comes home, he wants you to himself."

"And then he wants something to eat!" Mrs. Fleming teased her in a friendly fashion, brushing a crumb from the lap of her black silk as she rose to her feet.

Mrs. Clark blushed. The ladies, including Mrs. Clark, all laughed gently, knowingly, together.

The little Fleming girl, subconsciously aware that only the initiated sisterhood could share their amusement, ignored them.

"Madame Lisa," she said politely but firmly, looking up at her hostess with a serious light in her brown eyes, "I would like to meet Senor Lisa. There are questions I wish to ask him."

She appeared a smart, taking little girl. Donna Lisa liked her style. She hadn't even blinked to find her hostess was an American, much like Mrs. Clark, and not Spanish.

"Senor Lisa has been gone a long time," Mrs. Fleming said with mild reproval. "He would be polite, Mary, but not particularly pleased to find us monopolizing his wife."

"Another day you can come see Mr. Lisa," said his wife, smiling at the child, who was plainly disappointed.

"When?" the little girl asked with artless directness.

Mrs. Fleming made stern clucking noises with her tongue.

Reluctantly, Mary rose from her chair. She set the white and gold-banded tea cup and saucer carefully on the table with the rest of the handsome tea set, and joined the ladies in their bundling up before venturing out into the brisk November afternoon. She decided that even if she had been allowed to stay, Senor Lisa would have had other priorities, such as the new baby boy, a darling, and, from what she had overheard, an event that Senor Lisa had hoped to get home for, but was six weeks too late.

"You are fortunate to be forewarned," said Miss Judy, giving her hostess an affectionate hug in farewell, as Mrs. Bequette dawdled with cloak, bonnet and gloves, all in unrelieved black for mourning her mother-in-law. "William just strides through the house shouting, 'I'm home. Where are you?'"

As they waited on Mrs. Bequette, adjusting her bonnet before the handsome wall mirror, Mary said thoughtfully, "Papa always says, 'Where the hell's your mother?'"

The ladies laughed again in a way that shut her out.

"Mr. Lisa is going to feel real bad about Governor Lewis," said Polly Lisa quietly to the General's likable little wife. "Folks going around saying he committed suicide — they're full of prunes." She shook her head sadly. "Poor Rueben Lewis. Mr. Lisa will probably be the one to take the word to him, months from now."

After seeing her guests on their way, Polly spent some time with the cook and hired girl, giving them some strokes. Although some households had slaves, and Manuel had tried to interest her in such an investment, she preferred hired help. Even the negro nursemaid who was so dotty over little Manuel was a free woman. She had her own reasons, ones that made her tremble at times, for this aversion to 'owning' another human being. Her husband had been understanding in his way, but it was something they had never really discussed, what it was like to be 'owned' by someone. She knew and still had nightmares about it.

She left her helpers happily planning the menu for Manuel's

welcome-home dinner and made her way to her bedroom. As she entered she could see herself reflected in the gift mirror, which loomed large in the armoire against the farthest wall. She advanced upon her reflection, looking for traces of the late Polly Charles.

Nothing could faze that girl. Bright as a button, brought up not to make a show of herself, to keep a tight rein on her feelings and never let her firm spine loll against the back of her chair. The late Polly Charles, happily married, suddenly, bloodily the Widow Chew, and an Indian captive, had needed all her backbone to keep herself and her baby daughter alive.

Over a dozen years ago, Manuel Lisa had found her, one among the forlorn white captives, delivered through government intervention and set down in Vincennes, disoriented, haggard, apprehensive. Donna Lisa did not like to recall, nor had she ever let on, publicly or privately, how it had been for Polly Charles Chew, the secret heights and depths. After the initial desperation and panic she had been clear-sighted and pragmatic in her determination to save her infant daughter. Alone, the only steadying force her own judgment and patience, she had put aside her grieving and bent to dissimulation. Cold-bloodedly and swiftly she turned herself into a submissive, proper Kick-a-poo woman, and, protected and provided for, she and Rachel had both survived.

In the beginning, she had hoped for rescue. Two years later, when it came, she feared it was too late. She thanked God then, that just before she had been ransomed, her body had rejected the Indian implant. All she carried away from her Indian home was her own white child.

She was still weak and listless from the miscarriage, vulnerable in her sensitive awareness of the prejudices of frontier society, when she lifted her chin and put her shoulders back and went out to run the gauntlet: the self-conscious, compassionate and quickly averted eyes of the white men; the gimlet intensity of the probing eyes of the assessing white women. For one-hundred-fifty years, the brutal, the prurient details of captivity had been woven into frontier knowledge. Those descriptions, gabbled by rescued captives such as the Ferguson woman, gave frontier women nightmares. Bad dreams or not, they knew the scenario, and with doleful shakes of the head, they waited with self-righteous condescension to be sympathetic over the details. It was plain Polly Charles Chew was very ill, not up to giving details. Disappointing, in a way, but it left a lot of room for titillating speculation.

They said she had shown backbone. No one knew how much. Or in what fashion. There was talk, some of the ambivalent speculations designed to be overheard, and it rankled, but Manuel had been her shield. In the end, it was Manuel who got talked about.

William Henry Harrison, at Fort Washington, had inquiries made about the piratical-looking stranger, why he was in the area. He was a New Orleans merchant, it was said, captain of his own boat on the Mississippi, with a store in Vincennes.

Manuel said he had come looking for her. She doubted it. He said he had envied Samuel, which she conceded could have been possible, once upon a time. Other men had.

That day when he took Rachel, nearly three years old, gently from her arms, she was swaying back and forth on her feet. Mazy in the head, she sought for the English words to tell him Rachel was very, very sick. All she could summon up, peevishly, was, "Oh, Thunderation!" before collapsing into his arms, unconscious.

Samuel hadn't been there when she needed him, never would, never could be again. Manuel had taken charge, placed her and Rachel in the care of his mother, Donna Maria Ignacio de Lisa y Rodriguez.

That wise lady from the venerable Spanish settlement of St. Augustine had married one of the officials sent to Louisiana when Spain took over from France. A native of Murcia, Spain, the transplanted Christobal de Lisa made a home for his family in New Orleans where he worked as a customs official. The de Lisa sons, Joseph and Manuel, were born there, and Christopher was buried there.

The widowed Donna Maria divided her time between her two sons. An observant woman, who had wondered if her rapscallion Manuel would ever provide her with an acceptable daughter-in-law, she knew a lady when she saw one. He could do worse than this strange American, 'the charms of her beauty all fled.' She set about nursing the frail wraith back to health.

While Polly lay sick and helpless, Donna Maria and Manuel had seen to Rachel's baptism and care. Eventually Polly had summoned the strength to rise from her sickbed, and enter into a new life, the cherished wife of Don Manuel de Lisa.

Manuel was only twenty-four when they were married, with some upper-class connections and a bit of the grandee about him in style and sophistication. Unlike his father and his brother, Manuel's only interest in the civil service was in overcoming the bureaucratic restraints on his free-wheeling style of commerce. Already prospering, he was edging out the incompetent, disconcerting the complacent. A bit of a visionary, toiling long hours, he was even more of an opportunist.

In the decade since they had moved to St. Louis he had become a man of considerable property. He owned lots and houses in St. Louis, a warehouse, a flour mill, bought and sold slaves, provided employment for all manner of callings, from keelboatmen to bakers. When he bought sixty arpents of land from Joseph

Taillon, followed by a Spanish land grant of six thousand arpents, she hadn't been sure how much that amounted to in acres. Since the coming of the Americans, who put an arpent at close to an acre, there had been added Joaquin's six thousand arpents.

When Joaquin decided to take his family and return to the familiar environs of New Orleans, where he was now a US customs official, he had deeded his land grant to Michael. Which was only fair since Manuel had wangled the land grant for him in the first place. Roughly, it all came to twelve thousand acres which, except for some cattle, an undetermined number of hogs and squatters, remained rough and undeveloped, for Manuel was no stolid toiler of the soil. He was a wangler.

He looked to make a profit and usually did. Wholesale or retail, he handled everything from fine glassware to chamberpots, from coffee to guns. He had a knack for coming up with stock for his retail trade when other merchants couldn't.

He kept up with his old contacts in New Orleans, adding new ones as he broadened his base. In Vincennes, it was Francis Vigo and Touissant Dubois. In Kaskaskia, Menard and Morrison. In Louisville, Dennis Fitzhugh. In Philadelphia, Francis W. Geisse. In Pittsburg, Judge Brackenridge. In Detroit, Richard Pattinson. In Montreal, George Gillespie. In St. Louis, he had made common cause with most everyone at one time or another.

Polly remembered that in 1802 it had been the partnership with Charles Sanguinet, his son-in-law Francis Marie Benoit and Gregory Sarpy. In 1803 he bought out Sanguinet, Benoit and Sarpy. Manuel wangled a flour mill out of his partners and the Missouri Osage trade monopoly away from the Chouteaus.

The winter of 1803 and 1804 saw Manuel involved with men and supplies at Wood River, brought Lewis and Clark into their lives. 1804 saw the departure of the Spanish, rather slowly. From March, when the government was turned over to Major Amos Stoddard, representing the US, to October, Spain paid Manuel rent on the log house at Third and Elm, quartering there the Spanish troopers awaiting evacuation to New Orleans.

He wrangled with Joseph Robidoux over the Pawnee trade and a two-thousand dollar note, was thrown in jail by Governor Delassus in 1803 for lese majesty as much as anything, but she remembered 1805 and 1806 as his suing years.

To collect money due him, Manuel took over twenty people to court. He got $1,185.33 and court costs in his suit against Robert McClellan, and the man's enmity. He got on the wrong side of Major Zebulon M. Pike when he had the sheriff arrest and haul in Pike's interpreter, Baroney Vasquez, for a four hundred dollar debt. He didn't get the money but got the attention of Governor James Wilkinson, who went Vasquez's security, and on record as suspecting Lisa of despicable intrigues. Worse yet, Wilkinson, himself a shrewd conspirator, even then in the pay of the Spanish government, took a dim view of the Sante Fe expedition Manuel was planning with Jacques Clamorgan.

Manuel, with his Spanish roots, found nothing disloyal or injurious to the United States in the idea of promoting trade with Sante Fe. An associate of his, and an American, had already made the attempt. William Morrison, in 1804, had fitted out a small expedition headed by Baptiste La Lande to explore a suitable route and trading potentials. Unlike Morrison, who thought La Lande dead, or a Spanish prisoner, Manuel suspected La Lande had found the comfort and hospitality of Sante Fe, particularly its senoritas, too pleasant to leave, a conclusion eventually confirmed by Major Pike.

In 1807, when Jacques Clamorgan proposed Manuel join him in sending an outfit to Sante Fe, Polly had reservations, but Manuel was agreeable. If anyone could take on a complicated project and see it through with a minimum of disastrous mistakes, it was Manuel. He had a talent for taking on some scheme with a hundred dangerous, dangling loose ends and making it work, a talent Clamorgan recognized.

Polly, like many people, was ambivalent about the man Clamorgan. There was nothing unusual about the fact Clamorgan had been a slave trader in the West Indies, a merchant, a land speculator and explorer. Gossip said it was unusual, and a trifle reprehensible, for him to enjoy an exotic negro harem, four lively, natural, acknowledged issue of same, while a respectable church warden. Polly had said dispassionately, "What church *does* he belong to?"

From her contacts with the man, getting older and stouter, she thought he could be as much Welsh as Portuguese, his integrity as questionable as his ancestry.

"Stick to your last," she had told Manuel when Wilkinson's rancor surfaced. "You've got too many irons in the fire. Pull out of the Clamorgan deal."

Manuel, who counted on his mate being helpful in supporting his ambitions, was mindful of the possibilities of reprisals from Governor Wilkinson if he didn't stick to the last Polly had mentioned. This was the partnership with Menard and Morrison and the first organized trading and trapping expedition to journey up the Missouri to the Rocky Mountains.

Verbally and in person, he did pull out of the deal and headed up the Missouri. That was the time he was gone from home for eighteen months, leaving her and Hyacinte Engliz to deal with affairs on the home front. It was midsummer of 1807, with Manuel five months and hundreds of miles up the Missouri, when Clamorgan wrote to her and Hyacinte.

The Sante Fe expedition, headed by Louison Beaudoin, a veteran, unscrupulous St. Louis trader, was departing for Sante Fe, with Clamorgan himself going along. Promptly, Polly and Hy wrote back, reminding Clamorgan that months ago Manuel had told him he wanted nothing to do with the Sante Fe undertaking.

There was no getting away from the fact, however, that Manuel and Clamorgan had gone in debt to the tune of $12,000 to Francis Geisse in Philadelphia to outfit the Sante Fe expedition, and Manuel had obtained a license to trade with the Republican Osages, whose territory lay across the westward route to Sante Fe. In April, 1808, $6,459 of that debt was due and payable but neither man was around to do anything about it, so it was tabled until Manuel's return.

While he was gone Meriweather Lewis had replaced James Wilkinson as Governor. She had signed the petition circulated to incorporate the city of St. Louis. Hyacinte said Nathaniel Pryor, unhappy over having to scoot back down river with Shehaka undelivered, had put the blame on Manuel for the enmity of the Sioux.

Hy also said there was going to be trouble over the death of Antoine Bissonnette so Polly had a talk with Edward Hempstead, the lawyer and native of Connecticut. He was ready when Manuel and George Drouillard pulled into town the first week in August of 1808 and got them released from detention.

The trial of George Drouillard for the death of Antoine Bissonnette took place before the Honorable J.C.B. Lucas, presiding, and the Honorable Auguste Chouteau, associate, on September 23, 1808.

Polly didn't attend the trial by Hy did. It went pretty much as he had assured her it would. The hunters and tradesmen took a keen interest in the case for the prosecution; the traders, in the defense.

The facts, as they emerged, were covered thoroughly, with depositions, copies of agreements and personal testimony. Manuel Lisa, in partnership with Pierre Menard and William Morrison, two merchants of Kaskaskia, in the Illinois country, had been the leader of a trading and trapping expedition to the upper Missouri; George Drouillard and Antoine Bissonnette, employees. Menard and Morrison, remaining at home, made George Drouillard their representative.

George Drouillard, as the defense lawyers, Edward Hempstead, William Carr and Rufus Easton, brought out, had served Lewis and Clark with distinction. He was known as an honest, loyal man without ill will toward anyone. Antoine Bissonnette had deserted deliberately, making off with company property, after contracting legally to a three-year employment agreement.

When Lisa and company left St. Louis April 19, 1807, Bissonnette was one of the engages who had signed the typical contract to hunt, trap, unload, reload baggage, do guard duty and obey such reasonable orders as might be given him from time to time by those in command.

Bissonnette had not been with the expedition much more than two weeks when, for reasons he never revealed, he prepared to go awol, began squirreling away supplies in strategic caches for retrieval on his homeward flight.

On May 14, 1807, one-hundred-twenty miles upstream, at the mouth of the Osage River, Manuel discovered Bissonnette had deserted. Deciding to make an example of him, and an object lesson for any others thinking of taking such French leave, Lisa ordered Drouillard to bring the man back 'dead or alive'.

George tracked the man down, turning up the emptied caches in the process, and shot Bissonnette when he tried to evade capture.

"That's well done," Manuel was reported by witnesses to have said when Drouillard brought the wounded fugitive back to him. "That's a rascal who got what he deserved."

Witnesses also reported that Lisa tried to find out why Bissonnette had deserted but he would give no reason. Obviously in no condition to carry out his contract, Bissonnette was loaded into a canoe and launched downstream to St. Charles for treatment for his wound, while the rest of the expedition continued upstream. Before reaching St. Charles, Bissonnette died.

The jury took only fifteen minutes to arrive at a verdict of not guilty. George Drouillard was free.

"Somehow," said Hy sardonically, "everyone, including William Carr, for the defense, and George himself, consider Manuel to be the one who should be blamed for Bissonnette's death. Fortunately, no one asked Manuel himself. His fellow traders are too elated."

Polly could see why. The verdict put them in the driver's seat with a whip hand. They had all been hopping mad at deserters at one time or another.

You couldn't blame a trader. Once he had given a man supplies and credit he expected some return on his investment. To keep order and discipline, ward off Indian attack, a leader had to rely on force. They didn't cotton to being left in the lurch when the going got rough.

Shooting deserters in order to maintain discipline was a fact of life in the military. Now the traders, within the civil law, could be equally tough on deserters, if they could catch them.

The verdict would gall the hunters and boatmen. Polly thought it was too bad Manuel hadn't come down off his high horse to let such men know he had given some thought to their rights. He was working on a revision of the statutes concerning engages. There would be a registry for contracts and provisions for either party to the contract to sue for his rights. Deserters were to be jailed; anyone harboring a runaway, subject to a stiff fine.

Manuel, himself, didn't have time for re-hashing the trial or events leading up to it. He was faunching at the bit over the delay.

He wanted to get a move on, start back up the Missouri with hundreds of men to fan out from the Mandan villages to the Columbia bar, harvesting the wealth of furs there. He knew he would bite off more than he could chew if he tried to do it with just Menard and Morrison's backing. Oh, those two were pleased with their profit, as he was, and if all else failed, would continue the partnership. For what he had in mind, however, he was going to have to cast about for additional investment capital.

He took off for Kaskaskia to confer with Menard and Morrison, then, with their blessing, on to Louisville to sound out his friend, Judge Dennis Fitzhugh, Fanny Clark O'Fallon Thruston's third husband.

As a successful merchant, Fitzhugh made a qualified commitment. As a lawyer, he went into the pros and cons of corporation versus a partnership. For Manuel, a corporation would be best, give him management control. If he was serious about disarming his main competitors, the Chouteaus, he would have to offer a partnership. They believed in exercising as much control as possible over their investments.

When all was said and done, at the banquet to celebrate the signing of the Articles of Association and Co-partnership, Polly had a gander at the men who made up the St. Louis Missouri Fur Company. Except for Fitzhugh, they were all there, and some of the wives.

William Clark and his exquisite Miss Judy. Pierre Menard and his doll, his adored second wife, Angelique Saucier. Pierre Chouteau, Sr., and his second wife, Brigitte, another of the attractive Saucier sisters.

Clark and Chouteau, courageous and bold, especially in supporting anything or anyone they believed in, be it friend, cause or idea. The younger Chouteau, at twenty-five just half his father's age, but with the same assurance and charm. A trained, experienced military man who had resigned his commission to join his father in the fur trade, he knew how to take and hold the high ground in any endeavor. Once he adopted an idea, he was a most enthusiastic and convincing promoter, a practical thinker who quickly mastered all aspects of a situation.

Sylvestre Labbadie, the other young man of French family, was another kettle of fish. His late father of the same name had married the youngest Chouteau girl, shared in many Chouteau enterprises profitably. The son had benefited from his example, had done well in land speculation. He'd had some military experience under the Spanish regime as well as with Clark's Fire Prairie expedition. Young Labbadie made a good first impression, fair of face, with an athletic build, ready for adventure, smiling and laughing at the prospect. He gravitated to the powerful and influential, would work with anyone he thought would be of use to him in some way. If he became bored he would want to withdraw, move on.

Reuben, for the Lewis family, to whom he was genuinely devoted, was a steady fellow, his smile easy and generous. He was very proud of the accomplishments of his brother, Meriwether. He was pleased to have his friend and companion on the Fort Osage adventure, Labbadie, sharing in this endeavor.

Benjamin Wilkinson, like all the Wilkinsons, had enormous faith in himself. Unlike James, he had a permissive attitude toward others, and expected the same treatment. In a social setting, his attention moved from person to person, idea to idea, looking for new areas to explore. He had a taste for travel, successful deals, but would let others take on the responsibility of administration.

In contrast, William Morrison was an energetic man who inspired activity in others. Trained by his uncle and partner, Guy Bryan, Morrison had a reputation for hard work, perseverance and shrewdness. Still, underneath that ruddy open countenance there was a tremendous ego that thrived on success, one that would be resentful and critical of failure.

Pierre Menard, now, was plain and simply, a good man. Good features, good physical coordination, good mind, good manners, good-hearted, and a good husband, father and friend. He took pleasure in making careful plans, then in promoting those plans, and had taken personal pleasure in getting his brother-in-law's interest and support. With his easy-going disposition, he wouldn't like contention. It would pain, irritate and exhaust him.

The successful young man of the lead mines, Andrew Henry, neat and quiet, was an unknown quality. Vouched for by his fellow Masons, Clark and Chouteau, he had the manner and carriage of the well bred gentleman, dignified and erect, with a pleasant face, and intelligent, humorous gray-blue eyes. Menard considered him reliable and dependable. Morrison thought his greatest asset was his understanding and rapport with American frontiersmen. It was well to have a partner who'd had much experience on the frontier and possessed that force of character you see in men who have a successful undertaking or two under their belts. From hardy, stock, with proven leadership abilities, he'd be a valuable asset.

As for her Manuel, he was a workhorse, by nature competitive. She had no illusions about his strengths and weaknesses. Everything he did had a purpose and he was always going about his work even in a social situation. Discriminating, selective, critical, striving for perfection, single-minded, he was ruthless in eliminating anyone no longer useful to him. There was more truth than poetry in the rumors that he could be ungrateful and treacherous. With Indians, he was true-blue, and proud of it.

Restless and flamboyant, he was so different from Samuel. Contention. Litigation. Samuel had never gone to law about anything in his life. Manuel and his confrontations had been frightening at first. Sue and be sued. Denounce, defy authority, be taken into custody. Samuel had never gone about picking fights either. He had fought well when forced to it, but not well enough at the end, when there were so many Indians . . . .

The woman in the mirror glared at her. "Forget it!"

She closed her eyes making her mind go blank. When she opened them she didn't look into the mirror. Instead, she noticed for the first time some carving on the pale hardwood frame.

'Voir clair' at the top. At the bottom, winding in and out among a vine of some kind, it looked like 'avoir du cran.' Somewhere along the line, one of the previous owners had inserted the reminder to 'see clearly.' Another, and Polly grinned to herself, had been more forthright, acknowledging the need to 'have guts!' She was not given to flights of fancy but she could not help but wonder what those other owners had sought — and found — in the mirror to keep them going.

After all she had done to keep Rachel safe, shortly after they left Vincennes to settle in St. Louis, Rachel had died of the putrid sore throat. From then on there was no longer even an absent-minded exchange in Kick-a-poo to remind her of the captivity.

Manuel had wanted children. She did not catch easily. When she did, she did not carry well. With every embryo she lost, she suffered guilt, worrying that it was her punishment because she had not mourned the one conceived in captivity. After she had produced a son for Manuel, she had been less vulnerable, then last February they lost their eldest, little Sally. Manuel had been with her to share her grief which had helped some. Shortly thereafter, she was sure she was pregnant again but did not share the good news immediately.

This time there would be no disappointment for Manuel. She was in good health when he left in June, the baby boy quickening strongly. Her labor had been comparatively easy. This second son for Manuel was perfection itself, healthy, hardy and flourishing on the milk-filled breasts of his wet nurse. The ladies said they had never seen a happier, healthier baby, not quite two-months old. There should be no guilt for her.

"Where is your backbone?" she demanded of the woman in the mirror. "So you have had some ups-and-downs. Who hasn't? You've always managed to find a protector. You're that kind of woman. Not everyone has been so lucky."

She gave some thought to the original owner of her strange bequest, how she came to have this unusual piece of furniture. The poor girl spurned the opportunity to become the mistress of the Sun King in order to marry the man of her choice. That weak-livered man was furious when he found it meant exile to the New World for both of them. He abandoned her somewhere along the route, sneaking off the ship at one of the islands of the West Indies, with all their ready cash.

She ended up in New Orleans, alone and penniless. She made out somehow. When she sailed back to France after the Sun King died, she was well-to-do. She handed on the 'lucky looking glass' to another brave young woman.

Polly frowned. That lecherous, aging monarch, whose own plentitude of mirrors told him his own brightness and appeal of youth was gone forever, wasn't really being all that generous with such a gift. Oh, it was something special, all right. Even a hundred years later, a looking-glass was not a common household furnishing, particularly out here on the frontier.

There was malice in that choice, though. Every time that pretty girl who had spurned him looked into it she would see she was growing old, too. She fooled him, though. She made it 'growing up.'

"Mrs. Manuel Lisa, it's about time you did the same. Act like a grown-up instead of a big boobie. Show some backbone!"

She put her hands to her hair, smoothing back the sides. In trying to anchor some loosened locks back into the chignon, several more came loose, unfurling into waves over one shoulder. There was nothing staid-looking about her reflection now.

With an impudent toss of her head, she flung her arms up and hummed a measure of the flamenco air the guitarist had strummed for the Spanish dancer that had entertained at their last party. Holding her hands on high, she began clicking her fingers. In a surge of newfound gaiety, she essayed the steps of the dance, falling into the rhythmic rattling of her heels as Donna Maria had taught her, whirling about and looking arrogantly over her shoulder into the mirror.

There, suddenly, without warning, she saw her husband reflected, leaning against the doorjamb, his arms folded, eyes darker than his hair, savoring the moment. He had bathed and shaved and changed into his short jacket and form fitting pants before leaving St. Charles so that he appeared more Spanish grandee than returned rover.

"Ole!" she exclaimed, looking down her nose at him, not missing a step. She found him just as magnetic and vital as the first time she laid eyes on him.

"Ole!" he replied without hesitation, moving with easy-flowing masculine grace into the pattern of the dance. It had been a long time since they had danced together, encouraged by Donna Maria, who had discovered this introduction to Spanish culture was good therapy for her daughter-in-law.

She whirled away from him, as he hummed a measure. "How did you get here so quickly?" She rattled her heels. "We just had word you had arrived in St. Charles."

Bold, bright eyes meeting hers intently, Manuel advanced, his hands held at his side, his heels a staccato, passionate assertion. "You were making yourself bonita for me?" He tilted his head toward the mirror, standing very close to her. "Querida mia!"

She stomped her heels at him, feeling the positive warmth of his attraction.

"Remon?" he asked about their son, his face aglow with vitality and the joy of life. "And the new baby?"

"Bueno. Remon is spending the day with one of his playmates." She whirled away from him. "Your new son is a chip off the old block." She whirled back into his arms. "You can see for yourself — later."

"Ole!" cried Manuel exuberantly, gathering her up in his arms and carrying her to their bed.

Their reunion was deliciously carnal and abandoned, a happy match of two people well-acquainted with the responses of the other. Later, lying with her head on his arm, idly twining the hair on his chest into curls, Polly felt like a new person. This man was a constant in her life that had never wavered. His presence made her feel safe and secure. He could be an anxiety, an irritant, but life was both more exciting and more complicated when he was at home. All that abounding good health and vigor, the hearty appetite for the good things of board and bed, the enthusiasm he brought to all his undertakings. She took pleasure in watching him move, thinking, planning, seldom still for long.

Just as now, with, "Where did you get that monstrosity?" he padded, stark-naked, his olive skin gleaming in the light from the late afternoon sun shining in the window, to the armoire-with-mirror. Tapping, probing, he assessed it with the experienced touch and shrewd eye of a merchant. She summarized the history of the mirror and how it had come to be hers.

"Could be the mirror was made in France," he said. "The

wardrobe was not done by the same hand. One was an artisan. The other an artist. A shame to have cobbled up the original work."

Polly suggested that the wardrobe could have been built to hold the mirror, at a later date, to make it more stable, easier to transport. Perhaps when it belonged to Madame Chouteau, when she packed up all her household goods and jointed LaClede at his new town of St. Louis. Manuel thought it might have had something to do with the tax system under the Spanish, when mirrors, along with windows, chimneys and other amenities were heavily assessed.

"Not much resale value. Too many emigres dragging around heirlooms from the old regime nowadays."

"It isn't supposed to be sold."

He lifted a sardonic eyebrow. "You can only give it away?"

She nodded but didn't tell him that when she gave it away it was to go to someone who needed it more than she did.

"I'm hungry," he said, turning away from the armoire.

She giggled. Mrs. Fleming had named the priorities correctly. She suggested he get dressed, take a look at his new son, while she clothed herself. When she joined him, he was well-turned out, meticulous as always about his appearance, and had his baby boy in his arms. He was very proud of both of them, he told her, and would next week be too soon to have the christening party?

In the days that followed, the tempo set by the master of the house was closer to the fandango than the minuet. A man of enthusiasm, who liked to judge and shape events and people, with an innate belief in his ability to look after himself and those dependent upon him, he thrived on responsibilities and obligations that would have overwhelmed a lesser man.

They were both early risers, so the day started off with a hearty breakfast of ham, eggs, cornmeal mush, biscuits and gravy, and a favorite breakfast dish of Polly's which Manuel sampled occasionally, mince pie, even as he wondered aloud what it would do to his digestive system. All of it accompanied by lots of coffee.

The table was cleared by 7 a.m. While Manuel went about the town, Polly kept to her own routine. He came back at noon to eat dinner with her and review his morning activities, then he sometimes worked at home or spent some time with Remon and the new baby until time for supper, after which he might have business in town again. Lights were out by half-past ten.

Manuel wasn't one to dandle babies or horse around at childish games, but he was a conscientious parent. He did not take his responsibility for Remon's health, habits, learning and conduct lightly. Already Remon shared his father's love and respect for books and learning. The time spent together cemented the ties between them and Remon, after months of feminine companionship, revelled in having a masculine role model, and was walking and gesturing like a miniature Manuel.

Manuel was a hospitable man, enjoyed planning and hosting the well-attended christening party. They had people to sup with them frequently, sometimes with advance notice, sometimes not, but Polly was accustomed to this. Her larder was well stocked and she believed that business went more smoothly if those involved had the benefit of a relaxed social setting to put them at ease with one another.

Their gatherings were never on the scale of the French families such as the Chouteaus for she recognized that, first of all, Manuel was not a social animal. He liked to be out in the field and that was where the Chouteaus preferred to have him.

And that, while Pierre Chouteau revelled in the comforts of his mansion and prepared for "Jour de L'An", was what Manuel was planning: a trip to Canada to get trade goods for next year.

First, though, he had written a letter to Madame Menard to let her know how her husband fared. Menard, he told her, had lately left Fort Mandan with fifty men to join Henry, Lewis and Morrison at Fort Raymond. He was well and could be expected back in St. Louis sometime next July.

By New Year's Eve of 1810, Manuel was tidying up the last of loose ends in St. Louis.

In the French households, ever since Christmas there had been a frenzied period of cooking and baking and making ready for the overflow of visitors and relatives to celebrate the arrival of the New Year, beginning with midnight Mass just as on Christmas Eve.

The "Patriarch" or father, was an important man on New Year's Day. As each member of a French family arose on that day, he did not speak to anyone until he had been to the father of the house and asked his blessing. Individually, all members of the house came on bended knee to ask, "Father, give me your blessing," and the father would extend his hand and say, "May God bless you, my child; I bless you with all my heart."

Just as at Christmas, everyone in the family attended church, after which the family reunion got underway. Married sons and daughters began to arrive. They, too, went first to the head of the house for his blessing.

The dinner for the day was festive and plentiful, soup, turkey, meat balls, tarts, rolls, creams, nuts and fruit. After dinner, adults visited, the children played, welcomed other family members who had dined at their in-laws earlier.

Sometime during the first month of the year, all the married members of the family took a turn at inviting the family over for a "fricot," or get-together, cementing relationships, smoothing out any misunderstandings, laying the groundwork for sustained cordiality in the coming year.

Before the last of the 'fricots' had been held, Manuel was on his way to a different 'get-together.' In Vincennes, on January 23, 1810, he picked up his old friend, Touissant Dubois, and the two started off for Detroit.

During the long and dangerous ride across country, the travelers suffered greatly from the bitter cold. Lisa, in particular had to give attention to his health after his balky horse dumped him into icy waters two different times. Arriving safely, they crossed to the British side of the city, where they were guests of Richard Pattinson, a long-time friend and business associate of Pierre Chouteau.

Sometime later, with thoughtfulness that was typical of that French gentleman, Pierre Chouteau shared the news Lisa had written him, none of it good, with Madame Lisa.

"... generous offers have been made to us, but it is impossible for me to get a needle across due to the embargo ... If however the war is not declared after all, I shall continue my way to Montreal. I do not abandon my progress, and I will push it until I succeed.

"... Mr. Dubois returns to Vincennes by whom I write you, without having made any business at all. This damned embargo hinders all communications of the two sides. Guards are all along this river, who watch if one takes anything across, and the fines are very harsh, confiscation of the goods, $500 fine and 25 days in prison. I believe that this time I shall go to prison, because I could not bear that one would not let me take over merchandise. If by chance the embargo continues, for the $500 fine, I would do this in consequence. All that one could do to me would be to put me in prison. (One must joke sometime)."

Polly, who had schooled herself not to worry, shivered at the thought of Manuel continuing in the dead of winter to Montreal. She was a trifle awed, when he did get back, to learn that when he was unsuccessful in Montreal, he had gone directly to Philadelphia before completing the long loop back to St. Louis.

"Corsets!" Michael snorted on his return. "That's all I could find in Philadelphia."

"They're out of style," said Polly, considering the dismal prospects he had reported. "Josephine hasn't worn them for some time."

"Somebody must," said Manuel. "Michael Bequette bought all I brought back."

"I am pleased with the style book you brought me," said Polly. "Do you suppose it is true that fashionable women dampen those muslin dresses before putting them on — without corsets, or much else?"

Michael frowned and Polly held up her hand. "I won't do such a thing. I promise. Of course, the humidity here could achieve the same results."

"One nice thing about the mountains, it's never humid there," said Michael. "The days are getting longer. Soon the snow will be melting. But it will be cold still. And stormy."

And it was.

Chapter 13

With frostbite, the pain is fiercest when the flesh first thaws out. Even when there is no permanent damage, the feet, or fingers, nose, ears, cheeks, or, Heaven forbid, the privates, are tender and very touchy. When again exposed to the cold, they hurt like hell.

That first week in February of 1810, Thomas James was as sore as his feet.

The intense cold penetrated even his fur-lined moccasins. Every few steps, he broke through the thinly crusted snow. The jar sent sharp pains from the soles of his feet to top of his coyote skin cap.

As he struggled grimly to keep up with his rescuers, the three Company men on Company business, leading winter-weak Company horses up the south bank of the Missouri to the little Missouri, reviewing the circumstances that had led him to this miserable situation helped take his mind off the pain.

Born in Maryland in 1782, Thomas James was but a youngster when his Welsh parents, Joseph Austin and Elizabeth Hosten James, joined the flow of migrants to Kentucky, where his younger brother, James James, was born in 1798. James was a toddler of five and Tom, at twenty-one was more like a second father to him, when the family decided Kentucky wasn't living up to its promise of prosperity. They joined other American settlers moving into the rich stretch of land along the east bank of the Mississippi in southern Illinois, one hundred miles of fertile floodplain south from present-day Alton. A few years later, when their expectation of prosperity still had not been realized, Tom and his father moved everyone across the Mississippi to Florissant.

This old French settlement on the Missouri had succeeded in popularity the American Bottoms of the Illinois country as the land of opportunity for peripatetic Americans. By then Thomas James had known the frontier experience common to his generation, was good with a rifle, knew something of tracking and enough of the three 'R's' to qualify as literate.

When word reached him that the St. Louis Fur Company was looking for expert riflemen for the upriver expedition, Thomas James seized the opportunity presented, signed a three-year employment contract on March 29, 1809. In the succeeding months, his introduction to the specialized demands of the fur trade had left him feeling bitter toward most of the Company partners but had not entirely quenched his ambition to make a killing in furs.

Back in November, the day after the Cheek-Ride-Chouteau ruckus at Fort Manuel Lisa, Tom had told Cheek and his cronies to look him up when they got to Three Forks in the spring. Then, in driving rain, wielding a paddle briskly, he took off boldly up the Missouri River with Miller and McDaniel in their canoe.

Miller and McDaniel, the two American hunters he had teamed up with at the Company fort right after his twenty-seventh birthday, seemed the right sort. In the planning stages, they appeared as enthusiastic as he was about trapping the Upper Missouri.

Tom had cooperated with them in every way, making himself useful, expending energy, time and supplies. A hard worker, he expected his chosen associates to work equally hard and to produce exactly what they promised. He had been known to harass those who didn't.

After four days of strenuous canoe travel upriver in late November, during which the rain gave way to snow, and much of the river water turned to ice floes, Miller and McDaniel turned pessimistic. Being a practical man, Tom, too, could see they'd best wait for better weather before advancing further. There was plenty of game on the south side of the river and they had already taken some beaver pelts so Tom James agreed to a more prudent plan.

They built a rude log cabin, banked it with earth, and prepared to pass the winter months there. Tom felt they were quite comfortable, eating wild game, making moccasins and leggings from the hides. He would have been ahead if he had never ventured out until spring.

Instead, he went out in the intense cold of Christmas Day, 1809, and came back to the cabin with frozen feet. He was a man who, if his friends were sick or ailing, would be concerned and helpful. He expected the same consideration when he found himself painfully disabled.

While he believed he had as much fortitude as the next man, and set about proving it by hobbling about the cabin as best he could as soon as he could, it rankled that his companions were less solicitous with each passing day.

He didn't have much patience when companions revealed weaknesses and shortcomings. As a good friend, he felt entitled to criticize their behavior, and did so, for their own good.

They walked out on him, ostensibly to take the beaver catch back to the company fort and replenish the dwindling supply of ammunition. Obtuse, self-centered, he waited in vain for their return. It never occurred to him they might have had a bellyful of their association with him. He had always prided himself on his ability to inspire loyalty in family and friends.

They would be back, he kept telling himself, trying not to worry about his dwindling food supply as January drew to a close. He was surprised, but relieved, when Ayres and two other Company men came knocking at the cabin door.

"They changed their minds about going upriver with you," Ayres said. On his way with Marie and St. John and dispatches and supplies from Fort Manuel Lisa to Fort Raymond, Ayres had detoured to deliver the message. "Miller & McDaniel say they're going trapping down river instead."

They'd had a lot more to say than that, like know-it-all-son-of-a-bitch and bossy pain-in-the-ass, which Ayres, looking at the subject of their complaints did not repeat. Most of what he knew about James was hearsay.

An able American hunter and scout, with some first-hand experience at survival above the Platte, Ayres had been one of the men A.P. Chouteau and Sylvestre Labbadie had tolled away from Robert McClellan, Lisa's old antagonist, at the Oto camp.

From then on, Ayres had been too busy with his own duties to have more than a nodding acquaintance with Thomas James, and no reason to size him up. He was familiar with the self-righteous effrontery of the frontiersman, having a share of it himself. He, too, had been at loggerheads with management on occasion. If a man didn't wear well with his fellows, however, that was something else again.

From the looks of him, James had been on short rations for some time. If they left him to fend for himself, it was doubtful he would make it through the winter. He was also looking down his nose at Marie and St. John, as he was said to do with all French-Canadians.

When he fixed his sharp, piercing gaze on Ayres and flashed the magnetic smile he reserved for Americans, Ayres found himself warming to the man, getting a glimpse of the personality that had gathered a loyal band about James on the keelboat coming upriver from St. Louis.

The large, beaklike nose stood out in the bony face gaunt with hunger, the riveting eyes dark-circled and sunken beneath the over-hanging brows. Except for a couple passing Indians who had let him have some jerky in exchange for a twist of tobacco, James hadn't seen a really friendly face since Christmas. Nor had such strengthening venison stew as Marie and St. John were now dishing up.

"Be ye of a mind to, and iffen you feel up to it," Ayres offered in his characteristic offhand manner, watching James finish off his third bowl of stew, deciding the man was old enough to know the consequences of overloading a shrunken stomach, "y'could come along to Fort Raymond. We'll be getting there in time to join up with the Major and the men going to Three Forks for the spring trapping season."

Ayres had a cool, detached manner that could seem brusque but served effectively as a protective device to guard against an involvement he wasn't sure he wanted.

He didn't relish the thought of this man, who didn't know better than to go out in below zero weather in inadequate summer moccasins, complicating what at best would be a difficult journey.

Taking along a fourth man, one unaccustomed to such winter travel as they were undertaking, would cut into their supplies, and crowd them uncomfortably in their small sleeping tent. Just feeding him one meal had used up one hindquarter of venison already.

The three Company men, veterans of Canadian winters, had outfitted themselves for winter travel. Unless they did the same for James, who now accepted Ayres tentative suggestion with alacrity, he would freeze more than his feet.

James, his mind on what gear he should leave behind for Miller and McDaniel, dug a hole in the dirt floor in one corner of the cramped cabin, his broad, thin-lipped mouth moving now and then as if he were talking to himself. If Miller and McDaniel had thought the plan to trap the Upper Missouri imprudent, the least they could have done was come back and tell him so, man-to-man. Trapping downriver within reach of the Arikara could prove an even more imprudent plan.

James considered the six traps they had left. Being strictly honest, he decided he had enough for his own needs. He shoved theirs into the hole with the few meager belongings they had left behind, which, now he thought about it, should have given him a clue to their intentions. He began covering the cache with dirt, St. John helping him.

Marie, shaking his mop of curly black hair over James's footwear, fashioned a pair of winter moccasins for him. Clean shaven, for he had his grandmother's disdain for hairy-faced men, he had the hatchet-like profile of his French grandfather along with his mother's high cheekbones and healthy brown skin, and an open happy nature all his own.

From his own gear, Marie drew out a thick square of buffalo hide, and cut out a pair of moccasins for James. Turning the hair to the inside, adding a lining of soft rabbit fur, he made footwear to reach to James's knees.

From experience, Ayres knew Marie's handwork to be good for temperatures considerably below zero, and would be better insulation against the cold than anything James had. St. John loaned him hooded capote, Ayres gave him a pair of woolen pants outright. He did have a shirt or two of his own, linsey-wool, and an ancient knitted vest to wear next to his chest, as well as a pair of roughly fashioned muskrat mittens and the shapeless cap of coyote fur with ear flaps.

Just before leaving, James, using a charred stick, wrote on a log above the cache, "In this corner your things lie," even though he had finally realized there was little likelihood Miller and McDaniels would ever show up again at this spot to read it. They didn't show up any place else, either, although their rifles did, in the hands of some Arikaras, months later.

On February 3, 1810, Thomas James found himself out of the frying pan into the fire, and his feet felt like it.

He could have sworn the invitation to accompany the confounded Company men had meant the use of one of their horses until his feet were in better shape. Instead, he got to add his belongings to the pack of one of the stronger horses and lead it.

As Ayres pointed out, their horses, rough-coated Indian ponies, were absolutely necessary for transporting the supplies. Even these traditionally hardy animals, bred to endure and survive on cottonwood and willow bark in a bad weather, were feeling the harshness of this winter. They did well to travel burdened with packs only, so everyone was walking, three of them easily.

James was a gutsy man, and proud of it, with a strong physique and an equally strong will. By the time they reached the Little Missouri, and encountered some friendly Indians, he could keep up with Ayres and the two French-Canadians without wincing at every step.

These Indians, smoking the peace pipe with them, with straight faces and sign language, advised them to keep to the banks of the Little Missouri for two days travel, then turn northwardly, and a half-day's travel would bring them to the Gunpowder River near its head.

"The pace they had in mind must have been speedier than that of a white man. After five days of travel we hadn't come upon that branch of the Yellowstone," Ayres was to tell the Major later. "I think they were Crows — and not very good at geography."

"The Crows are very good at geography. And practical jokes," said the Major. "The Powder River would have been one hundred miles away — to the southwest."

So, on Tuesday, February 12, Ayres, Marie, St. John and the rescued James were still travelling northward in the undulating, sea-like loneliness of one of the world's great velds. The snow was blowing directly into their faces. No game was to be seen. They had to thaw snow for something to fill their stomachs, for they had nothing else. The snow piled up around the tent three feet deep when they lay down to sleep.

They were destitute, alone in a vast, desolate, limitless expanse of drifting snow.

For James, it was so cold the hairs in his nose were brittle, his skin purple and goose-pimpled. The hunger pangs of the first few days, gut-wrenching, unappeasable craving for food, had been bad. The next couple days, he suffered from a sinking and weakness of the stomach, accompanied by nausea.

Now, the fifth day without food, the physical effort of staying on his feet, staggering more than walking, left him weak and listless. For a time he had thought his feet were toughening up but, back at starvation level again, the healing process was interrupted, and the tender skin chafed easily. He was sure he could feel the blood oozing out to gurgle and bubble up and down in his tough moccasins with every step.

He wanted something to eat, even if it was only raw, stringy horse flesh, and said so, once again, when Ayres stopped to let the horses rest.

"Whose horse? Yours?" said Ayres bleakly. "D'ya think yer up to packin' yer own gear?" His cheeks were hollow and sunken, his color pasty, and his body appeared shrunken. He knew that another day without food would make his head giddy, and he'd have to fight off the tendency to give in to overpowering languor, his mind wandering, haunted by well-remembered feasts.

James, who had been eyeing St. John's horse, scowled. St. John said something to Marie in French, and they both chuckled. James glared at them.

"We'll decide tonight," said Ayres, getting to his feet carefully, for the effort made him dizzy. "We ain't on our last legs yet. Let's see if we can make it to that knoll before dark."

James, who had looked in vain for a tree or shrub, a hillock, on which to rest his eyes, now saw there was a slight change in the prairie that had rolled on and on before them for so long. Far off, there was a mound of some sort. Falling snow veiled it from time to time.

For Andrew Henry, ten days away as the Crows travel, on a ridge overlooking the Yellowstone River, the morning was bright and clear, the sky blue overhead, the storm blown to the east.

Cheeky, at heel, was having a fit. So was the young Crow warrior, face down in the snow at the Major's feet.

Bryan, from concealment, could see the fringes of the Crow's leggings flutter as his feet beat out the tattoo of the typical gran mal seizure.

He had known more than one heart-stopping moment in this country where the Indians had an uncanny ability to rise up, literally from the ground without warning.

He found it gratifying the way the Major had turned the tables and startled the Indian, but he was beginning to feel some concern as the seizure continued. He suspected the young Crow's concealed companion was, too. He sensed, more than saw, the faintest suggestion of movement in the depression on which he had his rifle trained.

In the open, the new snow was soft and damp over an old crust. It had broken the Crow's fall. It was also going to plug his breathing passages very shortly.

The Major knelt down beside the young Crow, holding his rifle in his right hand. His face, lean and imperturbable, was darkened by sun and weather so his gray-blue eyes, bright and clear, made a striking contrast.

Gently, he turned the Crow's head to one side, clearing the snow away from his face with his left hand. Cheeky, whining softly, came closer.

When the seizure passed and the young man opened his eyes, Cheeky, who didn't take to an Indian ordinarily, thrust forward and gave his face a swipe with his tongue. The Major helped the Crow turn over and supported him into a sitting position.

The Crow warrior, who looked about eighteen, was well built and well dressed, in the fashion of his people. He had an abundance of blue-black hair which had come partially free of its otter wrappings during his seizure and one long spill cascaded over his right shoulder to below his waist.

Like so many of his people, he was good to look upon, with a clear brown skin, a straight nose and bright, intelligent black eyes. As the latter met those of the Major's, his face became incandescent, as if he were being vouchsafed a vision.

"In my dream of power, you were not so brown," the Crow signed with broad gestures, speaking softly in Crow at the same time, and Bryan recognized a word or two. "The first time I looked upon you, there was a mighty forest all around. The next time the dream came, you were in a large canoe. This time, when you rose out of the ground, it seemed the most powerful dream of all. I could smell you."

"It is an honor to be recognized by a dreamer of power," the Major signed gravely. Aloud, in a careful monotone, he filled Bryan in, just as the Crow had been letting his hidden companion know what was going on when he augmented his sign language with the spoken Crow words. "Claims to have second sight. Says he is known as Looks Far and," the Major added wryly, "I am the Man Looked For."

With the passing of yesterday's storm, the temperature had risen close to, or just above zero. In his winter clothing, a man in his middle thirties, fit and hardy, of medium height, the Major was comfortably warm. The young Crow, more in reaction to his seizure, for he was dressed for winter, was beginning to shiver.

"Tell your companion to come out of hiding," signed the Major, continuing to speak aloud at the same time for Bryan's benefit. "Let us meet in peace."

"You have keen eyes," signed Looks Far, impressed. He called out to his companion to come forward, his voice, like that of most Indians, high and thin when pitched for any distance, more in the tenor than the baritone register.

The companion, belly down in the snow, head thrust into the meager cover of a tuft of grass, was not feeling particularly friendly. Looks Far did have a way of seeing into the future; in the process, however, he sometimes forgot to consider the present. If he lay out in the snow much longer, following the rigors of his seizure, he would come down with another of his chest sicknesses.

At least Looks Far, who had a reputation for remarkable visions among the people, had waited until after the blizzard was over to go out and prove the validity of his latest one.

Ever since Larocque had spent time in his mother's lodge, Looks Far had been seeing white men playing an important role in the future of The People. Lately he had been getting more specific and insistent. A white man was going to come into Looks Far's life with surprising suddenness and save him from an uncomfortable death. It sounded grandiloquent and impressive and the companion felt the contact should have been.

Instead, since early morning when they found the first trace of him, the white man had out-foxed them, moving like a wraith over their own terrain, and risen up from nowhere to tap Looks Far on the shoulder without warning.

One look at the white man had plunged Looks Far into one of his visionary collapses. Saving his life had been an act of mundane common sense. There had been nothing dramatic about it. Demeaning, that's what it was. The whole thing was the white man's fault.

Seething with resentment and indignation, Looks Far's companion arose abruptly.

As the companion did so, Looks Far's eyes narrowed in anger. He barked an abrupt, high-pitched tenor protest.

His companion, gripping a stout buffalo bow with arrow nocked and drawn, aimed at the Major, replied crossly, but in a soprano voice.

Looks Far was on his feet in one light movement, his body interposed between the Major and the weapon. This time, when he commanded with unyielding authority, the bow was not only lowered but the arrow returned to its case.

The Major, who had not moved during the exchange, rose to

his feet. He had seen an arrow from such a bow pass entirely through a buffalo. Such were not wielded by weaklings. Despite the girlish voice, there was little doubt that Looks Far's body guard was competent. There was a chill between his shoulder blades that was not warmed by the sparks shooting out from her black eyes.

"Now," said the Major aloud, his hands moving smoothly in sign language, "My friend will join us."

Bryan, who had been working on the Major's dictum that you have to believe that cold isn't any worse than heat, and you can stand either one, was glad to leave his chilly burrow in the snow. As he stood up, holding his rifle casually at his side, the eyes of the two Indians swivelled toward him. The quick blink of two pair of eyelids was the only indication of surprise that escaped them.

Bryan, too, kept his face carefully impassive, despite the fact he had not expected to find one of the Indians they had been trailing to be a teen-age girl. He was still slightly bemused at the Major's deftness at peaceful ambush. Wisely, he set aside a review of the steps that led to it for later cogitation.

The Major had made it a custom, every few days, whenever his duties permitted, to get away from the confines of Fort Raymond. He seldom went alone, for one or more of his recruits vied for the privilege of accompanying him, to scout out the surrounding country in person, instead of depending on reports, however accurate, of others. His ability to memorize the patterns of ridges, canyons, passes and streams and his preparations, care and watchfulness enabled him to travel long distances in this rough country, safely and quickly. By emulating him, his men were mastering impressive skills.

Among other things, Bryan had learned that ridges were the safest approaches and exits from unknown territory. He was developing a pattern of habitual screening, of automatic analysis of input.

His eyes, as he moved along, augmented by all the other senses, including an incipient sixth sense, screened and analyzed input, computed information, sifted out garbage. He had learned to move along the slopes *below* the ridges. Before every new summit, short of each new shoulder of a hill, or twist of a valley, he went forward cautiously.

If there was no cover to get behind to view the skyline, he thrust forward a cut branch or piece of brush, moving it into place an inch at a time, then lay on his belly and scrutinized everything before him, eyes moving back and forth, looking for any human in the valley, the pocket or hill. All movement must be made with great care so as not to disturb birds or animals.

From experience, he knew the Major expected him to figure out on his own the process that had brought them here. Only then would he take him, step-by-step over the terrain they had scouted all morning, and describe the signposts Bryan might have overlooked. The unnatural swirl in the wind-packed snow, the blade of dead grass turned over, the broken twig.

An apt pupil, Bryan was becoming an adept who could, even when part of his attention was occupied with other things, remember every fallen log, each clump of willow, every twist of stream and hill since they left Fort Raymond early this morning. He knew the Major could find this place in the dark, and that he was expected to be able to do the same. He hoped they wouldn't have to.

Bright, alert and a rapid learner because he was curious about everything and possessed an excellent memory, Bryan's smooth emergence from concealment would not have disturbed a bird or animal. It did surprise the two Indians.

His sweeping glance catalogued them swiftly. Teen-age twins, by the looks of them. And, by the calendar of their people, already adults: a young man of psychic powers; and an edgy young woman, of unknown powers.

Bryan wished he knew as much about the Crows as the Major did. In the past three months, the Major had been amassing a great deal of information, actual and theoretical.

The Crows were migrants, too, retaining the word for, and memory of, the alligator, that had been a menace in their original homeland. They had taken to mountain country and made it work to their advantage. Like the Swiss, they were great traders. The women were so skilled at making clothing, footwear, robes and skin lodges that even tribes at war with the Crows would postpone hostilities to trade with them.

Edward Rose, who claimed to be one of them by adoption, said they called their land Absaroka, land of the Sparrow Hawk people. The country of his people was in exactly the right place. Everything good was to be found there. There was no country like the Crow country.

Crow men were tall and good looking, he said. The women, not so good looking, were skilled at making a man comfortable, in or out of bed.

Their saddest commentary was, "S/He has no relatives." Relatives provided a built-in support system for all endeavors; they also provided a share-the-wealth system that discouraged the individual, capitalistic minded entrepreneur.

According to the Major, contact between the two cultures could be likened to a street with two sides and a lot of potholes. One of the potholes he had mentioned was that the Crows, men and women alike, had a keen, ribald sense of fun, and delighted in playing jokes. The Crows would go to great lengths to make their victims, friend or foe, look silly.

"D'you think we're heading into a pothole?" Bryan asked the Major as Looks Far signed 'friend' and 'come' and 'lodge' to both of them and gestured for them to accompany him and his twin sister.

"Looks Far wants us on his side of the street," replied the Major, indicating the girl should lead the way. Having Looks Far bring up to the rear made Bryan feel better.

Bryan moved out after the girl, who had her lower lip stuck out just like a sulky white girl's, which made him momentarily homesick for the potholes of Philadelphia, where a girl's lethal weapons did not include a buffalo bow.

In Philadelphia, young Bryan's father, Guy, could see that his wife was getting ready to read their son's letter for the nth time. Each time she did so, she came up with another question about the west he could not answer.

The fifty-six year old Free Quaker, a prosperous merchant with ties to men of power and influence in business and political circles, active in the western trade through his nephews, William Morrison, at Kaskaskia, and James Bryan, at St. Charles, usually found his wife's questions acute and thought-provoking.

He rather prided himself on seeking out answers. However, he did not relish the prospect of getting sixteen-year old Timothy started on the west, too.

In order to forestall those questions, Guy Bryan gestured with his newspaper to get his wife's attention.

"This is most interesting, my dear," he said. "Just listen."

Slowly and distinctly he read aloud paragraph after paragraph concerning the procedure for the third national U.S. census while young Timothy stifled a yawn. He would just as soon hear his mother read his brother's letter again. Perhaps this time she wouldn't censor by silence some pages, which he suspected dealt with ladies of the Indian tribes. "It is estimated that the population of the United States will be in excess of seven million people. Imagine that!"

Martha Matlack Bryan, who had been disowned at the regular Quaker meeting after wedding a Free Quaker, had a firm, inquiring mind, particularly when it concerned her offspring. "There's no problem with your nephews being counted in the census. They're still within reach of civilization," she said thoughtfully. "What about William P.?"

Their teen-age son stirred restlessly, enviously, thinking about his brother hunting buffalo with his new 'rifle gun.' Free Quakers claimed membership in the Society of Friends, and had also claimed it was permissible to take up arms in the War of Independence.

Timothy's maternal grandfather, the Revolutionary War veteran, Colonel Timothy Matlack, thought it permissible at any time. He'd taken an active interest in his grandson's choice of rifle before the young Bryan departed for Kaskaskia in 1808 to familiarize himself with the Bryan and Morrison western operation in order to take over part of the Philadelphia end of the business.

Instead of coming home, young Bryan had joined his cousin, Samuel Morrison, who had gone to Kaskaskia in 1807, on a fabulous trip that stirred Tim's imagination.

"James'll probably do the counting for St. Charles. To hear him tell it, he's doing most everything else," said Timothy, wondering when he would be allowed to join him. He looked toward the doorway to see if the tea cart was on its way, which it wasn't, so continued, with seeming casualness. "Besides, James is over twenty-one and counts as head of a household. You know, he went out there when he was seventeen. Young Bryan's been there since he turned seventeen. I'll be seventeen this summer —"

"And, so far, you are nowhere near as old as William P. was when he left here," said his mother, with deceptive mildness that made Timothy resolve to work at presenting a more mature impression. Unfolding William P.'s last letter, she continued, "Our son says right here," she fluttered the page, "that there are over three hundred men out in that wilderness with him. Tell me, husband, who is going to count them?'

Guy Bryan gave her a benevolent look over the top of his glasses. "The census taker, to be sure, my dear," he assured her, making a mental note to put the question to Judge Brackenridge at their next lodge meeting. Or better still, invite General and Mrs. William Clark to sup with them. Young Biddle had passed the word that when they concluded their visiting in Virginia, the General planned to stop over in Philadelphia and discuss the editing of the journals he and Lewis had kept.

Timothy Bryan decided, wisely, to ask his civics teacher the same question.

In his settlement on the Missouri River, Rebecca Bryan Boone's husband, Daniel, also of Quaker heritage, felt a great deal of satisfaction as he busied himself in the days remaining before he started east.

At seventy-six, he counted it as fourteen years since he left Kentucky. He had done well, served in various posts of responsibility in the new territory, had sons and grandsons who were giving a good account of themselves. He was going to make the trip back to Kentucky and, at long last, settle his outstanding debts there.

Rebecca, no known relation to Guy, Quaker heritage notwithstanding, had not liked leaving such debts behind them, either. In her fiercely gentle fashion she had been indignant that the man who led the way into Kentucky had not been allowed to retain an acre of it.

In St. Louis, Dr. Nicholas Fleming, entered Michael Bequette's establishment. Shaking the rain off the collars of his greatcoat, he looked around him, located the proprietor bent over a barrel.

"What are you doing?" he asked, as Michael, scrabbling in the barrel, tossed out several items. "Counting corsets?" he dodged as one of those items sailed past his head. "Mamán says to cancel her order. Corsets are out of style."

"Not Madame Fleming, too?" sighed Michael, not looking up, a strand of gray hair falling over his forehead. "Then you win your wager."

"You old fraud. Nothing doubled is still nothing," responded Dr. Nick. "Fashions are the devil to predict, aren't they?"

"Not today," said Michael, rising triumphantly from the barrel, cradling some china objects and a clock, which he set beside some rolls of wallpaper. "Look what I found packed in with all those corsets."

Dr. Nick removed his greatcoat, hanging it over a chair to dry, and joined him at the counter to examine the objects curiously. "Wallpaper? Snuff boxes? A clock?"

"Wallpaper with balloons all over it. A Montgolfier painted on the snuff boxes. And Blanchard crossing the Channel painted on the clock," said Michael his face wreathed in smiles. "Very opportune."

"You are thinking of those aeronauts and their balloon that everyone is talking about?"

Michael nodded. The objects he had found packed in with the out-of-date corsets that Lisa had brought from Philadelphia were not in demand there, either. In St. Louis, now that A. R. Hawley and August Post were finalizing preparations for their balloon trip to Canada, with lots of popular support, young blades rubbernecking at the site, the fashionable making it a Sunday afternoon outing, they would be.

There were expatriate Frenchmen here who could remember the first Montgolfier flight in 1783, watched by tens of thousand Parisians, and thoroughly chronicled and observed by the high, mighty and lowly.

The balloon had captivated the Continent. The mania had spread to England. Entrancing in shape, the balloon was embossed on wallpaper and fabrics, painted on china and porcelain, chandeliers and clocks, celebrated in song and memorialized in print and painting.

Balloons caught the public fancy in the New World, too. Clubs of aeronauts and stuntmen sprang up. Balloons in all shapes, sizes, colors and arrangements — and the daredevils to fly them — had been bobbing up all over ever since. This balloon ascent would be the first west of the Mississippi.

"Aeronauts — another dimension — a bit awesome, isn't it?" said Dr. Nick. "Too bad they have to go with the prevailing winds. If they were going west, toward the Rocky Mountains, I'd be tempted to go along, at least as far as Fort Raymond."

At Fort Raymond, twenty-year old Samuel Morrison, who was instructing eighteen-year old John Dougherty in double-entry bookkeeping, was counting off items on his fingers. "You have three major classifications to consider in merchandising: imported goods; country products; and peltry and skins."

"The vermillion Baptiste got for his squaw today: imported goods," said John, scratching away with his sharpened goose quill pen. Imported goods meant all articles coming into St. Louis, regardless of foreign or American origin, that were not a product of the West. "The bear tallow he exchanged for the vermillion: country products."

Menard, Vallé and Lewis, sipping hot coffee from even hotter tin cups at the other end of the trestle table, had been making desultory conversation. Francis said, sotto voice, to Menard, "Should I tell him what to watch out for in country goods, such as goose feathers and duck eggs?"

Menard chuckled, remembering the sack of goose feathers that had burst, giving a downy coating to everything from apples to beef suet, including the unexpected hatching of ducklings.

Samuel, resisting an impulse to swap hilarious anecdotes with them, grinned, and prompted. "Mr. Brown brought in some beaver pelts and a fine buffalo hide. There you have your third classification — and the most important category of all to the westerner."

"Invoices for imported goods list the first cost in sterling. So," John went on with his lesson, "here's the table you had me draw up. I took the sterling equivalents and the provincial currencies and converted them into the new federal money. You said the pound sterling stays relatively stable at $4.44 federal money. Or 22 cents per shilling."

"$.222 per shilling," corrected Samuel, who had learned to be very precise about figures after two years with his exacting merchant brother. He looked at John's table. "The Pennsylvania shilling at $.133 and the Virginia shilling at $.1666. Good."

"I couldn't remember what the New York shilling was," said John.

"Never mind the New York shilling," said Samuel. "It's less than either but is seldom seen outside that state."

John considered the lesson. "Back home in Kentucky, everything was based on deerskins."

"Right you are," agreed Samuel. "With a barter economy, you've got to have some kind of a base. That's the 'peltry dollar.' There are more deerskins brought in than any other peltry. The price varies the least. It's a reliable standard to use. You can figure good shaved deerskins at 40 cents; medium, 30 cents; inferior, 20 cents. That's book credit."

"Cash price is 33 and 1/3 cents. Is that the base I use for Mr. Brown's peltry and buffalo hide?" asked John.

Samuel shook his head. "Mr. Brown is one of the hunters who signed a promissory note. When you take promissory notes for delivery of some product, from beaver to lead, it's at 'peltry price.' You figure that at 20% over the cash price."

John groaned. "It's enough to addle a man's brain!"

"Wouldn't be any fun if it was simple and easy," said Samuel who revelled in working with figures. "If you want a really complicated system, you should take a look at one based on French money."

"Like Menard and Vallé's?" Francis flashed his cheerful smile. "John, you really don't want to hear about a three column-entry system built around the escalin, worth 12 and 1/2 cents, do you?"

John pondered. Not very much hard money was in circulation. Some French crowns and Spanish milled dollars. The US hadn't coined any silver dollars since 1806. In greater use in the Mississippi Valley were the fractional coins, or the use of terms for fractional pieces.

"You'd have eight bits to the dollar, American or Spanish," he said. "That part would be easy. If you want conversion from sterling and shilling currencies, though, the livre at 20 cents, based on the smallest unit, the sol, or the sou, at 1 cent, would be better in the center column," he went on, reaching for a sheet of foolscap. "For, say a pound of vermillion, you could get to dollars and cents in the last column by — "

Samuel, beaming at his pupil, reached out a hand to stay him. "Good for you, John. That's exactly the way my brother William went at it up until a few years ago. Merchants," he inclined his head toward Pierre Menard, "have to keep their accounts in units best suited to their trade."

"A pound of vermillion?" repeated Francis thoughtfully. "Samuel, John is going to need to know the difference between the

English pound and the French pound. Vermillion would be in the English weight, but most of our engages prefer the French pound for their deerskins."

"True," agreed Samuel. "Even if you don't do much clerking, you need to know the difference between the French and English measurements. The French pound is approximately 1.1215 of the English pound; the minot to 1.10746 bushels; the French foot, 12.7893 inches; and the arpent, about 4/5ths of an acre."

John didn't say anything.

"Right now, though, you'd best learn more about how to foot and cross foot," said Samuel.

John put his head in his hands. "Are you sure," he said wistfully, "that all this will be needed by an Indian agent?"

"Is that what you want to be? An Indian agent? Why didn't you say so before?" exclaimed Samuel. "I can help you there. The government demands more record keeping — in triplicate, usually — than my brother William and cousin James put together!"

Another James, first name Thomas, had, at long last, put the open plains behind him and was counting on breaking his five-day fast with buffalo steak.

Reaching the timbered mound at last, they had come upon a small herd of buffalo, and James and Ayres had brought down four of them. As James was re-loading, Ayres said mildly, "Don't you think one buffalo apiece will do us tonight?"

James grinned at him in a flash of comradely good humor and joined Ayres in the butchering. Marie built up a fire while St. John tended the horses and set up the tent.

James set the liver aside and from time-to-time paused in his work to slice off a chunk, dip it into the gall bladder and gulp it down. Ayres shared out a portion of the liver to Marie and St. John to munch on in the same manner, gave Marie the tongue and hump to set to broiling over the fire. They left the carcasses to the wolves and coyotes that were always to be found on the edge of a buffalo herd, even a small one such as they had found pawing away the snow under the trees to get at the grass.

James felt there was no limit to his capacity and no quantity could satisfy him.

He ate, and ate, and ate, until utterly unable to hold any more. It was midnight when he sighed, patted his stomach, belched and rolled up in his blankets.

The next morning, after a restless night, Marie and St. John crawled out of the tent and built up the fire. "The glutton," said Marie, using the patois word for wolverine, as the two of them went about their camp chores, "He did not sleep so well."

"He moans and groans when he is empty. He moans and

groans when he is full," observed St. John. "Me, I teenk he is a mon of gripes."

Ayres, rolling out of his blankets, and immediately subjected to Tom James' complaints, had come to the same conclusion.

"Couldn't sleep a wink," Tom was saying lugubriously, sitting up. "Stummick is pret' near in as bad way as when starving. See, I'm swole up like a bloated calf." He placed both hands on his distended stomach, fixing Ayres with an accusing stare. "Never heard tell of buffalo meat doing that to a man afore — not from those tales you hivernants spin."

"Guess you had too much of a good thing," said Ayres dismissively, turning away. "We'll take it easy today," he paused to say over his shoulder to the man still sitting hunched over in the little tent. "Give the ponies a chance to forage. We're on the right course now."

The next day they reached the Yellowstone, where the going was easier.

Impatient, James began taking shortcuts across the iced-over river from bend-to-bend until he nearly lost his horse. The horse, with all James' worldly good on it, fell into an air hole. James grabbed its tail and hung on.

He would make the most of that tail/tale ever after, acting out both roles, making sure his listeners realized what a hair-breadth escape both had, saved by his quick actions from being swept under the ice to drown in the swift current of the Yellowstone.

The Yellowstone Valley was an Indian commissariat. The country was an immense level plain, with the river skirted on either sides by woods. Among the woods were herd after herd of buffalo, nibbling on the buds of the trees and grazing on the grass the strong winds laid bare of snow in many places.

The Sioux, Cheyennes, Blackfeet, Nez Perce, Flathead and Shoshones all came here to hunt buffalo. Closer to Fort Raymond, the Crows had already begun to arrive, erecting their graceful lodges along the stream banks.

On February 18, 1810, at Fort Raymond, Francis Vallé viewed the backslapping welcome Thomas James got from Jamie Cheek, while others left of his boat crew gathered around. It had taken fifteen days of painful travel, the way James was telling it, to come from his cabin on the Little Missouri.

"Did you have to be *such* a Good Samaritan?" Francis asked Ayres sardonically, leading him to the quarters shared by the partners, where he told Reuben Lewis, "This good man has returned your bad penny, fitted out in his own pants and St. John's best capote. Fortunately, he doesn't expect any thanks —"

"Just the return of St. John's capote," said Ayres, unslinging his saddle bags from his shoulder, removing the waterproofed container of dispatches, handing them to Pierre Menard. "We brung ammunition, mostly."

"Merci, Monsieur!" said Pierre Menard, smiling. Opening the dispatch case, he saw it contained a letter to him from Sylvestre Labbadie. "Good news, I hope."

"What's this about good news?" said the Major from the doorway, coming forward to give Ayres a hearty welcome.

"You'd better have some!" exclaimed Francis. "Rose came in with some tale about you being the honored guests of some Crows — but five days! Samuel has been worrying about how to phrase a letter to his Uncle about the Crows carrying off his favorite son. Where is young Bryan? Still fraternizing?"

"He's very hale and hearty," said the Major, gesturing to the doorway where Bryan was doing his best to appear insouciant in a new buckskin jacket, the quill decorations done in the inimitable Crow fashion.

"When do we start for Three Forks?" said Bryan nonchalantly.

"The sooner, the better," said Rueben, walking all around him, fingering the jacket. "What happened? Some Crow chieftain adopt you?"

"Just his niece," said the Major. "She draws a real cupid's bow."

Chapter 14

Ayres brought the latest news from Fort Manuel Lisa.

Shehaka could have benefited from a Dale Carnegie course. The only Mandan still speaking to him, tartly, was his wife, Yellow Corn.

Urbane Sylvestre Labbadie, who thrived on winning friends and influencing people, was finding he preferred to do so in the more appropriate mercantile channels worthy of his talents, a civilized setting. Venting his feelings about Company policy and, uncharitably, about some of its makers, he wrote Menard that any junior clerk could do his work at Fort Manuel.

Le Borgne, the one-eyed, unscrupulous chief of the big-bellied Minnetarees, playing footsie with the British at Fort Pine again, was gleefully predicting that Manuel Lisa, far afield in Canada, would not have any luck getting supplies for next year's trapping season. Chief Red Hair, had lost his good friend, Chief Long Knife. If you could believe the moccasin grapevine, he should have chopped off at least one finger by now.

The Indians did have a way of being cognizant of affairs, such as the decent thing expected of a man in mourning, obscuring a nugget of information within their own overlapping interpretations of a news item.

In Tennessee, the coroner's jury found there were no eyewitnesses to the shooting and slashing of Meriwether Lewis the night of October 11, 1809.

According to Mrs. Robert Grinder, her husband was away. Except for her children and servants, she was alone when the stranger rode into the Grinder clearing, seventy-two miles from Nashville on the edge of Indian Territory, seeking bed and board.

There were only two rooms to her frontier dwelling, rude log cabins at right angles to each other, connected by a dog run. She let him have the bedroom cabin, served him supper, sent his servant and hers to sleep in the barn, spread pallets for herself and children on the floor of the kitchen cabin.

About three o'clock in the morning she was startled awake by shots, thuds and cries coming from the other cabin. Shortly thereafter, the badly wounded stranger was at her door begging for help.

Too terrified to open the door, she crept silently to a chink in the log walls and looked out. She saw Meriwether Lewis stumbling about in the yard between the two cabins. He fell over a stump, crawled on his hands and knees to a nearby tree, pulled himself up with its support, lurched back into his cabin. She barely had time to settle on her pallet before she heard him at her door again, not speaking now, just scratching weakly, then she heard him at the empty water pail.

Through the long hours of the night, she huddled fearfully with her children behind the barred kitchen door. At first light, she sent two of her children scuttling to the barn to summon the servants, who had, according to their testimony, heard nothing.

Lewis was found, bled white from shot and slash wounds, semi-conscious, sprawled across the bed in the second cabin.

"I am no coward," he managed to say with great effort, "but I am so strong, it is so hard to die." Just as the sun was coming up, Meriwether Lewis died, on October 12, 1809.

The dedicated English botanist, John Bradbury, arrived in St. Louis New Year's Eve, intent on making arrangements for a trip to the Upper Missouri. He was disappointed to find he would be unable to make use of the letter-of-introduction penned in August by Thomas Jefferson for hand delivery to his protege, Meriwether Lewis.

In Pittsburg, David McKeehan, the ambitious editor, was relieved. No longer would he have to cross pens with that obstinate Lewis on the subject of journals kept by uneducated privates. Instead, he could get on with making a profitable publication of Patrick Gass's Journal of the Voyages and Travels of a Corps of Discovery Under Command of Captain Lewis. No matter now that Patrick Gass had only nineteen days of schooling, lacked scientific knowledge and training in celestial observation. The reading public didn't know that and it was unlikely any other from the Corps would be pointing it out.

Indirectly, veterans of that Corps figured in a Northwest Company report. Leading a brigade of Peter Pond's Pedlars, as the Northwest Company was termed derisively by their rivals the Hudson's Bay Company, Alexander Henry arrived on the Saskatchewan River September 13, 1809. This Henry, no relation to Andrew, was a hard-bitten, experienced factor who had come to take charge of a new territory for his company. He found the Painted Feathers and the Cold Band of the Blackfeet, three hundred tipis of them, eagerly awaiting the new supplies he brought.

Trade with the Blackfeet, he wrote in his journal, ". . . is of little consequence to us. They kill scarcely any good furs; a beaver of their own hunt is seldom found among them; their principal trade is wolves, of which late years we take none, while our H.B. neighbors continue to pay well for them." About two thirds of the

Slaves, as he called the Blackfeet, traded exclusively with HBC, and ". . . I would willingly give up the whole of them."

"Last year, it is true, we got some beaver from them; but this was the spoils of war, they having fallen upon a party of Americans," likely Potts and Colter, "stripped them of everything, and brought off a quality of skins."

To the south of Alexander Henry, across the wide territory patrolled by the Blackfeet, at Fort Raymond, the resourceful John Colter was critiquing the map Major Henry and Reuben Lewis had been sketching.

Len Cather, listening to the voices of the men taking an interest in the map, absently catalogued the differences. He was finding he could place a man's origins through his spoken word, even get a feel for the man's ability and potential.

"Up the Yellowstone River making use of game and Indian trails," the Major was saying, using his brass pocket compass to line up the landmarks. The Major, along with Morrison and Bryan, had what Len thought of as Pennsylvania voices, consonants firm and clear, vowels well rounded. "We'll come to a gap through the mountains and onto the Gallatin River. From there it is only a short distance to the Three Forks."

"Wonder if anything is left of Cortin's post there?" Rueben Lewis had the gentle cadences of Virginia in his voice, much like Colter and himself, but Lewis's background and his Scot tutor had given an educated cast to his words.

Colter shook his head. "Mebbe the one in the Flathead country." Instead of the polysyllables of the upper class of Albemarle County, Colter used silence, gestures, monosyllables and the phonetics of a less well-educated man from the hill country.

Here and now, however, Colter, in mountain lore was the best educated, and the man to learn from. Len Cather, intrigued, had been learning all he could about him.

Colter's background, as Len pieced it together, was frontier Virginia, augmented as one of Simon Kenton's famed Rangers. That meant, before he was twenty, he'd learned to go for long spells without sleeping, and a good part of the time to get along without eating. Sometimes he'd have lain in one spot for eight-ten hours without moving while chewed on by mosquitoes. Other times he'd have run sixty-seventy miles in a day and fought Indians at the end of the run. Mostly, he'd go afoot. Sometimes in a canoe, or on a raft, or snowshoes, or even swimming. No fires. Poor pay. The five dollars a month Meriwether Lewis offered privates must have looked good.

Len calculated that Colter must have been ten years older than the seventeen-year old George Shannon when they boarded Meriwether Lewis's keelboat on the Ohio River as the first of his select volunteers in the fall of 1803. In the six and a half years since then, Colter had gone to the Pacific and been part way home a couple times, then changed his mind, returned to the mountains, each new venture promising a more profitable deal than the previous one.

The first time had been in August of 1806, when he discovered that an acquaintance from Cahokia, Joseph Dickson, had succeeded in the running the gauntlet from St. Louis to the Upper Missouri. Colter already knew that Joseph and his wife Susan, representative of the many Pennsylvanians of Scot ancestry who proved adept at adjusting to an isolated existence, flowing with the tide of emigration, had tried their luck first in Tennessee. After the birth of their first child, and the lean pickings in Tennessee, they were part of the leading edge that pulled up stakes and moved to Illinois.

It was there on the east bank of the Mississippi, opposite St. Louis, that Colter, stationed with the Corps at Wood River, and a frequent visitor to the convivial taverns of Cahokia, until sharply grounded by Lewis and Clark, had come to know Dickson. Shortly after the Corps departed, Dickson, still reaching for prosperity, had teamed up with Forrest Hancock, also seeking ways to turn a profit, in a trapping venture up the Missouri.

Before leaving, Joseph moved Sarah and the children to Shiloh, some ten miles inland. With a two-year absence in mind, he stocked up on supplies, including some of the new-fangled, but scarce spring-powered iron traps, and took off up the Missouri with Hancock in the spring of 1804.

Rangy, leather-tough and wary, they went about their business of harvesting furs. They did very well. As vital statistics, they did even better, surviving where many another did not. For two years running, they lost their furs to first one Indian ambush, then another, emerging, except for an arrow-wound in Dickson's leg, unscathed.

Intent on making up their losses, they got even more venturesome. In the spring of 1806 they paddled their dug-out canoe beyond the Mandan Villages and were nearing the mouth of the Yellowstone when they met Captain Clark and party, August 11, 1806. He gave them powder and lead and messages for Lewis, whom they met the next day. There they were when Colter and another of Clark's hunters, who had missed their rendezvous with Clark, came into the Lewis camp.

In a lone, unfamiliar place, it is good to see a familiar face. Renewing their brief acquaintance, Dickson and Colter spent the evening visiting, Hancock putting in a word now and then.

Colter was keen to hear the latest news, some of it two years old, of harvests, people, events and fluctuating alliances. In exchange, he began telling them about the places he'd been and the sights he'd seen until, very late at night, it was plain he'd only made a beginning.

Eager to hear more, particularly about the beaver-rich streams of the Yellowstone Valley, Dickson and Hancock were in no hurry to proceed on their own. They agreed to Colter's suggestion that they accompany the party downstream to the Mandan Villages.

With Lewis's permission, Colter joined them in their canoe, continuing the saga. As they floated quickly along on the current, he gave them the benefit of his expertise, showing an increasing, proprietary interest in their plans. They would need more traps, tools for building canoes, a two-year supply of ammunition and other items, he told them.

One of the items turned out to be Colter, himself. His motives, recognized by others of the Corps, who were thinking along the same lines, was the economic opportunity, not to be dismissed lightly, to remain on the scene, make a killing in beaver.

Dickson and Hancock, knowing Colter was no trapper at that stage of his life, preferring to harvest beaver with a well-placed rifle shot in the head, were surprised, but not averse to his proposal. Some of the items they needed could only be obtained from the Corps. The captains would be more amenable to providing those to Colter.

Colter petitioned and obtained his release, and such supplies as the captains felt they could spare.

The three men left the Mandan Villages together. In July of 1807 Joseph Dickson was back with his family, after an absence of almost three years, with a story of his own to tell. As he dandled his youngest, the two-and-a-half-year old namesake Joseph, born while he was gone, he related his experiences to his family and to interested friends and neighbors.

Over the years, inevitably, Dickson and Hancock had been having their differences, fuming at each other, then settling back into double harness. With the presence of a third party, there seemed less need to reconcile, and they were at odds with increasing frequency.

By October they were involving Colter, who wanted no part of such continuous wrangling. If the three of them couldn't get along, he was leaving. Forrest Hancock chose to accompany him.

Hancock and Colter, Dickson told his listeners, left him alone, with most of the supplies, and went their own way in a canoe obtained from a friendly Indian.

Dickson spent the winter of 1806-1807 by himself, in his dugout in the mountains, where the snow got up to eight feet deep on the level. He had a bad bout with snowblindness but toughed it out and made his way out of the mountains and back to St. Louis where he sold his furs for several thousand dollars.

"Enough to buy a good farm," he said proudly. And he did so, obtaining a flourishing piece of ground where his next child was born May 12, 1808, and christened Missouri, to commemorate his father's adventures on the Missouri River. Dickson didn't know what became of Hancock and Colter, and didn't much care.

Colter and Hancock were back at the Mandan Villages by the summer of 1807. By then, Hancock had a husky, dusky helpmeet, and a slew of impecunious in-laws living off him. He was planning to teach them to trap beaver. Colter, who doubted he'd have much luck at that undertaking among the Mandans, wished him well, and departed. Once again Colter headed for home, this time travelling down the Missouri alone.

What white men had been in the Yellowstone Valley before them? Allowing for the claims of Charles Le Raye, and counting Captain Clark's party, Dickson, Hancock and Colter would have been the fourth party of whites.

Charles Le Raye could have been there in 1802. Captured on the Osage River by the Sioux, the tale, told by another, had him travelling with his captors, the Bois Brule band, on a visit to the Gros Ventre villages on the Missouri for the spring trading fair.

While at this encampment, he persuaded his captors to allow him to accompany a French trader named Pardo, who lived with the Sioux, on a trip to the Yellowstone country. Le Raye and Pardo, in company with three Sioux, joined some of their Hidatsa host on July 3, 1802, and rode cross country to the Yellowstone River. Before returning, they visited a Crow camp on the Big Horn River where Pardo did some trading.

There was no question that Larocque had been there. In the winter of 1805, Francois Antoine Larocque, a Northwest Company employee from Fort de La Bosse on the Assiniboin River, paid several visits to Lewis and Clark at Fort Mandan. When he heard of their plans to travel to the Pacific, he asked to accompany them. When, for the second time, they turned him down, he departed for the Assiniboin.

In the spring of 1805, Larocque, with two companions, was back at the Five Villages for the annual fair. More than six hundred Crows, linguistic cousins of the Hidatsa, a.k.a. Gros Ventre, Paunch Indians and Minnetarrees, were in attendance for the annual bartering and socializing.

Le Borgne, of the sinister appearance and matching reputation, persuaded the Crows to permit Larocque and one companion, as well as several of the one-eyed chieftain's Hidatsa, to go home with them. The Crows took the trader and his companions with them on the return journey to the region they considered home, cross country by way of the Knife, Little Missouri, Powder and Tongue Rivers. Crossing the Wolf or Chetish Mountains, an offshoot of the Big Horn Range, the party forded the Big Horn River near the lower canyon and then continued to the Yellowstone.

The Crows had their own proud rites and rules. They welcomed their first white contact into their camps. Fed him. Smoked with him. Listened courteously to what he had to say.

With the Crows, fathomless dark eyes weighing him, Larocque observed all the formalities. The dark eyes warmed to this well-mannered stranger who knew something of polite usage, the correct way to enter a lodge, pass the peace pipe, and the propriety of the culinary compliment, the fulsome belch.

It was the men who met in council, but around the camp circle the women knew how to convey their concerns. Larocque, his tricorn at a raffish angle, assessed the men, and the women who would be likely to influence them, as he made his pitch.

As he expected, the Crows reached no hasty conclusions. They preferred to talk and talk, then adjourn and go to their lodges and think, while the women, obliquely, made their influence felt.

Then the men met to talk some more. They believed in taking time to reach a unanimous position rather than risk a majority ruling that would leave a division in the band, a division that might widen, weaken the band.

The Crows were not that big a tribe, numerically. Every able man was a warrior, and, on occasion, some of the women.

The greatest honor was not in the numbers slain but in the degree of risk to which a warrior exposed himself. Young men were expected to master the curriculum: raid the enemy, steal his horses and women, learn bravery and fortitude. Broaden the gene pool by assimilating the captured women and children, introduce new bloodlines into the horseherd. Share the spoils with those in need, acquiring the honor that comes with generosity.

Indians, as Larocque knew from bitter experience, could not be judged on white men's terms. They were men and women with strong feelings about home and family, but caught up in a life style very different from that of the white man, one that had given them a quite different perspective.

The Crows had a good country, choice camping places, where water, wood and pasture were in good supply, plenty of game. They also had some thoughtful kin elders. Men who had reached maturity, scarred and tested as youthful warriors, who carried the fire and chose where to camp, and looked to the well being of the people. They had seen the wheel and understood its utility but saw no reason for its adoption. The beaver trap was something else.

Indians had to have dreams to guide them. And someone to interpret the dreams correctly. If the dream was of a beaver swimming toward the dreamer, carrying in his mouth, not a willow wand, but a fine new gun, it could be a threat. Or a promise. The elder, a man of unusual and valuable intuition, the spiritual adviser, the clairvoyant chaplain, had a way of interpreting his own and the described dreams of his people, with shrewd practicality.

Like the Swiss, the Crows were outnumbered on all sides. Sioux to the east; Cheyenne and Arapaho to the south; Blackfeet to the west and north. They were friendly with the Flatheads and Shoshones but separated from such potential allies by the corridor the Blackfeet made unhealthy.

The national policy, when the chips were down, was to resist encroachment. Larocque's proposals could enhance that policy. Without losing what he was born with, the Crow could assimilate this new technology, get a toehold in the arms race, raise the NGP index, improve the standard of living, gain honor as a peacemaker, and acquire an ally with a vested, economic interest in the tribe's well-being.

On the Yellowstone in 1805, Larocque took lively, inquisitive apprentices and introduced them to a new medium of exchange, the "Crow beaver."

For bait, the castoreum innovation of the Northwest Indians first used successfully in the Canadian west in 1797; the correct manner in which to set traps; the care in removing and caring for the pelt.

Larocque, a painstaking taskmaster, turned out journeymen who took professional pride in piling up clean, stretched pliable beaver pelts for the fur trade.

At the final trading session on an island in the Yellowstone River, Larocque promised to return. When he did so, he would alert his Crow friends by lighting four signal fires on the mountain tops for four different nights.

Larocque's Crows looked for him in vain. The Anglo-Frenchman had every intention of returning and made plans accordingly. Company policy, always changeable, led to one postponement after another, year after year, until he wearied and left the fur trade, to retire to a monastery.

Colter, who had come to know some of those same Crows, spending time with them in their various camps, made no promises to return. Heading downriver, alone, going home, in the summer of 1807, he reached the mouth of the Platte.

There, hailed by his old friends from the Corps, John Potts and Peter Wiser, he guided his canoe ashore to join them in a smoke and palaver. They had been recruited in St. Louis by Manuel Lisa, who was leading a party to the Yellowstone River Valley to build a fur trading post.

Lisa, shrewdly, offered Colter an even better contract than was usual, triple his private's pay in the Corps. For three years he was to serve Lisa as a hunter, a far-ranging scout, Indian liaison — the professional skills that set him apart, made him a valuable asset to such an undertaking as Lisa had in mind.

After returning to the Big Horn with Lisa, Colter had a very busy time of it. While others were dragging logs into place to build Fort Raymond, or wading up-and-down beaver streams setting traps, Colter was ranging over the country with a thirty-pound pack on his back, afoot, often on snowshoes. He explored an area larger than his native state of Virginia, alone, or in the company of Indians, for he'd had enough of acquaintances who did not wear well.

The purpose of his long marches into the unknown Indian country on the upper Shoshone, Wind and Snake Rivers was to determine the fur resources and, where practicable, encourage the natives to catch, skin and trade beaver.

A white man could state his business to his fellows the minute he got within hailing distance. Colter, a patient man, had long since learned that an Indian could not. Therefore, Colter, in making his contacts, mainly Crows and Shoshone, in scattered bands and at established villages, timed the length of his visits carefully, diplomatically, and promoted the catching of beaver, advertised the trading opportunities to be found at Fort Raymond, and distributed carefully selected trade samples.

In the process of familiarizing himself with a few of the people and so much of the territory, a lot of it in the dead of winter, he got familiar with the ways of the Blackfeet. Every time he got within hailing distance of the Blackfeet, there was hell to pay.

Three times in one year they played hob with his plans. And his life. After his third narrow escape from their over-familiar ways, he promised fervently, by God, not to gamble with his life in Blackfeet country again.

Yet here he was, getting ready to lead some thirty men among Bug's Boys.

The party, in numbers, would be about the same size force as Lewis and Clark had led. Lacking the discipline. Without the esprit de corp.

The leaders, Menard and Henry, had proved capable, conscientious. A Frenchman of good family, Menard was without prejudice, a man of principle. Henry, a man of unknown antecedents, cool and tough and businesslike. Menard, even though he'd had experience as a colonel in the Illinois territorial militia, was inclined to be paternalistic and was esteemed by men who knew their gripes would get a sympathetic hearing.

Henry, who handled men with greater emotional detachment,

demanding that they have some alternative solutions to present along with any problem, had their respect.

In the next few weeks, they would choose the most experienced, able men, French, Indian and American, from those available to go to Three Forks.

Lisa, who had known the Blackfeet to be friendly on an occasion or two, had hopes of getting them to see the convenience of trading with a post closer home, weaning them away from the Norwesters and HBC. He had persuaded the partners that, with proper overtures and gifts, this expedition could neutralize, if not establish regular trade with, the Blackfeet. Colter was not so sure.

Len Cather, still listening to voices, caught the occasional subtle lilt in Francis Vallé's cadences that indicated he had not learned English at his mother's knee. Idly, Vallé had left the mapmakers to wander over into the corner where Belt Jackson sat cross-legged near the light from the fireplace, sketch pad resting on one knee, absorbed in what, off-handedly, he called his letters home.

"Col-tair?" Francis was saying, his eyebrows raised as he stared at Belt's pencil sketch, suspending in time something of Colter's character in his posture, something of his thoughts in the frown line between his brows. "When did you ever see that man looking worried?"

"Just now," said Belt absently, finishing off his drawing with his signature, a small cracked bell enclosing the initial 'J'. "Talking about Three Forks."

"Vair-y good," Francis said thoughtfully, dropping to the floor beside Belt, waving his hand toward the latter's portfolio of sketches that lay beside him. "May I?"

Belt hesitated. Francis said easily, "I've dabbled some, myself. It's a very useful talent to cultivate, particularly when you want to ingratiate yourself with a pretty girl. They find it flattering to be asked to sit — but the result must be flattering, too." He shook his head in mock despair. "If the likeness displeases, it can be very enlightening. Was surprised more than once to find there was really a shrew beneath a smiling, pretty face."

"Never done girls," said Belt, passing the portfolio to Francis. "I'm a real good sign painter, though. Done a lot of it. And interior house painting."

Francis settled himself with the portfolio. Belt, his concentration broken, looked off into space, thinking back.

He and Len Cather and Pet McBride had expected to be busy throughout the winter, wading in the icy water several times a day to unload or reset their beaver traps. Delighted to see the pelts of their catches getting thicker and thicker, they had been taken aback to have old hands assure them the pelts were too thick in winter.

Among themselves, they decided it was the human hide that was too thin for chancing the danger and discomfort of trapping in sub-zero weather.

Following the lead of the more experienced veterans, trappers who traditionally holed up in their winter camps or at the fort, the trio, except for the tramps they took with the Major, occupied themselves in various ways during the long winter days. By mid-February, they, like most of the other men around the fort, had mended their moccasins, made new ones; cleaned and polished their rifles and accouterments; patched their clothes and fashioned skin or stroud replacements.

Each, in his own way, found an interest to break the tedium. Len, with his ear for languages, was adding new words and phrases to his vocabulary, Crow, Shoshone, and the patois of the engages. Pet, acutely missing the physical activity, had taken to helping out in the smithy, pounding and shaping iron into all manner of necessities.

Belt, when digging out his extra woolen shirt, found his mother had wrapped it around his sketchbook with a note. "Son, we know you be no hand to write. Draw us some pitchers. Yore pitchers be near as good as a letter."

That made it easier to indulge himself. His fingers had been itching to catch a place, a moment or a person with his pencil. He set about doing so, unobtrusively. There was no need to feel self-conscious, defensive, for there was nothing effete about a man who wrote home to his Ma, albeit in his own fashion.

"Who taught you to sketch like this?" asked Francis, impressed, as he leafed through the portfolio of the young frontiersman he was more used to seeing holding a rifle in his large, capable hands.

"A limner," said Belt, which wasn't entirely true. He had been drawing pictures since he could walk, with anything that came to hand, charcoal sticks on Grandma's freshly scrubbed puncheon floors, fingers and India ink from Grandpa's desk on her whitewashed walls, in the comfortable times when they still lived in Pennsylvania, before Pa got the Kentucky fever. "Sam Smith. He travelled from place-to-place painting worshipful masters and butterflies. We'd have made better time if he hadn't stopped so frequent to paint butterflies. Took me nigh onto three years to get him from Kaintuck to Ste. Genevieve. Then he went gadding off into the swamp after a new kind of butterfly and that was the death of him."

"Hmm. I think I remember him," said Francis. "A successful portrait painter from Philadelphia who planned to bring out a book on American butterflies. Rather than finance him directly, the brethren in his home lodge got commissions from Blue Lodges along his route to do portraits of the respective worshipful master to hang in the Lodge hall. Some shrewd brother Mason suggested he prepare the paintings beforehand, the worshipful master complete in his regalia, only needing the addition of the face."

"Grandpa's idea," said Belt grinning. "The regalia is the same so it seemed a sensible shortcut. Grandpa was always on the look out for ways to help out his family and his Masonic brethren. He had enough of both to keep him busy."

Grandpa had eleven sons and three daughters and a successful establishment on the main route between Lancaster and Pittsburgh that had survived all the troublesome times. He took a purposeful interest in the prosperity of his offspring, even when it was a daughter who had insisted on marrying the man of her own choice, not his. From time to time, some of his children relieved the pressure of numbers at home by departing for greener pastures. Grandpa helped them make a start, kept in touch with them by travellers, and by occasional visits in person.

Grandpa had started out as a trader in peltry when everything around him was western Pennsylvania wilderness, then imported goods to exchange for skins, formed connections with merchants in Philadelphia. By the time he was seventy, hale and hardy still, he had a store, an inn, a blacksmith shop, lots of land and a sufficiency of sons to take on the day-to-day details.

Travellers sought and obtained shelter at his inn. Newcomers, magistrates and itinerant preachers came frequently, keeping Grandpa abreast of activities and trends. When Grandma died, he didn't sit and brood, but took to travelling about. Visiting the Blue Lodges, prevalent along the frontier, in his official capacity of leading its members into other select, higher degrees, he also managed to look in on his scattered progeny often enough to keep abreast of their circumstances. There was no telling when he would turn up, with whom or what ideas.

When Belt was fifteen, a good woodsman and shot, knowledgeable about wilderness survival, Grandpa rode into the Jackson clearing with a consumptive fellow Mason and some ideas for improving the lot of the Jacksons.

When he told the Jacksons, quoting from his extensive correspondence with Moses Austin and others, of the opportunities in Missouri, there was no doubt they liked what they heard. Pa had a lot of brothers. The single ones took off almost immediately. For the ones with families and property to pack or dispose of, it would take longer. There were ways and means of reducing the numbers and underwriting their expenses.

Grandpa found places for two of Belt's brothers to work their way west on a keelboat; for cousin George, who was good with an abacus, to accompany a trader in peltries.

As for Belt, "That boy who scribbled all over the parlor wall," said Grandpa, "I see he's still at it."

"Not on parlor walls," said his mother defensively. "He knows better than to do that now."

"He certainly filled in all the blank spaces on the privy walls," said Grandpa, hitching his belt more comfortably in place around his middle. "Don't get me wrong. I'm not finding fault. In fact, I —," he broke off, suspecting rightly that describing his contemplative enjoyment in such a setting, despite his appreciation of the boy's recognizable renderings of the pomposity of the teacher, the slyness of a travelling horse trader or the catamount eyes of a frontier scout, all known to Grandpa, would offend her sense of propriety. "I can find him something better to scribble on. He can take Sam to Missouri, earn and learn while travelling. Sam's a real babe-in-the-woods. It'll be the boy's job to see Sam doesn't get lost."

While preparations were being made for Belt to accompany Sam, Grandpa told the limner he was too poorly to go haring after butterflies. If he would stay at the clearing and rest up a bit, the Jackson young 'uns would fan out through the woods and bring the butterflies to him. As for those blank canvases weighing down the backs of two mules, Sam would save time here and now by doing the preliminary work, paint up bodies and suitable back grounds.

At first Sam, who had been a conscientious portrait painter, didn't cotton to the idea of *not* painting a worshipful master from scratch.

"Nonsense," said Grandpa. "No need to wear yourself out over each painting. There's not that many ways to do Masonic regalia or the all-seeing eye and other symbols. I'm an average size man. I can describe the first half-dozen men you'll be painting. I can give you some pointers about the differences there. Besides four my size, you'll need one short feller with broad shoulders, narrow little hands and feet; one tall one with big hands and feet and narrow shoulders. When you get down to these last ones on your journey, inquire about the next. There'll be someone who can tell you about the build of the ones ahead. Then you hole up and get some more canvases ready. After a few lessons, Belt can help you do that. Give you more free time to paint butterflies.

"Another thing. Those Masons have womenfolk. Do up some painting of a genteel lady pouring tea or holding a Bible or some such folderol. They'll sell, too. Ruth, m'daughter here, Belt's Ma, she's got a nice build still, is about average size, not too hefty, not too skinny, and there's some nice pewter to put on the table beside her. Do half a dozen of her, all but the face.

"Well, maybe one with her face to keep to make up for having to sit still so long when there's so much to do. And if you've got to put a butterfly in a picture, put it in with the womenfolk. Don't put it on the master's lapel. Didn't set well with the last one, the way folks that came to the unveiling tried to shoo off that butterfly."

On horseback, Grandpa accompanied Sam, astride a black gelding, Belt, on the spare nag Grandpa had brought along. Belt was in charge of the two pack mules, one carrying their supplies, the other laden with canvases, the blank ones Sam had held in reserve for butterflies, the rest portraits awaiting faces.

It would be no coincidence that, in after years, visitors to Lodges and Masonic homes would find a certain sameness in the portraits displayed, except for the butterflies. For Sam, once he found Belt could do it, left Belt to delineate the same figures over and over. Sam put in the butterflies, a different kind each time, some of them, as he pointed out enthusiastically, very rare and unusual.

Grandpa, a stickler for detail, giving pointers on travelling comfortably and safely, saw them introduced to the first of the worshipful masters, comfortably housed in the latter's own home, and stayed long enough to get them settled in. He took Belt around to the general store, blacksmith, tavern, livery stable, the typical establishments in a frontier village, and demonstrated how to get orders for sign painting.

Before leaving to go about his own affairs, he cautioned his grandson, "Don't be gettin' any high-falutin' ideas. Sam's not one to put on airs. He'd just as soon be called a limner as an artist, long as the supply of butterflies hold out.

"Some folks think of artists as sissified. Mostly, you'll be passed along from Mason to Mason, who'll know what Sam's about and can vouch for the two of you. There'll be times, and you can't help it, that you'll come up aginst some hard cases. They might not be too sure what a limner does but they know a sign painter follows a manly trade, nothing sissified about him. So don't you be puttin' on any airs around such folks.

"Something else to remember. Sam's a sickly man. You might have to get a tad bossy with him to make sure he remembers to eat and sleep like he should. He knows he's not long for this world. He's got this fool notion to paint all the butterflies he can before his time comes.

"If he dies on you along the way, have the nearest Masonic brethren take care of the last rites. Sell the mules and whatever gear you have to pay for his funeral. Pack up his paintings of butterflies and send them on to me. Anything left over, you can keep.

"If you can get him to Missouri, it's not your problem any more. He'll settle up what he owes you and you can leave him with some of the Masons there.

"You can go ahead and rejoin your folks. They'll already be in Missouri by then and will be looking for you."

They followed the route Grandpa had laid out for them, passed along from Mason to Mason. They liked each other, the ailing man with the artist's drive, the adolescent expanding his horizons.

Going from Kaintuck to Missouri, from a gangly fifteen-year old to a filled-out, assured eighteen year old, Belt had to be more than a tad bossy at times to keep them on the move. Before they got to Kaskaskia, they were having to hole up more and more frequently, for Sam kept giving out.

At those times, Sam, lying in bed, struggling not to cough, conscientiously proceeded with the training of his apprentice. From necessity, he had to leave more and more undertakings to Belt. He got to depending on Belt to make the initial sketches of the real face, then Sam prettied them up. Took out the pock-marks, softened a lantern jaw, put more space between a lady's eyes.

Sam was a painstaking, meticulous teacher. "You need to work more on perspective in those sketches of yours. You've got a good eye. However, as a portrait painter you'd starve to death — unless you overcome your tendency to make such autobiographical faces. You're good with pencil or charcoal. In the other mediums — chalk, watercolor or oil — you get impatient."

"They don't feel right," agreed Belt.

When they neared their journey's end, Sam summed it up. "Belt, you could do all right as a travelling limner, as far as your skills go. But a limner needs a more settled, prosperous country to make his calling pay. The further west we go, the less chance it seems to me you'll find enough folks. If you wanted to go back east, you'd find there's a market for sign painting and interior house painting, at least."

Belt shook his head. He was anxious to catch up with his folks. "I've learned what I need to know," he told Sam, careful not to tell him exactly what he meant. "Grandpa's idea was a good one. Tell him that when you write. He'll be glad to know."

Shortly thereafter, in Ste. Genevieve, they parted on that note. Belt sought out his folks, already settled into industrious activities near the lead mines, and told them much the same thing. "Grandpa's idea was a good one. I've learned what I need to know. There's not much money to be made in painting folks or signs. It's in the brushes somebody like Sam uses. One good mink pelt should have enough hair to make a bushel of those brushes. A man could make more out of a bushel of brushes than a stack of good signs. That's where the money is — in furs."

Now in a fur-rich land, where he had already made nearly a bushel of brushes to fill in the time this winter, Belt was recalled to the present by Francis saying thoughtfully, "You have a rare talent for illustration. If you were interested in making it pay, there are places where you could advance yourself, seek out teachers and markets — find out more about things you would need to know as an illustrator — "

"I've learned what I need to know," Belt said firmly. "These are for Ma — to pass the time until I can get out there and find a sable. Do you have any idea what those artist fellows pay for a sable brush?"

"Vaguely," said Francis. "But I don't think you can expect to find a sable closer than Siberia."

Pierre Menard looked over Francis's shoulder. "There's Shehaka chasing his rooster. Lisa yelling about his canoe." He gestured with the sketch to the Major. "Have you seen these?"

"Belt's letters to his mother? I've seen some of them." He joined Francis and Menard in spreading the sketches out on the floor and their exclamations drew Lewis, Morrison and Colter.

"There's Drouillard, catamount eyes and all," said Colter, and, "My God, is that what I look like?"

"Here's Cheek mixing it up with Ride," said Lewis.

"And Ayres bringing in James," said Morrison.

Len, observing them, realized that Belt's light was going to come out from under the bushel, and it pleased him. He had already seen that Belt, conscious of the fact his sketchbook had only a limited supply of pages, had filled in all the spaces with pencil drawings that lived and breathed, catching the essence of the men here at Fort Raymond.

"I suppose it is only coincidence — said Menard slowly, then paused, looking at the Major.

"Probably," said the Major. "But it does look like the roster we've been considering, doesn't it?"

There was Ayres, a hardy, quiet-spoken man, and the two French Canadians; Brown, gnarled and laconic; Bryan, a quick learner; Dougherty, who wanted to be an Indian agent; Drouillard, who was part Indian; Cheek, big and brash; Hull, who couldn't swim and was very cautious at fords; Immell, of the soldierly solid bulk and troop-reviewing eye; Fleehart, who liked beaver meat; Jackson, in a self-portrait, a good woodsman; Lewis, capable; Morrison, learning; Pelton, a lugubrious fellow good with horses; Luthecaw, a good-natured Shawnee; Menard, dependable; Henry, well-qualified; McBride, a good shot; Vallé, a good horseman. Doza and his engages. Some Delawares. The prickle-edged James.

Menard, restless, got up and went outside where he was greeted with "Colonel?" giving him the honorary title from his days with the Illinois militia. It was Thomas James. "You here, too? Didn't expect to see you."

"Really? And why not?"

"Expected Lisa," said James. "Damned glad it's you instead."

Menard came back looking puzzled. Somewhat later in the day, Len, overhearing Cheek boastfully bringing James up to date on events, conferred with his friends, Belt Jackson and Pet McBride. "Do you remember hearing anything about Cheek threatening to kill Lisa before we left Fort Manuel?"

"You mean that story Cheek has been spreading about scaring Lisa so that he got Menard to come in his place?" said Pet. "Maybe he did talk about killing Lisa. He ain't the only one, I guess. From what I hear tell, lots do."

"Lisa and Colonel Chouteau were the only ones of the partners who didn't have to stay in the mountains," said Len. "They were supposed to return to St. Louis. The way Cheek is telling it, he scared Lisa so he high-tailed it back down river and left Captain Menard to take his place here."

"What's this you say?" asked Menard, joining them as he overheard the last sentence.

The three looked uncomfortable. The Major, strolling up, said easily, "You know Jamie and his way with a tall tale."

He summarized the story that was making the rounds. Cheek had told James, that after he left Fort Mandan, there had been a confrontation.

Lisa was at the Company marquee when Cheek and some of the other Americans arrived to dicker for equipment. When Lisa said something about the terms Colonel Chouteau had set, Cheek claimed he said, "Jest let that goddamned Frenchie get a hundred yards outta that there fort and he's a dead duck."

"'Cheek! Cheek!' exclaimed Lisa, "Mind what you say."

"I do that," Cheek said he said. "As for you, Ee-saw, I've heard some of our boys say that if they ever caught you two hundred yards from camp they'd shoot you. If they don't, I will.

"Now Ee-saw, you are going to the Forks of the Missouri. Mark my words, you'll never come back alive."

Menard frowned. "Cheek's had it in for both the Colonel and Lisa for a long time. I suppose it could have happened. I just don't remember hearing about it."

The Major grinned. "Or how Lisa turned pale and rushed off to persuade you to come in his place?"

"Nonsense. We all know this was the duty I undertook when I left home."

"We know that. However, Tom James and some of the others are accepting it as gospel truth that Lisa sent you here in his place because he feared Cheek."

Menard snorted. "That's damnable, blackening a man's good name."

The Major grinned. "Lisa's? Better men than Cheek have been doing it for years."

"I don't suppose there's much we can do about it. They'll believe what they want to believe." Menard looked at Belt. "Let me see that sketch you made of Cheek again." With it in hand he frowned over it. "There's something there — is he really looking over his shoulder at something?"

"This country makes Cheek uneasy," said Belt, adding. "At least that's the way he looked when talking about how different it was from back home."

"It's a cold and savage and alien land," said Menard. "We're creating a business against high odds in a strange place. We've all come a long way, through difficult passages and coarse, jabbering, ignorant people. We still have a long way to go. Soon, thank God, we'll be too busy to fabricate tall tales." He dismissed the matter with a smile. "The pleasures of the out-of-doors are strictly limited unless you care for hunting or massacres. So, how about a game of cards?"

Sleeping, eating or playing long, inconclusive games of chance; bartering with the occasional Indian; fraternizing if the opportunity arose; bringing in wood and water. The days of February gave way to those of March.

With spring in the offing, and the roster pretty well determined, Andrew Henry made a deal for some extra horses with Edward Rose, who obtained them from his Crow in-laws. Belt, trying not to stare, got Edward Rose on paper, too, all his scars, as well as the two Indians that accompanied him, bringing in the horses. Cut Nose, and the twins looking right at you. The boy had an open face and his eyes smiled at the Major. The girl didn't smile, but she eyed the Major, long and intently

Belt sketched the cavalcade that rode out in mid-March. With two exceptions, they came up against nothing more than the usual, normal hardships expected in mountain travel. Belt illustrated both events, as well as some others.

Two Americans had been sent ahead with their Shoshone wives and in-laws. They were to hunt game, keep the main party supplied with meat.

When Belt and the rest of the party came up with them, they had just been raided by the Gros Ventres. Belt sketched in all the details.

After they reached the Gallatin River, painful snowblindness held them up for several days. Belt sketched that camp, squeezing into one corner a depiction of James leading the snowblind Brown. On a margin, he illustrated James's indignation upon discovering that some of the men had killed and eaten the dog given him by an Indian.

They arrived at the Forks of the Missouri the third day of April, 1810.

About two miles above the junction of the Madison and Jefferson Rivers, there was a half-mile point of land. Selecting a strategic spot, the south bank of the channel later known as the Jefferson Slough, they put up a double stockade of logs, set three feet in the ground, ten feet above, enclosing an area three hundred feet square.

Belt made a sketch of Fort Three Forks for his Ma. He put himself in it, with the Major looking over his shoulder, and Cheeky, a gangling big dog now, stretched out beside them. Captain Menard had promised to take his letters-home to his Ma in June and send him some more sketch pads. He only had part of a pad left now, and it had gotten damp, but it was better than nothing. He had a feel for what he was doing now and would hate to be reduced to using skins and war paint, like the Indians, to record events.

Chapter 15

In that first week of April, one of the resident bachelors of Three Forks came fully awake.

He was a handsome fellow. Healthy and fit, like most of his kind. Young, but of impressive stature, he came from a long-line of outstanding forebears. His clan, upon arrival some ten thousand years before, had established, and since maintained, undisputed sovereignty over this and other extensive rangelands of the West.

He had not been sleeping too well of late. Since mid-March, he had been rising at intervals, sticking his straw-colored head out of his dwelling, checking on the weather.

On a nice day, he even ventured outside for an hour or so. Revelling in the warmth of the sun, he sprawled out on a snowbank, all three-hundred sturdy pounds wrapped in his rich brown and beige pelage.

Scratching, yawning, stretching his notable shoulders, he sunned himself in joyous abandon. He rolled on his back, kicked up his legs, and took a gleeful slide or two down the snowbank.

Above him a fluffy cloud moved across the bright blue afternoon sky of the Month of Sore Eyes. About him was the dazzling blinding white of a sub-alpine world, still in the grip of winter. As the sun touched the tip of the mountain top above his hillside den and the shadows coolly lengthened, he returned to his bed of disintegrating leaves, grass and pine boughs.

In the Moon of New Grass, not a temperate month in the Stony Mountains, he came out of hibernation for keeps, a bit groggy after his winter of sluggish inactivity. A sub-adult male grizzly, three years old, still growing, who had wintered alone for the first time in his life, he was lean but in good condition.

The claws of last November, worn down from an active season digging for roots, tubers, beaver, ground squirrel, and repeated sharpening on the bark of trees, had grown out again. They were light amber in color, slightly curved. The five claws on the dexterous front feet were three inches long, the five on his hind feet, one-and-a-half inches, all steely sharp. The heavily padded soles and toes of his feet were pink and a bit tender, for the dead outer layer of skin had sloughed off during hibernation. He had a fine set of teeth — forty-two altogether, twelve incisors, four sizable canine teeth, sixteen premolars and the ten flat-topped molars for grinding up his vegetation intake.

His hearing was good. His sense of smell, superb. His vision, hereditarily myopic, was excellent for distances up to one hundred yards. His digestive apparatus could handle anything he decided was worth eating. He was a good swimmer. Walking, purposefully, he could move along at about four miles an hour; running, flat-out, he could do forty miles an hour.

Like others of his kind, Griz would suffer few health problems. Even the secretions of his skin, naturally acid, served him well, as disinfectant and insecticide. Barring the unforeseen, he had a life expectancy of well over twenty years. Omnivorous, he would spend most of that life seeking out a balanced diet. He would do considerable travelling, some of it just for fun. When fall came, he would begin moseying toward den site he knew. Come spring, he would head for the sites of remembered feeding grounds.

Griz and his litter brother had been conceived in the month of June, 1806.

In a meadow between the Madison and Jefferson Rivers, as the rampantly promiscuous grizzly social season got underway, their mother, reddish-brown with pewter highlights, broadcasting the tantalizing scent of nubility, had been approached by suitor after suitor, with decorum. She considered and rejected several before accepting the advances of a good-looking black male, who fathered Brother.

The black male was driven away, after a knock-down, roaring brawl that she found most exciting, by an enormous silver-tipped brown-and-beige champion, who fathered Griz. For several weeks this handsome king of the grizzlies stayed close to her side, easily driving off all other contenders, as protective and possessive and lustful as any rapturous honeymooner.

With the end of June, and changes in the female hormones, the sexually-stimulating, summoning scents of feminine receptivity came to an end, too. Everyone lost interest in togetherness. Unceremoniously, the mother grizzly and her mate ambled off, separately, to take up their solitary way of life again.

While the mother grizzly began the routine circuit of her home range, which varied according to the season, and available forage, the two fertilized eggs were put on hold. Tucked away in the tickler file of her reproductive system for consideration in November, they floated free in her womb, in undemanding limbo.

Instead of having to eat for three, their Mom, thanks to the delayed implantation of putative offspring, could concentrate on her own current, and her and their, future needs.

In seven months, Mom had to stock up on a twelve-month supply of food. She had a good summer and even better fall. In September she returned to the traditional denning area of her kin, on an isolated mountain side.

For as long as Mom could remember, her mother and her mother's mother had been, and still were, building dens here. She was careful not to impinge on their critical zones. So were her siblings, of various ages, sex and status.

Currently, in the grizzly hierarchy, Mom's own mother, with her three little cubs, had higher status than even her grandmother, with only a yearling cub. Mom, and her sisters, who had had cubs, ranked lower than those females with cubs, but higher than young females that hadn't bred at all.

Among the males, size and strength made for dominance, but even the dominant male gave way before the fiercely defensive mother of new cubs. Males and females, knowing their place in the grizzly pecking order, they were content, practicing a confident tolerance toward each other.

Mom constructed her den according to the specifications she had learned from her mother.

Mom's winter home was average size, an accommodating five feet deep by four feet wide and three feet high, excavated on an upward slant for better drainage. For the bed itself, she carried dead leaves, boughs and grass inside, spread them in insulating layers over the dirt floor.

Her chambermaid chores done for the season, Mom returned to the assortment of rich feed in the meadows of Three Forks, and ate her way through October. In November, in the midst of a snowstorm that covered her tracks, Mom retreated to her den.

As soon as Mom settled down for her long winter nap, well-bolstered with accumulated fat reserves, her efficient reproductive system retrieved the fertilized eggs from the suspension file. Reactivated, they attached themselves to the walls of her uterus and began growing, rapidly.

Sometime in January, after an active gestation period of little over two months, the cubs were born. Sleepily, Mom cleaned them up, disposed of the placenta, and gently, dexterously, with her forepaws settled them against her warm, ample midsection. There was nothing cute about them. Weighing about a pound apiece, not much bigger than a chipmunk, scant of hair, with tight-shut eyes, Griz and Brother rooted around until each found one of her six nipples.

They made contented little sounds as they nursed; Mom, licking them, made loud, slurping noises. Curled around her tiny newborns, an insulating incubator of warm, furry body and legs, she sank back into somnolence. As the days went by, she changed position from time-to-time, automatically cradling her offspring, licking them as they nursed, cleaning up their excrement, never entirely awake.

On the rich grizzly milk, which has a fat content ten times that of cow or human milk, Griz and Brother doubled, tripled, quadrupled their birth weight. Early in April of 1807, they came tumbling out of the den on Mom's heels. No longer hairless or sightless, they were as cute as any chipmunk and considerably larger.

Griz, weighing over five pounds, was blond about his head and neck, shading to the darker beige-brown of his sire on the rest of his body. Brother, weighing slightly less, was as black as his handsome father. Fetching, fuzzy and filled with curiosity, they got their first instructions.

Going more than a few feet from the entrance to the den was a no-no, right at first. None of them were real steady on their feet as yet. Mom needed time to regain her strength and energy. Griz and Brother needed time to learn to walk, to get their eyes adjusted to the out-of-doors. If there was trouble, Mom's reactions would be slow, the cub's inept.

Mom took it slow and easy until her metabolism returned to normal. Griz and Brother got to know, and heed, Mom's woof for 'Come!'; the gesture for 'Stop that!'; the grunt and gesture for 'Don't do that again!'. Griz, bigger, smarter, didn't get his ears boxed as often as Brother.

At the end of the second week when Mom's post-hibernation lethargy had worn off and her appetite returned, she sniffed the wind for the location of the nearest protein. She got the scent of a winter-killed carcass of an elk, still half-frozen, some distance away, on the bank of the Madison River, and led them to it. She dug out the liver for them to sample. Mom kept them there, all three feeding on the thawing meat, bedding down in a thicket, until it was gone.

Then, Mom, solicitous and vigilant, introduced them to the circuit she favored, bounded on one side by the Jefferson, on the other by the Gallatin, with the Madison and all its larder in the center. She showed them where and when to dig for roots and tubers; to locate the edible plants, the berry bushes, the pine nuts, and, whenever possible, the protein in one form or other. Sometimes it was ground squirrels; sometimes a surprised beaver; sometimes the carcass of one of the larger grass eaters. The latter were there in the valley in abundance, elk, deer and buffalo. Normal attrition, a weakling fawn, an ancient elk or buffalo, the carcass marked by a gathering of the ravens, put dinner on the table often enough that Mom did not have to stalk and kill her own meat. In the warm days of summer, she did, however, show them what fun it was to splash around in one or the other of the three rivers, and come up with a tasty trout.

Until May of their third summer, they followed, learned from and obeyed Mom. An idyllic existence, relatively permissive, during which they indulged their curiosity, romped and played exuberantly, nursed and napped, secure in their status.

Their status underwent an abrupt change that summer. Mom, inexplicably, lost all interest in their well-being. As her hormonal urges prepared her for the mating season, Mom cut the apron strings with impatient ruthlessness.

She told them, roughly, to "Go away!" and "Don't bother me!"

Bewildered, as one after the other was knocked, squalling, end-over-end, they hung about in her vicinity. They were careful to stay out of reach.

Griz, always the more independent of the two, to whom Brother deferred, was the first to accept the fact they could no longer count on Mom's solicitude and leadership.

Grizzlies will return year after year to places where they remember having found food in the past. Their memories are long and improve with age and experience.

Griz began searching out the feeding sites he remembered. Brother tagged along.

In a place and time where good food was abundant, there was also an abundance of grizzlies. Griz and Brother, accustomed to the top of the totem pole thanks to Mom's vigilant fierceness, now found themselves near the bottom. They learned their status quickly. Working in tandem, they presented a united front that summer which served them well in dealing with most of the single, larger bears.

Instinctively, Griz recognized the need to defer to the king of the grizzlies. As the dominant male, he would chase all other bears from a large carcass until he had fed.

Figuratively tugging at a forelock, Griz and Brother, practicing the body language of submission, turning their bodies sideways, dropping their heads to avoid making eye contact, acknowledged their lowly status.

By showing such good manners, Griz and Brother, maintaining lowered heads and averted faces, were permitted more than once by the dominant grizzly to dine on his leavings.

Blundering at times, still Griz learned quickly, more so than Brother. They went into hibernation in good shape.

Now, in the spring of 1810, Griz took his time shaking off the lassitude of hibernation. He sniffed the air. Not far away, Brother did the same.

Others of the clan, far and near, were up and about, a bit woozy and lethargic, too, like anyone after a deep, long-sustained nap. In a short time, this would wear off. The dens, on the isolated mountain sides, where it was still winter, would be left behind.

With the re-establishment of normal metabolism, Griz and all his clan would be hungry — very hungry. They would not deal gently with anyone or anything getting between them and the breaking of their long fast.

The grizzlies were not the only predators coming out of winter quarters that April of 1810.

Running Wolf was a black-eyed Piegan teen-ager, bright and bold. At the end of his eighteenth winter, he stood tall and straight in his deerskin leggings and moccasins, his buffalo robe around his bare shoulders.

With the professional eye of an All Brave Dog soldier, he watched his clan as the herald rode among them announcing the departure schedule. In his wake, there was a flurry of exuberant activity.

Today they would leave for their spring camp on the Jefferson River.

Running Wolf wore his dark hair in the Blackfeet fashion, unbound, shoulder length, except for a long, narrow bang trained to fall over the bridge of his nose. The nose was slightly askew, having been broken by a Crow, just before Wolf killed and scalped him, on his first raid, when he was a thirteen-year old novice in the Pigeon society.

Wolf had all his teeth, still white and regular, but only one and a half ears. The cornered mother of his pet wolf, aiming at his throat, had snapped the top of his right ear clean off, just before he throttled her with his bare hands, so as not to damage her pelt, when he was a fifteen-year old adept in the Mosquito society.

He had saved that pelt and others. His favorite sister had fashioned them into a wolf cape, part of the regalia he had worn on the proud day last summer when he had been made a member of the illustrious All Brave Dog society.

Long of muscle, foot, hand and face, he had a wide mouth that turned up cheerfully at the corners. As one of the camp police, even when he spoke sternly to someone, he never made anyone sullen and resentful. When he put on his war paint, he drew harsh red lines down from his mouth in order to look properly fierce.

As a member of one of the prominent Piegan families, Running Wolf was well-schooled in the social, moral, political and religious beliefs and customs of his people. He did them proud as a cheerful, popular participant in all the sports, games and chores. He was expected to, and did, live up to the unwritten code of honorable conduct for all members of the Blackfeet confederation: to be honest, fair and considerate toward Piegans, Bloods and Blackfeet. To others, he owed nothing.

The Blackfeet maintained a lethal policy of immigration control. They were death on any poachers in their game preserve.

Running Wolf had been raised on the assumption the game belonged to the people of the confederacy. From the Saskatchewan on the north to the Three Forks on the south, from the glaciers above Lake McDonald to the villages of the Big Bellies on the Upper Missouri, the taking of game was their prerogative. Running Wolf was one of the enforcers of the no-trespassing policy, a member of one of the warrior societies that enthusiastically policed a big hunk of southern Canada and a sizable slice of the northwestern plains.

The three divisions of the Blackfeet confederacy were essentially independent. When the need arose to repel an invader, they could act in concert. Piegans, Bloods and the Blackfeet themselves would rally to the call, stripped and striped for the glories of combat. In addition, following the annual summer gathering of the tribes, members of the warrior societies, singly and severally, would take on assignments with other divisions, riding the fringes of the Blackfeet empire, seeking out illegal aliens.

The Blackfeet, living farthest northeast, actively discouraged the Cree and Assiniboin encroachments from the east. On occasion, Kootenae Appe, the Piegan war chief, had led Piegan warriors in joint endeavors with the Blackfeet. Running Wolf's father's brother had returned from one such raid with a Cree captive, now his third and favorite wife and mother of Black Cloud, Running Wolf's favorite cousin and one of his peer group.

The Bloods, at the center, dealt roughly with trespassers from both the east and west. Black Cloud had taken a jaunt with them last summer and returned to sing and dance and shake three scalps.

The Piegans, the fastest-growing of the three tribes, held the frontier aggressively against the inroads of the Sioux, the Crow, the Flathead, the Kootenai and the Shoshone.

Running Wolf had stolen horses from the Sioux, fought the Crow, raided the Kootenai and the Shoshone, carrying off a scalp or two.

After the battle with the Flatheads two years ago, all he'd been able to carry off was the body of his younger brother, slain by the far-reaching rifle of a white man. His mother, assertive and vindictive, had never let him, or any of the warrior societies forget that it had been one of the Long Knives who had been responsible, just as it had been a white man, four year's earlier, on the White River, who had killed his father.

There were all manner of societies. Something for everyone and every occasion: the Medicine Pipe society, the Tobacco society, the Buffalo Cows. These were open to people of all ages except the children. Many a Piegan belonged to more than one.

Running Wolf's grandmother, Ay-Len, was a person of consequence in all three; his mother, Shining Doe, was influential in the women's societies, and an active supporter of the warrior societies.

In addition, there were the cults, in which Ay-Len had a certain ex-officio status. These, a loose association of individuals banded together on the basis of a dream or vision about the same 'helper' bird, animal, sacred stone or celestial being, were concerned with the physical and mental well-being of the people.

The men and women with the 'power' functioned as both priests and doctors. These were supposed to use their 'helper' or 'helpers' mainly for the welfare of the tribe.

Ay-Len, who had a 'power' uniquely her own, made sure the welfare of the tribe came first. Any 'healer' who wanted the benefit of the prestige of success and concomitant payment for his services showed her a certain deference, called upon her as a consultant frequently.

The warrior societies were the dominating factor in the tribal confederation. As a group, the societies were known as the All Comrades. The chieftain of a band, civil or war, got a large measure of support from his own society. Nevertheless, he was aware that the power he wielded depended largely on his cooperation with the All Comrades societies.

Except for a few, rare occasions, the warrior societies were reserved for the age-grouped males. Generally, young boys of ten or eleven entered the first of a series of societies as a group to begin a career as a defender and policeman of the tribe. The group then proceeded up the ladder of societies by selling and purchasing ceremonies and regalia at regular intervals every four years or so.

Each society had its own name, descriptive of its function, with its own Old Comrade. The Old Comrade, mentor, herald and instructor, held office indefinitely, advancing with his group of warriors as they passed from grade to grade through the system.

The wives, mothers and sisters of the members were an unofficial auxiliary, permitted to sing, but not dance, in the ceremonials. When their men went to war, some of them, such as Running Wolf's fierce mother, went along to cook and do the housekeeping chores, and, sometimes to take part in the fighting.

Running Wolf had moved up rapidly through the societies — the Pigeons, the Mosquitoes, the Braves — summa cum laude. Last year, at the annual summer encampment of the Blackfeet confederacy, he had been inducted into the prestigious warrior society, the All Brave Dogs, when only seventeen.

After the ceremonies were concluded with a feast of serviceberry soup, he had marched through the camp with the other All Brave Dogs, belting out their famous society song:

"It is bad to live to be old,
 Better to die young
 Fighting bravely
 In battle!"

When the great camp broke up into the various bands and clans and went their different ways to hunt, the thirty-five members of Running Wolf's society were spread throughout the tribe.

Along with another cousin, Horn-of-the-Bull, the Old Comrade, there was Running Wolf and Black Cloud of the initiated to represent the All Brave Dog society at the winter camp of the clan.

Now, the Old Comrade, hearing the herald's announcement, rode up, grinning with delighted anticipation. "Soon," he said to Running Wolf, "will come the spring meeting." Horn was looking forward to rejoining their society leader and the two assistant leaders who would be with the bands scheduled to join them on the Jefferson.

Whenever possible, society members rode together, hunted together, fought the enemy together and celebrated together. At the first great tribal encampment, the societies would come together, for reorganization and new assignments.

The rotation pattern kept any one society from becoming an all powerful, permanent police force. For governmental purposes there were civil chiefs, camp chiefs and society leaders who together made the basic decisions regarding the general activities of a tribe.

Few held the power, or were held in such respect and awe, to have their commands instantly obeyed. For the individual, the dispersement of power made for an easy-going, self-centered, permissive way of life; for the confederacy, as an entity, it would, in the long run, be a weakness.

"Every one made it through to green grass, elders and newborn," marvelled Horn. He was not much older than Running Wolf, born to Ay-Len and her third husband shortly after Shining Doe had set up her own lodge with Wolf's father. "Even Rotten Belly says Tall Elk has good medicine — and you know Rotten Belly."

Wolf nodded. Rotten Belly was one of those people who could only go so long without getting huffy over something and pulling out to go off on his own or join another band for a season.

The medicine of their uncle, Tall Elk, the civil chieftain, had been good. There were more Piegans leaving the winter camp than had come into it. His grandmother said it was good to have winter babies. Running Wolf didn't question that Ay-Len knew best. Few of the clan did, for most of them were related to her in one way or another, sister, aunt, cousin, mother, grandmother.

Few could remember when Ay-Len had not been part of the Piegan band.

Ay-Len could. The first twelve years of her life she had been Allen Scott's indulged daughter, raised in the comforts of a Canadian trading post, her Piegan mother secure as the white man's woman.

Best of all, she remembered Allen Scott, the happy-go-lucky

man who had taught her so much that had stood her in good stead. When the letter came, the one that changed her life and his, he had been elated until his glance fell upon his daughter.

"Helen, lass," he said, gazing at her sadly, "I need to talk to you."

And talk to her he did, about his duty and family obligations. "Never expected to be the Laird. Two cousins and five brothers in line before me," he shook his head in wonder. "Now, I must go home to head my clan. If you were a lad, I'd take you with me, see you were trained to be the next Laird. As it is," he shrugged helplessly, knowing he would be expected to marry when he returned to Scotland and sire sons, "you will have to go with your mother. They aren't bad people, the Piegans."

"Heathens, sure. But in their own way, a bit like the Scots, border lords reiving, wrangling.

"The dogs and a dowry will be yours. The dogs you take with you. They'll give you status.

"The dowry, now. To my way of thinking, it would be best for you to come to the trading post each year, brush up on your English, and buy whatever five pounds will cover.

"The dowry will be in a trust fund, the interest compounding. Should be enough for you — or your get — for an annual shopping spree for years to come."

Dogs and dowry, those were the tangible inheritance from her Scots father. The intangible, intelligence, shrewdness, strength of character and sense of duty would prove equally valuable.

Her father, who could have left her and her mother to fend for themselves, as many traders did when they had a chance to go home, made one last trading trip to his in-laws. During that visit, he made sure of their welcome and acceptance among her mother's people. Then he departed for his ancestral acres, a suitable wife and a bevy of sons.

Bonnie Eyes, and her farewell gift of ponies, was welcomed back into her place in the band, led by her eldest brother. Ay-Len, with her pair of Irish wolf hounds, had time to adjust to the new way of life, and, after a final talk with her father, accept it.

"Take an older man for your husband," her father told her. "You won't be able to put it off. Your uncle already has an overcrowded lodge. Bonnie Eyes and her ponies will attract the younger bucks and is smart enough to take one she can manipulate. But you take an older man. Twelve is awful young but these heathens don't waste time."

The older man Ay-Len gave the nod was all of thirty years old, a leader of the Kit-Fox society in which the wives were practically members. Shortly after her third child was born, their band, and others, were decimated by an epidemic of smallpox.

Ay-len and Bonnie Eyes, vaccinated long before, who had learned from Al-Lens-Cot that the sweat lodge and the following cold plunge were not the way to handle smallpox, managed to keep their men and a portion of their relatives from taking that path.

The nucleus that survived, with their awed respect for the knowledge of the mother and the daughter, drew others into the band, people who came to share that respect.

They made their annual treks to the trading post to trade wolf hides and to spend Ay-Len's dowry. Those were the years that Ay-Len absorbed all Bonnie Eyes could teach her before her accidental death by drowneding at a Sun River crossing. The years that followed established Ay-Len and her children high in the hierarchy.

Her first husband, uncharacteristically, died in his sleep. She'd had three more husbands since then, with children by each, and they in turn had presented her with grandchildren.

Now she had a fourth husband, one of the Painted Feather Blackfeet she had met on the Saskatchewan, who had a Piegan mother. A younger man, healthy and strong, with a large pony herd, he had brought new technology and experiences to broaden the horizons of Ay-Len's Piegan band, making a respected place for himself. She had given him sons, too, but this winter there had been unmistakable physical signs that it was time to look around for an acceptable younger wife if he was to have more children. There would always be an honored place for her in his lodge but there was going to be need of a stronger, younger woman to help with all the chores.

Running Wolf could see his grandmother packing up, along with the young woman he suspected she had selected for her man's second wife. Ay-Len was putting one of her toddling sons before her on a pony, the other on her back.

Accompanying her was a descendant of the first pair of the Irish wolf hounds. The dogs of the band for a number of years had been larger, smarter than most because of introduction of Ay-Len's wolfhounds into the camp. Inbreeding and attrition had left them few of the good stock.

Ay-Len was in sympathy with Running Wolf's desire to improve the breed. The wolf-hounds had done their best to infuse the breed with new blood but it was thinning out. There was need for new blood, just as there had been need through the years to introduce new blood into her band of Piegans. Ay-Len, in her own way, with her diversity of mates, had broadened that gene pool.

Running Wolf had an acceptable dam in the half-breed wolf he was raising. There were no dogs in the camp her equal. Nor were there any young women in the camp who were her grandson's equal. Running Wolf must be encouraged to look farther afield for a mate for himself and his wolf-dog.

At this rate of increase, there would soon be more Piegans than dogs in their camp. The dogs of the band had been important before the coming of the horse and they had taken pride in the ownership.

Few of the Blackfeet confederacy could remember when dogs had been the important method of transportation. This Piegan band had not forgotten and, although their riches were measured in ponies, they still took an interest in their dogs. They guarded the camp, helped with the hunt, pulled the travois still.

It was good to be a Piegan, even a Piegan dog, in the opinion of Running Wolf. Especially to be an All Brave Dog Piegan, with his pack of hand-picked dogs at his heels, his badge of office a small eagle-headed rattle, in his right hand, watching out for his people.

As his clan left their winter camp, Running Wolf looked back at the site. It had been a good location, with the small creek that came out of a shallow canyon onto the valley of a larger stream. The canyon mouth had provided shelter from storms. The creek had provided water. There were aspen groves, food for horses and wood for cooking fires. Grass available and usually some game around. Without all of these present, a group could not survive the winter, and there seldom was such an area that would support a large group. Therefore, those that rode out were a smaller group than the summer group had been, or would be.

Running Wolf was joined by another dog soldier, who said, looking at the part-wolf female, "When she has pups, I would like to have a male."

Running Wolf considered. Black Cloud was older than he was, the regulation twenty-two years, but slower. He had all the attributes admired by the Blackfeet confederacy. He was a thief, a killer and mean to captives. Fighting, feasting, fornicating was the way of life, like it or not.

Actually, what Black Cloud liked was dogs. Which was all right with Running Wolf. He couldn't remember a time when he had not liked dogs, ran with, slept with, played with the best of breed in the camp. The Piegan war chief, Kootenae Appe, liked dogs, too, and saw nothing eccentric about a tested warrior with fine ponies taking an interest in raising dogs. At the moment Running Wolf had one big, smart yellow Indian cur; one brindle mastiff stolen from a white trader on the Saskatchewan; two half-grown Malamutes, left behind by a Cree visitor last winter; and, the gem, his part-wolf female, who would soon be ready to breed.

"Help me find a worthy mate for her then."

"What's wrong with any — or all — of these?" Black Cloud indicated those around Running Wolf.

"Don't want her mated to just any ol' dog this time."
"What do you want?"
"A big dog. Intelligent. Brave. One who minds." The first wolfhounds had obeyed Ay-Len's gestures and her white man's words. That's what the tribe should have again.

"Now that we are both All Brave Dogs, we should have special dogs," agreed Black Cloud, not quite knowing how to put into words his recognition of the symbolic value.

Running Wolf nodded. When they joined up with the bigger encampment on the Jefferson, he might have time to go off by himself, fast for a day or two, seek some guidance. He and Black Cloud rode off to take up their positions in the line of march. In a few days they would join up with the bigger encampment on the Jefferson. Two different sets of hominid of the primate family and the mightiest of the ursidae family were coalescing, on a collision course.

On that same April morning, James Cheek faced the fact he might never leave the Stony Mountains alive.

He had awakened early. He caught a glimpse of the Major leaving camp, carrying his rifle, a double-bitted axe hanging from his belt, Cheeky at his heels.

Cheek felt the need to get away from camp, too, before Tom James started pestering him again to join up with him, help make a dugout canoe to float to the Great Falls of the Missouri.

Taking up his own rifle and an axe, Cheek had hastened after the Major and his dog. He could see they were headed for the stand of cottonwood about a mile away, where Reuben Lewis had located and blazed the trees he wanted for straight, long pole timbers.

Cheek did admire the way the Major worked as hard, or even harder, than those he assigned specific tasks. Even under the most trying conditions, he showed good sense and good faith which inspired confidence and a positive response to his leadership.

He would give the Major a hand in chopping down some of those trees this morning, in companionable silence. After working up a good, relaxing sweat maybe he'd feel easier in his mind, feel up to having a word or two with the Major about this gloomy feeling he'd had lately

He set his course to intercept the Major and Cheeky as they approached the three prime trees off by themselves on the edge of a game trail that led to the Madison River. The breeze was coming at right angles to them from the Madison River.

Those carcasses of winter-killed elk along the river bank would be smelling pretty high when it warms up, he thought idly.

A little over a mile away, Griz, with his keener olfactory sense, was following the same breeze toward breakfast. Brother, trying to get used to being on his own but still inclined to follow Griz's lead, was trailing along steadily, pausing now and then to sniff the beckoning, mouth-watering odors.

Cheek also moved steadily along on an intersecting course, watching the easy, ground-eating stride of the Major, and admiring the clean lines of the strong, obedient dog at his side.

That Cheeky sure had grown up and filled out. A downright handsome dog. And smart. The Major never had to say a word to him, just flick his hand, and Cheeky knew what he wanted him to do. You'd never guess he'd started life as an Indian dog.

Too bad Cheeky was one of a kind. He'd like to have one just like him. Most of the other men felt the same. One good rifle, at least one good dog, mighty comforting to a man.

They'd sought out other dogs, but no one had lucked out like he had. The other dogs in camp were Indian dogs, scruffy and not too smart. Like the one some Crow gave Tom James before they left Fort Raymond. Tom hadn't paid it much mind until it turned up missing and he discovered some of the boys had killed and et it while he was gallivantin' around, off the trail, lost as usual.

Now Tom had another, claimed it was a bear dog. To Jamie it looked just like any other scruffy, yellow cur. Sure didn't have the style of ol' Cheeky.

Cheeky, becoming aware of his approach, wagged his tail. The Major acknowledged his presence with a curt nod, not breaking stride. Cheek moved along quietly beside them.

The three of them halted before the three blazed cottonwoods, standing by themselves, with a tangled thicket reaching out on each side.

Cheeky, looking toward the thicket, growled, hackles raised.

The Major eyed the thicket as did Cheek, breathing shallowly, listening, sniffing. After a long, still, silent wait, during which nothing unusual was noted, and Cheeky relaxed, the Major placed his rifle against one of the trees, and took the axe out of his belt.

While the Major was walking around the right hand tree, calculating the way he wanted it to fall, Cheek put his rifle next to the Major's and pulled out his axe. Cheek took his place opposite the Major so their axes could be wielded alternately to fell the tree the quicker.

The Major swung and the axe bit deep. The tree went cra-a-a-ck, sharp as a rifle shot in the stillness. Cheek swung. His axe bit even deeper. Cra-a-a-a-ck!

On the other side of the thicket, Griz halted, turned his head toward the unfamiliar noise. Brother, on a parallel course, not exactly with Griz, as he had been the previous year, but not quite as ready as Griz to strike out on his own, swivelled about, curious as always.

Cheek's axe didn't come free. He tugged at it, but it moved only slightly, pinched tight in the trunk. He stepped closer to get better leverage.

"Look out!" said the Major but it was too late. Cheek had stepped on a dead branch, slick with ice, and his foot slid. He hung onto the axe, trying to get his balance. That axe gave further, throwing him entirely off balance. He slid onto his back, skidding toward the thicket, halted only by his grip on the axe.

"Lie still," the Major ordered Cheek, very softly.

Thirty feet to the left, Griz stepped out of the thicket. Cheeky growled at him. Griz, the better to see, rose on his hind feet and took a good look. Brother decided to do the same.

Jamie Cheek looked up at the bear standing tall above him and time stood still. He wished he had never left his blankets this morning.

The Major, his eyes moving from the black bear with the silver-tipped hairs to the bigger blond bear, spoke to them even more sternly than he would have to a disobedient dog.

"Beat it!" he snapped at Brother. Over his shoulder, he pitched his voice in parade-ground tones at Griz. "Leave my dog alone!" And again, to Cheek, "Lie still," he said softly but quite as firmly. "Don't try to get up."

There was something in his voice that echoed Mom's no-no in Brother's ears; something in his stance, the axe on his shoulder ready to swing forward, that reminded Griz of the bossy king grizzly.

Just then the breeze swept past their noses, redolent with odors of ripening elk, summoning Brother and Griz to a feast. The two young grizzlies gave the objects of their curiosity one last look, sniffed the wind again, wheeled around and, still on a parallel course, continued on their way to the Madison River.

Cheek scrambled to his feet. Watching where he put his feet this time, avoiding the icy branch, he moved quickly to take up his rifle.

"You saved my life," he said, holding his rifle before him, leaning against the tree, weak in the knees, "again."

"Nonsense," said the Major. "According to the Crows, there's not much danger from the young grizzlies. They were just curious about the noise we were making. Young ones aren't too sure of themselves. A sow with cubs — or a big male — it'd been a different story."

"When I go under," Jamie Cheek said fervently, "I want to do it with rifle in hand, not flat on my back hanging onto a useless axe."

"That you will, Jamie boy," said his Granny, just as plain as if standing next to him. Jamie Cheek shivered.

The Major had taken up his rifle, was scouting out the thicket. Cheeky, still abristle, was at his side. Cheek stayed put, struggling to master the empty feeling in his middle.

"They're long gone," said the Major, returning. He picked up his axe, once against set his rifle against the tree where Cheek leaned. "By now they're probably feeding on those dead elk along the Madison. Let's finish up with these trees and go get some breakfast for ourselves."

On the way back to camp, the trees chopped down to await men and horses to haul them to the busy fort site, Cheek said, "This country — 'n most everything in it — makes me feel like the bride after her wedding night." Andrew Henry lifted a quizzical eyebrow. "Said she knew what to expect. Just didn't figger on it being so big."

The Major grinned. Cheek confided he could not make up his mind whether to stay at Three Forks, go with James, or join the group going up the Jefferson

"Have this feeling it won't matter much what I do," said Cheek, looking off into the distance, "I won't be seein' St. Louie again."

"Your chances look better than they did a little while ago," said the Major drily.

Cheek thought over his remark. "You're right," he said. "One thing for shore, I don't want no more truck with bears. I'm gonna go right now and tell Tom James I ain't goin' up to that great falls with him. From what Colter says, that place is crawlin' with grizzlies in the spring. Brown and Dougherty can go with him if they ain't got better sense. I ain't."

Jamie Cheek went off to do just that. He gave Thomas James a glimpse of his foreboding about his chances of survival but he didn't mention the grizzlies.

As Thomas James would recall the event for publication, thirty some years later, Cheek's words, filtered through a pedantic ghost writer were:

"James, you are going down the Missouri, and it is the general opinion you will be killed. The Blackfeet are at the Falls, encamped, I hear, and we fear you will never come back.

"But I am afraid for myself as well as you. I know not the cause, but I have felt fear ever since I came to the Forks, and I never was afraid of anything before.

"You may come out safe, and I may be killed. Then you will say, there was Cheek afraid to go with us down the river for fear of death, and now he has found his grave by going up the river.

"I may be dead when you return."

If anyone else had a similar premonition, he didn't confide it to Thomas James. That serious, strong-minded man, intent on making the most of the six to eight weeks of spring trapping season remaining, turned to others who had been with him on the keelboat last year.

John Dougherty, not yet twenty, who had made his way from Kentucky to Missouri when he was seventeen, soft-spoken, with a natural ability to deal with people pleasantly, who found James in many ways likable, was one.

William Weir, broad shouldered and extremely powerful, not in the least imaginative, anxious to get on with the trapping that would make him some money, was another.

The third was the lean, laconic Ab Brown, who took each day as it came, with no feeling that the world owed him anything.

There was a great deal to be done, not only by James and his men. The fort needed to be palisaded and flanked by blockhouses, with a storehouse and stables.

As the trapping parties sorted themselves out, the record keeping had to be up-dated. The partners had to see that every article credited to a man, even his horse, was described down to the color of the spots on the rump, was entered in the ledger books. The partners, busy from dawn to late, lantern-lit nights, had neither the time nor inclination to worry during the lengthening days, and were too tired to lie awake doing so by bedtime.

By April 7, James, Dougherty, Weir and Brown had completed their canoe and loaded it with traps and supplies.

At the same time, about a dozen other men, which included Jamie Cheek, had made preparations to go in the opposite direction, up the Jefferson River.

Both parties were on their way the next day.

Chapter 16

"This," said Thomas James, breaking the spellbound silence of astonishment and admiration that had the four of them resting their oars and taking in the spectacular view before them, "is my idea of the Garden of Eden."

It was April 11, the third day of their voyage down the Missouri from Three Forks.

On the first day, even though they got a late start, James, Weir, Brown and Dougherty had managed to catch some beaver. On the second day, they were hemmed in by very high and desolate snow-capped mountains and did not try to do any trapping.

"On the third day," according to the account his ghost writer, Nathaniel Niles, lawyer, politician and newspaper editor, put into literary, lyrical prose for Thomas James, "we issued from very high and desolate mountains on both sides of us, whose tops are covered with snow throughout the year, and came upon a scene of beauty and magnificence combined, unequalled by any other view of nature that I ever beheld. It really realized my conception of the Garden of Eden.

"In the west the peaks and pinnacles of the Rocky Mountains shone resplendent in the sun. The snow on their tops sent back a beautiful reflection of the rays of the morning sun.

"From the sides of the dividing ridge between the waters of the Missouri and Columbia there sloped gradually down to the bank of the river we were on, a plain, then covered with every variety of wild animals peculiar to this region, while on the east another plain arose by a very gradual ascent and extended as far as the eye could reach.

"These and the mountain sides were dark with buffaloes, elk, deer, moose, wild goats and wild sheep; some grazing, some lying down under the trees, and all enjoying a perfect millennium of peace and quiet.

"On the margin the swans, geese, and pelicans cropped the grass or floated on the surface of the water. The cottonwood trees seemed to have been planted by the hand of man on the bank of the river to shade our ways, and the pines and cedars waved their tall, majestic heads along the base and on the sides of the mountains.

"The whole landscape was that of the most splendid English park. The stillness, the beauty, and loveliness of this scene struck us all with indescribable emotions. Nature seemed to have rested here, after creating the wild mountains and chasms among which we voyaged for two days.

"Dougherty, as if inspired by the scene with the spirit of poetry and song, broke forth in one of Burns' noblest lyrics, which found a deep echo in our hearts.

"We floated on till evening through this most delightful country, when we stopped and prepared supper on the bank of the river. We set our traps and before going to rest for the night we examined and found a beaver in every one, being twenty-three in all. In the morning we were nearly as successful as before, and were cheered with thoughts of making a speedy fortune.

"We determined to remain in this second paradise as long as our pursuits would permit. We skinned our beaver, ate breakfast, and started to go farther down the river in search of a good camp ground.

"Brown and Dougherty started in a canoe before Weir and I were ready, and after going about two hundred yards they struck a rock concealed under the water, overturned the canoe, and lost all our skins and ammunition except the little powder in our horns and the few skins left behind. They also lost their guns, but saved themselves and the canoe.

"Weir and I soon followed them and we all encamped at the mouth of a small creek on the left side of the river. Here Weir and I remained while the two others went back to the fort to procure other guns and ammunition, taking with them one of our guns.

"They reached the fort the first night, having saved a great distance by crossing the country and cutting off the bend of the river, which here makes a large sweep to the east. They went up on the west side, or that next to the mountains, waded Jefferson's Fork and entered the fort late at night."

The Major heard their report.

John Dougherty, enthusiastically, told of their good luck first. "More beaver than we'll be able to catch in a month of Sundays. And the game!" He went into detail about that quality and quantity, the beauty of the setting, and sketched a map of the terrain, showing the water route they had followed going, and the land route, returning.

Of their bad luck, he said. "Coulda been worse. Friday, the 13th, instead of Thursday, the 12th."

"Everything is quiet here," the Major told him. "The same day you left, Colter, Immell, Vallé and eight others headed up the Jefferson. The rest of us have been putting the finishing touches to the fort."

"Major, I guess we'll have to go on the books for the replacements for the guns, ammunition and supplies we lost overboard," said John ruefully, disliking the idea of going further in debt. "But we're bound to come out ahead once we get back there. Before this spring season is over, we can have enough beaver to repay everything we owe and then some!"

"Glad to hear it," said the Major. "We'll take care of your needs in the morning."

The morning, however, of Friday, April 13, brought the really bad news.

Shortly after daylight, Francis Vallé and his companions, Bryan, Doza and Luthecaw, rode in. They had travelled all night, with brief stops to rest the horses, watch their back trail.

The Blackfeet, out in force, had struck without warning. As far as they knew, they were the only survivors of the Jefferson party.

"After we left here, we followed the Jefferson for three days, trapping each day with good results. We'd gone about forty miles. No Indian sign," said Francis Vallé, pausing occasionally to make sure he was leaving nothing out of his methodical report.

"Yesterday we pitched our tents for the night near the river. I took some of the men to hunt for game. Others went with Immell and Colter. Cheek, Ayres and Hull stayed in camp, setting things to rights, getting in water and wood. Fleehart and Rucker took off, anxious to get their traps set before dark."

Francis leaned back wearily on the rough-hewn bench in the partner's headquarters, with young Bryan beside him, both of them sipping the coffee that Reuben Lewis had laced generously with whiskey. The partners were all gathered around them, listening intently.

"The Indians hit us the evening of the third day when all eleven of our party were scattered up and down and out from the river," Francis went on. "They appeared suddenly on the prairie south of us, already on the move toward the camp. Some were on horses. Some were running on foot. We were the first to spot their approach and set off to warn the others."

He took a generous swallow of his coffee royale.

"Soon as Francis yelled at me, I did just like he told me," said Bryan a little shamefacedly. "I left off stalking some deer and ran like hell for my horse and headed flat out for the fort."

"We all ran like hell," said Francis bleakly.

"That's not exactly true," said Bryan. "First you rode like hell to warn Cheek and Ayres and Hull at the camp."

"To no avail, I fear," sighed Francis, his hand tightening around his cup, the knuckles shining white with his repressed emotions. "We couldn't budge them. Cheek grabbed up his rifle and pistols, saying his time had come, that he was going to kill at least two of the devils. After that, he didn't care."

Francis sat with bowed head, wondering what he could have done differently in the crisis. "Hull didn't say anything. He just took up his rifle and braced himself for those screaming devils. Ayres, whose horse was within reach, ran around frantically, screaming, 'Oh, God. Oh, God. What can I do?'

"Cheek was the cool one. He said 'Get away while you can!'

Francis looked up at the Major. "The mounted Indians were getting closer and closer, mon ami," he said sorrowfully. "We did only as we had been directed."

"Everyone scatter and make his own way back to the fort as best he can," the Major agreed, nodding his head at the wisdom of the course Francis had taken. "That's what they'd been told to do, too, if they encountered a sizable war party."

"Thirty to forty, all painted hideously," said Francis. "They were close enough you could see the different colors, plainly."

"I thought for sure some of them would be right behind me." Bran held out his cup for a refill of the coffee and whiskey. "When I looked back, they were all lined out chasing Francis and his men. And getting uncomfortably close behind them. I expected to hear them firing away any moment."

"They chose to attack the camp instead." Francis picked up on his narrative again. "That wasn't the only party out, I'm sure. There could have been many more behind the ridge. We rode along the river, hoping to find others to warn in time, but saw no one else. From the camp, we heard some sharp reports of rifles."

"If Cheek got a chance to shoot, he wouldn't miss," said the Major flatly. "If Gil Hull held his fire, then Cheek might have had a chance to reload —"

"The Indians just rode right over them, I'm afraid," said Francis. "Shot them down at point-blank range with their muskets. We heard at least one volley. Then there was silence for a short time. Then came the wild yelling — you know, the awful noises the savages make over a successful kill."

"God Almighty, yes," said Reuben Lewis. "The Blackfeet are said to be as bad as they come. Still, anybody who ever heard the Shawnee celebrating a victory knows what you mean." Bloody scalping. Hacked up bodies. Gore everywhere. "Hope to God none of them were captured."

"There could be others who escaped," said Samuel Morrison, pacing around the table.

"Depending on where they were and how many Indians they had to avoid," said Pierre Menard, pacing around the table in the opposite direction, "some could be making their way back to the safety of the fort right now."

Some were.

Before the day was out Colter came in, accompanied by Immell and Pelton. They got an enthusiastic welcome and the coffee royale at the partners table, too.

"No sign of any Indians, Blackfeet or others, around here," he reported, which was good news to the fort, where all the men were standing on alert.

Lt. Immell didn't have any good news. "Cheek's dead," he said bluntly. "The Indians have taken at least one man prisoner. I couldn't tell who it was."

A large, powerful man, he stretched his big frame, wriggling his shoulders to loosen the tension that had begun building up the night before when he had come back from hunting and couldn't locate the camp.

"Me 'n Pelton, here," he indicated Archie, whose narrow eyes were blinking with nervous rapidity, "we got back from hunting about dusk."

"Seen Cheek's tent was gone," put in Pelton. "Got this creepy-crawly feeling up my scalp. The Lieutenant, though, he says as how they musta decided to move to a better location."

"We heard a noise down by the river," said Immell. "Things didn't feel just right." He didn't have to explain that feeling to his listeners. They were all here because more than once in their life their own sixth sense, generally a vague uneasiness, had warned of danger. "Pelton hunkered down behind a tree on guard. I crawled careful-like down to the bank, took cover in some willows. That's when I spotted the buggers. Thirty Indian lodges right across the river from where we'd set up camp."

There was a silence while his listeners were doing the mental calculations that John Dougherty, Samuel's prize pupil, now put into words. "Figuring a minimum of five to a lodge — Judas Priest, that'd be at least one-hundred-fifty Indians!"

"And there'd be at least one warrior for every lodge," said the Major softly. Another thoughtful silence followed.

"What else did you see?" prompted Reuben.

Immell drained his cup and held it out for a refill. "Damned if I didn't see a big fat squaw come down to the river with my brass kettle and fill it up with water. My brass kettle! You remember my brass kettle?" Nods indicated they knew what he was talking about. A sizable kettle, good for carrying a substantial amount of water or holding a delicious stew, that all of them had dipped into at some time or another. "Coulda shot her easy. Wanted to, the worst way when I saw what she did on her way back to the lodges."

He took out his pipe and filled it. When he had it drawing, he took a puff, went on. "She stopped by a tree and started poking at something with a stick. That's when I saw they had a prisoner tied to a tree." He drew on his pipe, exhaled fiercely. "Couldn't tell who it was but he swore in American."

"If Cheek is dead, then it could have been Ayres, Hull or — "Pierre Menard paused. "Who else is missing?"

"Fleehart and Rucker," said the Major.

"I crawled real careful back to Pelton. The light was fading fast so we couldn't see much around the camp except that Cheek's tent was gone," continued Immell.

"Lookit my hands," shrilled Pelton, holding up first one, then the other, never letting go of his rifle. "Creepin' around that camp, feelin' around, put my hands right into his bloody brains. Gotta wash the blood off."

"You've washed them at every ford," Immell said.

"Need soap," muttered Pelton. "Strong lye soap."

Bryan stepped forward, "I've still got a sliver of soap in my pack," he told Pelton, leading him out of the room.

Immell waited until they were gone, then said, "Findin' Cheek like that, the top of his head gone along with his scalp, and all hacked up, gave Archie quite a turn. Cheek was lucky, though. Appeared he was dead before they started carving on him."

The Major didn't say anything about premonitions. This was not the time for making any negative contributions.

Menard stirred. "We'd better let the rest of the men know what happened." Followed by the partners, he went out into the fort, climbed up on a barrel so all could hear, and described the events on the Jefferson.

When he climbed down from the barrel, amid a silence that was replaced by an occasional murmured comment, he called Dougherty and Brown to him. "John, you and Ab better go warn James and Weir, bring them in. Knowing we are not now so numerous, the savages may attack at any time. We will need all the able riflemen to stand them off."

"Be damned careful," said the Major. "Colter didn't see any sign of Indians around here when he came in but there's no telling how many may be roaming down the river."

Brown and Dougherty, well mounted, taking the short cut they had used earlier, reached James and Weir just as they returned to camp to prepare dinner.

"There's Indians out there, for sure," Dougherty told them. "There was this horse with a rope around his neck that ran up and snuffed around us as if in search of his master then trotted off."

"And an Injun dog that did the same," added Brown.

"Let's get back to the fort," said Thomas James.

They packed their supplies onto the two horses. Taking turns leading them, they proceeded cautiously up the river about four miles, screened from view by willows.

"We'll leave off following the river now," said James. He motioned for the others to precede him while he watched their back trail. He noticed sudden activity amidst the buffalo herd in the creek bottom far to their right.

He crept up to an opening in the willows, not watching the buffalo but letting his eyes roam over the ground at their rear. As he watched, eight Indians appeared, walking rapidly across the plain toward the camp they had just left.

He rejoined the others, quickly described what he had seen.

"Let's get away from here fast as we can," exclaimed Weir. "Dump the packs an' — "

"Two horses and four of us?" James shook his head. "All I saw was eight Indians. Maybe that's all there is. We could manage against eight."

"I dunno," said Weir doubtfully.

"If they attack, we could make a breast-work of the horses. You and I will fire upon them at a hundred yards," proposed Tom James encouragingly. "Then, Brown and Dougherty at fifty yards. With reloaded guns, we should be able to dispatch the third couple. Then we can all pitch in and finish off the seventh and eighth with our knives and pistols."

He was glad to see the others look more cheerful at the prospect he'd laid out before them. Having faced the worst of the possibilities before them, they were now willingly following his suggestions for making their way to safety.

While Brown and Dougherty led the horses, which travelled slowly with the packs as they retreated, James took Weir with him to a high spot. From there, in concealment, they watched the activities of the Indians.

"It was the smoke they saw," James told Weir, keeping his eyes on the Indians who were casting about the campsite in desultory fashion. "Remember, Drouillard said you could see smoke from an ordinary fire out here for three hundred miles?"

"Damn, why didn't you say so afore?" said Weir.

"I think that's stretching it some." James shrugged his shoulders. "It's something to keep in mind in the future."

"Providing there is a future," said Weir gloomily.

They travelled throughout the night. They moved along fairly rapidly for Dougherty and Brown had already been over the route twice now. All of them were edgy, filled with trepidation behind faces wiped clean of expression.

It was a relief when they reached the Jefferson River. Their goal in sight, they decided to ford it, which was not easy in the dark.

One of the horses stumbled, floundered. Dougherty got a thorough wetting as he clung stubbornly to the lead rope. He and the horse finally came ashore downstream, on the fort side of the bank, and he came squishing back to the others.

Their approach to the fort set off a canine cacophony. Weir swore. "Where in the hell did all those dogs come from?"

James, recognizing the leader as the dogs rushed at them, spoke softly. "Cheeky, it's me. Yore ol' friend, Tom James."

As Cheeky wagged his tail, James called the other dogs by name, quieting them.

There was a hail from the Major inside the fort. "Who's there?"

"James and party, Major," he answered promptly. "Let us in. We've got at least eight Indians comin' up fast on our tail."

James was relieved to see how alert the men were at the fort. All of them were on watch, rifles in hand, as they trailed in.

He was the center of attention as he told of their escape, described the Indians. Colter said they were probably Piegans, the branch of the Blackfeet that claimed sovereignty over this area. There was speculation about how many bands were on the move and whether they would join together in a mutual undertaking against the fort.

There was also speculation about the fate of the missing men.

"Gil Hull," said Pierre Menard sadly. "Do you suppose he might have escaped?"

"Don't count on it," said the Major. "We should try to find out what happened to him and the others. Give Jamie Cheek a decent burial. That's the least we can do."

"We should pursue the savages," said Menard.

"We should try to recover the traps," said Morrison. "And the horses and beaver pelts."

John Dougherty snorted. Samuel Morrison got red in the face. "I wasn't being callous," he said defensively. "Just realistic."

"Them dirty buggers'll ambush us," said Pelton when he heard the call for volunteers. "I don't like the idee a'tall."

Thomas James didn't hesitate. He volunteered immediately. He was one of the group that retraced the route to the camp on the Jefferson and found the body of Cheek, where Immel and Pelton had left it.

James was also present when another body, flung into the river, was found. This was identified as Ayres. James, thinking back to how Ayres had given him a helping hand just a few short months ago, shook his head dolefully. He'd been a good man, too good for this kind of an end. Still, the one he was going to miss was that big man, always getting into scrapes, James Cheek. Stoically, he helped dig the graves and listened to the burial service, brief and heartfelt, conducted by Pierre Menard.

"No trace of Gil Hull," Menard said sadly.

"No trace of Rucker and Fleehart either," said the Major who had gone with Colter to the camp Rucker and Fleehart had set up several miles from that of Cheek, Ayres and Hull. "We found four traps, traces of flight and pursuit. No sign of them being killed, or even wounded. The poor devils must have been overpowered and taken prisoner."

"I think there's a body concealed over here," said Drouillard, pointing. He began kicking away leaves and earth. The other men joined him, pulling aside some logs. They looked down upon the body of a young Indian brave. Drouillard examined the body roughly, showing his teeth in a savage grin. "Looks like Cheek managed to get one of the devils. He's got a couple bullets in him." Several of the men gathered around, maltreating the body with angry kicks. A knife was wielded furiously, the scalp passed from hand to hand.

"I think another was wounded," said Colter, casting around, pointing out the faint brownish marks on a blade of grass.

Grimly, they set out to trail the savages. For two days they persevered, then the trail petered out.

"We will go no further," said Menard. There was a chorus of protests. "It would not be prudent. We already know there are a lot of Indians ahead of us. The ones we have been trailing seem to be only a detachment from the main party. If we keep on, we might find ourselves surrounded by an army. I believe the main body of Blackfeet to be a very large one and not too distant from us or the fort.

"We have recovered a number of traps and several horses. I don't believe that, by now, we would find any of the other men still alive. I do not want to have our forces divided in this way any longer. It is best to return to the fort, which is undermanned, and be on our guard for an attack."

When they had returned to the fort, Colter made an unexpected announcement.

"I promised my Maker once before that I'd leave this country and now," said Colter, throwing his hat on the ground, his eyebrows drawn together in a frown like a pair of bleached caterpillars, "if God will only forgive me this time and let me off I will leave the country day after tomorrow, and be damned if I ever come into it again!"

Once it was determined Colter meant what he said, having put in his term of service as agreed, Pierre wrote to his Cher Papone, on April 21, 1810:

"I profit by the way of John Colter who leaves for St. Louis to let you know that I always enjoy perfect health although I am at this moment the image of a skeleton. I have not as much as an ounce of fat and have never felt better. I will not give you any news because the prospects which I have at this present moment are not as bright as they were eight days ago.

"The land is rich with beaver but the incursion of the Blackfeet discourages all our hunters. Two days after they started their hunt about ten leagues from here, the Blackfeet killed them and stripped them....

"Kiss our dear children for me. Tell them to expect me in July. Between the 5th and 10th of June is when I leave here to go down.

"Say hello for me to Mr. Langlais and his family as well as to Mr. Pepe St. Gemes & in other words to all my friends, Janet and his family & Brindamaure...

While Colter was making his preparations and conferring with Bryan and Francis, who were seriously considering returning with him, Pierre Menard wrote to Pierre Chouteau on the same day:

"I had hoped to be able to write you more favorably than I am now able to do. The outlook before us was much more flattering ten days ago than it is today. A party of our hunters was defeated by the Blackfeet on the 12th inst. There were two men killed, all their beaver stolen, many of their traps lost, and the ammunition of several of them, and also seven of our horses. We set out in pursuit of the Indians but unfortunately could not overtake them. We have recovered forty-four traps and three horses, which we brought back here, and we hope to find a few more traps.

"This unfortunate affair has quite discouraged our hunters, who are unwilling to hunt any more here. There will start out tomorrow, however, a party of thirty who are all gens a gage, fourteen loues and sixteen French. They go to the place where the others were defeated. I shall give them only three traps each, not deeming it prudent to risk more, especially since they are not to separate, and half are to remain in camp.

"... The resources of this country in beaver are immense. It is true we shall accomplish nothing this spring, but I trust we shall next autumn. I hope between now and then to see the Snake and Flathead Indians.

"My plan is to induce them to stay here, if possible, and make war upon the Blackfeet so that we may take some prisoners and send back one with propositions of peace - - which I think can easily be secured by leaving traders among them below the Falls of the Missouri. Unless we can have peace or unless they can be destroyed, it is idle to think of maintaining an establishment at this post.

"... We are daily expecting to see the Blackfeet here and are desirous of meeting them."

Reuben Lewis, writing to his brother Meriwether, who would never read it, felt the Blackfeet had been actively encouraged by British traders to war on the Americans. When William Clark, as administrator of Meriwether's estate, opened the letter sadly, he was encouraged to note that Reuben thought the prospects for success more favorable on the headwaters of the Columbia, where Champlain and Wiser had explored for Lisa in 1808:

"... Mr. Shamplain tells me that the martin abound in the mountains ... the upper branches of the Collumbia are full of Beaver, and the rout by the middle fork on Madison's River is almost without mountains. It is about 5 or 6 days travel to an illigable plane for a fort on that River where the Beavers, from the account of Peter Wyzer, is as abundant as in our part of the country."

Without any fanfare, Colter took the letters, the self-elected travelling companions, and started for the Big Horn.

Arriving at Fort Raymond, Francis Vallé, confided to Charles Davis, "I rather regret my decision now as I think about the Major. He is a brave, purposeful man. I don't really feel comfortable about leaving him — but I don't feel comfortable staying around Blackfeet, either."

"Bet ever' body'll be glad to get shet of Three Forks," said Charlie.

That wasn't entirely true. The Major and Cheeky were enjoying themselves, making daily, careful explorations. So was Belt Jackson, who had a nice thick notepad again, a farewell gift from Bryan who said he wouldn't need it for writing letters home. He'd be getting home as quickly as any letter, the Good Lord willing.

Belt was sketching everything in sight, including a wolf bitch who appeared now and then at a distance that he suspected was in heat. The dogs at the fort thought so, too, and went in pursuit, singly and in a pack, fighting fiercely. Belt wondered about Cheeky's lack of interest but the Major only shrugged.

"He's too young," he said.

"He's certainly big enough," said Belt. "I'd admire to have one of his pups."

"You certainly can — when we find the right female, one that has some really good qualities that would enhance his, then we'll raise us some pups," said the Major. "For now, he's still a growing boy and needs exercise. Let's go see if we can find some duck or geese. He dearly loves to retrieve birds. I swear he can count the ones that fall for he will not give up until he has found and brought back every one that does."

Thomas James wasn't enjoying himself. Frustrated, after having to abandon the rich beaver harvest in his Garden of Eden, he was one of the group of men who had ventured up the Jefferson once again. Every day, as he trapped, he mentally totaled his take against his indebtedness to the Company, and found himself still short.

Part of the problem was the three trap limitation. The largest part was having to trap as a group per Menard's orders. For a few days they tried it as a group, then by mutual consensus tempered the orders.

They divided into four-man groups, and spread out, going their separate ways each morning, two men to tend the traps while the other two kept watchful lookout for danger. During the midday, from a spot easy to defend, they would skin the catch, bundle up the pelts. In the late afternoon, it would be the turn of the guards to wade about in the cold water, retrieving the catch, resetting the traps, while the other two, their moccasins and leggings drying out, their rifles at the ready, swept the terrain with keen, discerning eyes. Again finding a place of relative safety, they would skin the afternoon catch before returning to the main camp.

The evenings were spent fleshing, stretching the hides, hanging the hoops of beaver up to dry, mending traps and clothing, sharing camp chores, eating, yarning. They slept in their clothes, rolled up in blankets, rifles at hand, rising only to take their turn at night guarding.

Inevitably, as the Indian menace did not materialize as expected, there was a restlessness, a tendency to take a risk, to venture farther afield, to throw off the imposed restraints.

George Drouillard, who was a law unto himself, with anthracite eyes in an unreadable face, went off on his own early one morning near the end of April without any by-your-leave. He found a thriving beaver colony about a mile up river from the camp, set his traps. Off he went the next morning, alone, returning with six luxuriant beaver hides.

"Mr. Drouillard," Thomas James said, "You are following a dangerous course."

Cheekbones casting their own shadows, imperturbable black eyes stared down the officious newcomer to this land. "I am too much of an Indian," said George flatly, a faint air of disdain about him for people who had to rely on other people to feel secure, "to be caught by Indians."

His father's people had been residing in this land for over two hundred years; his mother's, ten times as long. His father, Captain Peter Drouillard, held posts of importance in the British Indian Department of Detroit, including, among other duties, serving as interpreter to the Huron and other Indian tribes, which led to liaisons of short duration with at least two Indian women. The sons, one apiece, Peter took home to his French wife. She would, he knew, attend to their spiritual and cultural welfare, while he saw to their necessary survival skills.

George, raised in the Drouillard household in Detroit, had great affection for his stepmother, Angela Descomps dit Labadie, and her six children. He was related to Louis Lorimier and had visited him and his exiled Shawnees at Cape Girardeau, benefiting from Shawnee tutelage in the ways of the hunt and war. There was talk, Uncle Louis had said, on one of Drouillard's visits there, that the George Rogers Clark his father much admired had a brother heading for the Missouri on some sort of an exploration trip. George, an American citizen who liked to think he'd been named for Clark and not for a crazy king, looked into the matter. On November 11, 1803, at Fort Mason in Kentucky he had been enrolled as a member of the Lewis and Clark expedition. Clark's younger brother, William, and his partner, Meriwether Lewis, came to regard Drouillard as one of the most valuable members of their company.

The year he got back, he went to share his adventures with Uncle Louis. He found the Lorimier's all puffed up over cousin Louis, smart and sharp in his military finery, a West Point graduate of 1806. It was Pierre Menard, Uncle Louis's sometime partner, who not only insisted on hearing about Drouillard's travels but indicated he was more impressed with George's achievements than Louis. Menard and Morrison and Lisa got together with him to discuss future ventures, more promising than anything cousin Louis would ever envision. Menard and Morrison made George their representative in their partnership with Lisa for establishing the fort at the Big Horn River in 1807. In St. Louis, Lisa signed up two other Lewis and Clark veterans, John Potts and Peter Wiser, and, on the journey up river, intercepted and recruited John Colter. Even though George never paired off with any of them, going his own solitary way, it had been reassuring to have their expertise to fall back on. Counting the years with Lewis and Clark, George had been coming or going from the Stony Mountains for six years, most of them, profitably.

In order to show a profit this year, it was necessary to trap beaver, lots of them. He was here with a handful of human beings who felt dwarfed by the land and the sky, among them, but not one of them. He was an old campaigner in this land, strong, self-reliant.

If it had been Colter, raising one of those white eyebrows, one professional giving pause to another professional, he might have modified his course of action. He might not like the man. He did respect him. He had been taken aback at Colter's abrupt departure, his first reaction one of indignation: now he would have the chore of weaving these newcomers to the mountains through the tendrils of danger from Blackfeet, grizzlies and congenital incompetence. They probably thought he was getting in a dig at Colter, making out that his own Indian blood gave him an edge, when what he'd had in mind was the motto with which his admired step-mother went about dealing with her life: "J'ai du coeur," — "I am courageous."

George could write an adequate letter, read the Latin terms in his contracts and make a rough translation of "Dum vivimus vivamus," as a suitable motto, "We won't live forever so lets get busy living."

He kept in contact with his family in a desultory correspondence with his favorite half-sister, Marie Louise Parent, and regretted having postponed the promised visit, year after year, to Detroit for a joyful reunion. Let him get the next few weeks of trapping done, then he really would go home. In the meantime, he'd take care.

The next morning, however, James's beetle-browed disapproval was more a challenge than a deterrent. George, who could outstare a rattlesnake, outrun a jackrabbit, who was finding the officiousness of this obtuse man tiresome, just looked at him, long and silently until he turned away. No one said anything when George went off again, alone.

Returning with a good catch, he strove for a light, off-hand tone, saying, "This is the way to catch beaver." Even to his ears, it didn't sound conciliatory, as intended, and he turned away without inviting any of the trappers to share his undertaking on the morrow.

On the third morning, he really didn't intend to push his luck. He was killing time saddling up his horse, when a delegation, headed by James, approached him.

"The whole party is to move upstream today," James said. "We think you should wait until then to go check on your traps."

"Those two Shawnee buddies of yours say they're going off on their lonesome, too, after deer," said Dougherty, diffidently, sincerely concerned for the welfare of this dark, forceful man. "We don't think that's safe either. Couldn't you have a word with them?"

Drouillard looked at the two Shawnees, Elk and Wild Cat. These young men had never seen their homeland. Their parents had been among the some four thousand Shawnees that split off from the main tribe in 1779 and left the Ohio country forever to get away from the Long Knives. The majority had settled on the land grant Peter Loramie had obtained for them near Cape Giradeau. Elk and Wild Cat, born and raised in exile, had shown more than a passing interest in the siren song the Prophet was trumpeting on behalf of Tecumseh and his proposed confederacy. Their elders had actively encouraged them to join the expedition to distance them from the temptation to cross the Mississippi to join Tecumseh. With youthful enthusiasm, they had accepted Drouillard's dictum that life in the mountains was seldom easy. They had tended to ignore his qualification that life in the wilderness was never long if a man didn't act mighty careful all the time.

"Deer?" Drouillard said. "Is it necessary?"

Wild Cat, drawing his short, stocky body erect, gave him a

scornful look. Elk, his obsidian eyes flashing, spoke for both Shawnee warriors.

"We are too much Indian to be caught by Indians," Elk said, using the Shawnee language, phrasing it so his reply was not only mocking and a touch malicious but a challenge.

Drouillard didn't think any of those within hearing understood the words, but the tone, disdainful, superior, was unmistakable.

"Oh, merde," muttered Drouillard, who knew a dare when he heard one. He couldn't think of a graceful, dignified way to handle the situation without loss of face. Looking at the young Shawnees, ramrod with dignity, measuring him, he knew he was Indian enough to value their respect. "I gotta go," he said tonelessly to Dougherty. "Don't pay to let these or those other hellions out there think you're scared."

Turning on his heel, he mounted his horse, saying "See you up river," and rode out ahead of the Shawnees.

With misgivings, John Dougherty watched them ride off.

Several hours later, when the remainder of the party had packed up and moved out upstream, Dougherty looked upon the Shawnees again. He swallowed the bile that rose in his throat.

"Damn fools," said Weir, hawking and spitting, "got theirselves kilt."

Lying close together, it appeared that Elk and Wild Cat had defended themselves in the best traditions of their people, fighting back-to-back against the sudden onslaught of the Blackfeet. What remained of them had been savaged by lance, arrow and bullets. A few moments later, when he saw Drouillard again, John wasn't the only one who gagged at the sight.

In advance of Elk and Wild Cat by some one hundred-fifty yards, maintaining the same distance as when he had ridden out of camp, George Drouillard had gone down fighting, with rifle, pistol, knife and tomahawk. The signs indicated he had been able to stay on his horse, fighting in a circle, and probably killed some of the Blackfeet, before being overwhelmed.

The spot where he had been ambushed looked and smelled like a slaughterhouse. The remains of George Drouillard, drawn, quartered and beheaded were flung angrily about the scene of the ambush.

The trail of the victors was easy to follow, at least in the beginning but it got harder to discern toward evening. The trappers gave up the pursuit and returned, gloomily, to bury the dead, and make their way back to the fort.

There they saw for the first time the handiwork of the four-legged inhabitant of this area who also resented their presence here.

John Dougherty, who had been drawn aside by Cather, Mc-

Bride and Jackson, who were anxious to know in detail the disaster that had overtaken Drouillard and the two Shawnees, had been answering their questions stoically when he suddenly broke off to ask, "My God, what happened to that man?"

"Johnny Marie?" said Cather. "Looks like hell, don't he?"

With the right side of his face grotesquely re-arranged, right-eye gone, head and face lacerated and swollen, an open wound beneath his injured right jaw, the French-Canadian bore little resemblance to the nice looking young man who had made winter moccasins for Thomas James.

The latter, out in the open area of the fort was examining the injured man. In consultation with St. John, Thomas James was discussing treatment and a change of bandages, for Tom was discovering that he had a certain aptitude for treating injuries and prescribing for ailments.

Dougherty, whose roiled stomach had not settled down, gulped and turned his questioning gaze again upon his three friends.

"He was fool enough to stir up a big grizzly that was minding its own business," said Pet McBride.

"From what St. John had to say when he brought Johnny in, all the way from the Shields River, and more dead than alive, Johnny brought his trouble on hisself," began Cather, hunkering down on his haunches. "It happened about a week ago. That morning, after setting his traps around a beaver pond, Johnny went out on the prairie looking for game. He came up on this huge white bear who was taking a roll in the grass under a tree. Instead of getting the hell away from there, he started shooting at the bear. The bear ignored him and his bullets — until one connected. Then he reared up and took out after Johnny.

"The damn fool was out there in the open with the grizzly between him and the tree. He hadn't done any great damage to the bear, just made him mad as hell. Johnny tried to outrun him. When he reached the beaver dam, the grizzly was so close behind, Johnny dived into the deep pond, thinking he could outsmart the bear that way."

"Turns out a bear can swim near as fast as he can run," interpolated Jackson. "That was news to me."

"Me, too," said Dougherty. "The bear swam after Johnny —?"

"Sure did," said Cather. "Johnny swam and dove, swam and dove. But that was one smart bear. He waited and watched, caught Johnny when he came up for air. That bear fastened his big ol' jaws over Johnny's head, got a good tight hold. That's what put out his eye, mangled his jaw and the whole side of his face. With his tushes sunk into Johnny's head, the grizzly started swimming for shore with him.

"Sinjon, having heard the shots, came a 'runnin'. He shot and killed the grizzly and drug Johnnie out of the water. There wasn't much he could do for him so he brought him back here."

Dougherty was thoughtful. "What can be done for him?"

"Hard to say. You saw how swole up his head was. That ain't the worst," said Cather. "He just may starve to death. There's an awful hole under his jaw made by the bear's teeth. Whenever Johnny tries to eat or drink anything, the stuff gushes right out again."

All three of them considered the situation, wishing they knew of some way to help their fellow trapper.

McBride broke the silence, "One thing for sure. When anybody goes out from the fort, he better be almighty careful. It's bad enough to have the Blackfeet laying for us. Now there's all those bears out there, too, sure puts us between a rock and a hard place."

April went out. May sloshed in. Hunting parties ventured out daily, in small groups. They found themselves competing with the bears for both the trapped and untrapped beaver and for the right-of-way to reach them. There were disagreeable encounters with Griz and Brother's Mom, who caught Cather out by himself, fortunately near a tree, where he had to perch uncomfortably until she tired of trying to reach him; with Grandma, who only had one cub this year but was so fiercely protective she chased any trapper venturing into her territory, giving them no chance to loose off a shot.

For Griz, who tried to stay clear of these strange newcomers to grizzly country, there was Pelton, who screamed and yelled in a most unearthly manner when he ran into him in the bush. Griz pushed him down on the ground and sniffed him over thoroughly. The strong smells emanating from Pelton were neither familiar nor appetizing, particularly now that Griz, comfortably full from feeding on his own stash of elk, was not hungry.

Curious, Griz squatted over him, nose-to-nose. The weird noises issuing from the grimacing face assailed Griz's sensitive ears. He gave a disgusted snort, rose to his full height and looked down at Pelton. Even at his caterwauling worst, Brother had not made such ear-piercing sounds.

They almost, but not quite, masked the sounds of the hurried approach of other two-legged strangers. As Pelton drew a deep breath and let out another yell, Griz leaped over him, gave him one irritated backward glance, growled and padded away on all fours.

Pelton scrambled to his feet. Grumbling and cursing, he stumbled toward Thomas James who was coming to his rescue on the run. Weir and Doughterty, close behind James, were relieved to find Pelton unharmed.

As they escorted the man, dishevelled, with mud and dead leaves still plastered to his back, they listened to his disjointed description of the encounter.

Dougherty, who was striving to find some pattern in the behavior of these ubiquitous bears, said, "He didn't do you any harm. Why not?"

Pelton rolled his eyes, which were so close together, just like a bear's. "He looked into my eyes," he tittered nervously, "and thought he'd found one of his relatives."

Griz retreated to the island thicket where he had cached the elk carcass. He was there when William Weir came face-to-face with Brother, bumbling along in Griz's wake.

Brother was slow to react. When Weir, hastily, shot him, Brother took after him, moving quite rapidly considering the bullet had reached his heart. Weir saved himself by diving into the river.

Weir, looking back, saw Brother stumble down the bank in his death throes and fall into the water. He pulled him out, skinned him and was dressing out the meat, when he decided there was another bear nearby.

Weir hurried to the fort for reinforcements.

Thomas James brought his dog. When the dog located Griz for them, Griz charged the dog indignantly. When James's hasty shot creased and stung his shoulder, he was even more indignant. When James turned and ran, he chased him, until James ran pell-mell into others of the bear-hunting party. Everyone beat a hasty retreat.

While the two-legged strangers were taking to their heels, Griz watched and waited until they were out of sight and hearing. Dimly, he realized they had challenged and defeated Brother in some final way even beyond the strength of a king grizzly.

He crossed the river, travelling into a more peaceable area where, as his wound healed, he cannily put cause and effect together. As a result, he would live to become top grizzly.

The father of Brother, who was moving up in the grizzly hierarchy, would not. He was surprised and wounded by a group of hunters. In a great fury he plunged toward his attackers, who scattered quickly.

The Shawnee, Luthecaw, had the misfortune to stumble over some brush as he retreated and fell down helpless. The handsome black grizzly closed his jaws over Luthecaw's capeau and coat collar and rose up to grasp and crush him in his mighty forearms. The other hunters took aim and put six bullets in him before he fell dead. He fell on top of Luthecaw, who bellowed loudly at the crushing weight.

With some difficulty, the others of the party shifted the bear off Luthecaw. Before the Shawnee could rise, they had to help him slip out of his coat for the bear's jaws kept their firm hold, even in death.

"Sacre mote," said Luthecaw indignantly, when he was able to take a deep breath again, "l'est crazy monte." He yanked at his coat which didn't give any more than had the jaws. "Be-damned bear," he said, taking his tomahawk to the jaws that held it, "near mash me."

They were still adrenalin-high when they got back to the fort. The Major, listening to their tale, recognized the pattern: the terror at coming face-to-face with sudden death, the rage, when it's kill-or-be killed, and the relief when you look down at the kill and you feel great to be alive.

Like any other combat veteran, they were on edge. They were deep in enemy territory, under constant threat of attack, and the game they required for food was to be found further and further away from the safety of the fort. Small groups of hunters went out at daylight. Sometimes they had to travel twenty or thirty miles before finding an elk, deer or buffalo to kill, butcher, and load on horses for the return trip. They had to move fast and quietly or they were in real trouble.

The men who had come into this valley were changed. As Cather had put it, "Down inside, we're all a bit like Pelton. We go to sleep scared. We wake up scared. It makes a man damn mean when he does get a chance at the enemy."

The Major nodded. He could see they needed to work off their edginess. If Cather, McBride and Jackson wanted to go a short distance from the fort to hunt for wildfowl this day, he could see no immediate threat in their proposed jaunt.

"Just bring back a goose or two," the Major told them. "Don't take chances even if you spot a Blackfeet or two."

"Cheeky'll let us know if there are any around," said McBride as he and Jackson prepared to join Cather. "Last time, he saved our bacon. Seems like there's always a couple Blackfeet keepin' an eye on the fort. They're good at coverin' sign but Cheeky can smell them out."

Still, the Major was relieved to see them return, laden with geese and ducks but looking down-at-the mouth. "What happened? Where's my dog?"

The three men shifted uneasily.

"Two Injuns stole him," Cather blurted. "Leastways, that's what it looks like."

"We can show you where it happened. Cheeky won't give up when there's any bird to bring in. Those damn Indians sneaked out from their hidey-hole and dragged one of the geese we shot back there. When Cheeky come for it, they threw sort of a net over him. Bundled him up and stole off with him."

"Stole my dog? Indians? Whatever for?"

"I'm afeerd we'll never know," said McBride. "If we'da had horses we mighta been able to catch up with them. But they were mighty cute — took to the water and we lost the trail."

"I could understand if they'd stolen a horse or taken one of you prisoner," said the Major. "but to kidnap poor ol' Cheeky — that's like carrying coals to Newcastle."

In the Piegan camp, where Running Wolf and Black Cloud were proudly displaying their prisoner, Running Wolf's mother, in a voice that could shatter glass, said much the same thing. The clan did not need another dog. Shaking her brass kettle, she said that if they were not men enough to take scalps or real prisoners, this was the sort of loot they should have brought back.

No one paid her much attention. The sheer effrontery of the two Dog Soldiers tickled the Piegan funny-bone, as they clamored for details from the venturesome pair. When the prisoner seized the opportunity to bite Running Wolf's mother on her fat behind, there was even greater hilarity.

Ay-len intervened before her humiliated daughter could take vengeance on the fine dog Running Wolf had brought back.

"Come," said Ay-len, using the English words her father had taught her for handling the original wolfhounds, the ones she still used when she had time to work with a promising dog.

At the familiar command, Cheeky looked around hopefully.

"Good dog," Ay-len said. She took the rawhide thong that served as a leash from Running Wolf. "Come, boy," she said, turning toward her tepee. "Heel."

Cheeky looked at her with his intelligent eyes. She might smell like the enemy but she at least knew the correct sounds to make when communicating with a well-trained dog.

He went with her to his new home. There, after she watered and fed him, he sat close to her, listening as she practiced English phrases to be used later this year for the trading. The rest of the camp was noisy with celebration. There was many a tale to tell, of danger, bravery, and achievement. There was also a certain greedy anticipation of the rum and guns and ammunition to be acquired at the Rocky Mountain House on the Northern Saskatchewan in exchange for the goods stolen from the white men who had dared venture into the Three Forks land of the Piegan.

Chapter 17

By the first of June 1810, the men at Three Forks were ready to leave the fort. They lowered the American flag. They hoisted the Blackfeet scalp in its place.

The constant harassment by the Blackfeet and the frequent confrontations with grizzlies had been most discouraging.

The score read:

For the Blackfeet
Killed: Ayres, Cheek, Drouillard, Fleehart, Hull, two Shawnees, and Rucker. The lucky ones died quickly, before the torture and mutilations became really painful.
Stolen: All beaver, traps, firearms, ammunition, sundries, and seven horses of the above.
Intimidated: Most everyone, including friendly tribes who wished to patronize the post, and Colter, Bryan and Vallé, who left Three Forks April 21, after several narrow escapes and headed for St. Louis.
Lost: Weeks of good trapping, a good deal of equanimity, and some of Archie Pelton's wits.

For the Grizzlies
Severely injured: Marie, brought to Three Forks by St. John from their camp on the Shields River.
Mauled: Pelton and Luthecaw.
For the Expedition
Killed: One Blackfeet, for sure. Three grizzlies.
Recovered: Forty-seven traps, three horses; Luthecaw, entirely; Marie, somewhat; Pelton, not quite, mentally.
Discouraged: More of the expedition than Blackfeet or grizzlies.

For the British Traders
Profits: At his post on the Saskatchewan, Alexander Henry would dicker with some Blackfeet later in the year. From them he would obtain a supply of prime beaver pelts, and other furs, traps, and one appealing dog, part Newfoundland, who understood English.

Pierre Menard had completed his one-year stint for the Company and was looking forward to returning home to Kaskaskia, as planned. Reuben Lewis and Samuel Morrison were to go to Fort Raymond. Andrew Henry, however, was more determined than ever to spend at least another year, maybe two, in this rich beaver country.

June is a pleasant month for travel in the mountains. The somber mood that had set in during the last weeks at Three Forks was relieved as the men left the place behind them. They reached the junction of the Clark's Fork with the Yellowstone without incident.

There, as arranged earlier in the year, men from Fort Raymond were awaiting them with the expected boatload of supplies. Unexpected was an encampment of the Crow Indians.

Even after some much needed R&R, which included some mutually enjoyable fraternizing with agreeable Crow women, most of the forty men from Three Forks, engages and free trappers alike, were saying they wanted to go back east with Menard.

The Major didn't blame them. He just didn't want to talk about their problems. Or anyone else's. He wanted to get away by himself for a while and not have to think about anything.

He knew he was in a helluva mood that nice June morning. He had snarled at young Morrison over the grounds he found in his breakfast coffee, grumped at euphoric Menard who wanted to talk about the trip home, told Lewis, shortly, "Later," when he wanted to talk about the Wiser-Champlain route to the headwaters of the Columbia.

Andrew Henry recognized his acute need for privacy and isolation. He was emotionally exhausted by the events of recent weeks. Other men in the expedition had suffered from mood swings, indulged in them, going from being laughing and happy to being suddenly moved to tears or bellowing with rage. He could identify with them.

There were words to describe his feelings. Down in the dumps. Lower than a snake's belly. Ready to fly off the handle. Howl like a banshee. Thin-skinned, his mother had called it. And thin-skinned didn't mean you were entitled to act hateful. He'd learned acceptable behavior at his mother's knee, weeding out the frowned-upon responses, directing his energies into conformity, trying not to make excuses for himself, still fully aware of this inadequacy in himself. The best solution had been to withdraw into silence and secrecy, focusing on some small aspect of a problem, or simply escape into daydreaming.

He left the partners to seek out a place of privacy he knew of beside a small, hidden stream. He was intercepted by Pelton, who wanted a decision about a horse; by Cather, who wanted to know when they would be visiting the Crow camp; by Hoback, who wanted to talk about trapping beaver on the other side of the mountains. "Later," he told each of them, striding away, only to find Charles Davis at his side.

After hearing what Charles Davis had to say, he returned to the partners' tent, borrowed Menard's folding desk, then strode away from the raucous camp to his chosen place of solitude. He settled down on the grass under an enveloping clump of willows to do some pondering, regain his equanimity.

The Major was not dismayed at the prospect of another year in the mountains. From experience, he knew he could move over a far-flung spread of territory and live off the land, unobserved, with six or seven expert assistants. Increase that number and they would have to carry or cache supplies and move much more slowly.

He knew he could count on Cather, Jackson and McBride, doggedly determined men. He also knew he missed Francis Vallé with his enthusiasm, his vitality and his fount of laughter. If he'd had a change of heart, as Davis indicated, a letter might overtake him.

On June 5, 1810, Andrew Henry penned a letter of inquiry to Francis Vallé. The one-page letter, with precise margins, consistently parallel lines, reflected a good basic education in the principles of correspondence, and excellent eye and motor coordination. The handwriting, analyzed, tells more about Andrew Henry than he ever let on to any one person. Integrity, aptitudes, mental, mechanical, social dexterity, emotional quotient.

On that day, in that place, he was resenting the demands being made on him. His handwriting reflected his feelings of irritability, impatience. The loops, the slants, the downstrokes, the upstrokes said he was a very caring person, acutely conscious of the human needs of those around him; an honorable man who avoided shady practices, not in the least greedy; a man who gave generously of himself to many people in many ways, but would not delude himself to be all things to all people. What he did, he wanted to be able to do correctly.

It was a well-balanced letter, offering Francis as good or better terms than Manuel had given him. On the other hand, he said he knew the family would be glad to have Francis home, "altho the pleasure of your company for a year in this wild country would be to me inestimable...."

Thinking about that family, about the warmth and conviviality of Ste. Genevieve and its people, he moved himself back in time, savoring the memories. He could picture the right hearty welcome Francis would get from the Joe Pratte's. At Lodge, presided over by the beaming Dr. Aaron Elliott. At the militia muster, erect, compact Colonel Rueben Smith barking out orders. Terry Weber would be ready to show off his new house by now, furnished, bride burnished. George Bullitt, the lawyer, jovial at the bar of the Price brick building, toasting a fine, winning point of jurisprudence. He'd get news of Dr. Thomas, the acerbic surgeon who had been good company on the trip upriver, who had not been sure what he would do upon his return to St. Louis.

Andrew Henry sent his regards to them and to his other friends. Francis knew them all, the Flemings, the Fenwicks, the Austins, the Ashleys, a long list of people that reflected the regard in which he was held, more than there was room for on this one-page letter. At last he penned his distinctive signature.

He folded up the portable desk, stretched out in the shade, hands behind his head. Not a bad day. Warm, but not too warm. He gazed up at the sky, a lovely blue, cloudless, letting his mind go blank, his lids lowering slowly. He slept.

Len Cather, who had been keeping an eye on him, relaxed, too. He didn't think the Major'd had a decent night's sleep in weeks. Bound to make a man cranky, being rousted out to tend to some crisis or another, never letting on. Staying calm on the outside amidst dangers, toils, snares, repressing anguish, speaking quietly, considerately, even compassionately as he dealt with the irrational, the divisive, the opinionated, the obtuse, the obdurate.

The other watchers didn't stir until the Major did, as the evening sun was going down. "The man needed good dreams," Looks Far said to his twin.

"He will be needing a bedfellow now."

"I didn't think you liked him?"

Anthracite eyes met bituminous. "My mare doesn't like your stud. Their colts improve our pony herd. One must consider that."

When the Major rejoined the partners and the men of the expedition, the recovery of an essential inner tranquility made facing up to the burdens of command easier. No overt trace of pessimism or despair or even fatalism remained to cast a shadow over his characteristically cheerful, optimistic disposition.

He rounded up his three trustworthy lieutenants. They visited the Crow encampment, where they spent several days as honored guests, and emerged, rested, relaxed, with a cavvy of Indian ponies and the peaceful look and good humor of the sexually accommodated. Business correspondence and messages for home folks were entrusted to Menard, and mutual fare-thee-wells exchanged.

Major Henry, an able, pragmatic man, knew where he was going and how to get there. He would take the route Peter Wiser and Jean Baptiste Champlain, sent out by Lisa in 1808, had traversed. From Three Forks, up the Madison, over an easy pass and down to the Snake River plains.

John Colter had reached the same area in the winter of 1808 by a different route. He had told Henry of an ideal, hidden valley to winter in, and how to find it.

Several other men, in addition to Cather, Jackson and McBride, thought they would like to go into Idaho with Henry: Jay Day, John Hoback, Archibald Pelton, Jacob Reznor, Edward Robinson, Edward Rose and William Weir.

The two groups under Henry and Menard parted company. Menard returned to Fort Raymond for one of Lisa's keelboats left there two years before, repaired it, descended the Yellowstone to Fort Manuel Lisa. By August 1810 Menard was back in St. Louis and preparing a balance sheet for the Company.

Henry headed west again. At the Gallatin River, Rose, the mulatto who had married into Many Coup's band of Crows, said he knew of a short-cut the Crows took to reach the Madison and a pass over the Continental Divide. The Major listened but did not turn aside.

Henry and his men, with the addition of some other men headed for Flathead country, made it to Three Forks. There the Blackfeet appeared in force and were not driven off until twenty-two of their number and one of the trappers had been killed.

Everyone abandoned the fort and Three Forks. With no more than nine men, the number varying from time-to-time, depending on the individual inclinations of the men and the Major's forbearance, Henry took off to retrace the Wiser-Champlain route into Idaho.

Rose was right about the Crows having a short cut. One night, near a lake that would be named for Andrew Henry, the Crows took back all the ponies Henry had got from them, and a few extras.

Rose, who liked to boast of his standing with the Crows, was irked. He set out, afoot, to recover the horses. The Major did not have to tell Cather, Jackson, and McBride what to do. They immediately began redistributing the supplies into packs for the men and remaining horses.

Reznor and Robinson, Kentucky frontiersmen, who had been on guard the night the horses were stolen, were already on the defensive. Looking over the packs, they protested. They would be carrying the heaviest loads.

"Serves you right," John Hoback told his fellow Kentuckians, shouldering his own pack. "You went to sleep on the job."

Men and horses, laden, making their way along the winding fork of the Snake that in days to come would be known as Henry's Fork, came upon an open plain. They could see the Teton range to the southeast and the Upper Snake River Valley spread out to the southwest.

When it appeared they had reached the location Wiser and Champlain described, near present-day St. Anthony, Robinson and

Reznor threw down their packs. They were going to stay at the "illigible" site. Hoback, heretofore the third member of the Kentucky trio, hid his chagrin, when, pointedly, they did not invite him to join them.

Archibald Pelton, the Yankee from Connecticut, showing signs of increasing mental instability, talked sense about horses, only. Shaking his fist at Robinson and Reznor, he refused point blank to leave a lame horse "with them sinners."

Weir got the Major to go with him and Day on a sweeping exploration of streams and region below the fort site, confiding in him their interest in making their way to the Spanish waters.

Back at the fort site, the Major, despite the increasing resentment of Reznor and Robinson, saw to the redistribution of supplies once again, traps, ammunition and sundries divided up equally. Pelton, shoving aside the traps, gathered up his share. Leading the lame horse, he set off to make a solitary camp of his own. Weir and Day took their share and set out on their own.

The Major found the tributaries he was seeking, present-day Fall River and Conant Creek, and the valley recommended by Colter.

In September 1810, Andrew Henry and four men set up "Camp Henry" on Conant Creek, two-and-one-half miles east of today's village of Drummond, Idaho.

"In choosing a site for its winter camp, a trapping party selected a hidden, well-watered valley, sheltered as far as possible from wind and snow, and sufficiently wooded to afford shelter for the company's horses and mules and provide an adequate supply of grass," wrote Robert Glass Cleland in *This Reckless Breed of Men*. "Here the trappers erected skin lodges or rough log cabins and 'holed up' for the winter."

A beautiful spot, then and now, with its grassy meadow, clear stream and proud stand of aspen, "Camp Henry" fits his description of the kind of country these men would find suitable.

Those were halcyon days. Too early yet to do any serious trapping. Just right to explore the streams and valleys and locate the beaver and lay plans for the harvest.

They would be comfortable in the Major's tent, warmed by the portable charcoal-burning stove from a sea-going vessel, sold to the Major in St. Louis by a stranded sailor. They set the tent up next to a side hill, hollowing and bracing up a snug dugout, for storage, and later a retreat, when the weather turned really cold.

They hunted far afield, so as not to scare off the game, and found deer and elk, and occasionally, a buffalo. They dried meat and set it aside, along with any berries and roots they could find, reserving these supplies for the lean, snowbound days of winter. They took turns herding the horses out to fatten them up on distant, rich grassland, saving the nearby grazing for winter. They cut and stacked wild hay and built a sheltered corral near the dugout for later use.

Archie Pelton came in from the direction of the Tetons, riding a familiar horse, no longer lame, and leading three thin Indian ponies.

"For you, the black man said," he told the Major, who recognized his description of Edward Rose. "Watch for Crows. Come spring."

Hoback, also recognizing the description, had some harsh things to say about Rose, imputing the horse-stealing episode to him, planned with his Crow allies before he left Clark's Fork.

Pelton, wild-eyed, thin and scabrous-looking, ignored everyone but the Major and did not respond at all sensibly to him, repeating "Watch-for-Crows-come-spring," tiresomely.

They fed him, even got him cleaned up and shaved, and beginning to make sense, until, one evening he interrupted one Hoback's stories about his "Bloody Ground" of Kentucky adventures, with his Crows-come-spring litany.

"Kaintuck addled some folks' wits, too, for awhile," snorted Hoback. "How long you gonna stay taiched in the haid from those tussles you had with the Blackfeet 'n ba'ars, Pelton?"

Pelton leaped up and started loading up his pony, shrilly declaring he wouldn't remain in a camp that included Hoback.

"Hold yore horses," said Hoback whose old bones and inclination had not relished the unrelenting activity undertaken at Camp Henry. He missed his easy-going, more indolent peers and had been hoping to find an excuse to rejoin them. "I'll leave. This ain't my idea of a good place to stay, anyway."

Pelton suddenly looked alert. "Tell Hoback 'howdy,' they said."

The words made welcome sense to Hoback.

"Told you Jake 'n Ed'd be needin' me," Hoback, grinning, told the Major. "I'll just mosey on down there an' give 'em a hand."

The Major didn't try to dissuade him. The grizzled Hoback came from a long line of survivors, Rhinelander Germans who had emigrated to Pennsylvania early in the eighteenth century. There had been Hobacks with George Roger Clark at the taking of Vincennes. Hoback himself, born on the frontier in 1745, had been one of the Long Knives who ventured early into Kentucky, fought to stay there. In his reminiscences, Hoback had made reference to family back in Kentucky on his cleared acres, or plantation, but had given no specifics about wife, children or grandchildren. When civilization and his sixth decade overtook him, he left it all behind to venture into the wilderness. There was something irresistable in the urge to live again in the peculiarly heightened fashion of his salad days, unfettered and free. There was also a positive aspect, from the Major's standpoint, to Hoback being reunited with his wilderness-wise old companions. Old they were, too, in the eyes of the younger men, old as their grandfathers. A winter of unrelieved togetherness was likely to exacerbate, not bridge, the generation gap.

With Hoback gone to rejoin Robinson and Reznor at their camp on the Snake River, Pelton became more his normal self. He was still inclined to ramble, in mind and person, but never seemed to lose his instinctive survival skills. As long as no reference was made to events prior to his arrival at Camp Henry, Pelton did not become agitated.

Cather, McBride and Jackson could not help contrasting the serenity of Camp Henry with the disastrous days at Three Forks. Usually they made sure Pelton was not present when making such comparisons.

The four of them were trapping in earnest by then. The cold, coming in November 1810, had primed the furs.

"Nothing but beaver," said Cather, exultantly, as he came up to his companions at the end of a gray, overcast day and laid his impressive catch before them. As Pelton wasn't with them, he voiced his further satisfaction at the welcome feeling of safety and security they were enjoying in their snug camp. "No Bug's Boys here. No sign of white bears."

"Bears?" Pelton stuck his head out of the tent, looking around, wild-eyed. "Bears! Run for yore lives!"

Before they could stop him, he was on his horse, bareback, off and away, his mind reeling with fearsome images of grizzly claws and jaws closing on his living body, once again haunted by the stressful encounters endured at Three Forks.

As Archie pelted away, the first really fierce snowstorm of the season blew in. It covered his tracks before they could overtake him.

The depth built up for several days. They already had their hand-wrought snowshoes ready. As soon as the wind died down, they were out trapping, bringing in beaver pelts in quantities they had never dreamed possible.

By New Year's Day of 1811, they had a wealth of beaver, all of them caught on streams within a day's reach of Camp Henry. Ruefully, they agreed there was no use doing any more trapping. They barely had enough horses to carry what they had pressed into tight packs. If it weren't for the snow, and the snowbound passes, they could leave this instant for Fort Raymond with an assured, substantial profit in hand.

They put their equipment in readiness for the day they could leave, discussed the likeliest passes, wishing for spring. As if their wishes had been heard, they got a January thaw and, for a change, began worrying about being flooded out.

The weather turned cold, abruptly, freezing snow and flood waters solid overnight.

Just as suddenly, Pelton came stumbling into Camp Henry, afoot, in the bright sunlight of Ground Hog's Day.

"They killed an' et him!" Pelton gasped out indignantly, grabbing the Major's arm to anchor himself on the slick ice underfoot. "They killed an' et him! Them accursed sinners!"

"Who?" said McBride, aghast.

"Judas Priest!" said Jackson, appalled.

"No," said the Major dryly. "Pelton's horse."

"Are you talking about Day and Weir?" said McBride.

"No," said Pelton. "They said 'come along with us'. 'Not to the Spanish settlements,' I sez. 'So long,' they sez."

"So it was the other three, Hoback, Reznor and Robinson, who killed your horse," said the Major.

"Why?" said Cather. "There was more game there than here. What ails them? Too sick to go out hunting?"

"No gumption," said Pelton bluntly, his narrow, close-set eyes blinking rapidly. "Et every deer I fetched in. Wouldn't fetch them no more. Said I should."

His anger seemed to have cleared his mind. They let him tell it in his own way, having learned the hard way that abrupt questions unbalanced his thinking. He was vague about when he'd last seen Weir and Day, and even vaguer about how and when he arrived at the other camp. He was not vague in his assessment of Hoback, Reznor and Robinson. "Feckless lot. Et Hoback's horse. Told 'em where to find a deer. Sneaky sinners went for my horse. Couldn't stop them. They told me to 'git.'"

From what Pelton had to say, repeating his story as he ate, with some additional details, they concluded that Hoback, Reznor and Robinson must be in dire straits to have been callous enough to butcher the horse Pelton thought so much of, despite his opposition.

The camp Pelton had left was about thirty miles distant as the crow flies, over the hardened surface of the snow. This seemed an opportune time to pack up everything and begin their journey eastward while the snow would support the weight of their horses. It wouldn't be out of their way to stop off at the other camp and see what ailed Hoback, Reznor and Robinson.

They found the three Kentuckians huddled in a half-faced camp typical of the Kentucky frontier. Nearby, drifted over with snow, was the beginning of a small log hut.

"Told you so," said Pelton tartly. "No gumption."

The Major and his men got an ambivalent welcome. Making small talk, the Major joined Hoback, Reznor and Robinson at their inadequate fire. Cather, McBride and Jackson set up a camp of their own in their routine, efficient manner, Pelton helping with the horses.

The Major found the three men weak, undernourished and feeling sorry for themselves. They brightened up considerably when he poured each of them a medicinal tot of brandy. There didn't seem to be anything wrong with them that food and activity wouldn't cure.

He got them warmed up and fed. Then, exercising tact, backed up with a measure of good-natured firmness, he insisted they strip, wash all over, put on clean clothes, shave, and allow Pelton to trim their hair. While Pelton made short work of Hoback and Reznor's tangled mops, Edward Robinson joked about the convenience of never needing a hair cut.

Tough as whang leather, Robinson, at sixty-six, was the oldest man there. In the early days in Kentucky, he had been scalped and left for dead. He kept his scarred scalp tied up in a kerchief, with a woolen cap pulled down over his ears against the cold.

The Major let them know his group would not be staying long. However, he did think everyone would be more comfortable, considering the time of year, if all hands turned to and completed the log hut. Also, there should be a shelter for the horses.

Pelton, heeding an inner voice of his own, hunted while the others worked on the cabin and horse shed. He had a knack for finding game, large and small, and took pride in keeping the cooking kettle well-stocked.

February turned mean. They had shelters for men and horses completed, but far from weatherproof, when hit by a three-day blizzard.

All seven men took shelter in the cramped log hut, the wind whipping the horse-hide tacked over the doorway, blowing snow through the gaps in the log walls, piling it up in miniature drifts across the dirt floor.

By the second day, Hoback, Robinson and Reznor had retreated again to a minimum level of existence. Rolled up in their blankets, conserving energy and warmth like hibernating bears, there was no doubt they slept. All three of them snored, loudly.

Pelton, too, retired into a world of his own. He staked out a place for himself in one corner of the room, humming to himself, swirling the snow this way and that, patting it into first one shape, then another, sometimes scooping dirt up from the floor and mixing it with the snow. As the second day wore on, his humming became an audible sing-song, the familiar "black-man-said-Crow-come-spring."

The Major and his men took a good look at Pelton's creation and exchanged glances. Pelton was sculpting recognizable mountain ranges and valleys, creating a topographical map.

Pelton paused once, dissatisfied with the course of a stream. The Major held out his compass. Pelton took it, studied it for a moment, flattened a mountain range, wiped out part of the stream, began again.

Unobtrusively, Cather, Jackson and McBride retreated before the emerging map. They remained motionless for long periods of time. When one of them moved, it was slowly, quietly, and for only the most essential chores, adding charcoal to the Major's portable stove.

Pelton did not seem to notice their presence but that of Hoback, Robinson and Reznor made him uneasy. He glanced frequently over his shoulder at their slumbering forms. Finally, motioning for the Major to join him, he touched his forefinger to his lips, rocking back and forth on his haunches in secret glee.

Using the first two fingers of his right hand, he pantomimed walking from the beginning of his map along a detailed route to reach a distant goal, which he emphasized by patting it flat. From strips of bark peeled from one of the log walls, he fashioned tiny triangles, set them out carefully on the flat, a miniature Indian encampment.

"Ah," breathed the Major. "Thanks."

Pelton nodded curtly, stood up, and kicked his map into oblivion. He snatched up his rifle, eased out the doorway, and did not return, that day or the next.

Cather, Jackson and McBride looked at the ruined map and swore. The Major only smiled. Quietly, he began moving the snow this way and that, as Pelton had done, recreating the main features for them to see.

"We are to meet Many Coup's band there?" said Cather in a jubilant undertone, when they had gone over the Major's map carefully, memorizing the route. "When?"

The Major told him. The next morning they got ready to leave. By then the snow had nearly stopped, but the wind had turned warm, was blowing harder. It would be well to seek higher ground before this location became an island amidst the melting run-off.

He roused Hoback, Jackson and Reznor, who were thickheaded with sleep and grumpy. They could come with them, stay, or go their separate way, the Major informed them. He repeated himself with considerable patience when they were dubious about leaving the best quarters they'd had all year. Forced to make a decision, the three, petulantly, were very definite about preferring to go their own way, when they were good and ready to do so. The Major, carefully, refrained from heaving a sigh of relief.

Pelton proved more elusive. From a distance, he watched them prepare to depart, darting away when any one of them attempted to approach him. It was not the American way on the frontier to interfere with a man's exercise of his free will.

Regardless of his state of mind, Pelton had proved to be a survivor. In his solitary way he had come through the winter in better condition, physically, than the Kentucky trio.

There was little the Major and his men could do to keep him with them, short of hog-tying him and leading him on a rope, which would not benefit them or Pelton. So they waved goodbye to Pelton, too.

The route Major Andrew Henry took in leaving Idaho became one of his carefully guarded trade secrets. Nor did he, officially, account for his exact whereabouts during the spring and summer of 1811.

Once the Major and his three stalwart companions joined up with the Crow band awaiting them in their spring camp somewhere in western Wyoming, they had no urgent commitments to keep. They renewed established friendships and liaisons, took a certain paternal pride in the small, healthy occupants of some of the papoose carriers, hunted, fished and explored. They were outfitted in buckskin, fashioned by loving hand in the esteemed Crow style.

The Crows were cheerful, pragmatic and adaptive. Many Coups' band had listened to Francis Laroque when he was in the Big Horn country in 1805. From him they had learned how to use the new-fangled beaver traps. Unlike so many of the western Indians who did not take to trapping, they now had valuable beaver pelts to trade for the white man's goods. When the time came, they would make sure their friend Henry had enough horses to get his party and all the fur packs back to Fort Raymond. In the meantime, there was no hurry.

The Crows preferred to lift horses, rather than scalps. It was a game of upmanship with them. They ranged far and wide, over trails and passes that were still unknown to the white man, and derived mischievous merriment in making off with the horses of erstwhile friends and foes alike. They were courageous and had a strong warrior tradition. Horse-raiding was a good way to hone their skills, develop perseverance and test the leadership.

Above all, they enjoyed the hunt. Like most Indians, they were concerned with protecting their food supply, and, by extension, the land where the game could be found.

"The Crows live where it is not too hot," they told Henry. "Not too high and snowy, and not too low and dirty. Animals enjoy it here. Men enjoy it also. Of all possible places in which happiness can be found, only in the land of the Crow is true happiness found."

It *was* a happy time, refreshing to the appetite in more ways than one. Henry and his men made the most of it.

They encountered other white men, sometimes with other bands of Crows, occasionally with Shoshones. More often, they found them in small parties of two or three, on their own.

In addition, there were men who had gone to Fort Raymond with Henry, such as Benjamin Jones and Alexander Carson, who were heading for the Missouri after a successful trapping season; Jean Baptiste Champlain and his party of twenty-three hunters returning from the Arapahoes; Ezekiel William with a party of nineteen, planning to trap the headwaters of the South Platte and Arkansas.

These men drew maps on the ground to show where they had been and where they were going, described what they had seen and what they expected to see.

Along with the firsthand knowledge of trails and passes he was getting in company with the Crows, Henry added these other items to his growing store of geographical information, priceless to his trade. The area he was, and had been traversing this past year, contained the headwaters of the Missouri, the Colorado and the Columbia. Eventually, those waters would reach, respectively, the Gulf of Mexico, the Gulf of California and the Pacific Ocean.

Henry applied himself mentally to sorting out the complicated web of overlapping tributary streams, the trails and passes to reach them. By the time he left the mountains in 1811, he had a grasp on the topography of the Jefferson, Gallatin, Madison, all of the Missouri, the Yellowstone, and the headwaters of the Snake River. He had knowledge, too, of the passes: Bozeman, Lolo, Lemhi, Gibbons, Marias, Union, Togwotee, Teton, Raynolds, Targhee and South Pass.

As the bright days of summer turned lazy, hazy, Pet McBride, who had relatives interested in the Sante Fe trade, found a congenial party headed for the Spanish settlements. Over a period of time, such men made contacts in Taos and Sante Fe, unobtrusively, that led to a secondary, unofficial base for American free trappers and the initiation of fur trading in that area.

Len Cather, comfortable with his own housekeeping unit, Crow style, was quite adept at sign language. And, thanks to domestic pillow talk, was getting quite fluent in the Crow language. He decided to postpone his return home.

Belt Jackson, who knew he could find his way back to this happy land and be sure of a welcome, made plans to give Henry a hand in getting as far as the Arikara villages, whenever he decided to make the trip.

Of the other men who had entered Idaho with Henry in the fall of 1810, news had trickled in, by tribal grapevine. The black man had gone to bring back ammunition and other supplies for his Crow friends. The man-without-a-scalp and his two companions had followed the black man down the Missouri. Now all four of them, as well as Jones and Carson, were coming upriver, guiding, hunting and interpreting for a large group of white men. Henry concluded that the American Fur Company had finally got its projected overland expedition underway.

John Jacob Astor, with his international connections and global grasp of the intricacies of the fur trade, had planned two expeditions, one by sea, the other by land. The one by sea carried men and goods around the Horn, established the trading post, Fort Astoria, at the mouth of the Columbia. The other, travelling overland to Fort Astoria, was to seek out the best routes, beaver streams, friendly tribes, and potential sites for a string of interior trading posts.

Eventually, by slower, semi-official reports, Henry would learn that Astor had put Wilson Price Hunt, the St. Louis storekeeper, in charge of the overland expedition. Hunt and his partners, Stuart, Crooks, McClellan and Miller, as they encountered Henry men at intervals, recruited them for their expertise: Benjamin Jones and Alexander Carson, who had been in and out of the Big Horn and Wind River country; Edward Rose, who claimed to have influential status in the Crow nation; and Hoback, Robinson and Reznor, who said they could show the Astorians an easier, more practical route to get over the mountains than that followed by Lewis and Clark.

Jones and Carson agreed it was best to swing south of the Blackfeet country, but were not in agreement with the Kentucky trio on the course to follow. And the latter made Hunt uneasy by voicing their distrust of Rose. Dubious about the black man's trustworthiness, Hunt prudently made it profitable for Rose to get them an escort of Crows through Crow country, then encouraged him to remain with the Crows.

The five remaining guides finally got Hunt to the heights of the Wind River range. From there, the Kentucky trio pointed out the Tetons, which Hunt, primly, called the Pilot Knobs. Robinson told Hunt that just on the other side of those mountains they had wintered on a tributary of the Columbia.

They found it hard going as they neared the Tetons, down a canyon, crossing and recrossing the stream at the bottom. Hunt named both for John Hoback. They camped where the Hoback flows into the South Fork of the Snake. Hunt was hopeful that he could take the boats from there, but had to give up the idea.

When a couple of Shoshone Indians visited the camp, Hunt

was pleased to discover they not only knew about the site the man-without-a-scalp and others had abandoned in the spring, but knew how to reach it. After some dickering, they agreed to show him the way. They guided the expedition over Teton Pass through Teton Basin and arrived at the exact location of the abandoned huts on a blustery cold October 11, 1811.

Hunt decided to use the site for an American Fur Company trading post. Since the expedition would be taking to boats here, he would have to leave over seventy horses and their tack behind; the trappers, spinning off in small groups, could return here to dispose of their catches, restock for another trapping venture; the location, already known to friendly Indians, had a potential to serve the traders passing through on their way to and from the Pacific coast.

Hunt named his trading post Fort Henry and the tributary of the Columbia on which it was located Henry's River.

Hoback, Robinson and Reznor, joined by another trapper, Martin Cass, and the unpredictable Joseph Miller, one of Hunt's partners, stayed in Idaho to trap. The spring of 1812, eastbound Astorians rescued four of the five from starvation.

Martin Cass and his horse were missing. The conflicting stories told by survivors gave rise to some dark suspicions. Unconfirmed rumors had some of the trappers speculating, in low tones, "D'ya s'pose, jest maybe, they et both Cass and his horse?"

In January 1814, Hoback, Robinson and Reznor were killed by unidentified Indians on the Boise River, along with the former Astorian clerk, John Reed, and all the other men in the trapping party.

Archibald Pelton, still intermittently deranged, had been found by Donald McKenzie, late in 1811, wandering along Henry's Fork with a band of friendly Indians. The Astorians took him with them to Fort Astoria. Nothing further was heard of him after the British marched in and took over that American establishment in December 1813, renamed it Fort George, and put an end to Astor's plans for the Oregon country.

Long before that, men who had gone with the St. Louis Missouri Fur Company expedition to the Three Forks of the Missouri in the spring of 1810 were coming down river in dabs and dribbles to tell the home folks what had befallen them there.

Chapter 18

"You'll never guess who showed up at Lodge last night." Dr. Nicholas Fleming looked around the breakfast table, anticipating the reaction to his good news.

"Francis Vallé," said his sister watching him polish off his bowl of cornmeal mush. Dr. Nick always ate a hearty breakfast before starting his rounds of calls which sometimes took him far afield and late into the night with no opportunity to eat again until he returned home.

"Hmph." Her brother looked disappointed. His mother removed the empty bowl and passed him the platter of ham and eggs.

"Did he tell you he had many adventures in the mountains?" prompted Mary.

"He did," said Dr. Nick shortly. He had expected the news he had for them this June morning in 1810 to be a surprise. He was a bit surprised at himself for feeling grumpy because it was not. "What do you know about it?"

"A veritable odyssey, M'sieu Pratte said."

Madame Fleming handed her son the pan of hot biscuits. When he had helped himself to two of her light and airy biscuits, she passed him the butter, freshly churned by her hands early that morning while the day was at its coolest. "His mother and sisters are most relieved to have him safely home."

Dr. Nick frowned. "Don't tell me you've been visiting the Pratte's!" He spoke with his medical voice, sternly. "Didn't I tell you all Miz Marie's children were down with the summer complaint?"

"That's why we took some chicken soup to the Pratte's," said his mother serenely.

"Madame Vallé was there helping Miz Marie nurse them." Mary handed her brother the honey jar. "She wouldn't let me go in. She said you would scold her if she did."

Dr. Nick nodded his head, somewhat mollified. Madame Vallé, experienced in childhood diseases, had been advising and nursing mothers and children as long as he could remember. In her day it had been an achievement to raise a child to the age of five. Of the fourteen or fifteen children born to her, only Francis and his four sisters remained. The survival rate had improved considerably since Dr. Fenwick's arrival a decade ago to implement up-to-date medical procedures on vaccination, isolation, sanitation, drainage and safe drinking water.

"Mary sat out on the gallery and had a nice visit with Francis and Joseph Pratte. I could see no harm in that, " said Madame Fleming.

"Pass me the biscuits," Patrick Fleming instructed his son. "You can tell *me* about Francis." He took his third biscuit, split it open. "Now, pass the butter. And the honey." He helped himself liberally to both. "I hadn't heard that Francis was expected home so soon. What did he have to say?"

"After the meeting ended, we all stayed for hours, listening to him," said Dr. Nick. "Francis took a real chance, coming home the way he did. One of Lisa's hunters decided to leave the mountains after a narrow escape. Francis and another young fellow came with him."

"John Colter. And William P. Bryan. He's from Philadelphia," Mary interpolated. "Mr. Colter is from Kentucky. He went to the mountains with M'sieu Clark and poor M'sieu Lewis and hasn't been home since."

"He hasn't got home *yet*," said Dr. Nick. "He's thinking of taking up land upriver near the Boones. Young Bryan is supposed to go home right away. Now he's learned something about the fur business firsthand, Guy Bryan wants his son to put his knowledge to use on a larger scale."

"He's going to stop in Kaskaskia and give Madame Menard her letter. He needs some new boots and a new hat. M'sieu Hubardeau didn't have any to fit him at the Morrison store in Ste. Genevieve," said Mary. Baptiste Hubardeau had been placed in charge of the Morrison store shortly after William Morrison made the Ste. Genevieve girl, Euphrasie Hubardeau, his second wife. "I don't think he tried at Mr. Craighead's store."

"William Morrison is his cousin," said Madame Fleming. "It's only natural young Bryan would go to his store."

"He'll have to go to the one in Kaskaskia. Or Cahokia. M'sieu Hubardeau says he's got big feet. I don't know about his head."

"Whoa, there." Patrick held up his hand. His gaze swivelled from his wife to daughter. "Let Nick tell the tale, please," he said with courteous firmness. "Now, if I understood you aright, just Francis and this Colter and the Bryan boy made the trip by themselves."

"That's right." Dr. Nick held his cup out for more coffee. "The three of them left the mountains late in April. The first day out the Blackfeet almost got them. They escaped by taking cover in a thicket where the Indians were afraid to follow. By travelling at night, hiding out by day, they got to Fort Raymond safely." He added cream and sugar to the coffee his mother had poured him, stirred it thoughtfully, sipped. "Things weren't quite as hectic after that — just high water and a swamped boat now and then and different Indians chasing them along the banks of the Missouri from time-to-time. They made it to St. Louis in record time."

"Did Francis make any money out of his trip to the mountains?" asked Patrick. "The price of beaver is way down compared to last year."

"Francis said he decided to quit while he was ahead."

"Takes after his late father," said Patrick. "The Vallés keep a close eye on the profits. With all the irons they have in the fire, Francis is probably of more use here."

Dr. Nick nodded. "Francis says the company has made a profit. Not as much as hoped. However, it's expected that the Major will do well, make the company a substantial profit."

"The price of lead is going up," said Patrick. "If there's a war, like some say there will be, lead will be in great demand. Major Henry may make a greater profit from his mines than from his mountains."

"When will the Major get back from the mountains?" asked Madame Fleming.

"Sometime next year," said Mary.

"That's right," said Dr. Nick, getting to his feet. "Sometime next year."

Mary followed her brother into the next room, which served as his dispensary. She handed him the Peruvian bark and a package of lint she had prepared. "What's an odyssey?"

"The adventures of a Greek trying to get home to his wife and family after a war. There's the book if you want to read it." He gestured at his bookshelves. "What did I do with that medicine for Madame Azor — oh, thank you, my dear. When I get back I'll show you how to prepare some more. If you have time today, you can get some more lint ready."

"Oh, I'll have time," said Mary. "I like helping you with your medicines. If you have a piece of paper I'll write down Madame Vallé's receipt for summer complaint before I forget."

"Here. You can use this." He handed her a bound volume of blank pages.

"There are a lot of pages in this," said Mary dubiously, hefting it. "I just wanted a sheet or two of paper."

"I'll tell you what we'll do." Dr. Nick took the volume from her, labelled it neatly, *Mary Fleming, Her Journal.* "Put whatever you want in it — receipts, remembrances, details about the weather, events of the day. You need more handwriting practice, anyway."

"You'll be looking it over to check my spelling?"

"It's yours. Private. Instead of blurting out any unpleasant truths that occur to you, restrain yourself until you can enter them in your journal."

"Did you know that Madame Vallé uses some of the same herbs you do for summer complaint?"

Dr. Nick grinned. "That's where I learned of their efficacy. All that herbal compendium needed was a touch of mint to make it more palatable. Doctors really don't know very much, my dear."

"Oh, but you know lots!" said Mary. "People believe in you. Only the other day Mrs. Walter Wilkinson was saying how much faith she had in you."

"That's half the battle," said Dr. Nick wryly. "When people believe in their doctor, they get well, just like Mrs. Wilkinson did. Between you and me, I think Dr. Fenwick has the right of it: belief helps to heal as much as the treatment, especially if a doctor gives a body a chance to heal itself."

He left his sister giving some thought to the introduction to her journal. "Me, Medicine, and Many Things," she decided would do for the title. "A doctor needs to know Many Things," she wrote, forming her letters with care. "He needs to have Many Things." Using the check-off list her brother maintained for his leather instrument case she copied it: "2 searing irons, 1 pair of surgical scissors, 6 scalpels, 2 saw blades, 1 brass trocar, 1 pair of forceps, 1 packet of curved needles, 3 bundles of ligatures, 2 of catgut sutures, 1 spool of waxed linen thread, 1 dozen linen bandages, 1 bag of lint."

She was learning about some of them: the lint was for padding splints, pledgets or compresses. "Medicines: Peruvian bark, sulphur, ipecac, calomel, mercury and opium.

"Dr. Nick lets me clean his instruments and pack his medicines. Sometimes. Like he lets me go with him sometimes. He says I am a good helper, real handy when he has to set a broken leg and needs four hands. I have a strong stomach."

A few days later, she wrote, "I don't think much of this Odysseus, always getting into some fool scrape. I told M'sieu Vallé I didn't think he was much like Odysseus, even if he'd had an odyssey.

"He said there were some — I had to wait until Dr. Nick came home to find out how to spell this next word — parallels. M'sieu Vallé just chuckled when I asked if that meant one-eyed giants, sirens and men turning into pigs. I told him I hoped the Major wasn't having an odyssey. He said what I should keep in mind was that what went on in the civilized world had an impack on the Major's chievements in the mountains. I asked him if he meant the price of beaver. That and Company policy, M'sieu Vallé said, among other things."

Events of 1810 were having an impact. Young Auguste

Choteau returned on May 6 from the Mandans with some peltry. He had intended to bring a valuable cargo from the Cedar Island post but it had burned down at a loss estimated at close to $15,000. Pierre Menard reached St. Louis late in July with thirty packs of furs, worth about $9,000.

At the Company meeting on July 26, 1810, it was decided to sell the company's furs and merchandise to pay its notes and debts.

Morrison, acting for the Company, took beaver to retire five notes, totaling $6,271.14, given to one St. Louis merchant for merchandise sixteen months earlier. Morrison saved the beaver for shipment to Philadelphia. To settle the notes, which were on deposit in New Orleans, he paid $1,500 cash, gave Bryan & Morrison note for $3,567.40, and credited the merchant's account at Kaskaskia for the remainder.

Other members took company peltry and cash to settle other debts. When initial tabulation was complete and goods on hand inventoried on August 1, 1810, the Company met its financial obligations but did not have enough left to distribute profits.

However, they satisfied all wages and paid Lisa & Company for the merchandise and property at Fort Raymond without touching the initial capitalization promised each member, about $4,000 each, or the $7,000 due for the return of Chief Shehaka to the Mandans. Granted, receipts did not measure up to expectations, but each partner had a part of the $7,000 and a few goods stored at St. Louis.

The Company was reorganized at a meeting held September 10, 1810. Morrison, Lewis and Henry were the only ones not present or represented. Those in attendance unanimously agreed to send another expedition as soon as possible to aid Henry, Lewis, Samuel Morrison and their party. Clark, Lisa and Menard made all arrangements, and each partner was assessed $500 to cover the anticipated cost of $6,750.

Among 'other things,' Tecumseh delivered an ultimatum regarding Indian lands to Governor Harrison at Vincennes. Benjamin Howard was made Governor of Missouri Territory. Manuel Lisa got his boatman's act passed.

Further afield, Napoleon was annexing Holland, Hanover, Bremen, Hamburg, Lauenburg and Lubeck, and, while the divorced Josephine sulked and seethed, married the Archduchess Marie Louise of Austria on April Fool's Day. In Mexico and South America, the struggle for independence from Spain had begun.

Scott published "Lady of the Lake". The French chef, Nicolas Alpert, was making successful experiments in preserving food in sealed containers.

Closer to home, Dr. Nick was ordering the first American anatomy textbook, Wistar's *A System of Anatomy*.

Dr. Nick's sister was telling her journal, "Going with Dr. Nick today has had a great impack on my life. If I'd stuck to weaving like Penelope I wouldn't have to leave home."

Riding pillion behind Dr. Nick on a fall day in 1810, she had found his rounds had started off routinely, medicine for fever at the MacLindens, lancing a boil for Tom Oliver, until they were intercepted by Ben Farrell, husband of the local midwife.

"Mother needs your help," he told Dr. Nick. "She took a fall this morning, hurt her right arm bad just about the time a couple young folks turned up lookin' for a midwife. The baby ain't comin' easy. Mother thinks you're gonna need your forceps."

As they dismounted at the Farrells, Mary could hear the moans coming from the cabin. Mother Farrell, her right arm in a sling, hurried out to meet them, describing the condition of her patient briefly as she led Dr. Nick toward the door.

"Where do you think you're goin', mister?" The doorway was blocked by a narrow, lanky racehorse of a figure, barely old enough to have fuzz for a beard, speaking in the accents of the Kentucky backwoods. "This is woman's business. I ain't lettin' you near my wife."

Dr. Nick shrugged. This prejudice against allowing a male, even though a qualified medical practioner, to deliver a baby was to be found among the educated as well as the uneducated. "Let's see what we can do about your arm," he said to Mother Farrell leading her to a seat on the stump in her front yard, where Mary joined him, carrying the instrument case. "Bring us some whiskey," he directed Ben, a grizzled grenadier of man. "You've got a break in your forearm, Miz Farrell. Mary 'n I'll have it set in a jiffy. Take a big swig," he ordered Mother Farrell as Ben produced a jug. "Give him some, too," he nodded toward the putative father, standing irresolute in the doorway. "Best thing in the world for expectant fathers," he met Ben's gaze meaningfully. "Puts them to sleep. When they wake up the ordeal is all over."

"They're jest babies, them two. Bob Ray and Cindy Lou Harris," said Mother Farrell in an undertone. "On their way to join kin at Austin's mines. The gal thought she had another month to go but she took a fall a couple days ago. Pore thing. She ain't much older'n Mary here."

There was a screech from the cabin. Bob Ray, hurried inside, came back, frowning. He beckoned to Mary. "She needs help."

"What do you expect a little girl to do?" snorted Dr. Nick. Mother Farrell got to her feet. "I'll go," she said, swaying. Dr. Nick caught her, lowered her to the stump again.

"I could go in," said Mary looking at her brother. "You tell me what to look for. Then you and Mother Farrell could tell me what to do."

"Have another drink," Ben suggested and the young man did. Mother Farrell whispered, "I'm not sure we can wait until he passes out." She winced at the sound of another prolonged shriek. " I'm too dizzy to even walk in there. That pore gal needs help or she's gonna die."

"I've seen calves born," said Mary sturdily. "The cow does better if there's someone around who talks to them."

Dr. Nick strolled closer to the tense young man. "Mr. Harris, if it's all right with you, this is what we're going to do. Mary will go in, examine Mrs. Harris, let her know help is at hand. She'll come back out, confer with the midwife here, then go back in and follow Mother Ferrell's directions. You sit down here on the stoop so you don't block the light."

Squaring her shoulders, Mary entered the cabin. There was a murmur of voices, then Mary appeared in the doorway with an iron kettle. "Mr. Harris, it would help if you would fill this kettle from that pot boiling on the fire out there and bring it back to me." There was a moan from within the cabin. "Hurry."

The youthful, bone-lean Mr. Harris took hold of the door jamb, pulled himself up. He took a couple unsteady steps and tripped over Ben's outstretched leg. He didn't get up. Ben knelt beside him. "Needed more than liquor to put him out of action," Ben said, laying aside a chunk of firewood. "I'll pull him around in the shade, Doc, and you can see to his wife."

Dr. Nick was already pulling off his coat, rolling up his sleeves.

As Mary confided to her journal, "It didn't take Dr. Nick long to deliver the baby. A boy. After it was all over, Mother Ferrell had him give Cindy Lou some opium. Both Cindy Lou and Bob Ray were asleep when we left. If they remember anything, the Ferrells will blame it on the whiskey and the opium. Ben's sending word to the Mines for their kinfolks to come get them.

"Fathers should allow doctors to deliver babies. It's too much for ten-year old girls. Mamán and Papa were displeased with Dr. Nick. Now I can't go with Dr. Nick on rounds any more. I am to go to school in St. Louis. Mamán says I won't be too lonesome because I'll have so many cousins who go to the same school."

Later: "I have written to tell Mamán and Papa that I like school. I do. I miss Dr. Nick but like he said, I am learning things here I would never learn at school in in Ste. Genevieve.

"Another new girl started school the same day I did. She said she was real glad there were two of us to learn the ropes together, not be 'timidated by the old timers. I never knew anyone like Abigail Brewster before. She knows a lot, being 13 years old.

"Abigail said of course doctors should be allowed to deliver babies. She said Dr. Nick and Ben handled Mr. Harris in a 'deliciously humorous fashion.' I got her to promise not to tell anyone else, 'specially Cousin Marie and Cousin Margarite, who would boss us around if we'd let them. They were shocked when Abigail said she was delivered by a doctor. Marie and Margarite said they would not want to have a doctor deliver their babies. Abigail said, 'Suppose the doctor was a woman?' That left them speechless for two days. They never did ask if the doctor was. I did. He wasn't.

"Abigail comes from Connecticut. She doesn't think much of Penelope either. She is a great believer in 'progress.' She says all American are. I reminded her that we are Americans, too. She said maybe I could be but Marie and Margarite were Penelopes. If Penelope had been an American she would have figured out a way to get out of weaving all day, unravelling all night. Just no profit in it. That's one of her favorite words. Profit. When she says, 'You can only profit by this experience,' one better watch out — it's usually something that gets one in trouble with the nuns.

"Abigail is a Presbyterian. She says that all the leading Americans are. People who want to live in Missouri don't *have* to be Catholics any more now it's part of the US instead of Spain. Most of the girls here at school are, except for some who are in everything but name, Abigail says, being Piscopalians. We agreed not to talk about religion but sometimes she forgets.

"Her Mamán is a 'learned' woman and named Abigail after a 'learned' woman and Abigail intends to be one, too.

"If she does get married, it's going to be to a 'go-getter' like her father. She thinks the Major is a 'go-getter.' He is a Presbyterian. Mary Ann asked her father about him. They are both Masons and her father likes him, said he was a 'real honest gentleman.'

"Abigail's Mamán has written to my Mamán and got permission for me to spend Christmas week with her."

The visit to Abigail's was so successful that Mary was there often during the year of 1811. The father was a businessman with a wide circle of acquaintances and interests; the mother, who corresponded with other 'learned' woman, was organized, efficient, open-minded, interested in all manner of things. Abigail was their only child, treated as an adult, as Mary found she was. They and their guests conversed and took an interest in far ranging subjects, solemnly discussed Penelope and Odysseus and their shortcomings with Mary, delighted with her viewpoint. There were men who could talk about the world of medicine; there were men who explained the system of surveying to Mary, all the imaginary lines on the globe; Abigail's mother got a discussion going concerning the rights of women — French versus English — and Mary was able to contribute some items about the rights of a Frenchwoman of Ste. Genevieve to leave her husband and take back her dowry.

When the mother found she could recount a "It's Good to Tell You" French folk tale with dramatic zest, Mary was the center of attention on more than one evening. She and Abigail made a good team, Mary telling the tale in French, Abigail translating with verve. Most of the tales were new to her listeners. Some were familiar, sparking some sprightly debates about the difference, as did the tale of the French Cinderella, who, as Mary insisted, was sensibly shod in fur slippers, not glass. "Deerskin, trimmed with beaver, would look nice," Mary insisted.

"She's right," agreed one of the guests, a tanned young man who turned out to be William P. Bryan, back in St. Louis once again to collect money owed his father by the Chouteaus. "The English fairy godmother had more sand than sense." He bowed over Mary's hand. "I know a friend of yours. Drank a toast to your ninth birthday just before I left him at Three Forks."

Mary showed her dimples.

"He has a faithful companion who never leaves his side," said young Bryan. "Four-legged," he reassured Mary, then proceeded to regale the entire company with the tale of Cheeky.

Mary wrote in her journal. "No one seems to know where the Major is. Or just when he will return."

In March Hugh Brackenridge held the center of interest as he outlined his plan to accompany Manuel Lisa up the Missouri. That Company expedition, sent to the relief of the partners still in the mountains, left early in April of 1811, just three weeks behind Wilson Price Hunt and his Astorians.

Shortly thereafter, Dr. Nick, paying Mary a visit, was able to tell her that F. M. Benoit, the company factor at the Mandan villages, had made his way downstream in a small boat loaded with peltries. "He met Lisa, going upstream," said Dr. Nick, "and told him that Andy plans to be at Fort Mandan sometime this summer."

"Andrew Henry is on his way to the Mandans with a rich catch," Reuben Lewis told Lisa in July.

"That was the latest word," Henry Brackenridge reported in August. He had come from Fort Mandan to St. Louis, in charge of two boats, twelve men as a crew, in fourteen days. Mary read with interest Brackenridge's article about his experiences in the August 8, 1811 *Missouri Gazette*.

Mary recorded the news in her journal as well as, "We have had a meteor shower. Some folks think it is from the comet. Abigail says both meteors and comets are natural feenomna, no matter what Tecumseh is telling the Indians."

The next news was that "A gaunt and skin-dressed Andrew Henry appeared at the Mandan villages sometime in September and presented Lisa with a number of packs of beaver." Further word had it that the partners would be stopping off to rebuild the trading post at Cedar Island. This was of prime importance in keeping the good will of the Sioux. A promise made, a promise kept would go a long ways in the next few years to maintaining the balance of power on the Missouri.

Andrew Henry was interviewed for the *Louisiana Gazette* edition of October 26, 1811.

"Well, yes," Henry, tongue-in-cheek, told the reporter who wanted to know about his 'harrowing struggle for survival in the mountains.'

"As luck would have it, I did live on roots and wild meat, and at the last, dressed in animal skins." No one told the reporter he was talking about tasty vegetables, buffalo steak and expertly worked buckskins, all served up by doting hands in the Crow fashion, with Wm. Clark coveting the latter suit with its beaded and porcupine decorations for his Indian museum.

There was nothing tongue-in-cheek, however, about Henry's report on the potential of the vast country, its incalculable resources and the prospect of future success. He was most positive about that, particularly in the discussions after the meeting of the Masonic Lodge in which William Clark and Pierre Chouteau added their assessments.

The *Missouri Gazette* echoed his words in reporting that "the company had been placed on a better footing than it was generally supposed it could be; and that there exists the most flattering prospect for future success."

Early in December, Mary, visiting Abigail on the weekend, was demurely pleased to find the Brewsters entertaining a large company who hung on the tales of the guest of honor, Major Andrew Henry.

The entry in her journal read, "The Major said he didn't have an odyssey. Mr. Brewer said it was more a saga. He never gets tired of talking to the Major. It's very lightening to listen to them. They talked for a long time about the 'plications of the Battle of Tippecanoe.

"When I got the chance, I asked if I could see Cheeky. The Major looked sad, said 'the confounded Indians stole him.' You can tell he thought a lot of Cheeky, really misses him.

"Last night the Major said he was leaving St. Louis in a day or two. With Dr. Fenwick gone, he didn't know what he'd find at the mines. They both agreed Dr. Fenwick was foolish to fight a duel when it was his brother who had been insulted. Abigail's father said he'd certainly like to visit the mines.

"The Major said 'Pack up and come along. Belt wants to get home in time for Christmas so we thought we'd leave about the 8th or 9th.'

"I told Abigail I wished I could be home for Christmas. She

said 'Why not?' and took her mother aside. Her mother told her father this would be 'an opportune time' for Abigail to accept the 'standing invitation to visit the Flemings.' After her father talked to the Major, he said to me, 'I've missed my violin. Time I picked it up, don't you think?'

"So the three of us are leaving St. Louis tomorrow with the Major and Mr. Jackson. We are to travel just as they did on their spedition, camping out at night. Abigail told the Major we would profit by the experience. The Major just laughed, said, 'We won't be trapping for beaver this trip.'"

Mrs. Brewster had a word with the Major. Mr. Brewster took a keen interest in all manner of things, from the steamboat Nicholas Roosevelt was building in Pittsburgh for the river trade with New Orleans to the work of Audubon and Bradbury. "Don't let my husband get caught up in any of his 'enthusiasms' and forget to come home. He's already deep into cataloging the flora and fauna of Missouri. If your lead mines get him started on geology, too, beware. Mr. Brewster will have you making scientific measurements and keeping records and making reports before you know it."

"If it would contribute to mining efficiency, I'd be glad to participate in such an undertaking," said the Major who had found Mr. Brewster not only an able businessmen but of broad-gauged intelligence with an organized and energetic procedure for satisfying his curiosity about his 'enthusiasms.'

"The girls should be back in school right after the New Year. Show him the lead mines but don't let him get sidetracked and forget to bring them back then."

"I have to come back to St. Louis for the Company January meeting," said Andrew Henry. "If Mr. Brewster and the girls don't get bored and return before then, I'll bring them back with me."

The weather was mild for December. The girls were good riders, did not tire easily, delighted in every change of view, were particularly taken with Mr. Jackson. He was a whiz at setting up camp. He could cook. And his sketching delighted them, particularly the one of the hog drover, another of the Shawnee and the surprising gift he delivered to the Major.

"Them there hogs shore been acting funny," the drover told them as he exchanged news with the Major. "Squealing and chewing on each other's tails. Had a time bedding them down last night."

Shortly after sunset, just as they were settling down in their campsite for their evening meal, Mr. Jackson surprised the Shawnee reconnoitering their location, and escorted him to where the Major sat on a fallen log.

"Says he brung you somethin' from Luthecaw," said Mr. Jackson. "He's in a hurry to get back to his village. Seems worried about somethin' or other."

Thaniel Brewster and the girls watched attentively as the Shawnee was welcomed to their campsite and accepted the Major's invitation to share their evening meal. When it was over, the girls helped Mr. Jackson with the cleaning up, while the Major and the Shawnee, with a certain solemnity, smoked their pipes. When everything was in order for the night, Mr. Jackson indicated that the girls were to sit quietly next to Mr. Brewster while he went to the opposite side of the campfire, squatted beside the Shawnee.

After a long silence, the Shawnee said, "The night sky shines in a strange way."

"A peculiar brilliance, but easily explainable," said Mr. Brewster dismissively. "Just the twilight of the comet. It will soon pass off into the regions of space and become invisible."

"The earth is fearful," said the Shawnee.

"Comets have always been considered harbingers of disaster," said Mr. Brewster sententiously. "Shrewd men make use of the superstition. Take William the Conqueror. The comet in 1066 worried the Normans and Saxons alike. He made his Normans believe it was a sign favoring them. Much like I hear your Tecumseh has been doing with this one. Didn't do him much good at Tippecanoe."

"Tecumseh was not there," said the Shawnee.

"That's right," said Andrew Henry soothingly. "As for signs, seems to me most people look back, make much of something like lightning without thunder or the red sun we've been having."

"The year 1811 hasn't been all that great. More trouble at sea with the British. Bad flooding on the Ohio and Mississippi. Terrible tempest on the East coast. No sign of the comet then," said Mr. Brewster. "Don't need a prophet to explain our troubles. Years of embargo and nonintercourse, of idle ships, goods piling up on wharves. President Madison calling Congress into special session, recommending that the country prepare for hostilities. But the educated man realizes that is only coincidence. Comets are a natural phenomena."

The Shawnee turned his back on Mr. Brewster. How come such an intelligent man could be so obtuse, Mary wondered. Abigail put a hand on Mr. Brewster's knee as he made as if to rise. "Shush now, Papa."

"He is here to see the Major," Mary whispered. "He's come with some kind of message from the mountains."

The message, whatever it might have been, was delivered in tones too low for them to hear, and briefly. At its conclusion, the Shawnee rose lithely and going to his horse, removed some sort of bag, which he placed at the Major's feet.

The bag wiggled. Slowly, the Major reached down and widened the opening. A bright-eyed, dark-brown head poked out, looked around.

"A puppy," breathed Mary as feet, legs and body followed the head. The Major, speechless, ran his hands over the puppy, who sniffed those hands carefully, then wriggling happily, snuggled close.

"I'll be damned," said Mr. Jackson. "Luthecaw sent you another Cheeky. Even wrapped him up in a hunk of your old hunting shirt. That's so he'd know his master when he reached him."

The Major can't say anything. He's got a lump in his throat, decided Mary. He's really a lonely man. He doesn't have anyone to hug him when he's down in the dumps. She turned her gaze away.

Mr. Jackson, too, turned way, busying himself at the pack saddles, bringing forth several items which he presented to the Shawnee. The latter nodded gravely, accepting them.

The Major looked across the campfire. "Come meet Luthecaw, girls."

They hurried to his side, cuddling the puppy in turns, noting its features, giggling at the puppy ways. Hesitantly, Mary said, "Isn't that a funny name for a girl puppy?"

The Major looked surprised. So did Mr. Jackson. They both looked more closely at the puppy, then began laughing. Still chuckling, the Major said, "In that case, Mary, perhaps you should choose a name. What would be fitting?"

"Luthecaw found her for you," she said slowly. "Who is Luthecaw?

Mary found herself unaccountably relieved to learn that Luthecaw was a man, not a woman. She laughed dutifully with the others when Mr. Jackson, with droll anecdotes, including the bear mashing, provided further dimensions to Luthecaw.

"If you think Mr.Luthecaw found her somewhere on the Upper Missouri," said Mary patting the puppy curled up in her lap, "I think it's all right to name her for him. Me, I'd name her Luthecaw's Missouri and call her Missy."

"Missy it is," said the Major.

"Missy?" said the Shawnee. "Luthecaw said 'another Cheeky.'"

"Cheeky's twin sister," said the Major. "When you see Luthecaw, tell him I couldn't have made a better choice myself."

Everyone was tired, even Missy, and they soon bedded down for the night, Missy snuggling up close to her master.

The next morning the Shawnee prepared to leave them, indicating he was anxious to get to his village before some sort of impending deadline. Looking down at them from his horse, his intent black eyes moved from face to face, settling intently, deliberately upon Mr. Brewster.

"The land is afraid," he said sonorously. "When a man is afraid, he shivers. So it is with the land when the tortoise awakes."

"That," said Belt, looking after the departing Shawnee, "sounded like a warning. What's he telling us — to fort up against Indian troubles?"

"Maybe the tortoise is about to take a step," said Andrew Henry. "There's an Indian belief, you know, that the world is carried on the back of a tortoise. Whenever he takes a step, it shakes up the world a bit."

"Oh, my," said Mary, "I'd hate to think my world was rolling around on the back of a tortoise."

"The Indian world," said the Major, "would be flat. It might slip and slide a bit. So far, though, the tortoise has never been able to shake himself free of his burden."

"I always liked them stories about that Greek what's-her-name — Gaea," said Belt Jackson. He leaned reassuringly toward Mary. "Mother Nature."

Thaniel Brewster stared at the frontiersman. It was a bit unusual to find one acquainted with classical Greek mythology. He cleared his throat. "Men have been trying to explain the natural phenomena of the world for ages. We are closer to it than at any time in history because of men who are disciplined to use the scientific method. Soon, with the progress being made, the world will hold no secrets for men of science."

"We better be giving some attention to our own progress," said Andrew Henry dryly, "or we'll not get Mary and Abigail to the Flemings this night."

They gave their attention to their own world, which was far from being flat. They hoped to make this the last day of their travel. Therefore, they paused only to rest the horses and eat a cold supper, before riding on, under a sky clear and serene, in air so still that the squeak of saddle leather, the breaking of a branch under a horse's hoof rang out clearly.

They arrived late at the Flemings, where they received a hearty welcome. Everyone was still up.

"The animals have been having fits," said Patrick, exasperated, helping the men unsaddle and settle the horses for the night while Madame Fleming took the girls into the house, a welcoming arm about each one. "Geese honking. Dogs barking. The cows kicking the shed and each other. Never seen the likes."

Shortly after Madame Fleming had seen all her guests bedded down, Missy roused the household, growling, yipping and dashing about, ending up in bed with Mary and Abigail. As someone lit a lamp in the main room, Mary gathered the quivering bundle of fur into her arms, murmuring, "There, there. It's all right."

It wasn't. At 2:30 by Mr. Brewster's watch that morning of December 11, 1811, they began hearing a strange sound, as if a troop of cavalry were charging toward the house. The earth shivered. The shiver became an unsettling shake. The house creaked and groaned, the sounds lost in the hollow and vibrating groans arising from the earth itself, as it rose and fell. Trees bent down as if before a tremendous wind.

"Earthquake!" shouted Mr. Brewster, who had previous experience with earthquakes in the Kentucky and Illinois country. "Out of the house. Everybody!"

In their nightclothes, Abigail and Mary, holding tight to Missy, made their way over a floor that danced beneath their feet to the doorway. They were snatched up by the Major and Dr. Nick, carried out into the yard.

"It's getting dark," said Abigail. "The air smells funny."

"Dust," said her father wrapping a blanket about her, Mary and Missy.

"Stinks like the devil," snorted Patrick, putting his arm around his wife.

"Sulphur gases," said Mr. Brewster.

Madame Fleming crossed herself.

With an unseemly degree of elation, Mr. Brewster went on, "This is a rare opportunity to observe a natural phenomena. Don't be surprised if there are follow-up disturbances. We must keep track of them. Abigail, don't be afraid. Just brace yourself and help me keep count of the tremors."

As daybreak arrived, Abigail braced herself against Mary and the two of them chanted, "Seven."

"Are you sure?" said Mr. Brewster. "I thought that was number six. This will never do. We must approach this scientifically. Ignore the little shivers. Count only the shakings that disturb your equilibrium."

"What's that?" said Mary.

"If it knocks you off your feet, it counts," said Andrew Henry. Mr. Brewster and his 'enthusiasm' was serving to rein in the fears of all. "One of you could count off the seconds the tremors last."

"Capital idea. Abigail counts the shocks. Mary counts the duration. Mr. Jackson here can draw up columns on that sketch pad he's carried out with him. The first column will be unbalancing shocks. The second column will be the duration. The third will be for disturbance and damage. Brace yourself, here comes another at — note the time Mr. Jackson — 6:30 a.m."

"That," said Belt Jackson, picking himself up off his hands and knees and shaking the dust off his sketch pad, "disturbed me."

"It also," Madame Fleming said indignantly, "threw two stones at me from the top of my kitchen chimney."

"Note that, Mr. Jackson. Damage to the chimney. Anyone else notice anything to report?"

"The earth went up and down several inches," said Andrew Henry. "The other shakes were more to and fro sideways."

"Cracks in the ground," said Belt Jackson.

"Fissures," said Mr. Brewster. "Only a few inches deep."

"Thank God," said Belt, who had been atop one of them.

"One good thing," said Pat. "That old snag that I've been trying to get rid of fell over. Just missed the barn."

"The spring gurgled," said Dr. Nick, "and sloshed water every which way."

"Excellent. Excellent. The four of you have managed to command the occurrences in a complete circle. Keep those same directions in mind for the next tremor," directed Mr. Brewster. "I must set up a measuring device. Let's see, I will need springs and pendulums and bells," said Mr. Brewster. "Or perhaps some sort of automatic scribing device that will jiggle up and down across a piece of paper."

Thus it was that Thaniel Brewster took up one of his 'enthusiasms,' putting together data on the seismic seizures that rocked the globe in 1811-1812, and the subsequent tremors of diminishing intensity that continued for seven years.

In the third week of December 1811, however, his daughter voiced the prevailing lack of enthusiasm. After doggedly counting the two mighty shocks of December 16 and 17 and forty-seven lesser ones, Abigail shook her fists at the heavens. "That's enough. Stop it! Stop it!"

". . . one hundred ten, one hundred eleven," Mary kept on counting.

"I think that's it, Mr. Jackson."

Abigail threw herself at her father, wrapped her arms tightly about his waist. "I'm scared, Papa," she began to sob. "I want my Mama."

"You've every right to be scared," he said, comforting her. "Thousands of folks must be feeling just like you do at this moment."

Mary looked up at the Major. "It isn't just us?"

The Major, who had just returned with Dr. Dick from a survey of the neighborhood, put an arm around her. "I'm afraid not." He didn't tell her what he and Dr. Nick had seen: land up where it had been down, trees tangled together like tossed kindling, fissures in the earth, fearful, shaken folks afraid to enter their cabins, afraid to stay outside. Unsettled Indians on the move, adding to the anxiety. "It'll be some time before we know just what happened."

"Is happening," said Mary as the earth shivered again. "That only lasted a couple seconds. Won't it ever stop?"

It didn't. In fact, it went from bad to worse. The Flemings were on the outer rim of the disturbance. The center was close to the frontier settlement of New Madrid, which gave its name to the fault zone and the series of quakes. Spreading out in a one hundred mile radius, the shakings rocked the Mississippi Valley and the contiguous states of Missouri, Tennessee, Arkansas, Kentucky and Illinois.

Dr. Nick, concerned about his mother, who was showing the physical symptoms of many buffeted victims, giddiness, nausea, vomiting, prescribed a change of scene for her and the girls. Madame Fleming, Mary and Abigail were relieved to be transported to St. Louis for an indefinite stay with Mrs. Brewster, where, most days, the only reminder of the upheaval they had endured was the occasional rattling of the dishes in the china cupboard.

Mr. Brewster, recruiting Mr. Jackson to do illustrations, set out for the heart of the disaster. Dr. Nick returned home to tend to his patients, give Patrick a hand in shoring up the house and buildings and keeping tabs on the unsettled livestock. Major Henry stayed on in St. Louis to be on hand for the scheduled meeting with his partners.

One of the greatest of the series of shocks coincided with the final meeting of the St. Louis Missouri Fur Company. Damage in St. Louis was minimal, but Menard's house in Kaskaskia, Morrison's in Cahokia were badly shaken and cracked. As those homes were being rocked violently, the shaky future of the Company was discussed in St. Louis. It was decided to let the St. Louis Missouri Fur Company expire on March 7, 1812.

On January 24, 1812, the company was reorganized into the Missouri Fur Company. Signing the new body of articles creating the president and directors were William Clark, who remained as president; Sylvestre Labbadie, Pierre Chouteau, A.P. Chouteau, Jr., Andrew Henry, Reuben Lewis, Manuel Lisa and Pierre Menard. William Morrison was no longer interested in being a partner, Benjamin Wilkinson had died on board ship while sailing from New Orleans to Baltimore in 1809 and his substitute Walter Wilkinson had other pressing business, while Dennis Fitzhugh had never been active.

Pierre Chouteau and Manuel Lisa were commissioned to sell the assets of the original company. Pierre Menard was to assist Lisa and Chouteau in apportioning the proceeds among the several members.

After the mighty jolt February 7, 1812, Mary wrote in her journal, "Whatever is causing it — Gaea, the tortoise, or that strange electricity of Mr. Brewster's — the shakings haven't stopped."

The New Madrid Earthquake shook up a million square miles of North America. It jolted, flooded, devastated the village of New Madrid, created new lakes, and not only changed the course of the Mississippi but had it running backwards for a short time.

The seismic waves radiated outward to rattle windows in Quebec, move the floor under President Madison's feet in the White House, drive folks out into the open all along the frontier, and terrify the Indians on the Upper Missouri, where British traders told them the Americans were to blame.

"Maman worries about Papa but he says it isn't too bad at home. Folks do say it's been bad on the river, though."

The major loss of life suffered from the initial onset of the earthquake was visited upon river traffic. Hundreds of keelboats, barges and flatboats were as usual on the river. The banks of the Mississippi were strewn for hundreds of miles with debris of flatboats and their cargoes. Listing of casualties was not possible. The boats had been isolated when wrecked. Most of the voyage from the Falls of the Ohio to New Orleans was through uninhabited country. Friends and families of those lost could only begin to guess the worst when after months of waiting the missing still had not returned.

"Abigail swears that right in the middle of the earthquake *a boat driven by steam* made it from Pittsburgh to New Orleans. It belongs to Mr. Nicholas Roosevelt, her papa says. He boarded it at Natchez. He writes that he plans to come home the same way. It's the safest way to travel the river these days. Haven't heard any more about the meteor showers or the comet. Mostly people talk about the 'shakes.' There are lots of pieces in the newspapers about the terrible experiences folks had." She wondered what Janey would have made of all of it. Janey was gone so she couldn't ask her. When she had visited the Clark's, Miss Judy said the Charbonneaus had gone back to the mountains with Manuel Lisa. When Mary and Madame Fleming called on Miss Polly, they found her still wearing mourning for little Remon. He had been ailing when Senor Lisa had gone up river so she didn't remember for sure who went with him, whether it was Charbonneau and both his wives, or just the sick one. Mary remembered that expedition, the one Lisa made to bring back the Major.

"I asked the Major about Charbonneau's wife. She died. I don't think it was Janey. I hope not. She was too good for him. I hope she got away from him.

By May she was writing "People are getting used to the shakes, I guess. Anyway, they are talking more about the Indian troubles and what the militia should do about it. Most of the men are in the militia, even Manuel Lisa.

"Major took us out to visit his friend Mr. Ashley and the Buckskin Rangers. The Major has a very nice little man who has been a soldier a long time who looks after him. He cooked us a very delicious meal. His name is propriate — Private Cook. Missy would like to chase his cats but the Major told her not to, so she doesn't. We got to see all the volunteer companies. The Major calls them 'rearguard forces' maybe because they had to stay behind to guard St. Louis while the regular militia is off driving war parties out of the territory."

In October of 1812, Mary wrote, "Maman is going home. Not exactly home. Papa and Mamán are to live in one of the Major's houses at Mine á Breton. Dr. Nick doesn't think it would be good for Mamán to go back to our old home. Would upset her all over again just when she's getting to be her old self.

"The Major and his Buckskin Rangers are to escort her to Mine á Breton. The Major says if the Missouri frontier is quiet enough to permit the troops to leave, he thinks I'll be safe enough in St. Louis — as long as I don't follow Abigail's lead and get in trouble with the nuns again. He thought it was funny when I told him what the Mother Superior said, that Abigail could cause a greater disturbance than an earthquake."

Several months later, Mary summed up the year. "All the talk in 1812 was about the earthquake. Now it is 1813 and all the talk is about Indian troubles and what the militia should do about it. M'sieu Vallé was right about Tecumseh. He certainly got the Indians all stirred up. I am to join Mamán and Papa. Dr. Nick thinks we'll all be safer there. British schemers are giving out presents to every Indian who will promise to fight for them against St. Louis. The Indians have been raiding uncomfortably close to St. Louis. The Major is a very busy man, what with his rangers, the fur company and his mines."

It *was* a busy year for Andrew Henry. He went with Manuel Lisa up river to establish headquarters at a new Fort Lisa, near Council Bluffs. He was able to make the July meeting of Missouri Fur Company when it was decided to sell sufficient goods to cover the debts of the company, meet and dissolve the company in September. As Mary, living with her parents not far from the Austin showplace, Durham House, put it in August, 1813, "The Major comes and goes. He danced with me at Emily Austin's wedding. So did Steven Austin and Alexander Craighead and the bridegroom, James Bryan.

"Alex says he can remember when the Major left Nashville to come to Missouri. He was just a little boy then. His papa showed him on a map where Andrew Henry was going. Soon as he was big enough he followed that same map to come to Ste. Genevieve.

"Alex says he hopes we move back to Ste. Genevieve. He told me I was 'a pretty little miss.' Mamán let him know, nicely, when he inquired, that I was not yet allowed gentlemen callers. The Major said he'd just have a word with young Mr. Alexander Craighead. I told him to mind his own business. He said, since that meant he had to be leaving again, he'd best have the last dance with me. He did and I thought he might kiss me goodbye but he just gave me a squeeze and told me to be a good girl and mind my Maman."

The Brewsters were houseguests at the time and Abigail, at fifteen, was allowed gentlemen callers. "Maman says I am too young. Mrs. Brewster said to let me receive with Abigail. There was safety in numbers. Abigail smiles on all of them but likes Alexander Craighead best. He brings us chocolates, calls me the Major's petite cheri. When Abigail heard that she asked me a lot of questions but I didn't tell her anything.

"Abigail said if the Major was going to chase around all over the country for little or no pay, he better find a well-to-do widow to help him out financially. She thinks Francis Vallé would like to see the Major married to his sister Julie Fenwick.

"Dr. Nick, when I asked him, said he thought the Major's finances must be all right, the way he was buying up land. Once the war is over, land will be worth lots."

The Company meeting scheduled for September had to be postponed. The Major couldn't have made it anyway.

The business that called the Major away again was another phase of the war. The Buckskin Rangers were part of General Benjamin Howard's expedition. Howard, who was also Governor of the Territory, was the ranking army officer in Missouri. He organized a force of 1400 men who joined Illinois troops for a direct assault on Blackhawk and the upper Mississippi tribes. They sought out and destroyed enemy bases, burning several Indian towns, scattering their inhabitants, captured grain stores, skirmished with the enemy.

"It's hard to know zactly where the Major is," Mary noted about the time of the Company December meeting when the books were examined, a surplus noted and a dividend declared. The Major and his rangers were busy elsewhere on the frontier then and at the time the Missouri Fur Company was dissolved at a long-postponed meeting for that purpose on January 17, 1814.

In the spring of 1814 Andrew Henry's friend William Ashley was made a lieutenant colonel in command of the newly organized Washington County regiment. There were two battalion of about six hundred men with twenty officers. Major Andrew Henry commanded the First Battalion of the Sixth Regiment.

"They march through the Missouri frontier. Dr. Nick is with them," wrote Mary. "He says they are going where the Indians have been the boldest. They will make sure that part of Missouri will never suffer from Indian troubles again."

Both the Lt. Colonel and the Major learned a lot from those experiences, leading mounted troops some seven hundred fifty miles along the northeastern, northern and western borders of the territory and back east along the Missouri in the fall of 1814. Over bivouac fires, the Major reminisced about his experiences in the Rocky Mountains. Ashley, an ambitious man, listened closely, encouraging the Major to expand on the innovations he felt were needed to organize a successful fur brigade.

Based on his experiences, Henry had some practical ideas about the recruitment, training and recompense for a select group of men who would be a match for those Rocky Mountains.

Ashley, who had no first-hand experience as yet with the fur trade, and therefore, an open mind, found his ideas intriguing. There were other, more immediate priorities, for both men, however, and beaver was not one of them.

"Maman prays for them daily. At least it's taken Maman's mind off the shakings. We don't have that many nowadays but when we do she's got like the rest of us, just pauses to see if it's going to get worse, then takes up wherever she left off, spinning, making butter, or whatever."

For the first six months of 1815, until negotiations began with representations of each tribe at Portage des Sioux, the northern Mississippi frontier suffered the boldest assaults of the entire war.

Major Andrew Henry continued ready throughout those months to serve without pay should conditions to the north require it, but the Washington County regiment did not have to take to the field in actual combat.

Peace came in 1815.

Chapter 19

"Abigail has just turned my life topsy-turvy. I was enjoying helping Dr. Nick with the medicines again. The Brewsters came by, just for a visit, I thought. When I was telling Abigail how much I wished I could learn more about medicine, she said why not? When I said I was too old for any school around here, it would have to be somewhere back east and only boys get to go for they must learn things so they can make a living, she got real indignant. Turns out she is to go to this special school in Connecticut, where girls get real learning, Latin and such. She insists I go, too.

"She said she couldn't go back east to school and leave me here, meekly waiting for some man, probably one who was too old for me anyway, to get around to marrying me. We'd both go to school and hang the expense.

"There has been a family conference. Actually, a lot of people got involved. M'sieu Vallé. Mr. Jackson. The Major. And, of course the Brewsters. Mr. Brewster says he can't go right now, leave his earthquake compendium: 1,874 measurable tremors so far; 20,000 killed in Venezuela; California Missions destroyed. Anyway, it's Mrs. Brewster's mother who is dying and wants Mrs. Brewster to come home. Mr. Brewster said Mrs. Brewster was perfectly capable of seeing to her mother and ensuring a 'fair division of the estate.' The Major said Mr. Jackson should go back east and show his paintings which upset Mr. Brewster who wanted Mr. Jackson to accompany him down into Arkansas. M'sieu Vallé soothed everyone by saying he'd escort the ladies and the paintings back east, since he had some business to attend to. He assured Mamán he'd make sure the school Abigail has picked out isn't too 'avant garde', whatever that is.

"We are to ride the steamboat to Pittsburg, then go to Philadelphia and take a boat ride to Connecticut. The Major showed me the route on a map he has. He also told me, and I haven't told Abigail, that if I got too homesick, let him know, and he'd come after me. We agreed it would be about right for both of us if he came in time to celebrate my seventeenth birthday."

She celebrated her fifteenth birthday a long way from home, happily. That day in May 1816 was about the warmest day of that whole year for snow fell in New England in June, July and August. Natives assured her it was a freak summer. When half an inch of ice spread over Vermont and New Hampshire, the natives conceded that 1816 was the year of no summer.

The next year was nicer, weatherwise, but Mary was getting homesick. She wrote the Major that she hoped he would still be coming for her seventeenth birthday.

He did. Shortly thereafter, they were married with minimum of fuss. Abigail was her bridesmaid. Mr. Brewster, escorted home at long last by the Major, gave her away. Mrs. Brewster, who cried softly during the ceremony, and again at leavetaking said, "Your Mother should have been here. Whatever will she think?"

"That the Major is a man of his word. He promised to marry me when I was three years old," said Mary, vivacious in her going-away gown of apple green silk. Ostrich plumes nodded on the crown of her straw bonnet. She twirled a cream parasol edged with lace.

The Major had said wedding was a private commitment, not a public entertainment. Marriage was concerned with two people living in harmony and honest fellowship. When they differed, and even when they didn't, he would explain himself so she would understand his feelings. Then she could put forward her own case and they could reach some sort of compromise.

She loved him then in a new way. Not with desire which, despite her innocence, she already experienced as an unknown hunger, but with a knife turned against herself. She would always suffer his suffering, and suffer for him. She wanted him to have the world and at the same time, to protect him from it. She knew without being told, he would protect her from the world, but it would be much harder for her to do the same for him.

She took to love-making as to a natural element. It was an ultimate compliment, a supreme intimacy, which satisfied something deep and earthy in her. Once her initial shyness was over she excelled her husband at the love-feast.

People noticed her, and the Major noticed the difference. Her voice softened and slowed. Her thin body rounded. There was a seductiveness in the way she walked or sat, a languor in the way she smiled. She had a voluptuous air, that was expressed in acceptable terms as "What a lucky man Andrew Henry is!"

The journey back to Missouri was leisurely. Andrew Henry had come east with various commissions to discharge for merchants of his acquaintance, which would more than pay his expenses. In the boom times following the war, not only had these merchants prospered, but so had Andrew Henry.

One of their first stops was in Philadelphia where the Guy Bryan's were most hospitable.

Welcoming them into the comfortably appointed home at 223 Arch Street, Guy said jovially, "Glad to see you're not ten feet tall as William has led us to believe. Mother was all set to order in a special bed to accommodate you, Major."

"Young Bryan, what have you been telling these good people?"

The upstanding young man in the well-tailored business suit who was grinning with unconcealed delight at seeing the Major again, said, "Don't worry. I didn't tell all your secrets."

"Do the Crows really have women warriors?" asked Timothy, who still hadn't had his trip west, even though, as he groused from time-to-time, he was twenty-one and certainly mature enough by now. "Did you ever find out what became of your dog Cheeky?"

Deftly, Martha Matlack Bryan, intervened, insisting the Henry's have time to get settled in the best guestroom, have a chance to freshen up, change out of their travelling clothes if they wished. "Then it will be time for tea and lots of interesting conversation."

Mary enjoyed woman talk with Martha while the men talked of all sorts of things, including the business William P. and Timothy B. had been handling since Guy's retirement. Andrew Henry told them about the new town of Caledonia he and his partner, Alexander Craighead, were platting. William said to put him down for a couple lots on Henry street. Timothy said he'd take one on the town square. Guy wanted to know what they'd do with them. "Talk about them," said William lightly. "There's lots of folks who would be intrigued at the thought of owning a part of ol' Scotland."

Martha and Mary had discovered they had mutual acquaintances in the Austin ladies. Mrs. Austin found it difficult to write, Martha said, but she had let them know that Emily's second child, a boy, was flourishing, and doing much to make up for the loss of the firstborn grandson, premature, from measles.

"Poor lady, she was troubled with rheumatism in her right arm last time I saw her. Do you suppose it's gotten worse?"

At that moment, the maid entered with more hot water for the tea just as Timothy stood up abruptly, bumping into the kettle, splashing boiling water down his left coat sleeve.

Mary was at his side in an instant. "His coat," she said to her husband, "yank it off. Quick." She turned toward the tea table. "I need that cold water." Snatching up a vase from an end table, she filled it, and, as Andrew divested Timothy of his jacket, plunged his left arm, shirt and all, into the water. "Hold your arm in there," she directed, pushing him back down in his chair, setting the vase on his knee. "Did you get splashed anywhere else?" When he shook his head, she turned to Martha. "Do you have any ice?"

Martha nodded, went to the kitchen after it herself, taking the wailing maid and the offending kettle with her. When she returned,

Guy and William were just getting to their feet, still not sure what the emergency was. "This," said Mary, adding ice to the vase, "should help ease the pain. Maybe prevent some nasty blisters."

It did, to Martha's surprise. "Mary's brother is a doctor," said Andrew Henry. "She's been his right hand for years."

"Did all right with Timothy's left hand," said Martha, examining the bright red arm. She had seen some nasty burns from hot water in her time. "It's going to be tender for a few days but..."

"It could have been much worse," said Timothy. "My word, I never knew anybody could move so fast. Is that the latest treatment for burns?"

"Actually," said Mary, suddenly shy with all eyes on her, "it's Mamán's. Dr. Nick says it the best way he's ever seen. But you have to move fast. Not let the cloth cling to the skin. I didn't mean to sound so bossy..."

"Andrew Henry," said Guy Bryan, putting his arm around Mary's shoulders, leading her to sit beside him on the damask covered love seat, directing William to bring her a cup of tea, "your young lady wife is ten feet tall!"

The Bryan's took to the young woman, not your usual teenage bride, to be fobbed off with frothy entertainment and frivolous shopping. There was shopping, but it was for medicines and an anatomy book. As for entertainment, the Bryans planned more than the Henry's had time for. They did attend the theater, but Mary opted for Othello and not the light farce William suggested tentatively; a concert or two; and they met some interesting folks who took their cues from the Bryans and treated Mrs. Andrew Henry as an adult, albeit a most attractive one.

Nothing would do but they accompany William to Washington City where he had some business to attend to with the War Department. Mary thought it was well planned, but very incomplete, and the street signs looked better than the muddy streets. She said as much to John Scott, Missouri's territorial delegate to Congress, who took them sightseeing while William attended to his business. They exchanged news with him about home folks, hearing for the first time that Moses Austin was talking of selling out in Missouri, setting up a colony in Texas. Young Bryan, as the Major still called him, now an able businessman, arranged for them to visit Baltimore, take passage to New Orleans. There Mary found Bequette and Fleming cousins, alerted to expect their arrival by Dr. Nick, a recent visitor. After several hospitable days, highlighted by sightseeing and shopping, the Henry's then travelled upriver to St. Louis where other relatives of Mary's and friends of Andrew Henry made much of them.

They dined with the A.P. and Sophie Labbadie Chouteau, heard from A.P. some of the details of his disastrous venture the year before to Sante Fe. Sophie, who was also his cousin, shuddered. "Those awful Spanish kept him and poor Jules de Mun in a nasty jail cell for forty-eight day!"

"In chains," said A.P. dryly. "While they confiscated over thirty-thousand dollars worth of trade goods."

"They came home in rags. Revolting, those Spanish. And now the people are, n'est-ce pa?"

The Major and A.P. agreed that if Mexico followed the example of Chile and did succeed in throwing off the Spanish yoke, Sante Fe would open up to trade. A.P. said he'd had enough of Sante Fe, asked after the Major's trading post, which he thought was in a good location. He might be passing through there one of these days for he was thinking seriously of setting up his own trading post with the Osage in the Arkansas Territory.

They were guests of William and Mary Ashley who had recently sold out their holdings in Cape Girardeau and settled in bustling St. Louis. They took the Henrys to the theater, and the performance, Mary thought, was the equal of those she'd enjoyed in Philadelphia. Mary liked the other Mary instantly and found the fox hunt William led them on, in the English fashion, whooping good fun, particularly since the fox got away. Ashley looked a real squire, on his fine white horse. Along with his new mansion, he was working on his image, getting into politics, angling for a place in the social life to be found in the parlors of the first families.

Both Marys were luncheon guests of Miss Judy, who wasn't looking well but was as cheerful as ever.

Mr. and Mrs. Andrew Henry were invited to attend the August wedding of Manuel Lisa and Mary Hempstead Keeney, widowed daughter of the prominent St. Louis attorney, Stephen Hempstead. The Henrys, who truly had another commitment, sent their regrets. It was a fine wedding, they were told. The Reverend Salmon Giddings, the Presbyterian minister, presided over the ceremony, witnessed by the bride's brother, Charles Hempstead, a bright young lawyer; by William Clark and Pierre Chouteau, both former partners of Lisa, and by one of his new partners in Cabanne and Company, Bernard Pratte.

Mary's cousins, belatedly, told her that Manuel had become a widower earlier in the year. They didn't know much about the late Polly Charles Chew Lisa, who had become something of a recluse during the war years when Manuel was gone so much of the time upriver. Typically, they did know what the gossips had to say about Manuel. He had married an Omaha princess, said to be young and lovely, called Metain; brought the daughter of that union, Rosalie, home for Miss Polly to raise, then took off upriver again. Shortly thereafter, during a cold spell in February, Miss Polly had died. Her two surviving children, eight-year-old Michael and five-year-old Mary, and Metain's four-year-old daughter had been taken into the households of friends. In July, Manuel came down river, bringing a ten-year old Spanish boy, ransomed from the Pawnees. After a very brief courtship, even by frontier standards, he had persuaded the attractive American widow to accept him and a ready-made family. What the new Mrs. Lisa would do when he brought his part Omaha son, Christopher, home, too, made for interesting speculation.

The Henrys did pay a condolence call on the Lisa's, when, less than a week after the wedding, little Mary Lisa died.

While the men talked, the new Mrs. Lisa drew Mary aside. She wanted to know the story behind the mirrored armoir. Briefly, Mary told the lady, thinking that her predecessor must have had recourse to that mirror often in the last years of her life.

"She willed it to me," said Mary Hempstead Keeney Lisa. "To be precise, to 'the next Donna Lisa, white, red or black.' Manuel, when I asked, just said it was 'a good-luck mirror.' I wasn't sure."

"Miss Polly would never wish bad luck on anyone," said Mary Henry."Particularly anyone who could make Senor Lisa happy. She was devoted to him." From what Mary could see, the Lisa's were very much in love, something of a revelation to her, who had never supposed that it could be so on the second time around for people past middle age.

"We'll be going up river before long," said Mary Lisa changing the subject. She didn't seem to think it unusual that she would be the first white woman to do so. At least, Mary Henry thought, this new wife wasn't going to give Manuel an opportunity to reconcile with his Indian princess. "We don't want to be apart if we can help it."

The Henrys didn't want to be apart either. When they got to the Flemings and the joyous welcome there, Andrew decided to make a quick trip to his trading post, see how Alex was progressing with laying out the new town of Caledonia.

The land boom in the central Missouri valley which had the Major and many of his contemporaries speculating in real estate was bringing hundreds of new people into the territory every day. In St. Louis competition for choice tracts had been intense. Auctions were well attended. Settlers could pay one-third down on a quarter-section, the remainder due in five years.

The Major, who already owned a house and several lots in Austin's new town of Potosi, a prospering farm on Wallen Creek in the Irondale area, besides his lead mines, was considering investing in lots for resale in Caledonia. If the influx of new people continued, land values would go up. The sooner the auction could be scheduled in Caledonia, the better.

He suggested, half-heartedly, that Mary wait until spring when the auction would be held to visit Caledonia. Perhaps, recalling the reaction of his first wife, he was a bit dubious about the accommodations at the trading post. When he had left, it had been the typical frontier log cabin, two rooms with a dog trot between. One room had served as the trading post, the other as living quarters. Before he took her there, he was sure Alexander would want some notice; as for himself, he'd like to make some improvements, move in better furnishings.

"It won't be the first time I've been to Bellevue Valley. Nor the first time I've slept in a one-room log cabin," Mary reminded him. "Before Dr. Bryan started his practice there, I used to ride those trails with Dr. Nick when he was called to treat folks there."

She rattled off the names, McCoy, Reed, Crow, McLaughlin, Ashbrook, McMurtrey, Goforth, Wood, Gregg. "Methodists. Mostly from Tennessee."

She took a deep breath and went on: Stevenson, Sloan, Boyd, McCormick, Baker, Alexander, Campbell, Blain, Blair, Pettegrue, Robinson, Akins, Frizzle. "Presbyterians. Mostly from North Carolina."

"It's pretty country but some of those trails are awful narrow. You sure have to watch out for tree limbs. Got knocked out of the saddle one day when I was gawping around. In places, the path is barely wide enough for a horse."

Families were scattered along those narrow trails. Some had obtained Spanish land grants, some had only tomahawk claims. Within a decade of arrival, these upright, godfearing, hardworking people had made a start at establishing a stable society, a hamlet where both the Methodists and Presbyterians already had meeting houses and cemeteries, with ministers doubling as schoolteachers.

All built close to springs, or, as Mary went on, "Cedar Creek, Reed Creek, Saline Creek, Lost Creek, McCoy Creek, Furnace Creek, Clear Creek, Jane's Creek, Brock's Creek, Big and Little Hazel Creek, Trace Creek, Cub Creek, Indian and Courtois Creeks." She paused for breath.

"You forgot Goose Creek," said her husband dryly.

"It was McCoy Creek when I was there," said Mary. "Who changed it?"

"Buford, when he bought the property. Named it after the place he came from in Virginia."

"The man with the beautiful horses," said Mary. "He's not Scotch-Irish."

Nor was he. William Buford, for whom Buford Mountain was named, was a lineal descendant of John of Gaunt's Beaufort get by his mistress Catherine; and through John, Duke of Lancaster, third son of King Edward III, a descendant of Rollo, the Viking, who was granted Normandy by the French king in 911. Through the generations, the name had been modified from Beaufort to Beauford, then in Virginia, to Buford. He had emigrated to Bellevue Valley in 1812, bought one of the original Spanish land grants, and as was typical of the Beaufort / Bufords, prospered.

From Buford, and Ananias MCoy, who was Scotch-Irish, Alexander Craighead had purchased seventeen acres apiece for his town. Harking back to his own heritage, he called it Caledonia: the ancient, honorable name of Scotland, symbolically appealing to the preponderance of middle-class Scotch-Irish settlers already there, a drawing card for those he hoped would come.

Mary and Andrew went there in the autumn season when the colors ran riot. Sumac and sassafras, red gum and maple, hickory and tulip tree, sugar maple and oak paraded the warmest colors of an artist's palette.

It was not quite noon when they rode into the clearing around the trading post to an enthusiastic welcome from Alexander Craighead, who had been looking forward to their arrival.

Alexander Craighead, Mary's one-time dancing partner and tentative suitor, was an energetic, personable young man of twenty-six from an upper class Scotch-Irish family. Well-educated, fluent in both verbal and written French and English, he had proved himself an able businessman at an early age. In 1810, when he was only eighteen, he was running his own store in Ste. Genevieve; a year later, he moved to Potosi, opened his second store. He had gone into partnership with Henry Dodge, made money in the lead mines, been involved in a lawsuit with the ubiquitous John Smith T over ownership of Mine á Shibboleth. During the War of 1812, he had campaigned with Andrew Henry, establishing a rapport that had led to their partnership at the Caledonia townsite.

Proudly, he showed off the living quarters, which he was turning over to them during their stay. Mrs. McCoy, he said, had 'redded' the place up especially for them. There was a bed in one corner, covered with a woven spread; a chest against the wall; dish cupboards against another; stools setting about; pots hanging by the chimney; a ladder in the chimney corner going up to the loft room; a white scrubbed table in the middle of the room set with pewter for three, venison stew waiting to be dished up, fresh cornbread.

While they ate, he waxed eloquent over his townsite plans. Caledonia already had a modest start. Besides the Craighead-Henry establishment, Fergus Sloan had set up a blacksmith shop, Joshua Morrison, a distillery. Nearby the Ananias McCoy and Robert Sloan families had located their homes. The Presbyterian and Methodist meeting houses were within easy walking distance. Spreading out the map of his proposed village, he pointed out the two lots the Major had selected at opposite ends of the projected Henry street, then took them tramping through the autumn brilliance so Mary could view the lots for herself.

From the Craighead-Henry trading post, next to the beaten trail that connected Potosi with Arkansas and Texas, the postal route between Potosi and Farmington, handy to travelers, traders and local customers, the land sloped down to the crossing of Goose Creek then upward to the proposed town square.

"The stream," Alex said, gesturing, "bisects the townsite from north to south. It was the boundary line between the two original Spanish land grants. Runs sort of northeast to join up with the Big River a few miles from here."

There was flatter land away from the creek. The Major thought the town would likely grow along the north-south streets. Alexander, stepping off both Henry lots, each ten rods square, to show Mary the generous proportions available for dwelling, garden patch, stables, chicken yard, indicated that within a thirty-eight acre rectangle, there were fifty- four lots, many of them already spoken for, if not actually sold.

Back in the living quarters at the trading post where Mary picked twigs out of her hair and burrs out of her skirt, Alexander was optimistic.

"In no time at all, I expect to see a population of over two hundred people," he said positively, bringing out for their review the announcement he had prepared for the Missouri Gazette of October 10, 1818:

"The sale of lots, in the town of Caledonia, Belleview Settlement, Washington County, Missouri Territory, will commence on the 15th of May next. The town is situated in the largest tract of fertile land in the county; it is surrounded by many valuable farms the products of which have already found their way to New Orleans; a still greater number of farms are now opening; men of wealth from almost every state in the Union are making purchases. Land which 12 months ago sold for $1.50 per acre is now selling for $5.00 per acre. The main road by Potosi to Cape Girardeau, the County of Lawrence, Arkansas, Ouachita, Red River and all the southwestern country passes through the town. Within the limits of Caledonia are three excellent springs, the largest of which affording water enough for a mill is in the center of the town and within the square laid off for Public uses. Signed Alexander Craighead."

They had a pleasant week in putative Caledonia. The first night, as they had expected, and had prepared for, folks gathered to give them a fairly muted charivari, then trooped inside to enjoy the refreshments and the Major's fiddling.

"Figgered it should be more a play-party than one of them rough shivarees, you folks not really being newly wed," confided

Mrs. McCoy, watching Ananias taking his turn at the whiskey barrel Alex had broached for the occasion. "You know most of the folks here, don't you, comin' like you did when a little gal with the doctor brother?"

Mary, making their well-wishers welcome, was reminded by more than one, rather flatteringly, of those earlier visits. In the days that followed, she talked shop with Dr. John Bryan, an old acquaintance from Ste. Genevieve, contemporary of Dr. Nick's, and fellow medical graduate of Kentucky's Transylvania University; exchanged receipts with Martha Harris Sloan, who confided that they were contemplating a move to the Irondale area, asked about the fertility of the Henry farm there; was treated to a ride on one of the Buford pacing mares by the gentlemanly Virginian himself.

Alex, promising to visit them in Potosi at Christamstime, if not before, saw them off reluctantly. In autumn splendor, the Henrys made their leisurely way the twelve miles to Potosi.

The Major, whose lead mining interests were closer to Potosi than to Caledonia, thought Mary might like living there. She had last seen it shortly after Moses Austin had donated forty acres, John Rice Jones, ten, to provide a county seat for newly created Washington County. St. George they called it, with its public square, twenty-two blocks and one-hundred-forty-seven lots. The name just didn't suit. Everyone knew there was nothing saintly about the old mine site. Across Breton Creek, the village of Mine á Breton clung to its own name and identity, so the county seat couldn't use that name. Folks, having heard their location often likened to the Spanish silver mining town, founded in 1545 in Bolivia, opted for that name. After only a few short months, St. George was re-named Potosi.

Mary, after an absence of three years, compared the thriving new town to those she had seen in her travels. If swampy old Washington City qualified to be capital of the country, this principal inland town of Missouri with its public square, imposing courthouse, handsome homes and flourishing businesses had the makings of a state capital. It was at the hub of roads connecting with Ste. Genevieve, Herculaneum, St. Louis, and Bellevue Valley. The mail route from New Orleans to St. Louis passed through Potosi.

With Moses Austin headquartered at Herculaneum, Joseph Smith T making plans for a shot tower and other developments at Selma, they feuded in the courts instead of the streets. Neither had much political clout any more. Which was just as well for the relative political stability of Washington County and its county seat. Durham Hall, within its reserve of ten acres, was there for Stephen Austin as he came and went, the busy civic leader, legislator, lawyer, miner, trader, as well as for any other Austins or their guests. The courthouse was now the dominant feature of the landscape, however. It was making a lively place of Potosi, folks coming and going, county government a positive, contributing factor in the economy of the region.

The young scientist, Henry Rowe Schoolcraft, gathering material for his book on the lead mines of Missouri, thought Potosi built in a better style than villages generally. As the shallow surface mines played out, the miners had moved on to easier diggings, so the rougher element that had preyed on the miners in the early days were gone, too. Those that remained were more orderly, mature. Many of them took up farming, and as their families grew, a stable, responsible citizenry, interested in establishing schools and churches, was putting down roots in Potosi.

Mary thought the best thing about Potosi was their French-Creole style house. Of fairly recent construction, it had the post-on-sill construction and broad gallery favored by French builders, the lap siding introduced by American builders. A hop-skip-and-a-jump away stood the stone oubuilding for the kitchen and, to Mary's delight, the beginnings of a medicinal herbal garden. Inside, there were four airy room divided by a central hall; upstairs, the same. And, a special plus, all the walls were plastered. Log cabins, such as the one in Caledonia constructed of white oak, were sturdy and long lasting, but the chinking did crumble, and a variety of insects took refuge in the logs. As Mrs. McCoy had said, brushing an unidentified flying object off the bed, the creepy-crawlies that found their way into pots and pans, onto tables and beds, could give a body the jim-jams.

Mary had been raised in a comfortable home, with help inside and out, warmth and cheerfulness prevailing. She set about recreating that same atmosphere in her own household, while family networking provided her with the help.

Cousin Angus, a distant cousin on the Fleming side, turned up shortly after their return from Caledonia. Supplied with bed and board, as was expected, he made himself surprisingly useful as stableman, groom, blacksmith, and carpenter, which had not been expected.

Cousin Penelope, colorless and fortyish, came to visit with gifts of chickens, ducks and geese, and stayed on, tending them, taking over the garden patch, milking the cow. She helped with the housekeeping chores but Mary did the cooking, oversaw the free negress who came in to do the washing and ironing. Private Cook, who had attached himself to the Major during the campaigns of the War of 1812, came and went, working for the Major in various capacities.

Mary enjoyed a bustling little social life. What a delightful thing it was when any of her cousins or the ladies of the neighborhood came visiting. To pour tea from her own silver teapot, and ask how much cream; to giggle over clothes and husbands; to give matronly advice on the affairs of the heart to fifteen-year olds.

She and Andy drank tea together, too, in great harmony, and spoke of everything and everyone, with due consideration, without lingering upon a single person or event. Her parents were only ten miles away so they could ride over and spend a day with them frequently, or vice versa. Sunday afternoons at the Henrys were a convivial time. Cousin Angus played his squeeze box. Cousin Penelope, in a pleasing soprano, sang the old, familiar songs. Folks, from far and wide, came to enjoy the talk, the music, a game of cards, a glass of wine and some of Mary's plum cake.

Nature allowed Mary twelve months in Eden and then let her know the price of apples. She felt very cheerful, apart from being nauseated by the smell of food, and unable to eat anything but oranges.

Once her innate robustness saw an end to the nausea, she ate to make up for the diet of oranges. Pregnancy, like love, suited her. Jane was born at home February 19, 1820. Her arrival pleased everyone immensely, particularly her father, hovering over her in the cradle Cousin Angus had made for her out of hickory. Missy, who was getting along in years, lay down beside it and became her guardian. Jane's father, rubbing Missy's ears, praised her and took in her stead as his constant companion, one of her latest litter, another large brown, good-natured Cheeky. Cousin Angus was all set to begin carving out a rocking horse for her until Penelope pointed out she was going to need a high chair first. Beaming down at Jane, Penelope said she was a pretty baby, a good baby. Unlike her Greek namesake, Penelope had no husband, nor prospects, for which to spin out the years. The poor relation who could hope for little more of life than to be on the fringes, she was a born nanny, happiest when she had a child to do for.

Neighbors came with little gifts and snippets of news. Stephen Austin had tidied up his business affairs in Missouri, left to take charge of the Austin mercantile interests in Arkansas and Louisiana. After thirty-one years in Missouri the Austins were in dire straits. The homeplace at Hazel Run of James and Emily Austin Bryan had been auctioned off at a sheriff's sale. Moses Austin had been arrested by the sheriff and imprisoned for his debts.

Grandpa and Grandma Fleming came every week from Flat River, always bringing something for Jane, already looking ahead to the time when she would be old enough to wean and could then go home with them for regular, lengthy visits. Patrick said it was a downright shame, the financial troubles Moses was having, and damned the Bank of St. Louis. Its failure was going to break more than the Austins.

Considering the circumstances, Mary was touched when Maria Austin and Emily Austin Bryan sent two daintily embroidered lawn baby dresses and their apologies for not calling in person via Moses Austin. That beleaguered man, nearing sixty and looking it, released from imprisonment, much of his property in the hands of creditors, his lead enterprises in shambles, should have been downhearted. Instead, he talked enthusiastically of the trip he was planning to make to San Antonio de Bexar to lay the groundwork for his new enterprise, the establishment of a colony in Texas. In the meantime, he proposed that the Henrys give some thought to the opportunities some three hundred American families would find available in his pueblo and port there. He would be returning before the year was out to get the show on the road.

Packing a hindquarter of fresh venison and a tiny pair of beaded moccasins Alexander Craighead came with news of Caledonia. Business was so slow as to be almost non-existent. Except for Martin Ruggles, who had come to the territory with Moses Austin, hung onto the money he'd made, most folks who had purchased lots weren't planning on doing much in the way of building until times got better. Alex had been postmaster for fourteen months, then replaced with Dr. Bryan. There wasn't much mail to see to, anyway. Oh, he had heard several times from his brother. John wanted Alex to join him in the Arkansas territory, set up a store there where times weren't too bad, yet. Alex still had hopes for Caledonia, was philosophical about its slow growth. He was comfortable there, had a roof over his head, good neighbors. When the larder ran low, there was always the chase, turkey to stalk, the fun of a deer hunt, a pig or two fattening on acorns to round up.

Dr. Nick brought a fine wool shawl to wrap Jane in, predicted the census was going to show a surprising number of people west of the Mississippi. The US marshalls doing the census taking were already saying they were finding people in little clearings that had been uninhabited wilderness only a year or so ago.

The calico kitten Private Cook brought her curled up companionably beside Missy. He didn't know much about babies, he said, but he'd vouch they didn't come prettier than little ol' Janie.

Francis Vallé came, bearing a fine gold chain on which was hung a tiny gold coin, and slipping it over Jane's head, dandling her on his knee, was cheerful and amusing. Mary, thanking him, frowned as her daughter tried to put the coin in her mouth.

"That's the first thing my nieces do, too," Francis grinned at her, deftly removing the coin, slipping the chain off Jane and handing it to her mother. "I wasn't sure but what it was a Vallé trait — making sure the coin was the real thing."

Wryly, he observed that if Marie and Joseph didn't cease presenting him with nieces, he might have to find a substitute for the gold coins. Pragmatic Marie had sent a length of soft flannel and best wishes for Jane. There was only Marie and Francis left of the family now. Both the Fenwicks were gone now. Julie had not lived long after Walter was killed in the foolish duel. He asked Mary if she missed Ste. Genevieve and privately, told the Major he could sure use his help in the various Valle enterprises, any time he was so inclined.

John Scott, not having given much thought to baby gifts, for he came to talk to the Major about a pending lawsuit, made a graceful recovery and a nice little speech about hope chests as he placed one of the scarce US silver dollars in Jane's chubby little fist. Penelope, tut-tutting retrieved it before it reached Jane's rosebud mouth. John Scott didn't notice for he was already in low-toned converse with the Major on the gallery, wanting to know what he thought of this Texas scheme of Moses Austin's.

Abigail sent a silver spoon and a potpourri of news. Sir Walter Scott had published a historical novel, *Ivanhoe*, which was selling well. Better yet, there were American writers who were making a place for themselves in the literary world. She devoted a paragraph to James Fenimore Cooper's, *The Spy*; two paragraphs to Washington Irving's *Rip Van Winkle* and *The Legend of Sleepy Hollow*. She had something to say about the Missouri Compromise, Simon Bolivar, the founding of the Unitarian Church, and Emma Willard's plans for a college-level school for young women.

She was teaching in a private school that had been doing well until the past year. The east was suffering an economic depression. Many of the parents were retrenching, some of the students were being withdrawn. Her father, who didn't trust banks, hadn't suffered any losses, but many of his friends had. She hoped the Henrys had been wise enough not to put their trust in any banks, either.

Young Bryan sent baby Jane an amethyst, the February birthstone, set in a tiny gold ring, which arrived shortly before her first birthday. His short letter, more nostalgic than newsy, wondered if the Major missed the mountains. There were times, particularly in the heat and humidity of a Philadelphia summer when he thought longingly of that clean, brisk fresh air, unbreathed by other lungs.

From his Osage trading post in Arkansas, A.P. Chouteau sent a fringed and beaded papoose carrier, and a note extolling the opportunities of Three Forks in Arkansas over those at the headwaters of the Missouri, that between the lines indicated he could use the Major's know-how in his enterprises.

Silver dollars, one apiece, arrived from the Clarks, Labbadies, Lisas and Menards. The Major, hefting them, said wryly that was more cash than he had handled all year. It was not until William Ashley stopped by, bringing a dainty baby bonnet from the ailing Mary Ashley, that Mary Henry realized that she had been blithely ignoring some nightmarish threats to her comfortable way of life.

The Panic of 1819, as it was called in the east, had depressed the economy there acutely. During the following year, the Mississippi Valley began to feel the pinch. Migration slowed, agricultural prices fell, banks got demanding about loans, tight with credit, and the price and demand for land plummetted.

The Major had a lot of property, but like everything else it was not worth much now. The venture in Caledonia with Alexander Craighead had not worked out — or rather, the depressed economy discouraged speculation in such promising developments. All that was left of the Major's investment in Caledonia was a street named for him and debts. In order to pay those off, he sold off much of the land he had acquired at a loss. He hung onto their home in Potosi and the farm on Wallen Creek, where Private Cook had taken up residence, management and the raising of hogs. The market for cats was down, too, locally, but occasionally he still made a good trade with folks headed for Arkansas.

There were ways out of it, none of them easy. They could follow up on Francis's or A.P.'s offers. Give up everything and join the Austins in the move to Texas. Or, as General Ashley proposed, she could give up the Major to the mountains again, for two-three years.

In the twenty years since he had arrived in Missouri, a *Vide Poche* or *Empty Pockets*, William Ashley had forged ahead, an ambitious man of ability and determination. He'd had some setbacks, financially and politically but the war years had provided him with a profitable gunpowder business and a reputation as a military man. Back in the good graces of the territorial government, he made valuable political contacts. In the post-war years, he went out of the mining and gunpowder business, sold his holdings in Cape Girardeau, and moved to St. Louis. There, he and his partner, Lionel Browne, were just getting a good start in the profitable real estate market when John Smith T needled Lionel into a lethal duel. Firing his pistol on the count of one, as was his notorious custom, Smith effectively dissolved the Ashley-Browne partnership.

William Ashley took his partner's body home to the mines for burial, wound up the affairs of the partnership, returned to St. Louis to make a go of it on his own. While he had left the mines behind him, he had kept up his contacts there, was respected as a man loyal to the friends of his youth. Partly because of his associations in the mines, he could still identify with the average Missourian, in attitude and expectations. These qualities, when he entered politics, brought him the necessary votes to be elected the first lieutenant governor of the newly created state of Missouri and brigadier general of its militia. As a founding member of the first Episcopal Church in St. Louis, he had moved up socially into the ranks of the prominent who were not Roman Catholic, had a fine mansion, a private carriage drawn by matched grays, and slaves to do the inside and outside work.

Elevated politically and socially, he had come a long way from the days when he was a lowly mechanic's apprentice on the Chesapeake. Financially, now the bottom had dropped out of the real estate market, he was on the verge of finding himself a *Vide Poche* once again.

General Ashley, watching Mary try the bonnet on the wriggling eleven-month old Jane who was more interested in taking her first toddling steps, made no bones about the situation. He was ten times as far in debt as his old partner, Andrew Henry. However, he did have sources of credit he could draw on. Did Andy realize the fur trade was coming to life again? Did Andy remember those talks they'd had over bivouac fires when they had been soldiering together, when he had reminisced about his experiences in the Rocky Mountains, outlined the innovations he felt were needed to organize a successful fur brigade? Would he like to lead such a fur brigade?

Mary, looking at her husband, saw how the lines fencing the mouth which arrive as a man grows older had deepened. Worry about unpaid debts had added a v-shaped furrow between his gray-blue eyes. He prided himself on having never knowingly cheated a man out of a penny. Nevertheless, within the limits of a scrupulously honest man, he possessed a healthy, acquisitive nature.

Would he remove himself from a comfortable home and loving wife to go jaunting off to discomfort, inconvenience, squalor, hardship and danger? to cope with the undisciplined, willful, irksome and irresponsible he would lead, encounter, bargain with, red men and white? Venture again into the midst of a people and land of unstable and treacherous nature? Chance the various plunderings of his experience, his well-being, life itself for problematical profits?

Mary, remembering how the Major had always regretted having to leave the mountains prematurely in 1811 because of lack of supplies, knew the answer. Of course he would like another go at the fur trade. If the General was willing to take the gamble with him, so much the better.

Based on his experiences in the Rocky Mountains a decade earlier, the Major had some practical ideas about the recruitment, training and recompense for a select group of men who would be a match for that rugged country.

First of all, he felt the caliber of the men was the most important factor. They should be wilderness-wise, able to exercise judgment, exert concentration, defeat weariness, and push a task to completion against odds.

Second, there should be clear-cut personnel policies, job descriptions, and an efficient chain of command. Andrew Henry had his own ideas about the reasonable rules necessary for the sensible division of labor, both on the march and in camp; and at the camping sites, the defensive arrangements for men and livestock. He wanted policies and procedures best suited to establish and maintain order on the long journey to the mountains, while in winter camp, and for dealing with aggressive Indians.

As militia leaders, Henry and Ashley had coped successfully with the American attitude of free-will. Henry had found it best to let his men know at all times not only what he wanted them to do but why he wanted it done. The men recruited to go to the mountains should be allowed to make their common-sense contributions to developing workable rules of conduct. Even the most independent-minded would accept a system of quasi-military regulations as long as that imposed order made allowance for the necessary individual flexibility.

Third, and just as important as the first two considerations, would be payment. Men should be well rewarded for their hard work. Henry favored a form of commission, rather than wages.

With those considerations in mind, Andrew Henry teamed up with William H. Ashley once again to found the Rocky Mountain Fur Company. Launching the venture took up most of the year of 1821, speeding up to a very hectic pace the first three months of 1822.

They successfully petitioned the government for a license to 'trade' with the Indians. Their help-wanted ad did not mention 'trapping' either.

The selection of '100 enterprising young men to ascend the River Missouri, there to be employed for one, two or three years,' found candidates besieging the Major near the lead mines, and General Ashley, in St. Louis.

The old-boy network sent the Major relatives of the men from the 1809 expedition, such as Davy Jackson and two of the Harris clan, George and Black; veteran Indian fighters from the Major's own rangers and militiamen in the War of 1812, such as James

Anderson; neighbors of the late John Colter; and old friends, such as the reliable and trustworthy John H. Weber, as able to captain a fur brigade as he had a Danish naval vessel.

The Major interviewed them leisurely, sitting on the gallery when the weather was good, or took to the cabin behind the house that he used for an office, when it rained and blustered.

Dr. Nicholas Fleming, who was to serve as the company surgeon, did the physical examinations. Noting that this expedition could be something like doctoring in the army, where you came across every medical crisis known to man, excepting maybe childbirth, he rejected more than he accepted. There was no need to start out with problems, he insisted.

As for problems at home, Mary assured her husband there was no need to worry. She was not the first wife left behind to do all the familiar homemaking chores, nor would she be the last. She had ruled out the tentative suggestion that she and Jane make their home with her parents while he was gone.

No matter how much she would miss his reassuring presence, she was a grown woman now, with her own well-run household. With the garden, the chickens, ducks and geese, they would eat well. There would be hogs to sell this fall, or failing that, hams to cure and barter with. There would be no need to run up any large bills at Daniel Phelp's store. Never mind their cash shortage. She also figured, but didn't say so, that she'd now have time to make use of her healing skills. She could earn a bit now and then, midwifing. Aloysius might need some help at the farm, particularly at hog killing time. He had in mind this old acquaintance of his, a peg-legged veteran of . . . .

"Aloysius?" said her husband, pulling her closer in the old familiar way, in their old familiar bed that would soon be her big old empty bed.

"Penelope says he's tired of being called Private Cook. I think he's sweet on her. There was something else I had in mind to ask you about," said Mary, her breath coming a little faster under his pleasuring hands. "The taxes." She paused to nibble his ear. "You are distracting me."

"Precisely what I had in mind," said her husband. "Let me show you how sweet I am on you."

Afterwards, neither of them gave any thought to taxes. Instead, they made plans for her to travel to St. Louis at the end of March to see him off.

Chapter 20

On Wednesday, April 3, 1822, the Major left St. Louis with one boat, one-hundred-fifty men, and not as many horses as he would have liked.

In three weeks of travel that brought them to Fort Osage, he pointed out familiar landmarks to his brother-in-law, noting the changes since he had last seen them.

"Last time I was there was in 1813," he said of Fort Bellefontaine, located on the right bank of the Missouri River, the first US fort established west of the Mississippi. "The Commander had some mighty fine whiskey for toasting the newlyweds." Colonel Daniel Bissell's teen-age daughter had just become the third wife of William Morrison, the fifty-year-old successful Kaskaskia merchant and one-time partner of Henry's. "Mostly, though, I associate it with Shehaka. He got fat there waiting for transport home."

"Whatever became of him?"

"After all the trouble the government took to get him home, he up and left after a couple of years. Came back to St. Louis and got knocked in the head one dark night. Nobody seems to know who did it. Or care."

Fort Bellefontaine had served as the staging area for the Yellowstone expedition of 1819. Six hundred men of the Sixth Infantry from Plattsburg, Philadelphia and Detroit were moved in, moved out on steamboats to set up military posts at Council Bluff, the Mandan Villages and mouth of the Yellowstone. Along with the soldiers, a scientific expedition, consisting of botanists, a zoologist and geologists, under command of Major S.H. Long, arrived to ascend the Missouri in the steamboat.

"Steamboat? Then why are we travelling this old-fashioned way?" said Dr. Nick, gesturing at the men poling the keelboat along.

"All five steamboats broke down. The troops, short on rations, had to go into winter quarters near Council Bluffs. Hundreds of them died of scurvy. They did get Fort Atkinson built," said the Major. "Instead of going on upriver, Long and his bunch took off horseback for the Spanish waters. Didn't much like what they found. Too dry."

At St. Charles, Dr. Nick lanced a boil. St. Charles had not changed a great deal. The Morrison store and its manager, James

Bryan, were long gone. Still home for the boatmen, and the bibulous send-off, it had grown some, boasting now a newspaper.

"These adventurous young men," the editor of the St. Charles Missourian wrote after watching them pass without stopping, "are the yeomanry of Missouri, embarked on an enterprise profitable not only to themselves, but a benefit to the nation."

Zeke Williams, retired trapper, who had wintered at Fort Raymond with Henry, assessed the passing expedition from the river bank near his home. Arthritic and cantankerous, remembering his own close calls, "Bug's Boys'll get the Major," he predicted dolefully, "this time."

Before they got past Charette, one of the boatman broke his arm. Splinted and complaining, he was set ashore in the little settlement where Daniel Boone had passed on in his ninety-second year. Somewhere in the same general region, John Colter had taken up a farm, married his Sally, sired a son, Hiram, died before he was forty of hepatitis.

At a cabin in a clearing near Cote sans Dessein, they paused to give Dr. Nick time to deliver a baby. On April 25 they passed Boonslick without stopping. On the opposite bank was the western outpost of Franklin which had come into existence in the past decade.

At Fort Osage, after three weeks of travel, Dr. Nick pulled two teeth, dispensed medicine for chills and fever, diarrhea and gastritis while the Major wrote to his wife.

"Dear Heart,

I am writing this at a handsome desk, seated in a chair with an embroidered, padded cushion, with a purring kitten on my lap. The kitten is the only thing in Fort Osage that has not changed in 13 years.

The soldiers have gone. To military posts farther up the Missouri. There are no Osages about, not even keening ghosts. Harmony Mission started up this year, some 70 miles from here, to Christianize and school the Little Osages in white ways. They have a few students already, half Osage mostly, such as the two daughters of the interpreter, Bill Williams.

The factory system is going. With it, probably, my estimable host, George C. Sibley. My hostess sends her regards — says she met you at the Brewsters. Had some very nice things to say about your way with a French folk tale.

In case you don't remember, she was Mary Smith Eaton before her marriage. Eldest daughter of the Honorable Rufus Eaton. Very cultured and civilized. Has a piano with drum and fife attachments and an uncertain future.

It is sad. The Sibleys have made themselves a nice place here at Fountain Cottage. Very fine gardens, a well-stocked poultry yard and an ice house. They are known far and wide for their courtesy and kindness. Officers and their wives come to spend time here when they can get away from their posts up river.

Sibley would have liked the garrison to remain at Fort Osage. Settlers and the Indians need the soldiers to protect them. From each other and from the brawls and quarrels among themselves, he says.

The Sibleys see most of the travellers going east or west. Our old friend Belt Jackson was here late last summer. A group headed for Sante Fe, led by William Bucknell, came through about the same time. Sibley thought Belt decided to go with them, instead of up river. Would liked to have exchanged news with my old comrade, taken a look at his sketches. The Sibleys have a couple on display, one of Mrs. Sibley at her piano, one of her with a lapful of kittens.

This kitten is promised. The owners, a new family of settlers, will pick it up when they come to town for some more logs. Both kittens and logs are much in demand among the settlers who have arrived in place of the Indians and the soldiers. The logs are free for the taking, it seems. At the rate the settlers are yanking them from the post itself, it will soon be dismantled. New dwellings arise instead, at the Audrain place, the fields where Dr. John Robinson and Risdon Price had William Wells raising corn to fatten the hogs they sold to the garrison and passing traders, like Lisa. Yes, that's the same Price who took over Austin's Durham Hall.

All goes well with us so far. Our daily progress upstream was slower than I had hoped. The men are rubbing together reasonably well. No adventures to report — may it continue so.

Give my regards to all our friends. Tell Francis that Mr. Sibley now has a mandarin costume. He assures me this is what he wears, along with a cap decorated with feathers, when distributing largesse to the Indians. Between the mandarin costume and Mrs. Sibley's piano playing, especially her stirring rendition of marches, these folks will be long remembered among the Little Osage.

This goes downstream tonight and should be in your hands shortly. Part of me wishes I could do the same. The other part says I must press on, make a success of this venture for both our sakes.

All my love to you and Jane,
Your A. Henry"

The Major pressed on toward Fort Atkinson. Doing his best to get more mileage out of his boatman, he wished for Lisa's motivating presence. He was sorry there would be no Manuel to visit with when they reached Council Bluffs. Two years before, Manuel had spent the last winter of his life there, at Fort Lisa, close by the newly erected military post.

Always in the vanguard, Manuel had brought the first white women to ascend the Missouri River with him. His second wife, a capable woman in her mid-thirties of New England background, and her companion, were the star attractions of the 1819-1820 season. A great curiosity for the Indian groupies who followed them about, they were also a jolly addition to the dinners and dances of the military.

The Indians insisted on trading with Mary Lisa, or 'Aunt Manuel,' as she came to be known. The expert coaching of her experienced husband and her own innate Yankee shrewdness enabled her to gauge the value of a pelt, conduct the pleasantries, and turn a profitable deal.

Manuel was ill during the winter, slow to recover. His failure to wrest custody of his son, Christopher, from his Omaha mother, Metain, aggravated both Manuel's temper and his well being. Mary Lisa was relieved to get him, drawn and haggard-looking, back to St. Louis and into Dr. Farr's care. Shortly after their second wedding anniversary, on August 12, 1820, Don Manuel De Lisa died, in his fifty-eighth year.

His legacy to Mary included two step-children, a substantial estate, mortgaged to the hilt, and the his plans for the continuance of his treasured Missouri Fur Company. Her successful Hempstead brothers had rallied round the Widow Lisa, reorganized the Company.

With Lisa gone, the firm needed a coordinator to serve as field agent. Joseph Pilcher, a man of good standing in banking, business and social circles, had been at Fort Lisa that last year, learning the business from Manuel himself. The most recent word the Major had indicated that Pilcher had become one of the partners, agreed to take on the duties and responsibilities of field agent. The Major supposed Pilcher would make his headquarters at Fort Lisa, handy to the Omaha trade and the military. From there, Pilcher could be expected to send veteran trappers to fan out over the upper reaches of the Missouri in competition with the Rocky Mountain Fur Company. For the time being, however, the Major was getting up river ahead of all competitors.

That the Rocky Mountain Fur Company expedition was on its way was known at Fort Atkinson but only one man had more than a nodding acquaintance with the man who led it. John Dougherty, the doughty Indian agent, there on business from his headquarters at Fort Leavenworth, was on hand to welcome the Major when he came ashore. Once Dougherty had been a callow youth, set to mastering valuable skills under the tutelage of this flinty leader, the planner with flair and attention to detail. Rowing, hunting, trapping, fighting, his stint with Henry in the mountains had taught him a valuable lesson: surprising, the many things a man could do and endure to guarantee his survival. Perhaps, like Lisa, one paid for such physical stress and strain later in life.

Henry's arrival brought a sense of continuity to Dougherty, a strongly built man in his thirties. Well versed in Indian dialects and French, knowledgeable about the habits, manners and peculiarities of the various tribes generally, and his own charges, in particular, he made it his business to keep abreast of events and people, near and far. An Indian agent could never be sure what might spark off a volatile reaction.

"Don't you miss 'Ee-saw'?" said Dougherty, his boyish grin unchanged, as he shook hands with his one-time mentor who looked fit and well able to face the rigors ahead of him.

"Hell," said the Major, "I even miss Tom James."

"He's on his way to Sante Fe with McKnight," said the Indian agent who made it his business to know what many people were doing. "Got any wet-behind-the-ears Dougherty-like boys with you this trip?"

"Weeded those out before we started," said the Major, introducing Dougherty to his brother-in-law.

"There's some men you'd want on your side in a fight, feisty and fit," said Dr. Nick, shaking hands, "but you wouldn't like to see them hanging around your sister. Don't know what the hell got into General Ashley, signing up that Mike Fink."

It was a happy interlude, this encounter, larded with reminiscences of the first time they passed the Platte, talk concerned with events, people, prospects. Dougherty still exchanged news and heard from some of his former colleagues occasionally, filled the Major in on their doings.

Reuben Lewis had remained on the Upper Missouri in command of one of the fur trade posts until 1812. Upon his return to St. Louis he was appointed Indian agent to the Quapaws and Cherokees. In 1820 he returned to his native Virginia.

Last he heard, Cather had joined some Nor'westers headed for the mouth of the Columbia. Edward Rose, sometimes with the Crows, in recent years had been hanging out with the Arikara. Michael Immel and Benjamin Jones, with some other veterans of Fort Raymond, were expected at Fort Lisa, where Joseph Pilcher would give them their marching orders.

The Major relayed what news he had of Young Bryan and Belt Jackson, the rumor that Pet McBride was trapping out of Taos. While John showed Dr. Nick around, met some of the other members of the party, Andrew Henry penned birthday greetings to his wife to go downstream with Dougherty for eventual delivery.

All was well, he reassured her again, nothing of moment to report.

After leaving Fort Atkinson, there still wasn't much to report. They got past the Arikara without incident. Before reaching the Mandan villages there were some desertions, aggravating but not unexpected. As had happened when he came this way with Lisa, men were both fascinated and disturbed by their passage through a wild emptiness, unbroken by any reassuring signs of civilization.

A little above the Mandans, some uncivil Assiniboines, a roving band out for plunder that paced their progress upriver, went whooping off with nearly all their horses.

"Waste of time," the Major told the men, their dander up, who wanted to set out in pursuit. To Dr. Nick, "Would like to get where we're going without getting anyone killed. Get some walls up around us. There'll be time then to see about getting more horses. Good men are harder to come by than horses."

In the dry heat of late August, they reached their destination, the junction of the Yellowstone with the Missouri, and set to work constructing Fort Henry. Dr. Nick jotted down some of his impressions.

"Good defensive site, above the flood waters of the two rivers, on a narrow tongue of land. Rectangular, within picketed walls, projecting blockhouses at diagonal corners so riflemen can give covering fire to the entire outside wall. A spartan place with a redeeming view, a place to store furs, take refuge from the xenophobic.

"A vast land, impatient with the puny. 'It bitheth like a serpent and stingeth like an adder.' Gnats, mosquitoes, hornets, horseflies, rattlesnakes. Burning sun. Terrific winds. Thunder, lightning, rain, hail, sleet. Winters like a Norse God's curse.

"Not a puny here. Young. Physically fit. Some smarts but no intellectuals. Like a new group of plebes, sorting out their own peers, learning to be beaver men, class of '22. No upperclassmen. Immel, class of 1810, got all them. So, the superintendent of this mountain academy has to be instructor, disciplinarian, to teach them the ropes."

From the days when the Dutch place name for Albany was Beaverwyck, where beaver once could be found in abundance, the greed and encroachments of man had well-nigh made them extinct in the east. With each succeeding year, trappers in the west had to go further into the wilderness to find them.

Beaver had always had value as adornment but it was most in demand for making the finest felt for hat. The tiny, microscopic barbs on the hair from the muffoon, or underfur of the beaver, with their interlocking qualities, were ideally suited to the process of felting. As one of the earliest fabrics developed by primitive man, felt was made, not by weaving, but by pressing fibers, vegetable, fur, wool, tightly together. Further processing refinements had been added over the years, the use of heat, of chemicals. Until fashion popularized another fabric, profiting hatters would make it worth a man's while to catch beaver.

Dr. Nick was not particularly interested in the beaver, or its habits, but the class of '22 was.

They already knew some things about the beaver, some true, some fanciful. Congenitally driven to halt running water, he felled trees, gnawed off, floated tree hunks, branches into place, slapped mud and sticks and twigs into the barrier. As the water behind his dam deepened into a calm, marsh-fringed pond, he slapped more twigs and sticks and mud together to make his lodge with its underwater entrance. Inside, in the main chamber, raised about a foot above water level, the beaver wintered, the young were born and raised. In their turn, the young went out and found running water to dam up, and the cycle of establishing a colony, repeated itself:

Fell trees, chop off branches and drag them underwater to the pool, shove one end deep in the mud outside the lodge entrance, building up a food supply of soft bark for winter, sometimes weighing them down with rocks or mud. Slap more mud and sticks and twigs on the dam to keep it in repair. Deposit castoreum on the mud piles marking the territory of the colony.

"Medicine," said the Major to Dr. Nick, "the trappers call it. Made out of beaver glands. Used for bait," he nodded at the man dispensing castoreum from an antelope vial into wooden boxes held by two novices. "Anderson there is going to take those young fellows out to a likely spot early tomorrow, show them how you get a beaver to 'come to medicine.' Want to go along?"

"Come to medicine?" repeated the doctor. "Seems apropos for one of my calling. Since when did Anderson get so knowledgeable?"

"Since I took him and Weber out the other day," said the Major. "Unless you'd rather go with Weber. He's taking out a couple, too."

"Anderson is easier to understand. And jollier," said Dr. Nick. "Why is he having them cut off their buckskin pants at the knee?"

"Going to piece them out with cloth. A man has to wade to catch beaver. Can't go tramping around on the bank leaving his scent," said the Major. "Wet buckskin stretches to hell an' gone. Dries so tight near makes you a soprano. Better wear those old wool pants of yours."

Dr. Nick was out for nearly a week, returned a humbler man. Anderson and his trainees, the Harris cousins, George and Black, leading packhorses carrying their traps, food and bedrolls, set a ground-eating pace to the beaver stream Anderson had selected. Dr. Nick, carrying only his rifle, had to stretch himself to keep up. Most men of that time, and in particular the recruits Dr. Nick himself had helped the Major select, had some wilderness experience. In the days ahead, they would get some idea just how hardy they would need to be before they could consider themselves bonafide trappers.

Anderson showed the two eager young men, and the curious but not so eager doctor, how to clip a long stake to one of the five-pound traps, sling the trap over the back by the means of the long chains, and set it. Carrying his trap rather gingerly, Dr. Nick joined the others in wading upstream against the current.

At various strategic spots, slides, drags, underwater entrances, Anderson first demonstrated, then oversaw the placing of each trap, in water of a certain depth near the bank. He dipped a long switch in his castoreum vial of horn, planted it on the bank above the pan of the trap.

"When ol' Mr. Beaver smells that, he'll come a faunchin', all set to rise up on his hind legs to get a sniff of the nervy feller edgin' into his territory. The trap's set right where he's goin' to have to stand to do his sniffin'. So, wham, you got him."

Pulling the chain to its five-foot limit, he then drove the long, attached stake into the deeper water of the stream bed. When it came Dr. Nick's turn, the water was too deep for a stake to show, so Anderson attached a float stick to the extended chain to mark its location.

"Ef'n he dives, you got him, shore. The trap 'n chain'll hold him down so he can't come up for air. Ef'n he gets to the bank, he'll gnaw off his leg, get away."

"Poor damn beaver," said Dr. Nick.

"Quicker way to go than most critters," said the husky Black. "Fox or lynx or such, jest has to lie there, waitin' for you to come along and knock him in the head."

"After you catch him, then what?" said Dr. Nick, stifling a pang of pity for the other critters, too.

"Skin him, save his medicine. Stretch an' fletch an' dry the pelt. You'll see."

The boy in Dr. Nicholas Fleming rather enjoyed the outing but the man was glad it was not his chosen calling. It was a full time job. Up at daylight to make the rounds of the traps, emptying, resetting in a new spot. After wading awhile the feet turned numb, feeling ending at the cold ring around the legs, until, emerging from the water, circulation re-established itself. His surgeon's skills made quick work of the skinning, his fingers nimble at making a hoop stretcher, tying on the skin, scraping off the fat and clinging muscle fibers.

He was relieved when Anderson, pointing out some tributary streams he had scouted, said, "Time to get back to the fort, fetch out some new fellers to those streams. Give them a turn at larnin' how to get beaver to come to medicine."

"What about us?" demanded George.

"You an' Black get to do what I done for you. Take a couple apiece an' larn 'em," said Anderson. "Think you could, Doc?"

"Could," said Doc. "But," gesturing toward the Fort and the route downriver, he put his refusal into words that made them chuckle, "thar floats my stick."

As they neared Fort Henry, they weren't surprised to see many more men moving about than when they left. For weeks, they had been expecting Daniel Moore to show up with the Enterprise, loaded with more men and supplies. There was no sign of any keelboat. There were a lot more horses, and a familiar figure astride one.

"That looks like General Ashley," said Dr. Nick. "What's he doing here?"

Turned out the General was here because Daniel Moore, setting out a month after the Major, literally hit a snag. The Enterprise capsized some twenty miles below Fort Osage. Boat and supplies were lost, survivors stranded. Between the first week in June, when Moore reached St. Louis to report the $10,000 loss, and the third week, Ashley, with speed and ingenuity that Lisa would have admired, managed to get another keelboat, which were much in demand, and an extension of credit to replace the lost supplies. On June 21, with a forty-six man crew, Ashley himself took charge of getting the boat and needed supplies upriver to Fort Henry. By the time he picked up the survivors of the Enterprise, some stragglers of Henry's who had got lost on the prairies, and some recent military dischargees from Fort Atkinson, he had over one hundred men in his section of the Rocky Mountain Fur Company expedition.

On sea biscuits and bacon, he kept them going without hunting stops. He made the expected courtesy-cum-gifts calls at the Indian villages of the Omahas, Poncas, and Sioux. At the Arikara villages, freshly fortified, after the cautious, diplomatic amenities were over, he did some horse trading, mounted as many of his men as possible, took off overland.

The keelboat arrived two weeks later, the middle of October. By then the partners had their balance sheets done and plans made for the coming year. The Major would send trappers up the Missouri and Yellowstone to winter in the beaver country. The General would return to St. Louis with one of the keelboats, the boatmen, and the already garnered packs of furs. The prospects looked good. On the basis of their accomplishments so far, the General was optimistic about obtaining supplies on credit to outfit a new expedition in the spring.

Before Dr. Nick left the Fort to return home, as planned, he got to meet Michael Immel, the big, experienced man leading the competition, when Immel and Jones came rowing up the river on their way to the Missouri Fur Company fort at the mouth of the Big Horn. At the time, he thought it wasn't quite right that they got upstream with none of the difficulties of Rocky Mountain Fur. Afterwards, he searched his conscience, decided he hadn't really wished them bad luck. No matter how keen the competition, an end at Blackfeet hands was not something you wished on your worst enemy.

In late November Dr. Nick was back in St. Louis, bidding goodbye to the General and others who had accompanied them downriver on the keelboat. Carrying loving messages from the Major to his wife and daughter, Dr. Nick went directly to Potosi to deliver them. When his knock was not answered, he walked in to find his sister kicking the furniture, while her household stood around looking uncomfortable at such uncharacteristic behavior.

"It doesn't look good anywhere," said Mary, rubbing her toe, gesturing for Aloysius and Cousin Angus to shove the offending mirrored armoire into her bedroom. "For two cents, I'd send it back to the Widow Lisa."

"Here. Let me help." Dr. Nick added his strength to that of the two other men, got the armoire in place just in time for Mary to fling her arms around him.

"I take it all back," she said, mistily. "It just brought me good luck. Oh, I'm so glad to see you. Are you all right? What news do you have? Do you have a letter for me? How was everything in the mountains? Is the Major all right? Janey, here's your Uncle Nick, back from the mountains. Isn't that wonderful!"

Janey glared at her uncle. "Make Mommie cry!"

"She shouldn't go around kicking the furniture," said Dr. Nick, offering his handkerchief to his sister. "I'm fine. Got lots of news. Brought a long letter for you. Never really saw the mountains, so can't say how it was there. The Major is not only all right but lean and brown and busy as a beaver."

Still sniffing a bit, Mary dried her eyes, sorted everyone out, Penelope to serving coffee, everyone seated around the table, eager to hear the news from the mountains. They shooed her off to the privacy of her bedroom to read her letter, wipe away more tears before rejoining them to hear Cousin Angus saying, "That must have happened jist about the time we had to pull up the beans and burn 'em. Had to misinfect afore planting anything else."

As the highlights of his journey were touched upon, Dr. Nick's audience was able to relate to the events by recalling something that had been happening at home. In the end, he had a pretty good idea what had been going on with Mary during the months she had been running the household by herself. It also established a pattern for the future, giving perspective to the news that filtered down from the mountain.

"Right now, the Major's probably taking a trapping party up the Missouri," said the doctor. "Weber was going to take men and canoes up the Yellowstone."

About the time the Major returned to Fort Henry with eight men, leaving a baker's dozen to winter at the mouth of the Musselshell, Aloysius, who had just proposed to Penelope and been accepted, fell off the gallery and broke his leg. While he was laid up most of December and January, with Penelope hovering, Cousin Angus helped the peg-leg veteran out on the farm, and Mary had some angry things to say to the mirrored armoire.

Jedediah Smith had joined the men on the Musselshell, making entries in his journal, as was Daniel Potts. Like the other men, they were keeping their distance from the swaggering bully Mike Fink and his toadying cronies, Carpenter and Talbot. While the unpredictable trio were alternately quarreling and making up, Cousin Angus and the peg-leg veteran were doing the same over the proper care of the hogs. Aloysius was threatening to take his crutch to both of them. Mary threatened to sell the hogs.

In February, Mary mid-wifed three births at two-bits apiece, and wrote a cheerful letter to her husband which Dr. Nick took to General Ashley for eventual delivery. Ashley was advertising for men again, offering the impressive sum of $200 per year. Hugh Scott and George Jackson signed up. The doctor, eyeing the two keelboats, Yellow Stone Packet and The Rocky Mountains, remained ambivalent until the last moment.

When he hadn't returned by the middle of March, and word trickled back of Ashley's departure with seventy men, no accompanying land party since the General planned to get the necessary horses from the Arikara, Mary said, "Damn, he must have gone with the General after all."

She glared at her reflection in the armoire's mirror. "I forgot to ask either him or the Major about the taxes."

April and May, in Missouri and the mountains, had their incidents.

Ten days after the break up of the ice on the Missouri, Daniel Potts shot himself in the leg, accidentally. He returned to Fort Henry, as did Mike Fink, Carpenter and Talbot. Jedediah Smith with ten men in canoes trapped their way past the Judith, the Marias, to the mouth of the Smith River. On the Yellowstone,

Mike Fink, showing off his marksmanship in a fashion he favored, took aim at the cup of whiskey balanced on Carpenter's head, and shot him between the eyes, claiming it was an accident.

The Blackfeet jumped the Smith party, killed four men, stole everything. The remaining seven hastened back to Fort Henry. They got there in time to hear Mike Fink, in his cups, saying he had killed Carpenter on purpose. Instantly, Talbot drew his pistol and shot Mike through the heart, definitely and deliberately on purpose. The Major, seeing to the burial, knew he was going to miss Jim Anderson, hastily interred with the others slain by the Blackfeet near Great Falls, more than Mike Fink.

The Major dispatched Jed Smith off downstream with a report to be delivered to the General before he reached the Arikara villages.

Penelope, fretting over the fit of her wedding dress, caught the chicken pox from Janey, and, tearfully, put the wedding plans on hold. Aloysius booted out the peg-leg veteran, found a spryer, more dependable veteran to look after the hogs, started moving Penelope's fowls and furniture out to the farm. Mary, amidst a neighborhood epidemic of chicken pox, dealt out calamine lotion and advice, and postponed the trip to Flat River to ask Patrick about the taxes.

Jed Smith, traveling with the current, intercepted the General, delivered the Major's report and the letter to be sent on to Mary, which got lost in the hullabaloo of the next few days.

The same day the Ashley expedition reached the Arikara, May 31, up on the Yellowstone, Blackfeet ambushed the thirty men of Missouri Fur returning from a Three Forks trapping expedition. Bloods, they were, and bloody work they made of seven men, including Immel and Jones, wounded four men, and got away with horses, traps and furs. Aloysius Cook and Penelope Bequette were united in marriage that same day. Mary, taking Janey, left them bracing for the expected raucous charivari, and went home with her parents for week's visit.

Far from Potosi, the Arikara were mounting a much more lethal charivari for General Ashley, sleeping in his keelboat after a difficult day of trading for nineteen horses, his men divided between the boats and shore, all within rifle range of the village.

The Arikara, at sunrise, began taking potshots at one and all. Brief but hellish, the battle left Ashley with fifteen men dead, ten wounded, the horses slain or scattered, and his boatman quivering, cowering and useless.

Ashley got his keelboats downstream, reorganized. Jedediah Smith and a French-Canadian volunteered to carry Ashley's appeal for help to Major Henry. While they set out for the reinforcements Ashley knew he could count on, he penned a letter for delivery to Fort Atkinson in the forlorn hope of military aid. Crewing the one keelboat, The Rocky Mountains, with volunteers, he sent the letter downstream with unneeded supplies and the disaffected on the other keelboat.

The stars in their courses had favored the Indians with an ascendant Mars during the first two weeks in May. The tribes along the upper Missouri might be primitive, barbaric and unpredictable. They weren't fools. They didn't need the British to point out they were getting the short end of the stick from Americans since Lisa had passed on the torch. If they allowed the Rocky Mountain Fur and the Missouri Fur Company to concentrate solely on trapping, they would no longer be valuable customers; the trade and placatory gifts they had come to depend on would dwindle away.

The Indians attacked every major trapping party on the upper river and emerged victorious. Ashley's defeat was the last straw. The response to the alarming possibility that there was an Indian uprising in the making was immediate.

"To suffer such outrages. . . to go unpunished, would be to surrender the trade, and, with it, our strong hold upon the Indians, to the British," Major General Gaines told the Secretary of War.

Colonel Henry Leavenworth left Fort Atkinson with six companies of infantry, supported by a volunteer battalion of fur traders and Sioux horseman under Joshua Pilcher. Major Henry brought all the men he could spare from Fort Henry. Much to Mary's surprise, Aloysius Cook and Angus Fleming insisted on going upriver to give the Major a hand in 'larnin' those mangy Rees a lesson they'll never fergit!'

"Stop blubbering," Mary said to Penelope, "or I'll give you the mirrored armoire. They've got to do what they've got to do. We have to do the best we can."

Patrick, in whom she had confided the need to find hard cash to pay the taxes, found a buyer for the hogs, and then took to his bed with a bad bout of intermittent fever. The tax collector, crediting her with the pittance she got for the hogs, allowed her sixty days to come up with the balance.

On the first day of August, she was counting her money, including Janey's silver dollars, coming up very short of the needed amount, when Abigail surprised her by dropping in with her new husband who was taking her to Texas where he had, as Abigail put it, more land than an European monarch, but, "Sorry, we don't have any cash money to speak of, either."

"Nobody has," said Mary. "We will have, from the furs, but that could be another year or more."

"Can't you find a buyer for this fine antique?" said her husband, admiring the mirrored armoire. John Johns, a well-to-do acquaintance of Stephen Austin's from his New Orleans days and among the first of his recruits for his Texas venture, he had wooed and won Abigail along with some additional settlers on a promotional swing through New England on Austin's behalf.

"She'd sell the farm before she parted with that monstrosity," said Abigail, who was looking forward to establishing the first academy for young ladies in Texas. "What use is the farm to you, anyway? You can't take care of it. And, Heaven knows, the Major isn't a farmer."

"It's more an investment," said Mary. "Once times get better, it'd bring a good price."

"Let's go take a look at this investment," said Johns. Somehow, in the process, adjacent landowners got the idea the Johns were potential buyers. Almost immediately, Mary got two offers, one a complicated barter, minimum cash, and extended credit; the other, for considerably less, in silver.

She took the silver, paid the taxes, and tried to give the armoire to Abigail. "Let me see that note from the Widow Lisa first," said Abigail.

After reading the note, she declined on the grounds it was implied that Mary at least keep the ugly thing until her husband got back from the mountains. "Some day, you may need money more than you do now. Sell it to that Senator Benton. He's ga-ga over anything to do with Missouri history. Dotes on his little girl: he'd think it a great idea to give her such a good-luck piece."

August was a hot month, particularly at the Arikara villages, where the Sioux slaughtered a lot of them, then rode off to raid their cornfields. Aloysius Cook and Angus Fleming finally located Major Henry, attached themselves to his contingent, under Hugh Scott and Jedediah Smith respectively. Brigadier General Ashley and Major Henry had about eighty men. Colonel Leavenworth had made Hiram Allen and George C. Jackson, ensigns; Thomas Fitzpatrick, quartermaster; William Sublette, quartermaster; Dr. Nicholas Fleming, surgeon.

In the Missouri Fur contingent, Pilcher was a nominal major; William Henry Vanderburgh, former West Pointer, a captain; Moses B. Carson, first lieutenant; William Gordon, 2nd lieutenant; Angus McDonald, captain in nominal command of the Indian allies.

The mix — trappers, Indians and military — was given the impressive name of the Missouri Legion.

Everyone watched as the Army made a lot of noise with their little cannons. The chief who had instigated the raid on Ashley was killed. The other chiefs, feeling guiltless, begged for a truce. Colonel Leavenworth granted lenient terms but the Arikara were more concerned with the attitude of the trappers. Fearing their vengeance, the Arikara fled their villages, which some Missouri Fur men, including William Gordon who had buried Immel and Jones on the Yellowstone, promptly torched. The homeless Arikara settled two hundred miles away near the Mandans.

"Leavenworth thinks he did a great job. Avenged the slain, humbled the Rees, left peace and tranquility behind him," snorted Dr. Nick when he got home the middle of September. "Pilcher told him he'd behaved like an imbecile. Alienated the Sioux, sent the murderous Rees off to infect the Mandans."

"What does the Major think?"

"Won't be safe for a white man to show his face on the Upper Missouri for years to come. He's pulling out, heading for Crow country."

The way up the Missouri was closed. Rocky Mountain Fur was abandoning Fort Henry at the mouth of the Yellowstone, moving to Crow country. Aloysius was with the Major doing just that, would winter with him at the new Fort Henry at the mouth of the Big Horn where Fort Raymond used to be. Cousin Angus had struck out overland with the party the Major was sending directly overland to the mountains under a very able fellow named Smith. "Any thing been happening here?"

"Mamán and Papa aren't a bit well. Penelope has morning sickness. Don't you have a letter for me?"

"Sorry. Forgot," said Dr. Nick. "Aloysius penned one to Penelope, too."

"Oh, my God," said Mary, putting down her letter. "Another year at least before he gets home. I think I'll throw up, too."

"Keep it in mind as a means of making sure he doesn't go back. That's Tartar country. Full óf Tartars, Crows not excepted," said Dr. Nick "Let some of those men he's training take over. Some of them are regular Tartars, too."

Ol' Hugh Glass, a real Tartar, who didn't take kindly to supervision, blundered into a grizzly who was feeding chunks of him to her cubs when Henry and the rest of the party came to his rescue. After waiting a day and a night for Glass to die, the party made up an $80 purse as inducement for two rather reluctant volunteers, teen-age Jim Bridger and the slightly older John Fitzgerald, to stay with him until he did. For five days they waited for Glass to die, getting antsier all the time, and with good cause.

A Mandan war party, in a night attack, had whittled away at the Major's party, killing two men, wounding two, and stealing two horses.

At Fort Henry on the Yellowstone, men, horses and equipment were being whittled down further. By the time Bridger and Fitzgerald came in, the details of Glass's demise took second place to stripping the fort, embarking men and equipment in canoes.

Crow country at last, the renewal of old acquaintances over the passing peace pipe, and horses for a party to travel ahead of the canoes, trapping as they went, to winter on the Bighorn. Fitzgerald, declaring he would rather be a soldier than a trapper, and two other men took their leave and headed back for civilization in a canoe.

The Major got men busy erecting a new Fort Henry, trapping parties headed out to all the streams he remembered and some he'd only heard of, smoked the pipe and traded with the Crows that stopped by, took time now and then for some R&R with his Crow friends from the old days.

The year of 1824 was ushered in with a spirited celebration. When Hugh Glass walked in, asking for Bridger and Fitzgerald, the Major wasn't the only one who thought he'd had too much to drink.

Aloysius, in years to come would relate the saga of Hugh Glass just as Cousin Angus would relate the saga of Jed Smith, chawed by a grizzly, too.

For this was the year the Rocky Mountain Fur brigades, under the field command and leadership of Andrew Henry, caught the fancy of the media. In no time at all, word began spreading worldwide of their enterprise and achievements.

When the Major left the mountains in September of 1824, he planned to return. Certainly, Ashley wanted him to, planned on it. Certainly he was feted and made much of upon arrival in St. Louis. A cool one, they said, with an amiable expression that never gave away his inner thoughts. Able, skilled, braver than most men, and wholly faithful to his friends. No one, his men said, ever saw him angry or disgruntled or fussed in any way. Andrew Henry pointed out that his mountain men were already getting a reputation for stretching things more than a bit.

En route to St. Louis, he had six of his men killed by Indians firing from the river bank, which distressed him. When he considered his own narrow escapes, he became somber. His well-honed instinct for survival, like that of John Colter's a decade earlier, said, "Enough of this!"

He had made his stake several different times and was aware that regardless of the enterprise, there was no guarantee of an easy life or a comfortable one. The world of commerce never had been stable long. Of more immediate concern was his health. He had experienced the mortification of recurring bouts of illness that had sapped his vigor, blighted his optimism.

Mary, making light of her concern for his welfare, gestured at their four-year old daughter, Jane, who was getting reacquainted with her father. With a twinkle, Mary pointed out that having a mountain man for a husband did make for a long, dull time between "begats."

He did want to provide Mary and his children with a living of comfort and grace. He was approaching fifty and might not have all that much time left. He weighed the pros and cons, considered the alternatives, and finally decided not to return to the mountains. Instead, he would devote himself to his lead mining business.

Ashley reluctantly accepted Henry's decision to withdraw from the fur trade. Jedediah Smith bought Henry's shares. The Major settled into the quieter, less vulnerable life of a Washington County gentleman.

For nearly another decade Andrew Henry continued to like good whiskey, most people and to love and cherish his young wife and children. He never dodged a debt or reneged on a bet. Or, as his obituary in June of 1833, phrased it, he was:

". . . a man much respected for his honesty, intelligence and enterprise. Major Henry was one of those enterprising men who first explored the wild and inhospitable region of the Rocky Mts. and at that time was a partner of the first American fur company that was formed for the prosecution of the trade."

Recollections

Jane Henry Cain

The first time I really remember having anything to do with my Papa, he was a moose. He had just come back from the mountains. Mama was so pleased to see this strange man. Mama said this was Papa. I knew better. Papa was a black and white sketch Mama looked at every night before saying her prayers. This man was different and wouldn't be laid away on the bureau. He took my place in bed with my Mama and I had to sleep in the trundle bed.

"Play buffalo with her," Mama said. "She used to think that was such fun."

I didn't this time. I screamed bloody murder. Papa sat back on his heels, looking at me. I shut up. His look could do that. That's probably how he handled so many different kinds of men in his lifetime.

Mama sighed. "She's usually not that hard to amuse."

"I'll a-moose her," said Papa, and he began lumbering around in the funniest way I ever saw, comical and grand at the same time. I've always had a soft spot in my heart for the moose ever since. Some of my playmates had Papas who played horsie with them but I was the only one whoever got to ride a moose.

He was a nice man really, a bit strict but not stern. Very honest and upright. "The house the mountains built," Mama called our frame home in Webster, meaning that's all there was left over from the money he made in the fur trade after settling his debts. It was the only one for miles around with a room set aside for just sitting. Came in handy at election time as a polling place. There was Missouri between me and Patrick. Sickly, and gone quickly.

After Patrick, Mary, and just a few months before Papa died, little Georgie. Mama let me tend him all by myself for nearly one whole day in the spring while she went out with Papa to see the place he'd picked out for his burying.

He was laid away in that spot with full Masonic honors. Important men came to pay their respects. So as Mama would have some cash money, Mr. Scott saw to the auction of Papa's things. Before giving up his fiddle, Mama made it wail about the bear going over the mountain, then took all of us to visit Papa's grave until everything was sold up and carted away.

I was past thirteen, already knew Mr. Cain had his eye on me, so was thinking more of my future than Mama's. We'd always had enough of the world's goods for comfort. Somehow Mama kept it that way, at least until I was married and left home. I never got much of a chance to see how she was making out after that.

Too late I found out Mr. Cain didn't approve of Mama, her religion, her frivolity, her doctoring and midwifing, her raising hogs, and especially her dancing the highland fling with Cousin Angus at our wedding party. I did stand up to him when my own little Mary was due. I paid him no never mind when it was time for little Andrew, too. I sent for Mama and she came, both times, when I had Mary and again when I had Andrew.

Oh, the comfort of not having to weigh thoughts nor measure words with her. Pour them all out, chaff and grain together. Knowing that her kind heart took and sifted them, kept what was worth keeping, and with a breath of kindness, blew the rest away.

I guess she meant it kindly, what she said when she was leaving. Or maybe I'd talked too much. Mr. Cain tells me I do that.

"Don't suppose that husband of yours will allow us to get together again unless one of us in on her deathbed," Mama said, kissing me goodbye. "Or you show some backbone." She hugged Mary and Andrew. "If I'd had any idea you were going to need it so desperately, I'd never have sold that mirrored armoire."

Mr. Cain moved us clear to the other end of Bellevue Valley so I haven't seen her since. If I didn't feel so poorly all the time, I'd just up and go see her and ask her just what she meant about me not having any backbone.

Patrick Henry

Do I remember my Pa? Sure I do. Ma, too. She twinkled. He was ten feet tall.

Mountain man tales? Not from Pa. Ol' Cook could tell 'em, though.

An' Cousin Angus. Ol' Hugh Glass an' the grizzly. Jed Smith an' his grizzly. Mike Fink. South Pass an' Oregon an' Californy, afore ary another laid eyes on 'em. What? Speak up? What's he sayin', Sis?

He knows those tales? Then what the hell is he askin' me about them for?

He wants to know what? Did Pa drink? Christ-a-mighty, ever' man, woman and child drank in his day. Did he die broke? Sis, Sis, get this son-of-a-bitch out of here before, old as I am, I show him broke!

Got rid of him, did you, Sis? No need to apologize for his bad manners. What'd he want to know about Pa for anyway? He's been dead and gone over sixty years now. Ma's been gone, I disremember how long. Buried her in the Catholic cemetery in Potosi. Too broke to put up a marker. Always intended to.

You was named for her, Sis. Likely lady she was, too. Good manager.

Pa prospered greatly at one time, but hard times gave him a set back or two. Doin' all right there at Webster, getting ahead. There wasn't much my Pa didn't know about the lead mining business. We'da been settin' pretty if he had lived. The Masons gave Ma a hand, and Aunt Penelope and ol' Cook an' Cousin Angus were always there when we needed them. Uncle Doc took me in to eddicate when I was about 10 or 11 but that sourpuss of a wife and those two spoiled young'uns he had made my life such a misery I up an' 'prenticed myself to a plasterer.

Yup. I'm the only one left. Janey died afore Ma, left two young 'uns.

Her man never even let us know she was sick. Made us all madder'n hell so's we've never spoke to one of them Cains since. Mary's been gone a while, too. Saw her buried alongside her young 'uns. Georgie was Ma's least one. Never got to know him hardly a'tall, leaving home as young as I did. Next thing I know, he's dead an' gone, leavin' a young widow just like Pa did, four little girls and another born after he was laid away.

What was it like at home before Pa died? Warm. Fun. Oh, we was put to tasks early. Help with the stock, in the garden patch. Girls knit an' wove an' did housework an' cookin'. No one prosperous enough around there to have slaves. Most folks didn't cotton to the idee, anywise. Had as many pleasures as time and place could provide. Church meetings, play parties, corn huskings and house raisings. Pa read to us, then, after he was gone, Ma. Rooms large and airy. In the front, next to the sittin' room was the bedroom where Pa died. The kitchen was behind those, and stairs to a sleeping loft where Janey and I had our featherbeds. Mary slept in the trundle bed in the folks room, Georgie in the cradle.

We went on visits to the grandparents, to Uncle Doc's, and once Pa took us all clear to Ste. Genevieve for the wedding of an old friend of his, one of the Valles. The next day he took us on the ferry across the Mississip to see another old friend. Another Frenchie, he was, with the biggest, fanciest house an' layout I ever saw, not until I was growed and made a trip to St. Louis.

What was my Pa really like? Whaddaya mean? Oh. A medium-heighted man, probably like me. Been a bit wild in his time. Like me. Hell's Bell's, girl, I was only five years old when he died. For a long time I thought he was God. You know, from the Lord's Prayer. "Our Father which art in heaven . . ."

Interview

Miss Grace G. Henry

You are correctly informed, Miss. Retired teacher. Spinster. Granddaughter of Major Andrew Henry.
Of course I can understand why Oregon would be interested in him.
Not everyone in the Ozarks is illiterate, ill-informed or ill bred. I taught history, among other subjects, for thirteen years in the Flat River schools. Cult heroes, now, his mountain men.
His sex appeal? Indian women? I have no idea nor do I consider it any of my business. Or yours. They do say my grandmother fell in love with him when she was three years old and never wanted another man.
She had a what? There again, you have 'they say.' An antique bestowed on women married to men of destiny? My, my. From a French courtesan by way of Madame Chouteau and an assortment of other wives through my grandmother to Jesse Fremont? There again, you have 'they say.' You'd have thought they'd have included Napoleon's Josephine in the line up while 'they' were at it, wouldn't you?
You must understand I had very little opportunity to learn anything about the Henry family background or traditions. The Harris family, yes. My mother knew that upside down and backwards and recited it ad nauseum.
My grandfather died when my father was a baby. I don't remember my Henry grandmother. She was dead and gone by the time my father married my mother, and he died, not yet forty of a mining injury, two months before I was born. Left my mother to raise us five girls. We grew up cheek-by-jowl with our Harris kin, never did get well-acquainted with our Henry kin, though. There was a Mary Henry, a teacher, too, daughter of Patrick, who used to have the family Bible. There was another Mary - - a Cain, rather an eccentric. Drove all over in a horse and buggy selling Singer Sewing Machines. 'They say' Patrick had a couple boys who headed west as soon as they were of an age.
That wasn't exactly what you wanted to know? You wanted something personal about my grandfather? I do not see the necessity. If the mountain men are now our version of the epic hero, it follows that the man who led them to the mountains was. If I

remember rightly, the epic hero is a historical constant. Odysseus. Beowulf. Arthur. Sal-a-Din. Roland. He acts in accordance with the highest ideals of his society. Some circumstances demand the epic hero be hardheaded, other circumstances make him seem to be hard-hearted, but he follows a code that justifies his behavior; it is a comprehensible code that is provided for him by the culture he inhabits; and in following the dictates of this code he preserves the culture which produced it. Physical bravery is only one quality his role demands; he must also make difficult moral choices.

The years you speak of, when my grandfather led those epic heroes to the mountains, are well documented. You probably know better than I whether he fits the epic hero mould. And you know better than I the purpose of your prying questions about his personal life. I can't answer them. Even if I could, I would have no part in the debunking of my grandfather.

Andrew Henry was a Major of the Mountains and a Major of the Mines, a highly respected man at both locations. He was laid away in a place of his own choosing. Not many men of his generation were so fortunate. Sorry, miss. I never knew the exact location of his grave except that it was not far from his home in Webster. If you can find it, I certainly have no objections to Oregon erecting a marker over it honoring Andrew Henry's contribution to western exploration. Whatever you do, you won't be any closer to knowing the real Andrew Henry than anyone else of your ilk.

Hazen Hawkes kneels behind his original find, the rock roster of the men at the site of Camp Henry in 1810.

Epilogue

This land was their land. They were the pioneers who had grubbed out the sagebrush, dug the irrigation canals and the ditches yard-by-back-breaking-yard to carry the precious water to their homesteads. As far as they knew, or cared, they were the first. Someone in the government had named their creek Conant, for one of those ne-er-do-well squawmen who about drowned in it, no true pioneer in their sense of the word.

They were the Conant Creek Canal Company. This spring of 1917, as every spring for the past decade, they and their sons and grandsons had camped at the head of the canal, fanned out, repairing the damage done by winter, spring run-off and burrowing gophers.

From the canal bank where they had been assigned to fill gopher holes, two young men could look down upon a rocky hillside outcropping.

Hazen Hawkes, ten generations from the Saints who crossed the Atlantic to pioneer at Plymouthtown, four generations from the Saints who crossed the plains with Brigham Young to pioneer in Zion, second generation in Idaho, said,

"Shh. There's a couple of coyote pups down there. Must be a den in those rocks."

Leaning on their shovels, they watched the pups at play and wondered if they wouldn't make nice pets. With youthful enthusiasm, they decided to find out and scrambled down the hill to the coyote den.

After a lot more shovel work than anticipated, Hazen straightened up and saw before him a rock with writing on it. The powder monkey, who had been observing their fruitless efforts, volunteered to make their task easier. He elbowed the two young men aside, planted and set off a charge of dynamite in the rocks.

When the dust settled, they had nine stunned coyote pups and an intriguing rock. The names, as they spelled them out, A. Henry, J. Hoback, P. McBride, B. Jackson, L. Cather, weren't familiar. The 1810 date gave them pause.

"Let's show it to P-P-Pa," said Hazen's companion.

Since P-P-Pa was a mile or so away, they took a couple halfhitches around the rock with some halter ropes, figuring Hazen's strawberry roan, could pull it to camp.

Hazen, holding a gunny sack full of coyote pups in one hand, mounted. The roan rolled his eyes at the gunny sack, where the recovering pups were beginning to wriggle, and took several steps.

When the weight of the rock, anchored by the ropes to the saddle horn, pulled the saddle back into his flanks, he unloaded Hazen and the pups.

The pups fought their way out of the sack and scrambled safely away. The roan, bucking furiously, disappeared from sight with dust, sagebrush and the rocks flying behind him. When Hazen caught up with him two days later, the saddle was under his belly and there was no rock anywhere near him.

In the meantime, P-P-a and his generation gave them what for. Those cussed gophers holes needed seeing to. Nobody much had been here before them, anyway. Maybe Ol' Beaver Dick Leigh an' his Indian woman and kids.They knew their own history, the persecutions in Missouri and Illinois, the martyred Joseph Smith passing on the torch to the pragmatic Brigham Young. They didn't know, or much care, about any other history. What they did know was good farmland. Whoever had passed this way had sure been foolish to pass up some of the best farmland ever. If it had water. So never mind some ol' rock. Get the water flowing into the laterals and onto the crops.

"Somebody was here in 1810," insisted Hazen. "Who were they? Why did they come here? What happened to them?"

Thirty-five years later his daughter looked at the recovered rock, the Camp Henry markers and asked the same questions. In searching for the answers, she discovered that there are no absolute truths in history, only this evidence against that evidence. New evidence, wherever it might be found, looked at from a different viewpoint, may fill in some gaps but still will be no guarantee of the absolute truth, either.

For sure, though, there once was a man named Andrew Henry and he left his mark in Idaho.

Appendix

Letter
Photos
Maps

Dr Francis   5th June 1810

Sir

Since you left the fort I was told by Charlo Sanis that some days past you expressed some regret at going down. If that is the case & you have any wish to stay. You shall have the same bargain which Manuel gave you last fall. & better should you desire it

But on the other hand if you have realy a wish to descend I will by no means advise you to stay, but would rather advice you to go home to your family who I know will be extremely glad to see you, altho the pleasure of your company for a year in this wild country would be to me inestimable.

Should you continue down please present my respects to Joseph Pratt & family, to Terry cashier, the Doctr Thomas Coll'd Reubin Smith & all my friends George Butler Doctr Elliot &c

I am Dr Francis
very respectfully
your friend

Francis Vallé   A Henry

Copy of a letter from A. Henry to Francis Vallé, June 5, 1810.

Missouri Historical Society

Stones with incriptions;
"Camp Henry," "Sept 1810," & "L C."

Photos by L. B. Lindsley

Camp Henry Historical Marker.
Photo by Bruce Campbell

Camp Henry as it is today.
Photo by Bruce Campbell

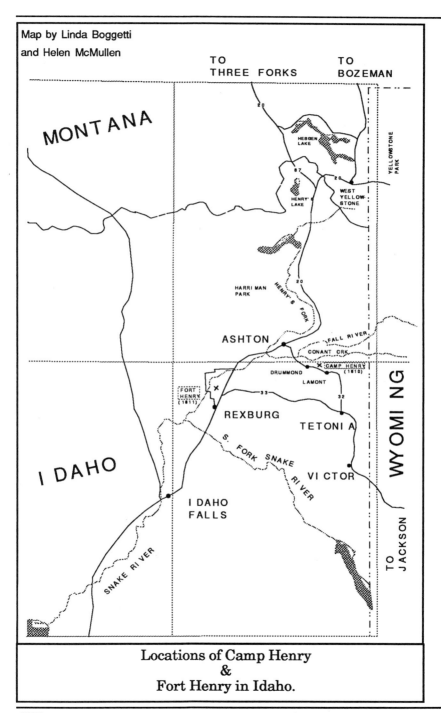

Locations of Camp Henry & Fort Henry in Idaho.